THE
HORIZON
HISTORY
OF
AFRICA

PUBLISHED BY AMERICAN HERITAGE PUBLISHING CO. INC., NEW YORK

A. ADU BOAHEN

J. DESMOND CLARK

JOHN HENRIK CLARKE

PHILIP D. CURTIN

BASIL DAVIDSON

STANLAKE SAMKANGE

STUART SCHAAR

GEORGE SHEPPERSON

MARGARET SHINNIE

JAN VANSINA

IMMANUEL WALLERSTEIN

JOHN RALPH WILLIS

JOHN HENRIK CLARKE, CONSULTANT

ELLIOTT P. SKINNER, CONSULTANT

ALVIN M. JOSEPHY, JR., EDITOR IN CHARGE

WENDY BUEHR, MANAGING EDITOR

THE
HORIZON
HISTORY
OF
AFRICA

Staff for this Book

EDITOR
Alvin M. Josephy, Jr.

MANAGING EDITOR
Wendy Buehr

ART DIRECTOR
Richard Glassman

ASSISTANT MANAGING EDITOR
Kaari Ward

ASSOCIATE EDITORS
Iris Eaton
Angela Weldon

RESEARCH EDITORS
Michael E. DuBois
Harold Head

ASSISTANT COPY EDITOR
Roxanne Wehrhan

PICTURE EDITORS
Maureen Dwyer
Joann McQuiston

ASSISTANT EDITOR
Mary Elizabeth Wise

EUROPEAN BUREAU
Gertrudis Feliu, Chief

AMERICAN HERITAGE

PUBLISHING CO., INC.

PRESIDENT AND PUBLISHER
Paul Gottlieb

EDITOR-IN-CHIEF
Joseph J. Thorndike

SENIOR EDITOR, BOOK DIVISION
Alvin M. Josephy, Jr.

EDITORIAL ART DIRECTOR
Murray Belsky

GENERAL MANAGER, BOOK DIVISION
Andrew W. Bingham

RAPHO-GUILLUMETTE–SABINE WEISS

ABOVE: *Berbers, harried by a sandstorm, scurry for cover at an oasis in Tunisia's hinterland.*

TITLE PAGE: *A Uganda shepherd guides his Ankoli cattle, still legal currency in his country.*

PHOTO RESEARCHERS–ARTHUR GRIFFIN

⮑ Contents

6 *Introduction:* THE EMERGENCE OF AFRICAN HISTORY — Dr. Philip D. Curtin
University of Wisconsin

16 *Chapter One:* AFRICAN BEGINNINGS — Dr. J. Desmond Clark
University of California, Berkeley

48 *Chapter Two:* CIVILIZATIONS OF THE NILE — Margaret Shinnie

96 *Chapter Three:* THE BARBARY COAST — Dr. Stuart Schaar
City University of New York

136 *Chapter Four:* THE SPREAD OF ISLAM — Dr. John Ralph Willis
University of California, Berkeley

176 *Chapter Five:* KINGDOMS OF WEST AFRICA — Dr. A. Adu Boahen
University of Ghana

216 *Chapter Six:* THE NIGER TO THE NILE — Basil Davidson

260 *Chapter Seven:* INNER AFRICA — Dr. Jan Vansina
University of Wisconsin

304 *Chapter Eight:* THE COMING OF THE EUROPEANS — Dr. A. Adu Boahen
University of Ghana

352 *Chapter Nine:* TIME OF TROUBLES — Professor John Henrik Clarke
Hunter College

400 *Chapter Ten:* WARS OF RESISTANCE — Dr. Stanlake Samkange
Fisk University

448 *Chapter Eleven:* UNDER COLONIAL RULE — Dr. George Shepperson
University of Edinburgh, Scotland

496 *Chapter Twelve:* AFRICA FOR THE AFRICANS — Dr. Immanuel Wallerstein
McGill University, Canada

530 Acknowledgments and Index

THE EMERGENCE OF AFRICAN HISTORY

By Philip D. Curtin

HISTORY HAS ALL TOO OFTEN been an ethnocentric subject written (often intentionally) to foster patriotism by emphasizing the deeds of ancestors. In Europe and North America this tendency has led historians to concentrate on national history, looking only secondly at the broader developments of Western civilization. Cultures beyond the West were either left out altogether or relegated to a minor place. The crucial and organizing question was "How do we come to be as we are?"—not "How did the modern world come to be as it is?" or "How do human societies change through time?"

African history fell under this blight, as did the histories of pre-Columbian America and of Asia. For Americans, "ancestors" include Africans as well as Europeans, but there has been a tendency to sweep the African heritage under the rug in a general pattern of Jim Crow history, negating the role of black Americans in the national life. Africa crept into the ken of European national interest during the colonial period, when Britain, France, Belgium, Portugal, and other nations had political commitments that seemed to call for a knowledge of the African past. But the African history these outsiders wrote tended to be colonial history, emphasizing the role of missionaries, merchants, administrators, explorers, and settlers.

Then, in the aftermath of World War II, people woke to the fact that relations between the Western and the non-Western world were rapidly changing. In Africa the drive for independence swept from North Africa to the south and east, where it stabilized in the early 1960's. Historians in and out of Africa began to take another look. Most had assumed that African history could not be investigated beyond the colonial fringe because it had to do with preliterate societies. In this they were three-times wrong. Most Africans before the colonial period lived in societies that were literate, at least to the extent of having a literate class of scribes or clerics. Even societies that were nonliterate often had a retrievable oral history. Finally, a good deal of African history had been written.

The "discovery" of African history after 1950 can be likened to the discovery of Victoria Falls or Mount Kenya by a European "explorer": its existence was suddenly publicized abroad, but the Africans knew it was there all along. Many African societies had institutions for preserving and transmitting oral traditions, but, even beyond that, Western-educated Africans had long been recording, gathering, and translating key works in Arabic by native writers on both sides of the Sahara. A small number of anthropologists, colonial administrators, and amateur historians also became fascinated by the depth and breadth of the subject. Working often in isolation, these people mapped the main lines of African history as it is still understood.

This is not to underplay the contribution of the last two decades. Intensive research has multiplied our knowledge of the African past many times over. And the new African history is not simply a matter of unearthing more data. Modern historians have new questions and new attitudes. Some are Africans seeking to integrate the modernizing present with its roots in the past. Others are non-Africans who have found that Africa's recent strides require new explanations, raising issues no one thought to consider at the high noon of colonialism.

Equally important, the study of history itself is changing. The ethnocentric bias is weakening, which means that historians—both African and non-African—have begun trying to see African history in the perspective of human history as a whole. The first step is to take an Africa-centered view of African history, and this adjustment is more difficult and more dramatic than one might suppose. It is not enough to turn colonial heroes into villains and resistance leaders into heroes. Instead, historians often have to go back to the original sources with new questions about the dynamics of African societies: "What recurrent patterns of change existed there that may have been different from those of the West?" "Why did various African societies react differently to the Western challenge?"

Much of the new, Afro-centric history could be written using European works, colonial records, travelers' accounts, and the like. It is simply a matter of taking a new point of departure. For example, instead of asking why the British took a certain line of policy in Uganda, the contemporary historian asks why the Ganda people reacted a certain way to conquest by Britain. Both questions are important to an understanding of the colonial period, but both had been seldom asked by the same analyst.

Along with the new attitudes have come new techniques. Before 1950 very little archeological work had been done in tropical Africa, but then the newly established governments and their universities began to sponsor research. With techniques like radiocarbon dating to place basic changes in material culture, such critical revolutions as the beginning of the iron age could be traced.

The new research techniques soon began to interact with a broadening field of historiography. Botanical history, for example, has a special importance in Africa, which was poor in indigenous, cultivable plants. The introduction of plants from southeast Asia and, much later, the Americas, brought to the African regions greater mastery of the environment and a food surplus over the needs of the farmers, leading to denser populations and the possibility of urban life, with its more complex civilization. Botanical history, therefore, becomes an important part of general history. In addition, historians came to realize that disease environments have differed throughout the world and that these differences influenced the way people moved about. As a result, disease was linked to migration, and Africa's demographic history could be explained by findings of epidemiologists. And much of the best evidence used so far to determine the movements of peoples within Africa has been provided by still another discipline: the study of languages.

Even more than new attitudes and new techniques, the new African history continues to explore the great riches of oral tradition. Most African societies have a sense of history and often a professional class of minstrels who remember and recite their communal past; but even where no professional class exists, many people are still alive who can remember the early years of the colonial period. And where Islamic civilization is found, African societies also have a literate tradition. This means documents written in Arabic (or in other African languages using Arabic characters) have often survived and are now beginning to be collected systematically. When these sources are used in combination with the reports of Europeans (who have, after all, been frequenting all the coasts of Africa since the beginning of the sixteenth century), it is possible to reconstruct far more of African history than anyone imagined only a few decades ago.

This work of recovery is far from complete, but the pages that follow will demonstrate its new depth. Africa no longer appears as a changeless continent lost in "barbarism"; rather, the reader will find that Africa has experienced a pace and quality of change similar to the pace and quality of change in human history as a whole. Nor is it split across the middle of the Sahara, divided into a White Africa to the north and a Black Africa to the south. Neither history nor color lent itself to such strict demarcations. North African history is, indeed, crucial to understanding the past of sub-Saharan Africa, for it forms a key link between Black Africa and the great bloc of intercommunicating civilizations stretching from the Mediterranean to China; Africa's relationship to this bloc of civilizations is often the key to understanding Africa's place in the history of mankind.

WHERE THERE ARE PEOPLE,
THERE IS HISTORY

"Africa is no vast island. . . . She has been closely connected, both as source and nourisher, with some of the most potent influences which have affected for good the history of the world." So wrote Edward Blyden, a prominent black nationalist of the nineteenth century. The world's second largest continent was probably the birthplace of man. From its tropical rain forests, silvery velds, undulating savannas, and parched deserts have sprung hundreds of societies whose traditions and histories have been handed down from generation to generation. In ancient times Africa was the "granary" of the Roman empire—a number of whose officials, including an emperor, were Africans. Monasticism, a vital Christian institution, was born on African soil. And out of Africa came the spectacular civilization of Moorish Spain. From Africa, also, came the inspiration for both jazz and cubism. In many ways, then, Africa's history is mankind's history, of import to all. It is the brilliant past of over 237,000,000 people that forms the story of this book.

PHOTO RESEARCHERS—THOMAS D. W. FRIEDMANN

Today's Africans, like those pictured in this portfolio, are maintaining many ancient traditions, but are also taking on the challenge of modernization and self-rule. Left, rebels of the 1960's patrol in northern Angola, where their forefathers resisted the Portuguese for five hundred years; opposite, children play below the guardian angel of a seventeenth-century Coptic church at Gondar, one of the pillars of Ethiopia's Christian heritage; page 10 education reaches Kenya youth via a rural school; 11 Congolese copper miners end their shift; 12 the emir of Kano, the ruler of over two million Nigerians, exits from his one hundred-fifty year old palace; 13 South African gold miners perform an age-old dance; 14–15 a Mauritanian nomad, the descendant of men who controlled the rich trans-Saharan trade, confronts the endless desert.

9 RAPHO-GUILLUMETTE—MARC AND EVELYNE BERNHEIM; 10 MAGNUM—GEORGE RODGER; 11 *Life* MAGAZINE © TIME INC.—DMITRI KESSEL; 12 MAGNUM—GEORGE RODGER; 13, 14–15 BOTH: RAPHO-GUILLUMETTE—MARC AND EVELYNE BERNHEIM.

Chapter One

AFRICAN BEGINNINGS

by

J. Desmond Clark

FOR CENTURIES MAN'S IMAGINATION has been captured by attempts, usually fanciful, to establish the exact locality of the place of origin of the human race—the paradise of ancient mythology. Scientific research of the last few decades, carried out by archeologists, paleontologists, and workers in allied disciplines, is making it increasingly likely that the legendary birthplace was somewhere on the African continent, probably south of the Sahara.

Today Africa is the home of many human cultural traditions, ranging from simple hunting societies to elaborate urban civilizations—a result of interaction over many millenniums and the selective use of the potentialities of the different environments. Indeed, the single most powerful influence on the lives of men, as of other creatures, is the environment in which they live. Temperature, rainfall and its distribution throughout the year—in short, climate—together with the kind of plant communities, the associated animal life, the availability of surface water sources or of economically important minerals not only shape the tenor of man's daily life but have been significant influences on his biological evolution.

Animals and plants are adapted to living in a particular habitat through natural selection and competition. Some creatures have succeeded in adapting to several different ecological niches, but by reason of man's culture and technology, only he and some life forms dependent upon him have been able to make adjustments that permit him to live anywhere he wants to in the world.

Man's emancipation from environmental controls has been a comparatively gradual process, though one of steadily quickening tempo. For nine tenths or so of human history, however, the rate of biological and cultural progress was extremely slow, almost imperceptible; only in the past

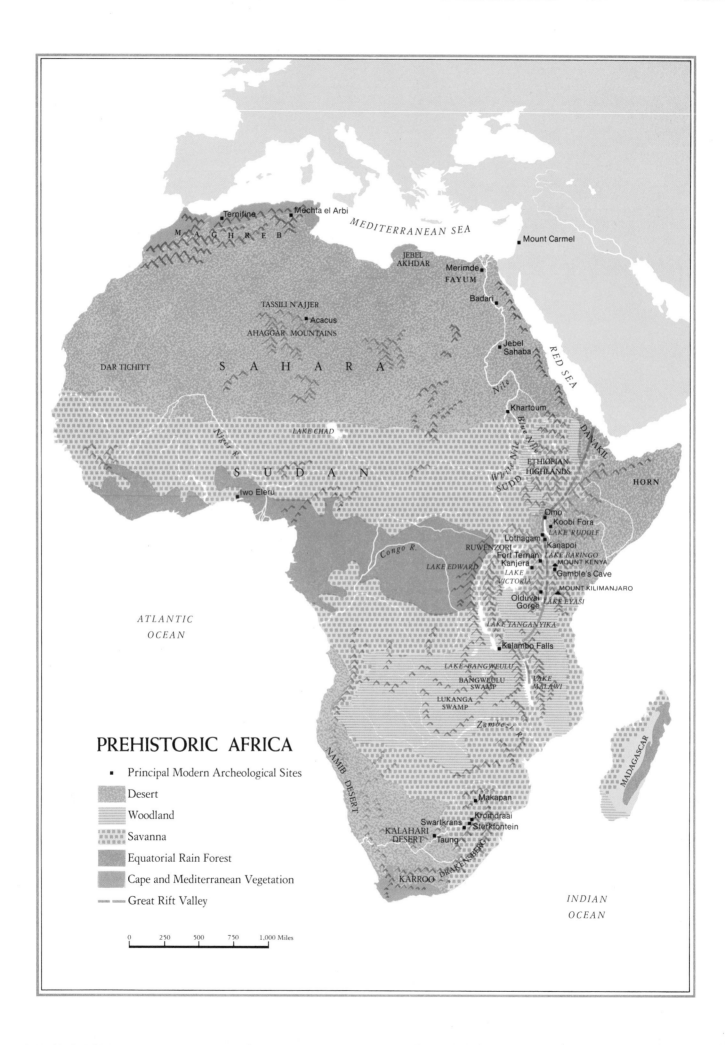

PREHISTORIC AFRICA

- Principal Modern Archeological Sites
- Desert
- Woodland
- Savanna
- Equatorial Rain Forest
- Cape and Mediterranean Vegetation
- Great Rift Valley

0   250   500   750   1,000 Miles

MEDITERRANEAN SEA

Ternifine   Mechta el Arbi   MAGHREB

Mount Carmel

JEBEL AKHDAR

Merimde
FAYUM

Badari

TASSILI N'AJJER
Acacus
AHAGGAR MOUNTAINS

Jebel Sahaba

RED SEA

DAR TICHITT

SAHARA

Nile

Khartoum

DANAKIL

Niger R.

LAKE CHAD

Blue Nile

White Nile

SUDAN

SUDD

ETHIOPIAN HIGHLANDS

HORN

Iwo Eleru

Congo R.

Omo
Koobi Fora
LAKE RUDOLF

Lothagam   Kanapoi
RUWENZORI
Fort Ternan   LAKE BARINGO
Kanjera   MOUNT KENYA
Gamble's Cave

LAKE EDWARD

LAKE VICTORIA

MOUNT KILIMANJARO

Olduvai Gorge   LAKE EYASI

LAKE TANGANYIKA

ATLANTIC OCEAN

Kalambo Falls

LAKE BANGWEULU
BANGWEULU SWAMP   LAKE MALAWI
LUKANGA SWAMP

Zambezi R.

NAMIB DESERT

Makapan
Swartkrans   Kromdraai
Sterkfontein
KALAHARI DESERT
Taung

KARROO   DRAKENSBERG

MADAGASCAR

INDIAN OCEAN

few thousand years has man developed the abilities that make possible today's sophisticated urban civilizations. Nonetheless, man remains an integral part, though by far the most influential part, of the many different eco-systems in which he lives, and he now has it in his power to destroy or to conserve and improve them. Moreover, from the beginning man's relationship with his environment was one in which he always had the freedom to choose how he could make best use of the natural resources and which of them he should select.

It is the possession of a rational intellect and of culture—the ability to manufacture artifacts and the skill to use them—that gives man the opportunity to exploit the resources offered by the different habitats, and this finds expression in the patterns of behavior that control the lives of every human community. Depending on social, legal, and religious sanctions, all of which affect the way a population reacts to innovations and the pressures of external influences, a culture may be sympathetic or conservative in its acceptance and modification of new beliefs, tastes, or technologies.

In any community the cultural tradition is made up of the social structure, the economic pattern, the learned ways of behavior, and the influence on these of technology and material culture—all of which are handed down from one generation to the next. For example, in Africa the peoples south of the Sahara may be separated generally into two geographical culture areas: those in the south and east, where hunting, wild food gathering, and the herding of livestock determine the culture; those in West Africa and Equatoria, where the economy is based upon cultivation by sedentary populations. The ways of life of the peoples in each of these main culture areas are broadly similar except where historical interaction has brought about some modification or displacement.

The concept of culture areas is of great value for the study of cultural evolution. Except in the latest, prehistoric periods, however, little evidence, other than the less perishable parts of the material culture, has survived. But as research becomes more advanced, archeology—the science that seeks to interpret these material remains—is able to provide a time perspective for some of the culture areas. An understanding of the main geographical regions of the continent is not only essential to an explanation of the varied ways of life of the African peoples today but is even more important for understanding the evolution of man and his culture in prehistoric times and his preference for and selection of some habitats rather than others.

Geographically, Africa can be divided roughly into a highland and a lowland zone by drawing a line from the mouth of the Congo river in the west to the Ethiopia-Sudan border in the east. South of this line, High Africa comprises mainly an interior plateau, most of it between 3,000 and 5,000 feet above sea level, but with higher ridges and mountains. The bedrock is formed of pre-Cambrian crystalline metamorphic rocks that also commonly obtrude, and some of them provide important sources of mineral wealth. North of our imaginary line, Low Africa composed largely of plains and basins of sedimentation in which are found the younger sedimentary rocks of Cretaceous and early Tertiary periods, is generally between 500 and 2,000 feet above sea level.

In the depressions on the plateau are large, relatively shallow lakes and swamps containing a seemingly inexhaustible supply of fish and, formerly, large numbers of hippopotamuses. The major rivers have their sources in the higher mountain ranges, from which they descend to undulating savanna, meandering in broad, deep valleys until they reach the escarpments, where they fall in a series of rapids and waterfalls, often through narrow gorges, to the coastal plains. Thus, the rivers are never navigable for any great distance from their mouths. This feature was directly responsible for the general failure of alien peoples—travelers, traders, soldiers, and geographers—from classical times into the nineteenth century to penetrate the interior and relay knowledge concerning the country and its inhabitants to the outside world.

The eastern part of Africa is split by a huge trough, or fault, that runs nearly the whole length of the continent. This is the Great Rift Valley, which starts in Asia, in Syria, and continues southward down the Red Sea, through Ethiopia into Kenya, Uganda, and Tanzania, and finally loses itself beneath the alluvial sediments in the lower Zambezi valley in Mozambique. In Kenya and Uganda the trough splits into the Eastern Rift and the Western Rift; in a shallow basin on the plateau between the two branches lies Lake Victoria, Africa's greatest lake.

The bottom of the Great Rift lies at extremely variable elevations. In the Danakil section of the Ethiopian Rift the bottom drops in places to nearly 400 feet below sea level, but southward the floor rises in a series of steps until in Kenya, in the Eastern Rift, the elevation is over 5,000 feet. The volcanic rocks and sediments of the area support short grasses and thorn bushes, which are highly favorable to wild game and the pastoralist way of life.

The Great Rift is a tectonically unstable zone where compression and tension of the earth's crust have pushed

up the land bordering the trough into high ridges and mountains. The deeper portions of the trough are filled by great lakes, some of which, such as Lakes Tanganyika and Malawi, are among the deepest and longest in the world.

Although there exists now only one active volcano in the rift zone (Ol Doingo Lengai in Tanzania), there are numerous dormant and extinct ones, two of which—Mount Kilimanjaro (19,565 feet) and Mount Kenya (17,040 feet)—are perpetually snowcapped. Another huge snow-covered mass —this one a crystalline rock thrust of nonvolcanic origin —is the Ruwenzori range. Its highest peak, Mount Stanley, rises to 16,795 feet. The vegetation zones of the rift run in belts around the mountains, changing with altitude from rain forest at the foot to alpine tundra near the top, and the scenery is some of the most beautiful and varied in the world. The very rich fossil record preserved in the Great Rift Valley is due to the accumulation of deep sediments in the bottom of the trough and to the rapid burial of land surfaces by ash and dust from the volcanoes.

Elsewhere in Africa the climate and vegetation zones generally fall in a similar system to the north and south of a central, equatorial region of high rainfall and evergreen forest, though altitude, monsoons, and other factors have modified this pattern, especially in the eastern and southeastern parts of the continent. Africa is not the all-over forest-covered steaming jungle that popular belief often assumes it to be, and the zone of rain forest is now greatly restricted as a result of some two to three thousand years of cutting and burning by man. Most of the continent is covered by a wooded savanna where deciduous trees predominate. The further removed from the equator, the longer the winter, or dry season, lasting up to six months or more. The ubiquitous green cover, stretching over mile upon mile

of undulating plateau, varies in the thickness of its tree communities from a nearly continuous canopy with only sparse grass beneath, or the gallery forest, to park land, where the grasses predominate over scattered bush.

The savanna zone north of the equatorial forest is known as the Sudan belt, and that to the south as *miombo* woodland. These savanna lands are the home of a mammalian fauna uniquely rich not only in the great variety of its species but in the size of the herds of its gregarious animals: antelopes, buffaloes, horses, elephants, and many others. The variety of this "Ethiopian fauna," as it is called, indicates the continuing favorability of the habitats in which the animals evolved over many millenniums and which we now think were also the original home of man himself.

To the north and south of the savanna belts the climate becomes drier, supporting only sparse grass and low bushes —steppelands. In turn, these give way to true desert, the Sahel grading to the Sahara in the north and the Karroo to the Namib and Kalahari deserts in the southwest.

All these tropical and subtropical regions of Africa enjoy a summer rainfall system; but in the north, along the coast of the Mediterranean, and at the southern end of the continent south of the Great Escarpment, or Drakensberg range, the country is fed by winter rains and experiences a much more temperate climate.

There is evidence for considerable past fluctuation in these vegetation zones, with their closely adapted animal communities, in response to changes in rainfall, temperature, and the intensity of winds and ocean currents. Plant and animal species and even communities, now isolated sometimes by hundreds of miles from the main center of distribution, are evidence for a previously more extended and continuous spread of these forms at a time when the climatic conditions favored this. Such changes in the habitat of prehistoric man were of considerable importance in influencing his biological and cultural evolution and thus inducing variations in the pattern of his behavior. It becomes of great importance, therefore, to be able to reconstruct past habitats in order to understand the way of life of the human populations.

There are many ways in which it is now proving possible to reconstruct Africa's past habitats, and these involve scientists in a number of different disciplines. The sedimentary history of a lake basin, a river valley, or a cave is interpreted by geologists and soil chemists. Botanists identify the microscopic pollen grains of plants, sometimes preserved in muds and silts recovered from the basins of existing and former lakes and rivers. Zoologists and paleontologists examine the assemblages of animal bones to determine to which point in the time scale these belong. By comparison with the general habitats and behavior of similar species and communities today, they can deduce what type of faunal community might have existed at that time.

It is essential to be able to arrange all these data into a logical, historical sequence within an established chronological framework. Since 1950 several methods have been developed by physicists and chemists to provide a radiometric time scale of the greatest significance. Two methods are of particular importance for African prehistory. The first is that of potassium-argon; it is based upon the measurable amount of argon in rocks rich in radioactive potassium (K_{40}), which, over time, decays at a regular rate into the isotopes of calcium (Ca_{40}) and argon (A_{40}). This method is valuable for measuring the age of rocks and of formations of volcanic origin, both those that are geologically very old and quite young—as recent as a quarter of a million years or less.

Of more universal use, but more limited in time range, is the radiocarbon method, based upon the measurement of the radioactive isotope of carbon (C_{14}), which remains in a plant or animal organism after death. Animal bone, or shell, or charcoals from hearths are, in varying degrees, suitable substances whose age can be determined, back sometimes to a maximum of sixty thousand years. The time scale thus achieved provides the basis for understanding the rate at which man's biological and cultural evolution took place.

The prehistorian is in much the same position as a man trying to reconstruct the picture of a jigsaw puzzle of which half the pieces are missing. It is both challenging and exciting, and the degree of success is determined by recognition of the pattern and the significance of the missing pieces. For the more recent periods the record is obviously much more complete than it is for the beginning, where little evidence of man, other than stone and bone, is preserved. However, much can be learned from the tools and waste material at the sites where they were manufactured, the dispersal of dwellings, the disposition of bone fragments from meals, and from the other kinds of artifacts.

It is also fortunate for the prehistorian that Africa has preserved in contemporary society a number of different ways of life, techniques, and tools, the origins of which lie deeply buried in the past. Of course, the present way of life of all these economically simpler societies, such as the hunting-and-gathering Bushmen of the Kalahari Desert or the Pygmy peoples of the Ituri forests, has been affected by contact with peoples of more complex institutions and technologies so that no *direct* comparisons between ancient and modern societies are possible. But, through analogies, archeologists can construct models that make it possible to surmise how prehistoric man behaved.

Another means to rediscover the past, though of more limited extent both in space and time, is the interpretation of the rock art of the Late Stone Age, some of which is incomparable for the liveliness of its styles and its portrayal of events and customs. Later in time other sources, such as historical traditions passed on by word of mouth, the evidence of linguistics by which the history of a language can be deduced, and, finally, written documents, all combine to create a better understanding of the past.

When it is assembled, all this evidence provides a record of man's activities that covers some four to five million years. It shows that Charles Darwin was right when he suggested in his *Descent of Man* that it was somewhere in the tropics, perhaps in Africa, that man the toolmaker first evolved, and leaves no doubt that man shares a common ancestor with the great apes, or Pongidae.

This ancestor, who lived at some distant time as yet not precisely identified, must have been a small, unspecialized apelike animal, probably similar to the subfamily of fossil apes known as *Dryopithecus*, a term meaning "tree ape." The earliest of these dryopithecines was found in sediments of the Oligocene epoch of the Tertiary period (about twenty-eight or thirty million years ago) in the Fayum depression not far from Cairo in the Nile Valley. This fossil, named *Aegyptopithecus zeuxis*, is a quadrupedal ape with a tail and an apelike tooth pattern. *Aegyptopithecus* was an arboreal ape, as were later forms found in East Africa, and dates from the Miocene epoch (about twenty million years ago); the Miocene apes, however, show some modification of the hand

and forelimb, suggesting that they may have been partly terrestrial. A smaller species, known as *Dryopithecus africanus* (sometimes less formally referred to as Proconsul), appears to have been adapted to living in gallery forest along the streams and in the savanna, while a larger form, *Dryopithecus major*, occupied the forests on the slopes of volcanoes.

In 1961 the Kenya-born British prehistorian Dr. Louis Leakey found pieces of an upper jaw and two isolated teeth in late Miocene deposits at Fort Ternan in western Kenya that have since been dated to fourteen million years old. This fossil, which he named *Kenyapithecus wickeri*, showed unmistakable human characteristics of the hominid branch of the Hominoidea family, from which man and apes are descended. Later it was demonstrated by Dr. Elwyn Simons of Yale University that Leakey's discovery differed in no essential respect from *Ramapithecus punjabicus*, a form discovered earlier in India. Although the India fossil is unfortunately known only from fragments of the upper and lower jaw, the modifications of the face and the tooth pattern that these exhibit have given rise to the suggestion that *Ramapithecus* (to which species the East African find was subsequently assigned) was not only a hominid but a tool user. A further indication was the discovery at the same site of a long bone that had been fractured in a manner suggesting crushing; close by lay a piece of lava with a battered ridge on one side. Proof of man's tool-using ability, however, must rest upon the discovery of limb bones showing whether *Ramapithecus* was a quadruped or a biped.

Professor Sherwood L. Washburn of the University of California has recently postulated the likelihood that the earlier hominids were knuckle-walkers like the apes. This would not only allow for more specialized use of the forelimbs for manipulating objects but would suggest, as does the estimated size range, that *Ramapithecus* lived mostly on the ground.

The place of both the dryopithecine apes and the more advanced *Ramapithecus* is yet to be conclusively determined. Some physical anthropologists consider the dryopithecine apes to be ancestral to the chimpanzee and gorilla. If so, they probably lie close in time and not far removed biologically from the common ancestor of apes and man. However, certain recent biochemical studies have cast doubt on this theory. These studies, based upon the analysis of blood serum proteins and on the chromosome composition of the higher primates, suggest that species have evolved at a constant rate and that man and the African apes split off from a common ancestor as recently as the Pliocene epoch (some five million years ago). If this were

the case, then *Ramapithecus*, a savanna dweller, would be an aberrant ape that left no descendants. It is to be hoped that the search of newly discovered Pliocene formations in East Africa will provide evidence to show whether the long chronology for the time of separation of the hominid and pongid lines, suggested by the earlier fossil finds, or the short one based upon the biochemical studies is likely to be the correct evaluation.

By the beginning of the Pleistocene epoch (some three and a half million years ago) there were present in the savanna land of East Africa, and probably also of South Africa, hominid forms known as australopithecines, or man-apes. There can be no doubt that through natural and social selection processes, which bred out the less desirable genetic characteristics and encouraged the increase of those more highly favored, the man-apes became ecologically well adapted to life in the open savannas. They were possessed of an upright carriage, using the forelimbs for tool manipulation and the hindlimbs for bipedal locomotion. It can be inferred that these fundamental changes were brought about by the greater potential of the woodland and grassland environments, with their wider opportunities to experiment and the greater excitement of a life in the open over one in the forests.

These hominids are the best known of any of the fossil ancestors of modern man, being represented today by several hundred specimens. The first of these fossils was found in 1924 at Taung in the northern part of the Cape Province in South Africa in brecciated cave deposits that were being exploited for limestone. Here, uncovered by a blast, was found the cast of the greater part of a juvenile skull; it showed characteristics that, in the opinion of its discoverer, Dr. Raymond Dart of South Africa, placed it midway morphologically between the apes and the oldest definitely identifiable human fossils.

Some believed Dart was wrong and considered the skull to be that of a fossil ape. Others, including Dr. Robert Broom, also of South Africa, thought that "In *Australopithecus* we have a being also with a chimpanzeelike jaw but a subhuman brain. We seem justified in concluding that in this new form discovered by Professor Dart, we have a connecting link between the higher apes and one of the lowest human types."

A few years later Dart was proved correct when Broom discovered the first adult australopithecine fossil at the cave of Sterkfontein in the Transvaal. Systematic investigation of similar limestone caves at other sites in the Sterkfontein area and in the Makapan Valley in the northern Transvaal

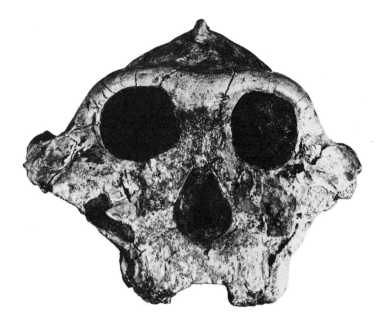

This ancient skull of Australopithecus boisei, *or man-ape, found in June, 1969, by Richard Leakey on the eastern side of Lake Rudolf in Kenya, is slightly older than 2.6 million years. An ancestor of modern man, this East African type of the robust hominid walked upright and manipulated stone tools with his forearms.*

produced a number of other man-ape fossils in association with many bones of animals.

On the basis of the fossil fauna, the earlier South African deposits could be no younger than the Lower Pleistocene and might be as old as two million years or more. The later deposits appear to belong in the Middle Pleistocene and could be half as young again. The earlier sites—Sterkfontein, Makapan limeworks, and Taung—contained the remains of a small, slender form, *Australopithecus africanus*, whereas at the later sites—Swartkrans and Kromdraai—only a robust form was present. At Swartkrans were also found the remains of a more advanced hominid, which has now been shown to represent an early form of *Homo* species. It is this form that is believed to have been the maker of the stone tools found in these breccias. No implements of flaked stone have yet been discovered with the gracile form (*Australopithecus africanus*), but what are claimed to be clubs and cutting, piercing, and chopping tools have been found among the many thousands of bones of other creatures in these deposits.

The australopithecines were small-brained hominids with cranial capacities of between about 435 and 530 cubic centimeters—around the average for the gorilla and about one third the size of modern man. Their rather muzzlelike face shows a number of apelike features, but the tooth pattern is essentially human, as are many features of the brain case. The head was centrally placed on the spinal column. The pelvic girdle and bones of the lower limbs show that the man-apes walked upright on two feet, and the arms and hands show that they were capable of simple toolmaking. *Australopithecus africanus* measured an average 4 feet 6 inches tall and weighed about 60 to 70 pounds; *Australopith-*

ecus robustus was taller, about 5 feet in height, and weighed about 130 pounds.

It appears now most likely that the Transvaal caves were not the dwelling places of the man-apes but rather the sites where carnivores, possibly leopards, brought their victims. In this case the australopithecines were not the aggressive hunters that some have claimed them to be.

East African discoveries that have been underway since 1959 have greatly enhanced our knowledge of these earliest hominids. There, australopithecine fossils are known from a number of different localities in the Lake Rudolf section of the Rift Valley (Omo, Lothagam, Kanapoi, and sites on the east side of the lake), from Lake Baringo (Chemeron) in Kenya, and from the Olduvai Gorge and Garusi in northern Tanzania. The oldest of these fossils dates from about five million years ago, and by the beginning of the Pleistocene both a slender and a robust form were living in the Lake Rudolf rift. The oldest stone tools, made some 2.6 million years ago, are from Koobi Fora on the east side of Lake Rudolf. At a nearby site have been found one well-preserved skull of the robust australopithecine and parts of another representing a more gracile form. Stone tools are also present at one layer in the Omo beds, about 1.8 million years old, and in the bottom of the 350-foot sequence of Pleistocene lake sediments at Olduvai Gorge.

Olduvai is unique for what it can tell us about early man. Here, since 1931, Drs. Louis and Mary Leakey have recovered the remains of a number of hominids associated with concentrations of animal bones and stone implements. These lay on land surfaces that had been rapidly covered either by ash and dust from periodic eruptions of the nearby volcanoes or by the rising waters of the lake, thus sealing

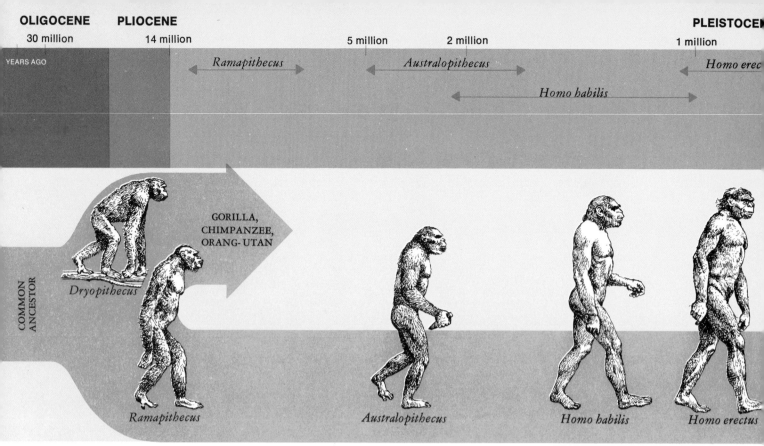

Ramapithecus   *Australopithecus*   *Homo erec*

Homo habilis

GORILLA,
CHIMPANZEE,
ORANG-UTAN

Dryopithecus

COMMON ANCESTOR

Ramapithecus   *Australopithecus*   *Homo habilis*   *Homo erectus*

THE EMERGENCE OF MAN IN AFRICA *(conjectural)*

the remains in a remarkably fine state of preservation.

The base of the Olduvai sequence begins about 1.9 million years ago, and in the lowest level (Bed 1) *Australopithecus robustus* was found together with a more advanced form named *Homo habilis*. The name implies the ability to make tools, and it is the association of this form with evidence of stone toolmaking that has justified including it with *Homo* rather than with *Australopithecus*. His remains are known from six sites and include three fairly complete craniums and lower jaws, together with bones of the lower leg, a nearly complete foot, and a number of the bones of the hand as well as isolated finds of teeth.

Homo habilis was possessed of a larger brain (640–650 cubic centimeters) than either of the australopithecines. However, in the remainder of the skeleton, so far as can be observed, the differences are not very great. *Homo habilis* resembles *Australopithecus africanus* in its slender build, and since it is of a later date, it could have evolved from the latter form; as yet, no certain identification of a slender australopithecine has been made at Olduvai. Alternatively, the evidence can be interpreted as showing three distinct and evolving hominid lines of which only the third, *Homo habilis*, survived to become a competent toolmaker and to be the ancestor of modern man.

The remains that are found at Olduvai provide almost the only evidence for the technological capabilities and activities of the Lower Pleistocene hominids. Concentrations

of animal bones, split to extract the marrow, and numbers of stone tools, together with the waste resulting from their manufacture, can be seen as their living places or home bases, to which were brought back the results of hunting, scavenging, and other gathering activities to be shared among the members of the group. Some time in a previous epoch, therefore, most likely in the Pliocene, which immediately preceded the Pleistocene, some of the ancestral hominids turned from a largely vegetarian to an omnivorous diet in which the hunting of animals became the most significant activity. In fact, it is likely that the need for sharp cutting implements to skin and dismember a carcass was the factor that made these groups take the momentous step involved in working stone to make tools.

The home bases were more than the transitory sleeping places of the hominids. The numbers of individual animals and species represented there suggest that the sites were occupied for several days at least. They were also the places where the juveniles were taught the skills and behavior that made for the successful perpetuation of the species, and it is now apparent from a study of the age when the young's permanent teeth erupted that they were dependent upon their parents for about the same time as those in simpler societies are today. The nature of the learned behavior can be gauged from several different lines of evidence—from the morphology of the fossils themselves, from artifacts, and from what is now known of the behavior of the gorilla

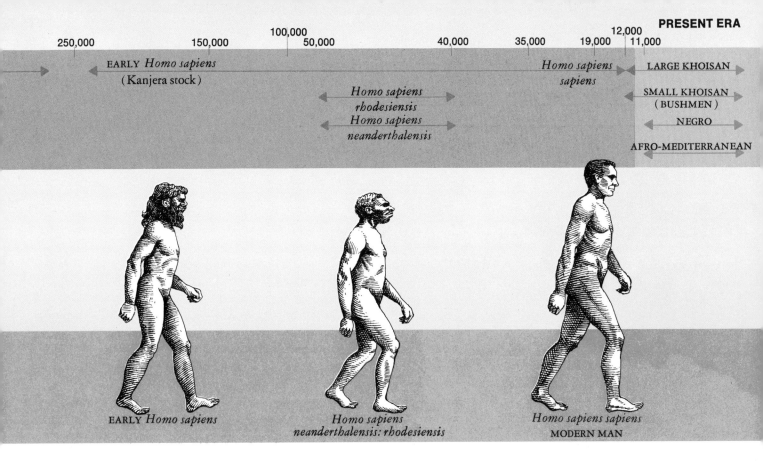

EARLY *Homo sapiens*
(Kanjera stock)

*Homo sapiens
rhodesiensis*

*Homo sapiens
neanderthalensis*

*Homo sapiens
sapiens*

LARGE KHOISAN

SMALL KHOISAN
(BUSHMEN)

NEGRO

AFRO-MEDITERRANEAN

PRESENT ERA

250,000　150,000　100,000　50,000　40,000　35,000　19,000　12,000　11,000

EARLY *Homo sapiens*

*Homo sapiens
neanderthalensis: rhodesiensis*

Homo sapiens sapiens
MODERN MAN

and chimpanzee, the latter in particular.

Studies of free-ranging groups of chimpanzees in wooded savanna (by the English ethologist Jane van Lawick-Goodall in the Gombe Stream Reserve in western Tanzania) and in forest (by English zoologist Vernon Reynolds in Uganda's Budongo forest and by others in West Africa) show that these animals live in highly sociable groups that are continually changing in composition. They do not indulge in any regular defense of territory, and they use some twenty-three different calls, together with facial expressions and gestures, for communication. They manufacture and use simple tools—peeled sticks and grasses for extracting termites from their nests, sponges for sucking water contained in hollow trees, sticks for breaking open the nests of tree ants or for defense; they also throw stones and regularly weave sleeping platforms. These observations, in combination with the fossil evidence, provide a basis for assessing the capabilities of *Australopithecus* and other early hominids, since what the chimpanzees are capable of doing, the australopithecines were biologically equipped to do appreciably better, and much else besides. Already it is probable that we can differentiate between the activities of the males and females, the males engaging in hunting and the females and young gathering wild plant foods.

It is, however, man's toolmaking ability that places him above all other forms of life, and his first great step in the manufacture of simple stone tools required a mind capable of inventing and transmitting a rudimentary knowledge of how stone is fractured so as to produce sharp fragments, or flakes, from the parent lump, or core, and a hand that could do the work. Such tools belong to what is called the Oldowan industry (after the site at Olduvai), and they consist of choppers, flakes for cutting, and rounded, many-faceted lumps for pounding or breaking bone to extract the marrow. Sometimes a flake will show a small amount of fashioning to form a scraper, or more rarely, a bone fragment may show signs of having been employed as a tool. These represent domestic equipment used at the home base, and there has been little, if anything, found to support the view that man was from his earliest beginnings the armed aggressor he has become today. Stones and sticks for throwing at game are likely to have been the only weapons, if such they can be called.

Fossils of early hominids in South and East Africa, and another in the basin of Lake Chad, show them to have been widely spread over the savanna and drier regions of the continent by the beginning of the Middle Pleistocene (about a million or more years ago), about the time that the australopithecine forms had given place to the biologically more evolved *Homo erectus*. So far, australopithecine fossils have not been found outside the continent of Africa; however, *Homo erectus* forms, with their toolmaking skills, were widely distributed throughout all the inhabited regions of the Old World.

Two fossils from Olduvai (classified by archeologists as Hominids 13 and 16), the one from the upper and the other from the lower part of Bed II, were originally grouped with *Homo habilis;* but they have more recently been shown to have more evolved features, indicating that they could be forms intermediate to *Homo erectus.* As known from sites in China and Java and from a third example found in the middle of Bed II at Olduvai (Hominid 9), the skull of *Homo erectus* shows quite a variation in cranial capacity (therefore in brain size), ranging from about 750 to over 1,000 cubic centimeters, with a longer, broader, and thicker skull, a larger palate, a low vault, and projecting brow ridges. *Homo erectus* was taller and had larger bones; indeed, there appears to be little difference between the rest of the skeleton and our own. This Olduvai specimen is probably about half a million years old, though the earliest of the *Homo erectus* fossils probably is as old as a million years or more.

At a site on the edge of what was once a small lake at Ternifine on the Algerian plateau, *Homo erectus* is represented by three lower jaws and one of the side bones of a skull. These jaws are massive and lack a developed mental eminence, or chin, but the pattern of the teeth is not markedly different from that of modern man. Biological changes of the magnitude that occured between the australopithecines and *Homo erectus* typically take about eight million years to effect in other animal species, but in the case of these ancestral human fossils, they seem to have transpired in not more than one million years. There is small doubt that the reason for the evolutionary speedup lies in man's cultural abilities and the attendant potential for improving his way of life. Once the great initial step had been taken—and it is likely to have been a comparatively sudden invention whereby the finished stone tool was envisaged in the rude block or cobble from which it was to be manufactured—it was inevitable that the innovator's descendants would dominate the less gifted species and that genetic changes would be further accelerated.

At much the same time as *Homo erectus* appears on the African scene there also appears a new bifacial technique for making stone tools, and we find the first characteristic tools of the Middle Pleistocene: the hand axe and cleaver. They were made from boulders fractured into large flakes; the pieces were then retouched and shaped on both sides with a hammer stone or by striking them on a stone anvil. This Acheulian industrial complex (named after a site in France) lasted for more than 750,000 years. Sites are found throughout Africa, southern Europe, and Asia. The bifacial tools often show considerable skill in manufacture, and the de-

gree of symmetry and finish of some of the later ones reveals the beginnings of an aesthetic appreciation among the makers.

Camping and flaking sites of Acheulian man are known in almost all parts of the continent with the exception of the primary rain forest, showing that by this time the hominid populations were able to live in a number of different ecological niches. The sites are nearly all in the open, close to water, and cover larger areas than do those of the makers of the Oldowan industry. Many hundreds of hand axes and cleavers may be found on the living sites, along with a range of other tools, and it would seem that the number of individuals making up the social group had by now increased and that some of the camps were revisited seasonally.

The stone tools still appear to be domestic equipment rather than weapons. We know from sites in Europe that simple pointed wooden spears were in use by this time, and a site at the Kalambo Falls in Zambia has produced a wooden club as well as primitive digging sticks.

The makers of Acheulian tools were more competent hunters, if the increased variety of species of animals and greater number of carcasses represented by the bones found at the dwelling places are acceptable as evidence. Improved methods of communication (signs and grunts), and so, more efficient group hunting techniques, were probably the chief factors behind the extended "awareness" of *Homo erectus.* At Ternifine many large and medium-sized animals had been dismembered and eaten, and their bones thrown into the water from the lakeside camp. At Olduvai and other East African sites there seems to have been some definite selection of the animals that were hunted, and at one of these, near the top of Bed II, herds of sheeplike and giraffelike creatures (both now extinct) were apparently driven into a muddy stream and there killed and butchered. At another of these artifact concentrations in Kenya the remains of some eighty giant baboons have been found among the food waste.

The different tool kits and the activities they represent suggest that individuals were now beginning to communicate with each other by means of some form of language. This protolanguage was, no doubt, essentially connected with staying alive and securing the immediate necessities of the moment, but, nonetheless, it provided the foundation on which language as we know it developed in the Middle Pleistocene. However, the fact that at this time one cannot see any regional specialization suggests that man continued to make only rather limited exploitation of the resources of his habitat. Very similar living patterns existed wherever the

Acheulian, or hand-axe, industry is found.

Homo sapiens makes his first appearance at about much the same time in Europe and Africa, about 150,000 to 200,000 years ago. European forerunners of modern man (*Homo sapiens sapiens*) are associated with Acheulian hand axes at Swanscombe in the Thames valley in England, and it seems likely that the fragmentary skulls and tools found at Kanjera on Lake Victoria were also those of *Homo sapiens*. Most of the other fossils are unassociated finds. Recently two almost complete craniums have been found from late Middle or early Upper Pleistocene sediments in the Omo valley in northern Kenya and probably date to about 200,000 years old. Though they represent the oldest *Homo sapiens* fossils from Africa, they do not look alike. Clearly, there was considerable genetic variability within a single population at this time.

A similar situation is exhibited by the later (about 50,000 years old) human fossils from the Mount Carmel caves in Israel, where both modern and primitive *sapiens* features are present in the same population. However, wherever it was that modern man originated, perhaps in southwest Asia or perhaps distributed over a wider area, it would seem that his intellectual and cultural abilities were such that the *Homo erectus* form was replaced with remarkable rapidity. By 50,000 or 40,000 B.C. Neanderthalers (*Homo sapiens neanderthalensis*) were present in North Africa, and a closely connected race of Rhodesioids (*Homo sapiens rhodesiensis*) in the southern part of the continent.

We can now see clearly for the first time the beginnings of a broad, regional specialization in stone tool manufacture. The cultural pattern of the North African population was not unlike that of the other contemporary peoples in Europe and Asia in that they made much use of light cutting and scraping equipment, such as has been associated with hunting camps and the working and flensing of skins. South of the Sudan modifications of the old Acheulian bifacial technique continued in use, together with a quantity of light wood-working equipment. In the open grasslands of the Horn and the South African Highveld an evolved expression of the Acheulian tradition (the Fauresmith) is found, while in the forests and woodland savannas of Equatoria and West Africa, now occupied permanently for the first time, many heavy-duty and denticulated (toothed) flake tools (the Sangoan tradition) are found. It has been suggested that the Sangoan tools may be those of a carpenter, reflecting a growing use of wood and such byproducts as bark and resin. The working of wood with stone tools is made appreciably easier by the discovery of a technique of controlled charring with fire and scraping. Utensils can be hollowed out by this method, and weapons and tools made with comparative ease.

Firemaking also has important implications for codifying the social behavior of the groups. Evidence from sites in the Far East and western Europe shows that fire was definitely used by *Homo erectus* in the colder regions close to the ice sheets during the Middle Pleistocene. None of the Acheulian sites in Africa shows indisputable use of man-made fire before the Upper Pleistocene (about 70,000 years ago). It is from the end of the Acheulian also that we begin to find many occupation sites in caves and rock shelters, and although weathering will have destroyed much of the older evidence for cave occupation, these kinds of sites appear to have been more frequently sought from this time onward.

About 40,000 to 50,000 years ago, therefore, three "races," or subspecific forms, of man were present on the continent: Neanderthalers in North Africa; Rhodesioids in southern Africa; and a stock tentatively identified as the ancestors of modern man to be seen in the Kanjera and Omo fossils from East Africa. However, by about 35,000 years ago the Neanderthaloid and Rhodesioid populations had been largely replaced, it would seem, by modern man (*Homo sapiens sapiens*). The disappearance of these Neanderthaloid populations is most likely to have come about, not as a result of wholesale replacement, but through long-term natural and social selection.

The tool kits are now more complex and exhibit a diversity of regional variations within several more general patterns, but it must be in the greatly stimulated intellectual life that the superiority of these Upper Pleistocene races lay. Whereas in the time of Neanderthal and Rhodesian man it is possible to see the beginnings of a concern with abstract beliefs, ritual, and a superior technology, these find full expression only with the coming of modern man.

It seems probable, though as yet the evidence is insubstantial, that the distinctive success of *Homo sapiens sapiens* lay in his possession of language, in the true sense of the word, without which man's life could never be complete. After 35,000 B.C. we have evidence of consciousness in art, music, ritual, as well as care for the dead and a counting system. More sophisticated tool kits speak of more efficient and extensive exploitation of the natural resources of the habitat, and the increased number of sites that are known to belong to this time suggests an overall increase in population density.

The fossil record for the Upper Pleistocene in Africa is not a particularly complete one; though a number of fossils are known, mostly from the drier parts of the continent, their precise age is often a matter for dispute. However, by about 10,000 B.C. the relatively unspecialized ancestral stock of modern man in Africa, which is generally identified with the Kanjera type, had undergone genetic changes, resulting in the appearance of the large and small Khoisan, or Bushman, types, the robust and gracile Negro stocks, and perhaps also the tall, long-headed Afro-Mediterranean stock.

The large Khoisan type was probably the oldest, dating to about 17,000 B.C., and the most unspecialized. It had evolved in the more open savanna and grasslands of southern and East Africa, even as far north as Khartoum. The small Khoisan—the Bushman proper—appears to have evolved out of the larger type in the southwestern parts of the continent only some 11,000 years ago.

The earliest remains that show Negro characteristics come from the West African forest country and the western branch of the Great Rift Valley. The first of these, from a burial site in a rock shelter at Iwo Eleru, near Benin in Nigeria, dates to about 9000 B.C. The second, at a site on the shore of Lake Edward, discloses skull fragments that are more robust, but with limb bones that show the slenderness of the West African Negro; these date to about 6500 to 6000 B.C. Unfortunately, the rain forest is not favorable to the preservation of bone, so the ancestry of the Negro is very imperfectly known as yet.

The Afro-Mediterranean type appears at about the same time in the Eastern Rift at Gamble's Cave, and both Negro and Afro-Mediterranean are present in the Sahara after 5000 B.C., being known from a number of burials and settlement finds.

In North Africa the population of the Maghreb, during the closing stages of the Upper Pleistocene and later, is known from many remains found buried in settlement middens and in caves. The physical type was tall and robust, and is known as the Mechta el Arbi stock—from the name of the shell midden in eastern Algeria where some of the first remains were found. These people show a general likeness to the type of man from the Cro-Magnon shelter in southwest France (of a much earlier date), but the associated cultural remains are very different. The oldest Mechta el Arbi skeletons date from about 10,000 B.C., but there was also present in northwest Africa by about 6000 B.C. a more slenderly built type representing an early Afro-Mediterranean stock that would ultimately dominate the area.

Both of these local races were associated with stone tools known as microliths, made by using parallel-sided flakes, or blades. These microliths included various kinds of scraping, grooving, and cutting tools, many of the last devices having the back blunted so that they could be held in the hand or, since many of the blades are quite small, mounted in a series. An ingenious notching technique was used to reduce long blades to sections of the required length. The sections were trimmed to various shapes to form the barbs of spears and arrows, the blades of sickles, and so on. Several sickle handles of bone have been found in the Maghreb, one with the microliths still in position, though the tree gum, or mastic, with which they had been held firm had long since disappeared. Microliths became considerably more common after about 15,000 B.C. They are indicative of fundamental changes in the technology, and it is hardly surprising that their use spread rapidly.

It has been suggested that technical innovation of this kind must have been accompanied by population migration, but this is not necessarily the case. Since hunting-and-gathering populations maintain regular contact between their various component groups, an innovation, if it is a sufficient improvement on the existing system, is likely to spread and be quickly adopted. Its progress is especially rapid if it concerns more efficient ways of food getting, for this allows more leisure to devote to intellectual pursuits. In this case it was a change to lighter equipment: microliths were very easy to make, they could be quickly hafted, or mounted, in the most effective manner. The bow and arrow was invented somewhere about 9000 to 8000 B.C., and because of its greater efficiency in some types of country (for example, low grass savanna), it was widely, though not universally, adopted.

From the beginning of the Upper Pleistocene epoch, the coastal regions of North Africa were the home of cultural traditions that differed from those found south of the Sahara. The North African Neanderthalers were associated with industries known as Mousterian, in the pattern of those found in the Levant and in Europe. It is as yet unknown whether Mousterian technology (successor to the Acheulian tool culture and also named after its earliest discovery site in France) developed independently in each area or whether some population movement was involved. By about 40,000 years ago, however, we find present in northeastern Libya a blade industry typologically in the Upper Pleistocene tradition of the north side of the Mediterranean basin. This would seem to have been an introduction from outside the continent, but, since it is known from only two caves in the Jebel Akhdar, it is unlikely that it was widely distributed, nor can it be seen to have had any profound influence on the essentially local traditions of the African

Middle Stone Age or on the contemporary North African industrial complex. This last culture—known as Aterian—developed out of the Mousterian and spread throughout the Sahara; it is distinguished by the use of different kinds of tanged, or stemmed, points, suitable for inserting into handles or attaching as heads of spears, and similar projectiles.

Several local industries based on blades, sometimes employing microliths, have been recently found in the Nile Valley north of Aswan, and it seems probable that there was not a little interaction between Egypt and the Levant from about 15,000 B.C. onward, and possibly earlier. The effect of this is also manifest far to the west throughout most of northwestern Africa. The similarities between the two regions, however, remain at the general level rather than the specific. As in the Mousterian, it was more probably the knowledge and innovative behavior that spread, rather than any significant group movement. Some of these blade industries are found south of the Sahara: one site on Somalia's northern coast; another in the East African Rift, where it is associated with a fishing as well as a hunting economy about 7000 to 6000 B.C.; and others, though as yet scarcely explored, in Ethiopia.

It is from the desert-confined Nile Valley at this time that there comes the earliest evidence of intergroup warfare. Two cemeteries in the Jebel Sahaba area of the Upper Nile contained a number of burials that had microliths associated with skeletons in such a way as to suggest death as a result of injury. Some even had broken microliths sticking in the skull, pelvis, and thigh bone. It was probably economic pressure on an increasing population of culturally distinct units that brought about the need for each group to seek to preserve its own territory intact and steal some of its neighbors'. Since groups could exploit, but not move permanently into, the desert, it would seem that defense of the more desirable flood plain by force of arms was necessary. Another outcome of this economic pressure was the much greater use of wild cereal grasses, as seen in the large numbers of grindstones in the equipment inventory of some of the hunting camps. Large quantities of wild grain could be harvested by means of primitive sickles, and when stored, could serve as a main food source for several months.

The savanna and forest lands south of the Sahara do not appear to have experienced similar economic pressure, and, indeed, these have always been among the richest natural environments in the world. Most of the Bushmanoid and early Negro populations that exploited the unlimited plant and animal foods of these habitats would have had little cause to encroach on each other's territory. Those occupying the West African savanna and forest were also hunters, made microlithic tools, mostly from quartz, and had both axes and adzes. They experimented more specifically with wild plant foods, so that by perhaps about 3000 B.C., if not earlier, selective genetic processes had resulted in the development of early forms of African domestic cereals.

In the Congo Basin the characteristic stone implement was a trapezoidal piece of stone that could be used in several different ways. It could be fashioned into the head of an arrow to cut the hide of prey, leaving a blood spoor; it could also be used as sickle or knife, as a chisel for hollowing or a drawknife for smoothing wood.

In East Africa and the southern African savanna and steppe the population was mostly of Bushman, or Khoisan, stock. Here also many of them used microlithic stone tools, including scrapers and hand adzes—tools of the woodworker. They made arrow points, linkshafts, and ornaments of bone; ivory and shell were commonly used for beads and pendants. Among other regional groups larger scraping tools and pounding and grinding equipment were common, and the microlith rare or absent. In Zambia and Malawi, for example, there was an emphasis on grinding equipment, presumably because of the greater reliance on plant foods; in the Highveld of South Africa the emphasis was more on cutting and flensing equipment and on bone arrow points, showing the greater importance of game herds to the hunting groups there.

The rock art of Africa gives us a very good indication of the activities and beliefs of these hunting-and-gathering peoples. The pictures are engraved on rocks in the open or painted in caves or rock shelters. Women are shown gathering wild plant foods, sometimes with the aid of a digging stick on which was occasionally set a stone with a hole pierced through the center for weight. The all important occupation of the men was hunting, and many paintings are scenes of stalking with animal-head disguises or the killing of antelopes, elephants, giraffes, and hippopotamuses with bows and arrows, and less frequently, with spears. Honey gathering was another male occupation. Dancing and social get-togethers also played a part in the way of life that one authority has called the "master behavior pattern of the human species."

Still more complete information of the prehistoric life patterns can be collected from the example of modern survivals of primitive hunters, though their continued existence has often depended upon accommodation to more advanced neighbors. The later Bushmen of the Drakensburg range in southeast Africa persisted, a dwindling population until the

1870's, when they finally succumbed to the pressures of Bantu and European farmers who had taken over their hunting lands. On the other hand, the Bushmen of the central and northern Kalahari demonstrate successfully how hunting groups can make a living out of dry, near-waterless country. The relatively unattractive character of their environment to other, economically more advanced peoples has saved them. So, too, the Hadza people demonstrate how much leisure the rich, though dry and tsetse-ridden, game country of the Lake Eyasi Rift in Tanzania permits to those hunters with six-foot bows. The Pygmies of the Ituri forests, and to a lesser extent the Nderobo of the montane forests of Kenya, show how hunting peoples can adopt and develop a system of exchange relationships with their Bantu agricultural neighbors.

A rare instance of peoples who have made few apparent modifications of the hunting and gathering way of life are two communities of OvaTjimba people, who were recently discovered in the Baynes Mountains in the extreme north of South West Africa. Their only contact has been with pastoral Hottentots, and they still make and use stone tools— the only people in contemporary Africa known to do so. What a wealth of information exists here for the archeologist and ethnographer to link directly the past and the present.

Elsewhere in Africa, in the region of the many lakes that existed in early post-Pleistocene times in the southern Sahara, as also along the seacoasts, man turned from strict hunting and gathering to exploiting the food resources offered by the water. Special equipment was developed at the close of the Pleistocene, and we find spearheads, barbed harpoons of bone, and fishhooks and gorges of bone and shell. Abundant fish and shellfish could be caught in tidal weirs, and stranded sea mammals supplied quantities of meat, as on the South African south coast. In the lakes and rivers fish and shellfish were taken, and the hippopotamus and other water mammals were hunted with spears and harpoons. Some of the waterside camps, such as those just mentioned and others on the Upper Nile at Khartoum or on Lake Edward must have been near-permanent settlements. Today some of the Batwa peoples of central Africa (for example, those living in Zambia's Bangweulu and Lukanga swamps) persist in a way of life that can give an idea of what some of these late prehistoric fishing camps were like.

There would have been small reason for the sub-Saharan peoples to exchange the hunter's way of life for that of the cultivator, especially if the farming tools were not very effective ones for dealing with the tropical woodlands and forests. How strong is the excitement of the hunt can be seen the world over by the amount of hunting that is still done today even in the most sophisticated societies. This is primarily the reason why farming came to sub-Saharan Africa fairly late in time.

As yet, no evidence has been found of food producers anywhere on the continent before about 5000 B.C., several millenniums later than their first appearance in southwest Asia. Whether domestication of plants and animals is, in fact, later in Africa will not be known until further work on settlement sites of this time has been carried out, especially the Nile Valley, where circumstances were most favorable.

The Nile Delta is only some three hundred miles from southern Palestine, where the incipient stages of domestication go back to 7500 B.C. and further, and it is difficult to understand what barrier could have prevented the spread of the experimental techniques that were already widely dispersed in the Near East. Was it the abundance of natural food supply? Perhaps so along the Nile, but this cannot have been the case in other parts of North Africa. Was it the fact that the Nile was then flowing in a channel now covered by many feet of alluvial sediment and that these earlier stages are buried and have escaped detection? Or is it that the evidence is already present in the archeological record but has not yet been recognized as such? The initial steps toward domestication form the substratum of urban civilization and have manifested themselves very differently in the New World from the way they have in the Old. So, too, the first advances may have been different in Africa from the now well-known pattern of southwest Asia's agricultural revolution; remembering the trend in the use of wild grains after 15,000 B.C. in the Nile, it seems not unlikely that earlier farming settlements, making use of local grains, may eventually be found there.

The settlements at Merimde in the Delta (dating to about 3600 B.C.), at Badari in Upper Egypt (about 4000 B.C.) in the Fayum depression (about 4500 B.C.) are of groups of farmers cultivating emmer wheat, barley, and flax. Flint-bladed sickles in wooden handles were used for harvesting the grain, which was then stored in basketwork silos. These people made pottery and lived in permanent and semi-permanent villages. Bones of cattle, sheep, and goats, probably domesticated, have also been found. At Badari careful burial of animals suggests the emergence of animal cults, which later became such a feature of the religion of dynastic Egypt.

Whether the first farmers in the Nile were migrants from Asia or of indigenous African stock has been much debated.

A group of Bushmen, living much as their ancestors did 10,000 years ago, are pictured in the Kalahari Desert of Botswana. Nomadic hunters and gatherers of wild food, they possess only what they can carry, using poisoned arrowheads to fell game and transporting their water in huge ostrich eggshells from one water hole to another.

There are a few cultural traits that suggest connections with Asia (for example, some of the pottery, a type of barbed harpoon, and notched arrowheads), but most of the material culture exhibits a characteristically African tradition of bifacial stone flaking, as in the axes and adzes, the sickle blades, knife blades, and scrapers. Sheep and goats as well as cereals, however, must have been introduced from elsewhere since there are no wild forms known in Africa from which they could have come. This is not the case for the cattle, for two wild species were present in northern Africa; cattle bones, said to date to 5400 B.C., have been found in the Sahara. The bas-reliefs in the tombs of the Old Kingdom in Egypt (3200–2900 B.C.) show what appear to be experiments in domesticating native species of gazelle, hyena, ass, and various birds. How far back this goes is not known; with the exception of the ass, these experiments came to nothing, presumably because of the greater potential of the Asian domesticates.

By 5000 B.C. there were certainly domesticated sheep or goats, though not cattle, in eastern Libya, but we have as yet no means of knowing whether the people also cultivated grain crops. It is interesting that, except for the introduction of pottery and a more refined manner of making flint tools, the material culture of these early farmers shows very little change from that of the immediately preceding hunting population. It is likely that the new economy resulted from the diffusion of outside ideas, rather than from a substantial change of population. In the same way northwest Africa probably acquired domestic animals, wheat, and barley about the same time that the Sahara was also populated by nomadic pastoralists with herds of sheep and cattle.

All these peoples have been described as being in possession of a Neolithic economy: they owned livestock and sometimes cultivated plants, made pottery, and ground and polished their stone axes and other implements to produce tougher cutting edges. There is little or no substantial evidence of cultivation by the Saharan pastoralists before about 1100 B.C., when bullrush millet was being grown by the Neolithic peoples living in defended villages at the western edge of the Sahara along Mauritania's Dar Tichitt escarpment.

The Sahara at this time, as during most of the Upper Pleistocene, was a much more favorable place to live than this arid desert landscape is today. Up to about 2000 B.C. the large Ethiopian game animals abounded and were regularly hunted, as is evidenced by the many different forms of arrowheads that occur in large numbers at desert sites. The grazing by lakes and swamps and in the wadis supported not only wild game but large herds of cattle besides. Cattle bones have been found dating from the middle of the sixth millennium B.C. in the Acacus caves in the Saharan desert of southern Libya and from 2000 B.C. in the Dar Tichitt. The people were mostly nomadic, living in easily transportable dwellings, probably made of mats or skins laid over a bent wood framework. Sometimes, as in the Tassili caves of Algeria—among the greatest storehouses of art in the world—these pastoral peoples are portrayed as Negroes, at other times they are shown as Afro-Mediterraneans.

These Neolithic pastoralists spread throughout the Sahara, and it can be expected that they made contact with the hunting communities living in the savanna belt to the south, where much of the country was unsuitable for live-stock because of the tsetse fly. Intradesert movement, evidenced by the wide distribution of certain traditions (for example, that of the dotted wavy line pottery motif), would also have led to the spread of knowledge of domestication. Since, however, the wheats and barleys are winter rainfall crops and do not do well in the tropics (other than on the high plateau of Ethiopia) except under irrigation, local cultigens had to be developed.

Although the evidence for the stages of incipient agriculture south of the Sahara still has to be found and documented, it is clear from the stone tools that have been uncovered that there must have been from about 3000 B.C. onward considerable experimentation. At first this was random, but later it was planned. Eventually, by hybridization and selection, indigenous wild prototypes were converted into staple West African and Ethiopian food crops. How long this took is unknown, but it was the essential basis for all large-scale settlement.

Dry rice in Guinea, sorghum and bullrush millet in the Sudan savanna belt, yams in the forests of West Africa, and the indigenous teff (a grain) and ensete (African banana) were cultivated similarly in the highlands of Ethiopia, as were also emmer wheat and barley, which presumably spread from the Upper Nile. Sites in northern Ethiopia and rock art depicting long-horned cattle suggest the likelihood that food production had spread to Ethiopia by at least the beginning of the second millennium B.C., if not appreciably earlier.

In the first millennium B.C., perhaps due ultimately to the desiccation of the Sahara and the consequent exodus of peoples, pastoralists appear in the Eastern African Rift with herds of sheep and cattle, introduced probably from the southern Sudan and Ethiopia. These herdsmen were long-headed Afro-Mediterraneans who buried their dead in communal graves under stone cairns or sometimes cremated them in caves. They had ground stone axes, made several

different kinds of pottery, and used pestles and curious thick platters and bowls made of lava, probably for cooking food. They made a range of implements from obsidian, the black volcanic glass.

As their handiwork shows no obvious break with local tradition, nor do the physical remains of the people themselves suggest a new physical type, it seems likely that it was the economy rather than the population that changed, as in Libya and West Africa. Some of these early peoples may even have penetrated into the southwestern parts of the continent, where they introduced cattle and sheep. Some of the large Bushmanoid peoples, including ancestors of the Hottentots now living there, were not slow to become pastoralists themselves.

The bushlands are yielding up a unique record for the understanding of our human origins. The seemingly unchanging and limitless expanse of Africa's savanna lands would appear to have been the cradle of mankind, and it was here about two million years ago that the first technological advances were made that led to the complex civilizations of the twentieth century.

By 8000 B.C. the ethnic and linguistic maps of the continent as we know it began to take shape. Berbers occupied North Africa and the Sahara, and Ancient Egyptians the Nile Valley. Sudanese Negroes lived in Nubia. Other Negro types lived in the West African savanna, the Sahara, and the rain forests. Long-headed proto-Nilotes and proto-Kushites inhabited the drier parts of East Africa and the Horn. To the south in the savanna grasslands were the Bushman races, who spoke Bush and Hottentot languages; and small-statured Negroid peoples occupied the equatorial forests.

Each had its individual cultural tradition and developed those skills and patterns of social and economic behavior that were dictated by the record of the past and the exigencies of the surroundings. So there emerged the naturalistic art of the Bushman hunters; the plastic art of the West African potter; the simplistic, but highly symbolic, skills and craftsmanship of the artists in wood carving in the equatorial and West African forests; the self-sufficiency and knowledge of animal husbandry of the Berber peoples. Each was in turn affected by contact with peoples of different races and different traditions in other culture areas, and so the way was paved for the appearance of more complex civilizations in the more strategically situated and economically richer parts of the continent. These new civilizations and cultures were also influenced by external factors, but they were, nonetheless, essentially African, with their roots buried deep in the land of Africa.

TONGUE, *Bushman Painting*

STONE AGE ARTISTS

Some of the world's oldest and most wondrous art exists in various parts of Africa. Painted or engraved by Stone Age peoples on rock surfaces, including the walls of caves and rock shelters, it was done over many millenniums, from approximately 6000 B.C. to perhaps as recently as the eighteenth or nineteenth centuries. Thousands of paintings and petroglyphs record with vigor and beauty the activities of primitive societies of hunters and gatherers and of early pastoralists and farmers. In South Africa prehistoric rock art of Bushmen, and possibly other groups, has been known to the world for two hundred fifty years. Scenes like the one above, of Bushmen trapping a hippopotamus (shown in a copy made early in this century by M. Helen Tongue from a wall painting in the district of Molteno), range in age from at least two thousand years old to comparatively recent work. Similar paintings, skillfully executed by Bushmen and other Stone Age artists, have also been found in many parts of eastern Africa, from Transvaal and Rhodesia to the Upper Nile. In North Africa in Algeria's Tassili plateau, rock art is the work of ancient peoples who occupied the Sahara before its desiccation forced them to migrate elsewhere. Their work was revealed only in the late 1950's, following the expeditions of the French explorer-ethnologist Dr. Henri Lhote. At Tassili and at other sites in the Sahara vast numbers of paintings and engravings, like those reproduced on the next two pages, provide a vivid and surprising picture of that now arid region at a time when it abounded with human and animal life. The polychrome paintings were done with pigments extracted from ocherous earths, mineral oxides, and powdered schists found locally. Representations of hunters, dancers, symbolic figures, wild animals, and cattle herds often overlap, the different subjects and styles revealing a steady development of these people toward more complex societies.

The powerful, charging rhinoceros at
right was painted by an artist at the
Tassili's Ozaneare site at a time in the
past when a wetter Sahara was the habitation of big game animals and cattle.

JEAN-DOMINIQUE LAJOUX, *Merveilles du Tassili N'Ajjer*

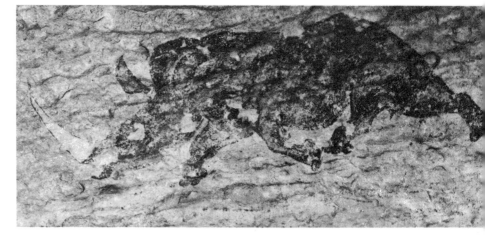

Prehistoric Saharan bowmen (left) race across a rock wall at Sefar in the Tassili region. The rhythm and excitement of the mural are heightened by the running archers' greatly exaggerated stride.

The graceful dancers below, evidently in ritual dress, were painted on cliffs in the Libyan Sahara. Their discoverer, Fabrizio Mori, places them before 2000 B.C.

A hunter stalks a giraffe in the copy at right of another painting from the Libyan Sahara. Killed for their hides and meat, giraffes probably vanished from the arid wasteland in the first century A.D.

SEEKING MAN'S ORIGINS

BLACK STAR—CONSTANCE STUART

THE TWO GUELAS

The creation of the world and of human life is one of the most popular subjects of the myths and legends handed down from generation to generation by the various peoples of Africa. The following tale is from the Ivory Coast.

There lived, before all things were on the earth and in the sky,

Two very powerful creators.

There was the Guela on High!

And there was the Guela Below.

One day the wind did not blow.

The Guela Below became bored; he began to yawn—

And some clay issued from his mouth. He said:

"I will make some men, women, fish, animals, and plants with the clay."

And with the clay he made some men, women, fish, animals, and plants. He said:

"I will put blood into the bodies of the men, women, fish, animals, and plants that I made in clay so that they can live by my doing."

The Guela Below poured blood into the bodies of the men, women, fish, and animals, but they did not come to life! The Guela Below became angry; and he left the clay men, women, fish, animals, and plants outside.

He grew impatient. He went away. He left all the clay statues outside.

One day the rain fell. Many of the clay men melted in the rain. The Guela saw what had happened to many of the men, women, fish, animals, and plants that were of clay. The Guela said:

"They melted in the rain because they are clay."

Sadness grew in the heart of the Guela Below. He took the clay men, women, fish, animals, and plants that were still in one piece. He took them and put them in a cave.

At that time the night was always on the earth.

At that time the earth was always in the night.

The Guela Below had only fire by which to see.

At that time the day was always in the sky.

At that time the sky was the day. The Guela on High had the sun to light his way.

The Guela on High saw that the Guela Below had some fine playthings. He said:

"Give me some of your clay men, women, fish, animals. I will give them life, and to you I will give the light of my sun."

The Guela Below said:

"I will give you only the clay fish, ani-

Ceremonial mask from the Ivory Coast

ABIJAN MUSEUM; RAPHO-GUILLUMETTE—MARC AND EVELYNE BERNHEIM

mals, and plants. I will not give you clay men and women." The Guela on High said:

"I also want the men and the women—"

The Guela Below said:

"So be it. You will have them, but first you must give them life."

Then the Guela on High brought life to the bodies of the men, women, fish, animals, and plants.

Then the men and the women arose and began to walk, the fish arose and began to swim, the animals arose and began to leap, the plants arose and began to grow.

The Guela on High said:

"Now, Guela Below, keep your promise. I gave life to the men, women, fish, animals, and plants that are of clay; I gave you sunlight; now keep your promise!"

But the Guela Below did not wish to hear of it. Then the two Guelas argued. Both of them became angry for all the time to come until the end of time.

Since that time the Guela on High tries to take back the life he gave to the clay men, women, fish, animals, and plants shaped by the Guela Below.

Each time the Guela on High appears to take back the life that he gave to the men, women, fish, and animals, and plants, a man, a woman, a fish, or a plant dies.

But since the Guela Below contests the life the Guela on High gave to the clay men, women, fish, animals, and plants, the time of their quarrels is the time when the men, women, fish, and animals, and plants are sick.

It is also the time of the sirocco.

It is also the time of war.

It is also the time of storms—

The stars are precious stones that the Guela on High makes shine to attract women to him.

The moon is the eye of the Guela on High.

With its eye open or half-open, the Guela on High watches the Guela Below, his enemy—even in the night, when he takes away the sun from the Guela Below, the sun he gave him along with life to the men, women, fish, animals, and plants of clay.

This was before all things were on the earth and in the sky.

THE REVOLT AGAINST GOD

This vivid creation myth, related by the Fang people of Gabon in West Africa, tells of a being whose ambition causes his fall from grace.

At the beginning of Things, when there was nothing, neither man, nor animals, nor plants, nor heaven, nor earth, nothing, nothing, God *was* and he was called Nzame. The three who are Nzame, we call them Nzame, Mebere, and Nkwa. At the beginning Nzame made the heaven and the earth and he reserved the heaven for himself. Then he blew onto the earth and earth and water were created, each on its side.

Nzame made everything: heaven, earth, sun, moon, stars, animals, plants; everything. When he had finished everything that we see today, he called Mebere and Nkwa and showed them his work.

"This is my work. Is it good?"

They replied, "Yes, you have done well."

"Does anything remain to be done?"

Mebere and Nkwa answered him, "We see many animals, but we do not see their chief; we see many plants, but we do not see their master."

As masters for all these things, they appointed the elephant, because he had wisdom; the leopard, because he had power and cunning; and the monkey, because he had malice and suppleness.

But Nzame wanted to do even better; and between them he, Mebere, and Nkwa created a being almost like themselves. One gave him force, the second sway, and the third beauty. Then the three of them said:

"Take the earth. You are henceforth the master of all that exists. Like us you have life, all things belong to you, you are the master."

Nzame, Mebere, and Nkwa returned to the heights to their dwelling place, and the new creature remained below alone, and everything obeyed him. But among all the animals the elephant remained the first, the leopard the second, and the monkey the third, because it was they whom Mebere and Nkwa had first chosen.

Nzame, Mebere, and Nkwa called the first man *Fam*—which means power.

Proud of his sway, his power, and his beauty, because he surpassed in these three qualities the elephant, the leopard, and the monkey, proud of being able to defeat all the animals, this first man grew wicked; he became arrogant, and did not want to worship Nzame again: and he scorned him:

Yeye, o, layeye,
God on high, man on the earth,
Yeye, o, layeye,
God is God,
Man is man,
Everyone in his house, everyone
  for himself!

God heard the song. "Who sings?" he asked.

"Look for him," cried Fam.

"Who sings?"

"Yeye, o, layeye!"

"Who sings?"

"Eh! it is me!" cried Fam.

Furious, God called Nzalan, the thunder. "Nzalan, come!" Nzalan came running with great noise: *boom, boom, boom!* The fire of heaven fell on the forest. The plantations burnt like vast torches. *Foo, foo, foo!*—everything in flames. The earth was then, as today, covered with forests. The trees burnt; the plants, the bananas, the cassava, even the pistachio nuts,

everything dried up; animals, birds, fishes, all were destroyed, everything was dead. But when God had created the first man, he had told him, "You will never die." And what God gives he does not take away. The first man was burnt, but none knows what became of him. He is alive, yes, but where?

But God looked at the earth, all black, without anything, and idle; he felt ashamed and wanted to do better. Nzame, Mebere, and Nkwa took counsel and they did as follows: over the black earth covered with coal they put a new layer of earth; a tree grew, grew bigger and bigger and when one of its seeds fell down, a new tree was born, when a leaf severed itself it grew and grew and began to walk. It was an animal, an elephant, a leopard, an antelope, a tortoise—all of them. When a leaf fell into the water it swam, it was a fish, a sardine, a crab, an oyster—all of them. The earth became again what it had been, and what it still is today. The proof that this is the truth is this: when one digs up the earth in certain places, one finds a hard black stone which breaks; throw it in the fire and it burns.

But Nzame, Mebere, and Nkwa took counsel again; they needed a chief to command all the animals. "We shall make a man like Fam," said Nzame, "the same legs and arms, but we shall turn his head and he shall see death."

Ancestor head of Gabon's Fang people

This was the second man and the father of all. Nzame called him *Sekume*, but did not want to leave him alone, and said, "Make yourself a woman from a tree."

Sekume made himself a woman and she walked and he called her *Mbongwe*.

When Nzame made Sekume and Mbongwe he made them in two parts, an outer part called Gnoul, the body, and the other which lives in the body, called Nsissim.

Nsissim is that which produces the shadow, Nsissim is the shadow—it is the same thing. It is Nsissim who makes Gnoul live. Nsissim goes away when man dies, but Nsissim does not die. Do you know where he lives? He lives in the eye. The little shining point you see in the middle, that is Nsissim.

> Stars above
> Fire below
> Coal in the hearth
> The soul in the eye
> Cloud smoke and death.

Sekume and Mbongwe lived happily on earth and had many children. But Fam, the first man, was imprisoned by God under the earth. With a large stone he blocked the entrance. But the malicious Fam tunneled at the earth for a long time, and one day, at last, he was outside! Who had taken his place? The new man. Fam was furious with him. Now he hides in the forest to kill them, under the water to capsize their boats.

> Remain silent,
> Fam is listening,
> To bring misfortune;
> Remain silent.

MAN'S NOBLE PEDIGREE

The great nineteenth-century English naturalist Charles Darwin shocked the world and revolutionized science by proposing that all life can be traced to a common ancestry. His two most famous works are The Origin of Species (1859), *in which he outlines the theory of natural selection, and* The Descent of Man (1871), *from which these passages are taken. Darwin was accused of denigrating man by relating him to apes and of hav-*

ing underminded the credibility of science through "flimsy speculation." However, as is shown here, the scientist was a profound admirer of all life, especially his human brethren.

The most ancient progenitors in the kingdom of the Vertebrata, at which we are able to obtain an obscure glance, apparently consisted of a group of marine animals. . . . These animals probably gave rise to a group of fishes, as lowly organized as the lancelet; and from these the Ganoids, and other fishes like the Lepidosiren, must have been developed. From such fish a very small advance would carry us on to the Amphibians. We have seen that birds and reptiles were once intimately connected together; and the Monotremata [egg-laying mammals such as the platypus] now connect mammals with reptiles in a slight degree. But no one can at present say by what line of descent the three higher and related classes, namely, mammals, birds, and reptiles, were derived from the two lower vertebrate classes, namely, amphibians and fishes. In the class of mammals the steps are not difficult to conceive which led from the ancient Monotremata to the ancient Marsupials; and from these to the early progenitors of the placental mammals. We may thus ascend to the Lemuridae; and the interval is not very wide from these to the Simiadae. The Simiadae then branched off into two great stems, the New World and Old World monkeys; and from the latter, at a remote period, Man, the wonder and glory of the Universe, proceeded.

We are naturally led to enquire, where was the birthplace of man at that stage of descent when our progenitors diverged from the Catarhine stock? The fact that they belonged to this stock clearly shows that they inhabited the Old World; but not Australia nor any oceanic island, as we may infer from the laws of geographical distribution. In each great region of the world the living mammals are closely related to the extinct species of the same region. It is therefore probable that Africa

was formerly inhabited by extinct apes closely allied to the gorilla and chimpanzee; and as these two species are now man's nearest allies, it is somewhat more probable that our early progenitors lived on the African continent than elsewhere. But it is useless to speculate on this subject. . . .

Thus we have given to man a pedigree of prodigious length, but not, it may be said, of noble quality. The world, it has often been remarked, appears as if it had long been preparing for the advent of man: and this, in one sense is strictly true, for he owes his birth to a long line of progenitors. If any single link in this chain had never existed, man would not have been exactly what he now is. Unless we willfully close our eyes, we may, with our present knowledge, approximately recognize our parentage; nor need we feel ashamed of it. The most humble organism is something much higher then the inorganic dust under our feet; and no one with an unbiased mind can study any living creature, however humble, without being struck with enthusiasm at its marvelous structure and properties.

EMERGING MAN

In the century that has elapsed since Darwin published his studies of evolution, dramatic progress has been made in anthropology and related disciplines. Although much data is still conjectural and controversial, scholars can now piece together, with a fair degree of accuracy, the fascinating story of man's African beginnings. The following essay, recently written by Dr. C. Loring Brace, curator of physical anthropology at the University of Michigan's museum, is a lucid survey of what has been learned to date. It suggests how man originated in Africa; why all his forebears were black; and why some, through adaptation, have what we call white skins.

Central to any definition of man, and the key to his evolutionary success, is a phenomenon not immediately visible when specimens of the creature are scrutinized. This phenomenon is what the anthropologist calls culture. It includes not only the high points of art, music, and literature, but also all those things that result from the cumulative efforts of other people and previous generations. Tools, the traditions regulating their use, vital information, and language itself—all are included in the concept culture. Man is not just an animal that possesses culture, but an animal that cannot survive without it. Men could not exist if each had to discover anew the control of fire, the manufacture of clothing and shelter, the sources of edible sustenance, and the guidelines for workable interpersonal relationships, to say nothing of the mechanics, electronics, chemistry, and physics on which human life depends today. These elements of culture are a cumulative continuation of simpler counterparts in the past.

In the beginning our ancestors, like other animals, must have been faced with the problem of surviving without the aid of culture. So much of culture is perishable or intangible that there is no way to determine when culture as a cumulative phenomenon began. Nonperishable cultural elements have an antiquity of about two million years in Africa. The cultural tradition of which they are a part continues without break, expanding to occupy the tropical and temperate parts of the Old World around 800,000 years ago, and ultimately developing into all the cultures in the world today.

From this we postulate an African origin for all mankind. The existence of crude stone tools in Africa a million and a half to two million years ago allows us to suppose the existence of culture at that time. Our guess suggests that the possessor of this culture could not have survived without it; therefore, he deserves the designation *man*—however primitive and crude he might have been.

We further postulate that culture existed a long time before the initial appearance of recognizable stone tools. This is speculation, but not idle specula-

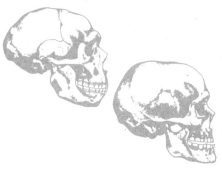

These skulls represent, in descending order, three critical stages in evolution: Australopithecus, *Neanderthal man, and Cro-Magnon man, an early* Homo sapiens.

ROMER, *Vertebrate Paleontology*, SMITHSONIAN INSTITUTION

tion, because we could not otherwise account for the transformation of ape to man. Although small in quantity, supporting evidence exists in the form of skeletal material. Fossilized remains, including skulls, jaws, teeth, and a few other skeletal pieces have been found in association with the oldest known stone tools both in Olduvai Gorge in East Africa and in the Transvaal of South Africa. Since the discovery of these fossils in 1924, argument has continued over their status—ape? man? human ancestor? extinct side line? Brain size was within the range of that for the large modern anthropoid apes, but these early hominids walked erect on two feet as does modern man. Molar teeth were of gorilloid size, but the canines did not project beyond the level of the other teeth.

Despite continuing arguments over whether the balance of traits was on the human or simian side, it is apparent that the survival of these early hominids depended on a distinctly non-apelike adaptation. Bipedal locomotion did not enable hominids to escape predators by rapid flight. Neither could these hominids seriously threaten to bite a potential

predator. Contrast this with such modern ground-dwelling primates as baboon and gorillas where the enlarged canine teeth of the males represent formidable defense weapons. We can guess that these early hominids depended for survival on something not visible in their anatomy, and our guess is that they used hand-held tools.

Possibly they defended themselves with the crude hunks of worked stone found at the sites where their skeletal remains have been discovered, but more likely they relied on pointed sticks. To use a rock as a defensive weapon requires close contact with the attacking creature, while the defender probably preferred to face his tormentor from the far end of a pointed stick. Not only is the pointed stick a simple and effective weapon—devisable with a minimum of manufacturing effort—but it can also double as a digging tool. Edible roots and bulbs are a substantial part of the diet of baboons that live today in the savanna, an environment typical of the areas inhabited by the earliest hominids. The addition of a simple digging stick of the kind used by the surviving hunting and gathering human groups—and probably by the early hominids—could easily double the baboons' food supply.

The huge, worn molars of the early hominids indicate that they relied on gritty, uncooked vegetables for subsistence. Unlike any other primates, their canine teeth are functionally indistinguishable from their small incisors. Assuming that the remote hominid ancestor had enlarged canine teeth like all other primates, then the creatures associated with the stone tools in East and South Africa two million years ago belonged to a line in which the selective pressures needed to maintain large canines had been suspended for a long time. Cultural means of defense must have existed long before the earliest stone tools.

Within the last three years jaws and teeth have been found in southwestern Ethiopia that are so like the Olduvai and Transvaal finds that they must be related. Their antiquity, however, extends back nearly four million years, and no stone tools are associated with them. The canine teeth in the fragmentary remains are not enlarged, leaving us to infer that defensive weapons must have been used some four million years ago—two million years before the earliest stone tools existed. Reliance on hand-held weapons for defense (and perhaps also for food getting) did not automatically convert apes into men, but it altered the forces of selection so that evolution in the human direction was a consequence. For one thing, occupation with tool wielding reduced the locomotor role of hands. Legs and feet, as a result of natural selection, assumed the entire burden of locomotion. Tools usurped the defensive role of canine teeth, and, with an accumulation of mutations, these teeth were reduced. The vast majority of mutations interfere with the development of the structures that depend on their control, but usually these "deleterious mutations" are eliminated by selection. When selection is reduced or suspended—as when tools reduced the defensive role of teeth—the reductive mutations simply accumulate in the ongoing gene pool of the population. The structure controlled by the genes—the canine teeth, for example—eventually fails to achieve the full development once characteristic of the remote ancestral population. . . .

The evidence from Olduvai Gorge in East Africa shows that crude stone tools were added to the limited cultural repertoire toward the end of this long early hominid phase—a period I prefer to call the australopithecine stage. These tools belong to the incipient part of a tradition of butchering large animals in the Middle Pleistocene. At the end of the Lower Pleistocene, however, they occur mainly with the fossilized remains of immature animals. We can guess that this records the beginning of the adaptive shift that was largely responsible for the development of *Homo sapiens*, a shift related to the development of hunting as a major subsistence activity.

In the Middle Pleistocene, somewhat less than a million years ago, man emerges as a major predator. This adaptation is unique among the primates, and it is not surprising that many of the physical, behavioral, and physiological characteristics that distinguish man from his closest animal relatives are related to this adaptation. While we cannot make direct behavioral or physiological tests on fossils, we can make inferences based on their anatomy, on their apparent ecological adaptation, and on conditions observable in their modern descendants.

Anthropologists generally agree that the men of the Middle Pleistocene are properly classified as *Homo erectus*. The first specimen to be discovered was classified in the genus *Pithecanthropus* at the end of the nineteenth century. While we no longer accept this generic designation, pithecanthropine remains a convenient, nontechnical term for Middle Pleistocene hominids.

Brain size was twice that of the preceding australopithecines and two-thirds that of the average modern man. With the absence of a specialized predatory physique, natural selection probably encouraged the evolution of intelligence. While brain size had increased, the size of the molar teeth had reduced, although they were still quite large by modern standards. This reduction may have been related to the shift from a rough vegetable diet to one with a large proportion of meat. Meat, needing only to be reduced to swallowable pieces, requires far less mastication than starches, which begin the process of conversion to simple sugars by mixing with salivary enzymes through extensive chewing.

Evidence, although fragmentary, also suggests that bipedal locomotion in its modern form was perfected at this time, the Middle Pleistocene. While man's mode of locomotion may not be speedy, it requires an expenditure of relatively little energy. To this day, primitive hunters employ the technique of trotting persistently on the trail of an herbivore

until it is brought to bay, often many days later.

Several correlates of this hunting life are suggested. Man, reflecting his primate heritage, is relatively night-blind and must, therefore, confine his hunting activities to the daytime. A tropical mammal (and physiologically man is still a tropical mammal) pursuing strenuous activities in broad daylight is faced with the problem of dissipating metabolically generated heat. The hairless human skin, richly endowed with sweat glands, is unique among terrestrial mammals of much less than elephantine size, and I suggest that this developed under the selective pressures of regular big game hunting early in the pithecanthropine stage.

The elimination of the hairy coat by natural selection left the skin exposed to the potentially damaging effect of the ultraviolet component of tropical sunlight. The obvious response was the development of the protective pigment melanin. Consequently the Middle Pleistocene ancestors of all modern men were probably what in America today is called black.

The conversion of this being into what is technically known as *Homo sapiens* requires only the further expansion of the brain from the pithecanthropine average of 1,000 cubic centimeters (actually well within the range of modern variation) to the average today of 1,400 cubic centimeters. Fragmentary fossil evidence suggests that this transition had taken place by the beginning of the Upper Pleistocene, about 120,000 years ago. Men at that time—referred to as Neanderthals—still had an archaic appearance. In general these early representatives of *Homo sapiens* were more muscular and robust than their modern descendants—particularly the males. Jaws and teeth were large, especially the front teeth, which, from their wear patterns, evidently served as all-purpose tools.

Since the first appearance of *Homo sapiens* in his Neanderthal form, human evolution has been characterized by a series of reductions. Whenever human ingenuity made life easier, there was a relaxation of the forces of selection, and these reductions followed. More effective hunting techniques lessened the burden on the hunter's physique, and an eventual reduction in muscularity was the result. Manipulating tools lessened the stress on the anterior teeth, and the consequent reduction of these and their supporting bony architecture converted the Neanderthal face into modern form. In parts of the world where manipulative technology is a late phenomenon, such as aboriginal Australia, faces and teeth have remained large. Where clothing was developed for survival in northern climes, the significance of protective skin pigment was lessened, and the consequent reduction produced the phenomenon that is euphemistically called white.

The only thing that has not been reduced is the number of human beings. We cannot even guess at the population density of the australopithecines. Throughout the Middle Pleistocene, the archeological record suggests a fairly constant population for the hunting pithecanthropines. Evidently the population increased dramatically with the Neanderthal form of *Homo sapiens*. The diversification of food resources and the increase in cultural complexity that accompanied the first appearance of modern *Homo sapiens* just under 35,000 years ago also signaled another sharp jump in population. This set the stage for the tremendous population growth made possible by the development of agriculture after the end of the Pleistocene 10,000 years ago.

Thus did *Homo sapiens* emerge—a manifestation of ecological imbalance, literally shaped by the consequences of his own impact upon the world. His fate, too, will be shaped by his future impact on the world—the result of his numbers and his actions. Malthus sounded the alarm nearly two centuries ago, but few listened to his warning. One who did was Ambrose Bierce, who added to his definition of man that "his chief occupa-

tion is extermination of other animals and his own species, which, however, multiplies with such insistent rapidity as to infest the whole habitable earth. . . ."

"THE MISSING LINK"

Misreadings of Darwin and other evolutionists led many people to the erroneous conclusion that man is directly descended from the gorilla and chimpanzee. This idea provoked a world-wide search for the fossil of a creature that stood halfway between ape and man. Even after it was known that man and the great apes (Pongidae) are descended from a common hominoid ancestor and stand in a cousin to cousin, rather than grandfather to grandchild, relationship, people continued to seek "the missing link." In 1938 the late Dr. Robert Broom, a physician and paleontologist who excavated extensively in the Transvaal, unearthed an ape-man fossil that seemed to confirm earlier suspicions. In this excerpt, from a 1950 report, he describes his discovery of the "Kromdraai ape-man," which he called Paranthropus robustus, *recently reclassified as* Australopithecus.

On the forenoon of Wednesday, June 8, 1938, when I met Barlow, he said, "I've something nice for you this morning"; and he held out part of a fine palate with the first molar-tooth in position. I said, "Yes, it's quite nice. I'll give you a couple of pounds for it." He was delighted; so I wrote out a cheque, and put the specimen in my pocket. He did not seem quite willing to say where or how he had obtained it; and I did not press the matter. The specimen clearly belonged to a large ape-man, and was apparently different from the Sterkfontein being [an *Australopithecus africanus*].

I was again at Sterkfontein on Saturday, when I knew Barlow would be away. I showed the specimen to the native boys in the quarry; but none of them had ever seen it before. I felt sure it had not come from the quarry, as the matrix was different. On Tuesday forenoon I was again at Sterkfontein, when I insisted on Barlow telling me how he had got the specimen. I pointed out that two

teeth had been freshly broken off, and that they might be lying where the specimen had been obtained. He apologized for having misled me; and told me it was a school-boy, Gert Terblanche, who acted as guide in the caves on Sundays, who had picked it up and given it to him. I found where Gert lived, about two miles away; but Barlow said he was sure to be away at school. . . .

The road to the school was a very bad one, and we had to leave the car, and walk about a mile over rough ground. When we got there, it was about half-past twelve, and it was play time. I found the headmaster, and told him that I wanted to see Gert Terblanche in connection with some teeth he had picked up. Gert was soon found, and drew from the pocket of his trousers four of the most wonderful teeth ever seen in the world's history. These I promptly purchased from Gert, and transferred to my pocket. I had the palate with me, and I found that two of the teeth were the second pre-molar and second molar, and that they fitted on to the palate. The two others were teeth of the other side. Gert told me about the piece he had hidden away. As the school did not break up till two o'clock, I suggested to the principal that I should give a lecture to the teachers and children about caves, how they were formed, and how bones got into them. He was delighted. So it was arranged; and I lectured to four teachers and about 120 children for over an hour, with blackboard illustrations, till it was nearly two o'clock. When I had finished, the principal broke up the school, and Gert came home with me. He took us up to the hill, and brought out from his hiding place a beautiful lower jaw with two teeth in position. . . .

The spot where the skull had been found was much more carefully examined within a few days. All the ground in the neighborhood was carefully worked over with a sieve, and every fragmentary bone or tooth collected. . . .

When the skull was restored, it was seen to be larger than that of the Sterkfontein ape-man, and to differ in a number of respects. The face is flatter, and the jaw more powerful. The teeth are larger, and in a number of characters different. I therefore made this Kromdraai skull the type of a new genus and species, *Paranthropus robustus*. A preliminary account of the discovery appeared in *The Illustrated London News* of August 20, 1938, under the heading "The Missing Link No Longer Missing"; for which title I think I was not responsible.

There are a number of characters in which this new skull is more human than the Sterkfontein. In the Sterkfontein ape-man we know that the lower canine, at least in the male, is rather large and with a well-marked posterior cusp. In the Kromdraai jaw, though the canine has lost the crown, we have the impression of it on the matrix, and it is about as small as in man, with apparently no posterior cusp. . . .

The teeth of Paranthropus are almost fully known. The incisors and canines are relatively small, but the pre-molars are very large . . . and the molars are also very large, and a little different in details of structure. . . .

In February, 1941, I sent a new assistant with a couple of boys to clean out a little pocket of bone breccia near the spot where the Kromdraai skull had been found. They brought the breccia back to the Museum, and when this was broken up and examined we found a badly preserved lower jaw, but with perfect teeth. Except for the first incisor the whole milk set is preserved and the first true molar crown is shown, but it had probably not yet cut the gum. The milkteeth are practically unworn, and the little being who had them was certainly a little younger than the Taungs child—perhaps three years old.

We do not, of course, know for certain whether this is the jaw of a Paranthropus. As we get the specimens, they are not labeled. But, as it is certainly the jaw of an ape-man child found within two yards of the spot where the adult skull of Paranthropus was discovered, we can re-

fer it with much confidence to the same species. It is most unlikely that two species of ape-men were contemporaries in the same locality. . . .

In the block of matrix in which the Paranthropus skull lay, I was able to find a number of important post-cranial bones. I got the distal end of the right humerus and much of the proximal end of the right ulna. These are so very human that had they been found isolated probably every anatomist in the world would say that they were undoubtedly human. Yet they were found in the matrix only a matter of inches from this remarkably man-like skull; and no trace of any human teeth or implements have been found.

Further, against the maxilla lay a second metacarpal bone with a number of phalanges. These show that the hand was so slender that it could not possibly have been used for walking on.

In the same block of matrix I found an ankle bone—the astragalus, or talus. This bone differs markedly from that of the chimpanzee, and is nearly human, but not quite. It confirms the view that Paranthropus walked on his hand-legs, and used his hands for the manipulation of tools and weapons.

CAVE-KEEPING 20,000 B.C.

Years of research in East Africa have enabled Dr. Louis Leakey to produce the following reconstruction of the life of a caveman.

A Stone Age hunter is wandering down the valley in search of game when he espies a rock-shelter in the side of the rocky cliff above him. Carefully, and with the utmost caution, he climbs up to it, fearful lest he may find that it is occupied by the members of some other Stone Age family who will resent his intrusion, or possibly even that it is the lair of a lion or a cave bear. At last he is close enough, and he sees that it is quite unoccupied, and so he enters and makes a thorough examination. He decides that it is a much

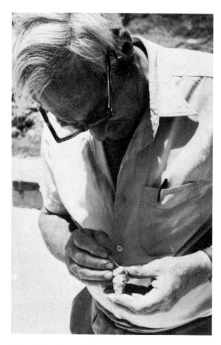

Dr. Louis Leakey examines a fossilized specimen on one of the sites at Olduvai.
RAPHO-GUILLUMETTE, CAMERAPIX, DAR ES SALAAM

more suitable habitation than the little shelter where he and his family are living at present, and he goes off to fetch them.

Next we see the family arriving and settling into their new home. A fire is lit either from some embers carefully nursed and brought from the old home, or else by means of a simple, wooden fire drill. (We cannot say for certain what methods Stone Age man used for obtaining fire, but we do know that from a very early period he did make use of fire, for hearths are a common feature in almost any occupation level in caves and rock-shelters.)

Probably some of the family then go off to collect grass or bracken to make rough beds upon which they will sleep, while others break branches from bushes and trees in the near-by thicket and construct a rude wall across the front of the shelter. The skins of various wild animals are then unrolled and deposited in the new home, together with such household goods as they possess.

And now the family is fully settled in,

and the day-to-day routine is resumed once more. The men hunt and trap animals for food, the women probably help in this and also collect edible fruits and nuts and roots. Gradually, rubbish starts to accumulate on the floor; decaying vegetation mingles with wood ash scraped from the hearth, and mixed with all this are the bones and teeth of the animals that have served for food. The stone and bone tools, which comprise the weapons and domestic implements of the family, break or become blunt through use, and they are discarded and new ones made. Blocks of suitable material collected during hunting expeditions have been brought to the new home, and from these flakes are knocked off to make new tools. This process involves the scattering of many waste flakes and chips over the floor, and these soon become incorporated in the debris in the same way as the tools that have become too blunt for further use. When the weather is fine a great deal of the work is done on the platform outside the shelter, so that deposits accumulate there too.

Years pass, the older members of the family die and—according to custom—are buried in the floor of the shelter; the younger members of the family grow up and marry, and all the time the home continues to be used, so that more and more debris accumulates on the floor. A large part of this debris is perishable material which by the process of decay turns into soil, throughout which imperishable objects of stone and bone are scattered.

Naturally enough, the deposits so formed do not accumulate evenly over the whole floor, and although the floor may have been level to start with (and even this is seldom the case) it very soon ceases to be so.

And so generations pass and a considerable depth of deposit is formed representing an occupation level, and then something happens which results in the shelter being vacated. When this occurs the shelter may perhaps be taken over almost immediately by some other Stone Age family—possibly of a different tribe and with a somewhat different culture—in which case we shall get a somewhat different occupation level superimposed upon the first one. On the other hand, the shelter may remain untenanted for a considerable period of time, in which case dust and leaves and other purely natural material will collect and gradually build up a sterile layer covering the occupation level, until the place is once more selected as a living site.

THE ART OF THE BUSHMEN

The naturalistic rock paintings and engravings of South Africa are among the richest and best preserved in the world; they provide invaluable information regarding the Bushmen and their ancestors. The surviving paintings and carvings were probably executed no earlier than 2,000 years ago; however, they are based on traditions that date back to the beginning of the Late Stone Age, about 11,000 years ago. The following description of the life of the Bushmen and Late Stone Age hunters was written in 1963 by Alex Willcox, a noted interpreter of South African rock art.

"**B**ushmanoid" peoples occupied most of Southern Africa, except the heavily forested areas, for many centuries before the pastoral Hottentots and the Bantu arrived.

Their culture, it has already been said, was non-pastoral and non-agricultural, the natural resources of the veld alone providing their food and their whole equipment. Hunting and fishing secured their protein requirements, but their very varied diet included innumerable varieties of berries and other fruits, bulbs, roots and nuts, seeds, insects, ant and termite eggs, birds' eggs, shell-fish, honey, etc. Some of these were sources of liquid also (or at least they are now), e.g. the body fluids and stomach contents of animals and the juices of fruits such as the tsamma melon. Although a hard struggle in their latter days and now, their life must have been easy enough before being disrupted by new-comers, for the earliest travelers found immense herds of game roaming the still unravished veld in the Bushmen territories.

Their habitations were natural rock shelters where these were found and small crude shelters of branches elsewhere; their clothing, loin cloths, aprons and cloaks (karosses) of animal skins, their ornaments, beads made from ostrich eggshell, bands of leather or rings of ivory about their limbs, or simply body paint. Having to trek whenever, because of local drought or over-hunting, the game became scarce, the Bushmen kept their equipment to a minimum in quantity and weight. A typical camp would have, in addition to clothes and ornaments, only the women's digging sticks and the spheroidal bored stones which weighted them, leather bags to contain the collected foods, calabashes, ostrich eggshells or the sewn-up skins of small animals as water containers, probably an upper and nether grindstone for crushing seeds, melon pips, etc. and perhaps a crude pot or two. There would also be the men's bows and arrows, quivers, knob-kerries, fire-sticks and painting equipment. Stone implements for cutting up and skinning their kills, for scraping the skins and for wood working (e.g. making bows and arrows and knob-kerries) would lie about but would not be transported when trekking, others being made in a few seconds when required.

The short weak Bushman bow with its bow-string of twisted sinew, the quiver made of leather or by hollowing out a section of a branch of Aloe Dichotoma, and the reed arrows, are too well known to need further description here. The arrow heads were most commonly of bone and latterly formed by a small triangle of iron beaten flat, but a few perfect tanged and barbed stone points have been found and there is good historical evidence that arrow heads were also made of laurel-leaf shaped points and by a pair of *crescents* placed together and cemented to the foreshaft with vegetable mastic. These were barbed with quills, thorns or small splinters of stone. The minutest crescents might have been used thus. It is difficult to see any other use for them. The poison spread behind the point was from many sources including snake venom, spiders, grubs of a certain insect and the juices of various plants.

The curious implement often seen in the rock paintings made by fixing a jackal's tail to the end of a short stick, which served various purposes from wiping perspiration from the brow, to swatting flies and signaling, was commonly used also by Hottentots and Bantu.

Naturalists to a man the Bushmen had names for the flora and fauna of their environment and knew well the habits of the animals, birds, and insects, and the properties as food, medicine, poison and perhaps as paint media, of the plants. They had even discovered a plant which by its smell would keep lions away. They were geologists enough to know where to find the minerals from which they made pigments and the best stones for making implements; and they were astronomers enough to name the principal stars and planets and know their peculiarities. As meteorologists they became renowned rain-doctors. In short they had an impressive body of practical knowledge and knew their environment better than most civilized men know theirs.

Their amusements were dancing, mime, music, storytelling and the graphic arts. Rhythmic clapping accompanied the dances which often took the form of one or a few dancers dressed in the skins of animals miming their actions, sometimes solely for entertainment, but sometimes no doubt, also for ritual and magical purposes, as in the case of the eland bull dance of the Naron.

STONE AGE SURVIVORS

Ethnographical studies are often valuable supplements to paleontological and artistic materials. The following excerpt is from a 1965 report by H. R. MacCalman and B. J. Grobbelaar describing two stone-working

OvaTjimba groups that still exist in the Kaokoveld mountain range of South West Africa. Despite long contacts with the pastoral Hottentots, they remain hunters and gatherers.

Living with these OvaHimba was a group of fourteen people who, it was immediately apparent, did not correspond to them either physically or culturally. They spoke Herero like the OvaHimba but in a dialect form, and said that they were of the Tjimba tribe. The group consisted of three men with their wives, three adult daughters, three small children and two babies. On questioning we learned that they normally lived in the heights of the Baynes Mountains, but had come down because of a sick child and were now liv-

ing with the OvaHimba, helping in the village and herding goats in return for medicine and food. They informed us that they owned no cattle but lived by hunting and gathering. On being asked to show their hunting weapons they produced bows and arrows with crude iron arrowheads and demonstrated that for other activities they used stone tools. . . .

The most important aspect of the Okombambi group technology, however, is the use of stone as an habitual and integral part of their material culture. On being asked what implements they used they replied that they made knives and choppers from stone, and voluntarily demonstrated their manufacture. . . .

Kaupatana regarded his stay at Otjinungua as merely a temporary move.

This Bushman woman transports her youngest—and probably all her household belongings—in a pair of leather slings. Typically, her people own no domesticated animals, and the task of providing sustenance is sharply divided between the hunters (male) and the gatherers (female). The life of Bushmen is one of mobility; they travel in small, semiautonomous groups under the leadership of a headman and come together in larger assemblies only during the melon season, the occasion for joyous celebration.
BLACK STAR—CONSTANCE STUART

When the rains came, he told us, he would take his family back up the Baynes Mountains and they would continue to live, as before, by hunting and gathering.

Kaupatana does the hunting using a bow and poisoned arrow, and the same range of animals are hunted and trapped as by the Okombambi group. He is also responsible for the collection of wild honey. The two women collect *veldkos* [vegetable foods] and this also comprises the same species as the Okombambi group collects.

When a big animal is killed it is first skinned and then the meat is cut off and the carcase dismembered, in all cases using stone flakes. As Kaupatana's bow needed restringing, a springbok was shot by the stock inspector and given to Kaupatana so that he could demonstrate how he would skin and butcher the animal while living in the mountains.

First, Kaupatana selected a suitable pebble from the river bed and struck some twenty flakes from it using the block-on-block method. These he examined very carefully and selected four flakes, all between two and three inches in length, which had a suitable shape and sharp edge. No further sharpening or shaping of these flakes was done.

Using one of the flakes Kaupatana slit the skin of the belly of the springbok from throat to tail and proceeded to cut the skin, which he held in his right hand, from the carcase. The flake was held between the thumb and first two fingers of the left hand, Kaupatana being left-handed, with the forefinger resting along the top and was used with short slashing strokes. In this way he skinned one half of the springbok, the skin on the legs being slit and taken off up to the hoof. The other half of the springbok was then skinned and the animal was turned over so that the complete skin could be detached along the back. Finally, Kaupatana cut off one shoulder, still using a stone flake, in order to demonstrate how the carcase is dismembered. The carcase was then carried back to the camp place . . .

BUSHMAN'S PRAYER

This prayer reflects the Bushman's age-old activity: hunting. These hardy peoples still live in the Kalahari, which covers large areas of Botswana and South West Africa.

I do not know
What will happen to me
Regarding food.
I do not know
What I shall do
To get something to eat.
Let us eat and become big.

HUNTERS OF MODERN AFRICA

When the first Europeans arrived in South Africa in the fifteenth century, they found groups of hunters who had not yet entered the Iron Age. Indeed, some hunters, having retreated into the Kalahari under Bantu and European pressure, have even today continued to perpetuate ancient modes, barely altered by outside influences. The following excerpt by Monica Wilson, professor of social anthropology at the University of Cape Town, describes the present economy and social structure of southern Africa's hunters and collectors, notably the Kung, the San, and G/wi peoples. It is based in part on reports of colonists and travelers up through the 1800's, but it also draws on contemporary scholarship, such as L. Marshall's studies of the Kung Bushmen.

The hunters and collectors described by the early travelers and settlers inhabited the mountains and the sea-shore. They had no domestic animals except the dog and lived off game, of which there were enormous herds in southern Africa; wild roots and berries, commonly called veldkos; caterpillars, termites, and locusts; wild honey; and fish. . . . Recent studies in the Kalahari show that, even in the desert, vegetable foods play a major part in the diet of hunters, and this is likely to have been the case when they occupied better-watered country. A digging stick, tipped with bone and weighted with a bored stone, and a skin cloak which also served as a bag, were the women's equipment among the

mountain people, and these are still used in the desert, though the stick is not always tipped and weighted; in the desert ostrich eggshells, used for storing water, are a housekeeper's essential utensils.

Honey was so important that wild hives were marked as private property and a thief who stole from one might be killed by the owner. . . . The hunters of the mountains fished in the rivers with harpoons made of bone, and trapped eels, when opportunity offered, and the Strandlopers [hunters and collectors on the shore] lived off shellfish and other fish caught on lines, and in the fishgarths which are still visible along the Cape coast. All the hunters used bows and poisoned arrows. The effective range was small—twenty-five yards among the G/wi—and hunters crept up on herds, sometimes disguising themselves in buck-skins or ostrich feathers. Then they followed the wounded animal until the poison took effect; they were highly skilled in tracing a spoor. They dug traps for large game, and built stone or brushwood fences, or posts or cairns, the height of a hunter, and surmounted by feathers, to form converging lanes through which game was driven. This suggests co-operation between a considerable number of men. . . .

The hunters also burnt the grass during winter to attract game to the fresh pasture and to make them more visible, and to encourage the growth of spring bulbs. This firing of the grass was a common cause of friction with the herders, who likewise burnt for fresh pasture, but who needed to preserve some areas of long grass to maintain their cattle. The hunters were fair-weather men, because their bows were not serviceable in the rain—the gut string snapped—and they always lay up in their caves during rain in the mountains and, where they had the choice, selected drier rather than wetter country.

The hunt supplied not only food but clothing, which was made of skins, and the furs and feathers which were, and still are, traded to other peoples for iron and tobacco. Even the every-day utensils of ostrich-eggshell and tortoise carapace were hunters' trophies.

The hunters lived and still live in bands, each independent of the next, and their characteristic is isolation. . . . In the Queenstown district in the nineteenth century every band used a cave as its headquarters, and in each of these there was a painting which was sacred and from which a band took its name. One painting was of a python, another of springbok, another of eland, and so forth. The desert bands, on which we have evidence, have no headquarters, but each has a name, which continues through time, and each moves within a defined area. All the hunting groups have, and had, territories over which their prior rights are recognized. . . . Mrs. Marshall's statement fits very closely with that of Kolb who reported in 1707 that "Hottentots of every kraal and nation have the liberty of hunting throughout all the Hottentot countries."

However, neither isolation nor the recognition of territory precluded movement over a hundred miles or perhaps much further. San living in the Drakensberg [Mountains] painted boats which could only have been seen near the coast, a hundred miles away, and mounds of shells from shellfish have been found on middens fifty miles inland. Hunting expeditions typically lure men far afield, and in the traditional histories of Africa it is most often the hunter who explores and settles in a new territory. The San were surely no exception. Interaction with only a small number of people is not to be confused with confinements to a limited area.

Among the !Kung, marriage between neighboring bands is approved, and movement of families of parents and children from one band to another occurs, but only within the area recognizing some common unity. This includes thirty-six or thirty-seven bands and a thousand persons. The diversity in language among the hunters, even neighboring bands sometimes not understand-

ing one another . . . is surely a reflection of long isolation.

Control over rights in water and vegetable foods is vested in a custodian among the !Kung. The office is hereditary, passing from father to son (or failing a son to a daughter and through her to her son), but there is no chief with power to adjudicate in disputes and enforce judgments. The custodian's precedence is recognized by his taking the head of the line when the band moves, and making the first fire in a new camp, from which others take brands, but he does not necessarily organize hunting parties or trading trips, and when theft or adultery occurs the wronged person will kill the one who has injured him, or they fight until both are killed. The whole band, however, is concerned to reconcile quarrelling members, for the loss of a hunter means a serious loss in food and, if weapons are used, the smallest scratch may mean death, since the poison with which arrows are smeared is deadly. Mrs. Marshall describes very vividly how men and women gather quickly, seeking to compose any quarrel that arises. A fight once begun is feared almost like atomic warfare. Taking fire from the custodian is a recognition of his leadership among the !Kung, as among so many peoples in Africa. He himself starts the first fire at each camp with firesticks, and even where hunters are clients of herders there is no fiction of inability to ignite a fire as among the pygmies.

No matter how wide the territory they occupy, or how much individual families may have to scatter during drought to find food, when a band moves as a group the members camp and build their shelters close together—so close that sisters in different households can hand things to each other. . . . One of the jibes of the Sotho against the San was that all slept together without regard for decency, but eyewitness evidence shows that the !Kung camp in a regular order, each married couple establishing their shelter, or a symbol of it, beside their fire, and people sitting in their set order, men to the

right of the fire facing the entrance to the shelter, women to the left. Boys from about the age of puberty sleep by their own fire with other boys of the band, and girls of the same age with some single woman, unless they themselves are already married. Each person may indeed hollow out a sleeping place to escape the biting night wind. The shelters and fires are huddled together in the wide expanse of the desert, and it might be that a stranger, coming on a deserted camp, would suppose that the whole band slept promiscuously. He would be mistaken, but relationships in an isolated band are necessarily intimate. . . .

Among the !Kung each woman cooked the veldkos she had collected for her own husband and young children, but the meat of any animal shot was distributed, the man whose arrow had first struck the animal allocating portions, according to set rule, to individuals in the band, for no one eats alone "like a lion."

The family of parents and children held together until a son married, when he went to live with his wife's band, and to hunt for his parents-in-law. Only after the birth of several children was he free to rejoin his own band, but he did not always do so, and no large descent groups, such as are common among the herders and cultivators, developed. . . .

At her first menstruation a girl, even though already married, was secluded and observed various taboos, and a great dance miming the courtship of the eland bull was performed in her honor. Circumcision was not a general practice among the hunters (though the Sotho claim to have learned it from the San), but a ritual which marked the attainment of adult status was celebrated for groups of boys. The elements emphasized by various writers are the testing of a boy's ability as a hunter; treatment with medicines to give him skill in hunting; and the performance of certain dances. The boy's rite preceded marriage, and among the !Kung it was a condition of marriage, for he must have proved himself as a hunter before he could marry, and bring to his bride's parents a large animal he, himself, had killed. . . .

Property that could be inherited did not exist—except for certain rights over the water and veldkos in a given area—and kinship bonds in time, which are so closely tied to the inheritance of wealth, were not treated as important. Nor was there a veneration of the ancestors comparable to that general among the Bantu-speaking peoples. . . .

The gods spoken of by the San of the Cape were Kaggen (Cagn, Qhang, 'Kaang) who made all things, and the mantis which was his embodiment. To J. M. Orpen's query: "Where is !Kaang?" a hunter replied: "We don't know, but the elands do. Have you not hunted and heard his cry, when the elands suddenly started and ran to his call? Where he is the elands are in droves like cattle." It is as though Pan and the mantis held the poetic imagination in the south of Africa as on the Mediterranean shore. The hunters danced at the new moon and full moon, and prayed for good hunting. . . . But these ideas were not held by all the hunters, and from the scanty material it is not possible to formulate any general beliefs which have continued through time. . . .

For all that their food supply was precarious and search for food occupied most of their time, San hunters were prolific artists. They painted or engraved on stone and ostrich eggs; they made thousands of ostrich eggshell beads to adorn themselves; they told myths; and above all, they danced. The myths and paintings were connected and so, perhaps, were the dances, for they painted dances as well as animals and hunting scenes. . . .

Men and women, daily engaged in the strenuous search for food, nevertheless found strength at night to dance. . . . In the dances the hunters regularly mimed animals: the courtship of the eland bull; the kudu; a gemsbok hunt; a hyena feeding off a carcass and keeping jackals at bay; vultures at the carcass of a zebra; ostriches. It seems as if the acute obser-vation of animals, necessary to a hunter, had to find some expression in artistic form, whether it be painting, or dancing, or myth. The Naron say "in olden times the trees were people, and the animals were people . . .", and the world view of all the hunters depicted a time when animals spoke like men, and there was friendship between them.

TRACKING FATHER ELEPHANT

The spirit and drama of the chase is expressed in numerous tribal poems. This one, chanted by the Gabon Pygmies, evokes the mystery and stillness of the black forest night.

Elephant hunter, take your bow!
Elephant hunter, take your bow!

In the weeping forest, under the wing of the evening
the night all black has gone to rest happy:
in the sky the stars have fled trembling,
fireflies shine vaguely and put out their lights:
above us the moon is dark, its white light is put out.
The spirits are wandering.

Elephant hunter, take your bow!
Elephant hunter, take your bow!

In the frightened forest the tree sleeps, the leaves are dead,
the monkeys have closed their eyes, hanging from the branches above us:
the antelope slip past with silent steps,
eat the fresh grass, prick their ears,
lift their heads and listen frightened:
the cicada is silent, stops his grinding song.

Elephant hunter, take your bow!
Elephant hunter, take your bow!

In the forest lashed by the great rain
Father elephant walks heavily, *baou, baou,*
careless, without fear, sure of his strength,
Father elephant, whom no one can vanquish:
among the trees which he breaks he stops and starts again:
he eats, roars, overturns trees and seeks his mate:
Father elephant, you have been heard from far.

Elephant hunter, take your bow!
Elephant hunter, take your bow!

In the forest where no one passes but you,
hunter, lift up your heart, leap and walk:
meat in front of you, the huge piece of meat,
the meat that walks like a hill,
the meat that makes the heart glad,
the meat that we'll roast on our coals,
the meat into which our teeth sink,
the fine red meat and the blood we drink smoking.

Elephant hunter, take your bow!
Elephant hunter, take your bow!

DEATH OF THE HUNTER

This poem, also included in the repertoire of the Gabon Pygmies, is called "Death Rites." It implies belief in the ascendance of the soul.

The animal runs, it passes, it dies. And it is the great cold.
It is the great cold of the night, it is the dark.
The bird flies, it passes, it dies. And it is the great cold.
It is the great cold of the night, it is the dark.
The fish flees, it passes, it dies. And it is the great cold.
It is the great cold of the night, it is the dark.
Man eats and sleeps. He dies. And it is the great cold.
It is the great cold of night, it is the dark.
There is light in the sky, the eyes are extinguished, the star shines.
The cold is below, the light is on high.
The man has passed, the shade has vanished, the prisoner is free!
Khvum, Khvum, come in answer to our call!

Chapter Two

CIVILIZATIONS OF THE NILE

(c. 4500 B.C.-A.D. 350)

by

Margaret Shinnie

THE ADVANCE FROM A LIFE OF FOOD GATHERING and hunting to one of agriculture brought far-reaching changes to the people. Nomadic life, with its urgent search for food, was replaced by permanent agricultural communities and a greater sense of security. Villages gradually gave rise to towns and the organization of forms of government, and the reliability of seasonal crops and animal herding provided leisure time in which to practice all the arts and crafts, a noticeable feature of this stage of man's development.

Agriculture probably came to Egypt from western Asia, where it had been practiced since about 6000 B.C. or possibly earlier. Although the Nile Valley is particularly well suited to agricultural pursuits, the earliest known farming settlements there date from as late as about 4500 B.C. By about the middle of the fourth century B.C., however, the Egyptians had become dependent on agriculture.

Once this advanced stage of life had been established in Egypt, more sophisticated social and cultural achievements rapidly followed, partly because farming was so unusually easy in the Nile Valley: grain scattered on the silt deposited by the river's annual flood grew of its own accord and had only to be harvested. It has been calculated that by sensible exploitation of his land an Egyptian farmer could produce three times as much grain as was needed for his domestic purposes. As a result, society could support craftsmen, officials, priests, and landowners. Another reason for Egypt's progress was that the Nile Valley, enclosed by infertile land, was slightly remote and easy to defend except in times of internal weakness. Lastly, because of its location, Egypt could share in the advances of the countries of the Levant, whose perpetual struggles with one another may well have given rise to technical achievements that they, involuntarily perhaps, placed at Egypt's disposal.

e mortuary temple of Ramses II *at Luxor, with a statue of the great ruler*

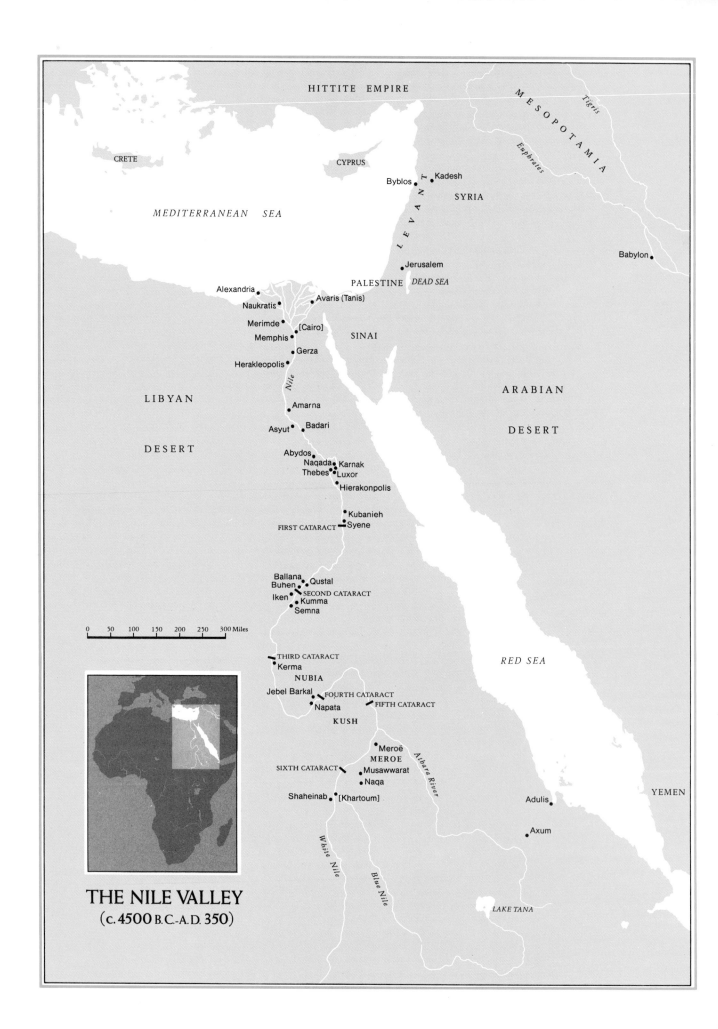

HITTITE EMPIRE

MESOPOTAMIA

Tigris

Euphrates

CRETE

CYPRUS

Byblos • • Kadesh

SYRIA

MEDITERRANEAN SEA

L E V A N T

Jerusalem •

PALESTINE *DEAD SEA*

Babylon •

Alexandria •

Avaris (Tanis) •

Naukratis •

Merimde •

[Cairo] •

Memphis •

SINAI

Gerza •

Herakleopolis •

Nile

ARABIAN

LIBYAN

DESERT

Amarna •

Asyut • • Badari

DESERT

Abydos •

Naqada • • Karnak

Thebes • • Luxor

• Hierakonpolis

• Kubanieh

FIRST CATARACT • Syene

Ballana • • Qustal

Buhen •

Iken • SECOND CATARACT

• Kumma

• Semna

RED SEA

0 50 100 150 200 250 300 Miles

THIRD CATARACT

• Kerma

NUBIA

Jebel Barkal • FOURTH CATARACT

• Napata FIFTH CATARACT

KUSH

Atbara River

• Meroë

MEROE

SIXTH CATARACT • Musawwarat

• Naqa

Shaheinab • [Khartoum]

Adulis •

YEMEN

• Axum

White Nile

Blue Nile

LAKE TANA

THE NILE VALLEY
(c. 4500 B.C.-A.D. 350)

Although ancient Egypt seems separate from the rest of Africa, isolated in the narrow valley of the Nile and unique in its culture and achievements, there was nevertheless contact with other African peoples—with Libyans to the west and with Kushites and the inhabitants of Punt to the south and southeast. In the earliest days of Egyptian agriculture the neighboring Sahara was not the arid expanse of desert that it later became. Climatically, there was a wet phase. The Saharan rock drawings make this clear, for the many animals portrayed, including cattle, would not be able to exist in the current environment. The people of the Sahara were not only pastoralists but also hunters, who must have hunted over land that was savanna. About 3000 B.C. the wet phase came to an end, and desiccation set in, accelerated perhaps by overgrazing as the aridity increased. It is not unlikely that the Saharan people learned the practice of animal herding and domestication from Egypt, and as the encroaching desert forced them to search farther and farther for better grazing lands, this knowledge was carried slowly to other areas by peoples whose identity is still something of a mystery. (In 1907 the remains of three previously unknown cultures were discovered in the region of Aswan; they were designated as A-, B-, and C-Group people.) The C-Group people, who moved into Nubia from the western desert about 2300 B.C., may have been one of the tribes who were forced southward; others may have gone toward the fertile banks of other great rivers. At Ntereso in northern (modern) Ghana arrowheads of a type common among the Saharan people were found, very much farther south than had been earlier supposed.

Traces of the various peoples who lived in the Nile Valley are prolific, and it is hardly possible to walk along the banks of the river without treading on antiquities—almost every part of the river's bank was inhabited at some time or other. For most of its course the Nile flows through a valley made cultivable by the deposit of silt that the flood brings down from the Ethiopian highlands following the summer monsoon rains. In a year of heavy flood, enriched soil extends some way up the wadis, thus providing further areas for cultivation. Back of the valley lies the desert sand, and at various places, particularly in Upper Egypt and the northern Sudan, a barrier of rocky cliffs separates the flood plain and the desert. Proceeding south into the area of annual rains, the desert lands and the scrub and seasonal grazing lands of the central Sudan give way to wide savannas, and even farther south, near the headwaters, to tropical forest. There is a barrier to river travel in the south in the shape of a tangled mass of floating papyrus and aquatic grass, known as the sudd (meaning in Arabic "obstruction" or "dam"), which even today must be cleared if boats are to pass. It has always been possible to travel overland, however, though the terrain might seem uninviting for such a trek.

Although the Nile would appear to be a natural link between the lands and peoples along its banks, river travel south of Aswan is made difficult by a series of cataracts or, more properly, rapids. The First Cataract at Aswan and the five more cataracts in the Sudan are all unnavigable; even small boats have frequently met with disaster in their attempts to negotiate the currents. All these natural barriers probably impeded the Egyptians from penetrating as far south as they might otherwise have done; but they did have constant contact with Nubia (the lands along the Nile south of the First Cataract) and are known to have traveled as far as the Fifth Cataract.

The earliest agricultural settlements in the Nile Valley are those discovered in the Fayum in Middle Egypt. Here, on the edge of a lake, were village communities that grew wheat and barley—staples of their diet—and possibly herded livestock. Tools and weapons of stone and spear points of bone indicate that they engaged in hunting, which must have played a large part in their lives. They made simple, rough pottery for cooking and storage—useful rather than beautiful—the shapes patterned on leather bags and baskets familiar from times when there was no pottery. If there was a more rudimentary agriculture at an earlier time, evidence of it has either been buried deep in the Nile silt or eroded away by subsequent exploitation of the land for farming and grazing.

Later settlements, whose inhabitants had more sophisticated skills such as carving bone and ivory into spoons and combs, decorating pottery with painted designs, and grinding jars out of alabaster and basalt, have been discovered at various places, the best known being Merimde, Badari, and Naqada. Much of this work reveals a growing appreciation of artistic design and expression, and there must have been craftsmen with tools adequate to practice it. There is also evidence that trade with outside peoples was beginning, for copper objects and fragments of cedar and juniper wood (materials not indigenous to Egypt) suggest contact with other lands, probably by an overland route that presumably crossed Palestine to Syria and the more advanced cultures of western Asia. Arrowheads of a type found widely in the Sahara were also found at Merimde, so there must have been contacts with people to the west of Egypt as well. Malachite, used in the preparation of eye paint, may have come from Nubia or Sinai.

Much farther upstream, in and around Khartoum, hunting and fishing and food-gathering communities lived on the riverbank. Two sites that date from fourth century B.C. have been identified, similar in many ways to those of Egypt, but later by a thousand years. Neither crop growing nor animal herding was practiced, though there is a possibility that at the later site, Shaheinab, the domestication of animals had just begun, as evidenced by the discovery of bones identified as those of a domesticated goat. Similarities in the stone tools of this village with some of those of the Fayum villages suggest contact between them, even though the Egyptian influence would have taken about a thousand years to take hold in the Sudan.

Up till this point in time, 3500 B.C. in Egypt and a little later in the Sudan, these small farming communities grew and developed their skills without much contact with the civilizations around them (particularly the more advanced cultures of Mesopotamia). Although agriculture presumably came to Egypt from western Asia, further influences are not apparent at this stage, despite some evidence that small trading activities were beginning. Another factor limiting the development of Egyptian technology was that many of the raw materials, such as hardwoods and metals, essential to the more advanced techniques of Mesopotamia, were not available in Egypt. Vague references in the later literature of early dynastic Egypt allow the inference that these small settlements were products of a social system essentially African in character, with a rainmaking god-king as leader. It was probably very similar to practices that still survive in parts of southern Sudan, where the leader is

invested with the power of bringing rain and is ritually killed when his powers begin to wane. (In Egypt it was not so much the bringing of rain that was desired as the control of the Nile flood, which itself is dependent on rain far upstream.)

Physically, the Egyptians at this time were typical North Africans, lightly built brown-skinned people. They were predominately of Afro-Mediterranean type, though in Upper Egypt skeletons of Negroid type have been found. (By pharaonic times a mixing of peoples would take place, and the careful depiction in the tomb paintings of skin color, facial features, and kinds of hair make it clear that there were Afro-Mediterranean, Southwest Asian, and Negroid types among them.) The people of early Khartoum were Negroid, and they shared a distinctive custom of the modern southern Sudanese, that of extracting two incisor teeth. The custom is still observed today to signify manhood.

The next period, starting about 3400 B.C., was one of great development in Egypt; it contained all the fundamental advances that would lead to the brilliance of the Old Kingdom. The most impressive features almost certainly arose out of contacts with Mesopotamia and are well seen at the Nile settlements of Hierakonpolis, Naqada, and Gerza. While it had been possible earlier to make trading ventures by overland routes, the development of a seagoing ship was vital in encouraging and widening the scope of such activities. It was at this time that seaworthy ships capable of sailing the tideless Mediterranean Sea were probably first used; they were most likely built in a well-wooded

The clay models at right, of what may have been fertility figures, were fashioned in the fifth and fourth millenniums B.C. by predynastic Egyptians. They were principally hunters and fishermen, but also primitive stockbreeders and farmers, and their small, agricultural villages were scattered throughout the Nile Valley before the formation of states and the rise of the great dynastic kingdoms. Also found at ancient sites were the objects on the opposite page: a pottery jar decorated with drawings of human figures, boats, and ostriches; and an assortment of flint knives, including one whose carved handle depicts warriors and boats engaged in a fierce river battle.

area such as the Lebanon. Other innovations found at prehistoric sites included a distinctive wavy-handled pottery, which is related to similar ware from Palestine. Still other innovations came seemingly from Mesopotamian sources: for example, building with sun-dried mud bricks, thus making possible more substantial houses than the earlier light reed or matting huts; using cylinder seals as amulets to protect personal belongings; and, most important of all, developing a pictographic form of writing. Though Egyptian writing was entirely different from that of Mesopotamia, it may well have been inspired by the concept of literacy derived from that culture. Trade, however, was not all in one direction, and Egyptian wares found in Palestine testify to the passage of their goods into wider areas.

During this period the first small states probably emerged in the Nile Valley (on the evidence of ruins found, it looks as though they fell into conflict.) Towns grew up and some of them were apparently fortified. Excavations at Naqada have revealed part of a town wall standing below the enveloping sand, and a little clay model found in a tomb shows a similar wall being guarded by soldiers. Rectangular-shaped townhouses were built of mud brick, though no doubt in the countryside the traditional reed or matting huts, usually approximately circular, persisted, as they still do today. Technological skills increased, and the working of flint reached a standard of perfection that has never been surpassed; the thinnest of knife blades were finished with regular ripple flaking, showing a mastery over material that is truly astonishing.

Toward the end of this period, about 3100 B.C., the coalescing of small towns gave rise to two main states: Lower Egypt, from the Mediterranean to the apex of the Delta; and Upper Egypt, from the south to the First Cataract. These became unified under the first pharaoh, Narmer, but the duality of two states continued down through Egyptian history. In times of internal dissension the rivalry between Lower and Upper Egypt asserted itself until a powerful leader came to the fore with the ability to reunite the country. The pharaoh was known as Lord of the Two Lands, and his two-tiered crown expressed this duality, the white mitre of Upper Egypt being superimposed on the red crown of Lower Egypt. Our conventional division of Egyptian history into dynasties is that given by the third-century B.C. Greek historian Manetho, who also gives the names of royalty and some account of events occurring in the various reigns. The dynasties in turn are conveniently grouped into kingdoms: the Old Kingdom (2664–2155 B.C.); the Middle Kingdom (2052–1786 B.C.); and the New Kingdom (1570–1075 B.C.). The periods between the kingdoms, called Intermediate Periods, were times of confusion and dissent, and it is in the three kingdoms that the mainstream of Egyptian history and culture developed.

Preceding the Old Kingdom was a time known as the Archaic Period, which was one of great development in many fields, and Narmer was the first known king of this period. His monuments have been found at Hierakonpolis, Abydos, and in the robbed tombs at Saqqara near Memphis. He also built a city called White Walls (later Memphis) as his residence; it was to become one of the great cities of ancient Egypt. Throughout the Archaic Period trade with the

Osiris, seen at left in a wall painting at the tomb of the Nineteenth Dynasty queen Nefertari, was the chief god of the dead. He carries his traditional emblems—the flail and crook—traceable perhaps to the Egyptians' nomad origins. Anubis, guardian-god of the necropolis, appears below on a chest from Tutankhamon's tomb.

EGYPTIAN MUSEUM, CAIRO

Levant increased. Wood in particular was imported and employed in building. Another major import was copper, turned to new uses for making tools, vessels, and even statues. Expeditions penetrated far south, and a rock-cut inscription of the First Dynasty pharaoh Djer near the Second Cataract in Nubia records an invasion and conquest of local tribes, though it may be a rather boastful description of a successful raid. Technical skills increased, and building became more magnificent, large stone blocks being hewn for funerary monuments and temples. In the making of smaller scaled artifacts craftsmen became more competent, not only at making jars and ornaments but also statues from various kinds of stone. The potter's wheel was introduced and ceramic styles became more varied. Most important of all, however, was the use of writing and the manufacture of a kind of paper from the papyrus reed, so that records could be kept, instructions sent, and all the business of state noted down.

During this time foundations were laid for the role of the king, the pharaoh of Egypt, as a divine god-king who embodied the spirit of ancient Egypt. Originally, simply the most powerful among regional leaders, he became associated with divine functions, in particular the control of

the Nile flood, which meant life to the country. (The powers of the Nineteenth Dynasty pharaoh Ramses II were thought to be so great in this respect that he was credited with the ability to affect rainfall in the far country of the Hittites.) A well-known stone plaque, the Palette of Narmer, found at Hierakonpolis, shows the contemporary view of the pharaoh: the typical stance, huge in proportion to the other figures in the picture, smiting his enemy before the hawk-god Horus, and treading on two captives beneath his feet. Even at this early time the extraordinary power of the pharaoh was evident.

The seeds sown during the Archaic Period came into full flower in the Old Kingdom. An impression of peaceful development, together with a broadening of trading activity, is conveyed. Royal burial customs became elaborate, as illustrated by the Great Pyramids of Giza (about 2600 B.C.). Organizing a sufficient labor force, and conceiving and carrying out the architectural plans, testify to the prosperity and order of the country and to the divine omnipotence of the pharaoh, who could command such resources for his personal use.

From the pyramids and from temple reliefs and wall paintings much can be inferred of religious beliefs. For example, the tomb structure—be it pyramid for the royal or rich, or brick-lined grave for the poor—was seen as a house to live in forever, where objects serviceable or precious in life were placed with the dead for use in the afterlife. Gods other than the pharaoh appear in the reliefs, most commonly Hathor, protectress of the City of the Dead, and Osiris, god of the dead, and the pantheon became established. Much of the artistic endeavor of the time must have been devoted to funerary building, and wall paintings and reliefs on tombs and temples show aspects of daily life, of the running of the country estate and country crafts, amusements, and even the arrival of the tax collector. Statues were also placed in tombs; they were carved of wood or limestone and often painted, and many appear to be realistic portraits, for physical defects are not disguised and there is little suggestion of flattery.

Trading activities were more venturesome, and expeditions were sent to Kush (the Egyptian name for Nubia), to Punt, probably along the coast of the Gulf of Aden, and into the Levant. Egyptian penetration into Palestine is revealed in tomb reliefs, which show Asian fortresses being stormed. At Byblos in the Lebanon a temple was built by the Egyptians as early as the Fourth Dynasty, about 2600 B.C., perhaps for a local community of their people, implying peaceful contact with this great trading center.

Nubia was invaded on several occasions, and early in the Fourth Dynasty the Pharaoh Snefru launched an invasion that cost the Nubians 7,000 prisoners and 200,000 head of cattle. It subdued the local population for some time to come. The wealth of the country was exploited, particularly gold, and at Buhen, near the Second Cataract, an Egyptian settlement was established that was in effect a trading post, and at which copper smelting was carried on. Nubia had been settled by a population archeologists call the A-Group people for lack of more information. Such evidence as there is suggests an appreciable increase in the population of Nubia in the third century B.C. due to settlement by the A-Group people, who may have drifted in from Egypt or from Saharan areas. Physically they were similar to Egyptians, and their culture was much like that of predynastic Egypt, based on small agricultural communities. They were probably not subject to a central authority, though each community would have had its leader.

The basis of Egyptian interest in this land was trade, and Mernera, a pharaoh of the Sixth Dynasty, sent four peaceful expeditions into Nubia, led by a nobleman named Harkhuf, that were of a more ambitious nature than before. The purpose was to open up communications with a country called Yam, whose exact geographical location is uncertain, though it must have been south of the Second Cataract. Harkhuf's fourth journey took place in the time of Pepi II, then a young ruler, who was delighted with the offer of a Pygmy. He wrote to Harkhuf, giving instructions for the care of the Pgymy on the journey northward and adding: "My Majesty desires to see this Pgymy more than all the gifts of Sinai and Punt." All control of Kush was lost, however, during the period of anarchy that followed the Old Kingdom, and the Egyptians withdrew into their homeland.

Up till the Fourth Dynasty power and government had been centralized in the pharaoh, aided by officials whom he chose and to whom he delegated various responsibilities. During the Fourth Dynasty the post of provincial governor and some local offices came to be accepted as hereditary, and the holders of these positions were very conscious of their power. It needed only an old or a weak pharaoh for the whole structure of government to collapse under the jealous ambitions of an anarchic elite. This very situation caused the downfall of the Old Kingdom. At the death of Pepi II, an old man, reputedly a centenarian, who had ruled for many decades, a formidable blow was dealt to the achievements of the Old Kingdom. A vivid account is given in *The Admonitions of the Prophet Ipuwer:* "Behold, they that had clothes are now in rags. . . . Squalor is throughout the land: no clothes are white these days. . . . The Nile is in flood yet no one has the heart to plow. . . . Corn has perished everywhere. . . . Men do not sail to Byblos today: What shall we do for fine wood. . . . Laughter has perished. Grief walks the land, mingled with lamentation."

All the artistic achievement of the Old Kingdom withered, and much of the work of craftsmen ceased to be practiced except in poor and debased forms. Various leaders made unsuccessful attempts to restore peace and order. Finally, a powerful family from Herakleopolis managed to unite Middle Egypt and also bring the Delta under its control. However, Upper Egypt seems to have maintained virtual independence, ruled by the Theban princes. (Thebes was the most important city in that area and the capital of Upper Egypt in times of disunity.) The Herakleopolitans (Ninth and Tenth Dynasties) made an impressive attempt to restore order out of chaos, expelling numbers of Asian and Libyan settlers from the land around the Delta, fortifying their northeastern frontier, reopening trade with Byblos, and re-establishing Memphis as the capital city. Nevertheless, there was sporadic warfare with the Thebans throughout this time, fortune favoring first one side and then the

The Egyptian artists and craftsmen were often organized like common workmen, laboring in gangs under the direction of a foreman. They produced one of the world's richest art legacies, ranging from tiny jewel masterpieces to works of monumental grandeur. The head at left, which once adorned a harp, was probably carved during the New Kingdom. Opposite, a copy of a wall painting in the Eighteenth Dynasty tomb of a Theban prime minister and governor, named Rekmire, shows artisans chiseling and polishing royal statues with tools made of dolorite, a hard stone.

other. After a decisive battle in about 2061 B.C., the Thebans defeated the people of Herakleopolis, and Mentuhotep I became pharaoh of a reunited Egypt. This marks the birth of the Middle Kingdom.

During the time of conflict a secular literature grew, in which appeals were made to the peoples' feelings by means of artistic expression. At a time when the divine guidance of the pharaoh was lacking, this had a particular relevance. Elegant and poetic as it was, much of the writing was inspired by a deep pessimism, an expression of the tremendous misfortune that had befallen a land bereft of its god-king. Titles such as "An Argument between a Man Contemplating Suicide and his Soul" or "The Complaints of the Peasant" give a hint of the sense of depression experienced. "The Instructions for His Son, Mery-ka-re," thought to have been written by one of the Herakleopolitan kings, is concerned with promoting a code of conduct based on moral principles. "Do right," he says, "as long as you are on earth. Calm the afflicted, oppress no widow. . . . Do not kill; but punish with beatings and imprisonment. . . . Leave vengeance to God. . . . More acceptable to Him is the virtue of one who is upright of heart than the ox of the wrongdoer. . . ." Yet another piece of advice praises the art of speaking, "for power is in the tongue, and speech is mightier than fighting."

The Middle Kingdom was a period of further expansion and development in all fields of activity. It was not entirely peaceful, for a bout of anarchy intervened before long and abated only when Amenemhet, who had been a governor of

the South, claimed the throne as first pharaoh of the powerful Twelfth Dynasty. A prophecy attributed to the time of Pharaoh Snefru had forewarned that a period of disaster in Egypt would come to an end only "when a king shall come from the South called Ameny"—but this prediction was contained in a papyrus of Twelfth Dynasty date and is more likely to be a piece of royal propaganda aimed at supporting Amenemhet's ambitions.

About this time a determined effort was made to subdue Kush. A series of remarkable forts was built to control the river passage and quell any insurrection by the local population. The southernmost of these was at Semna, above the Second Cataract; some were built on the eminences along the banks of the river and some on islands in it. The fortifications were strategically placed so that should any be attacked, it could call for help by signaling with a beacon to its neighbors. They served as trading posts as well as military garrisons, for the purpose of Egyptian excursions into Kush was as much for trade as to secure the southern frontier of Egypt. An inscription of a governor of Middle Egypt says that he followed his lord when he sailed south to overthrow his enemies: "I passed through Kush in sailing southward and reached the borders of the earth. I brought back tribute. . . . Then His Majesty returned in safety having overthrown his enemies in Kush, the vile." Efforts to subdue Kush reached their peak in the time of Sesostris III (1878–1843 B.C.), who rebuilt where necessary and consolidated the line of forts, and whose connection with the area was so close that he was later worshiped as a local god.

LEPSIUS, *Denkmäler . . . .*, 1860

The people of Kush at this time were the earlier mentioned C-Group people, a cattle-owning people living in small communities. Although their culture was dissimilar from that of contemporary Egypt, it had, nevertheless, affinities with the pastoral civilizations of late predynastic Egypt, including a distinctive pottery, much of it black with incised geometric designs, by which their settlements are easily recognized. Their animals were of such importance to them that they sometimes buried the skulls of cattle around their own graves and scratched pictures of them on pots. The C-Group were a non-Negroid people, and their settlements and cemeteries have been found from Kubanieh near the First Cataract to as far south as the area of the Third Cataract. One concludes from the number of fortresses built that they were extremely troublesome to the Egyptian forces occupying their land. In an inscription at the fortress of Semna, Sesostris III instructed his men "to prevent any Nubian from passing downstream or overland or by boat, [also] any herds of Nubians, apart from any Nubian who shall come to trade at Iken or upon any good business that may be done with them." (Iken was the name of the fortress at the Second Cataract.) Even their most trivial movements were reported back to Egypt, and the almost daily accounts end with, "All the affairs of the king's domain are safe and sound."

At about the same time, around 1900 B.C., a trading post was set up at Kerma in the neighborhood of the Third Cataract, but whether by the Egyptians or by the local people is not known, though it was certainly a native entrepôt.

The remains of the material culture found there are entirely different from that of the contemporary C-Group people. A spectacular burial mound revealed the interment of an important chief with the accompanying sacrifice of over three hundred others, mostly women and children. The pottery of Kerma, a very fine, highly polished, black-topped red ware, was unique, as were the little ivory and mica figures of birds and animals, which seem to have been used decoratively, the former as inlay for furniture, and the latter attached to leather caps. In the rooms around the trading post were found a variety of raw materials together with manufactured objects, including fragments of Sixth Dynasty alabaster jars, which had no doubt gone out of fashion in Egypt and were foisted off on the natives of Kush in trade. Various Egyptian statues, including one of the Lady Senuwy, wife of Hepzefa, a governor-general of Kush and prince of Asyut, and a fragment of a statue of Hepzefa himself, were discovered; these had probably also been passed in trade.

While the southern border of Egypt had been secured to some extent by deliberate expansion and subjugation of the native population, the northeastern border, which was frequently crossed by Asians, had still to be strengthened. To this end a series of fortified positions, named the Walls of the Prince, was set up along the frontier; but there was no attempt to conquer land or peoples, merely to define the frontier and protect it. Egypt's main interest in Palestine and Syria was undoubtedly a commercial one, though there are evidences of occasional wars; there was, however, much interchange of products of countries in the eastern Mediterranean, including Crete, most of which was conducted through an entrepôt city, such as Byblos.

After the death in 1797 B.C. of Amenemhet III, the last great ruler of the Middle Kingdom, the strength and prosperity of Egypt declined. After about 1785 B.C. a number of Asian names appear in the king lists, and evidently by about 1750 B.C. an Asian people, the Hyksos, had established a principality at Avaris in the eastern Delta. Hyksos control spread over Egypt, and Memphis, the capital city, was seized. Egyptians continued to rule Upper Egypt from Thebes, paying tribute to the Hyksos and holding an uneasy independence only as far north as Asyut. The Theban rulers had apparently also lost their hegemony to the south of Aswan, the land being ruled by a prince of Kush, probably from Kerma. His people had stormed and destroyed that great system of fortresses guarding the First and Second Cataracts, and had evidently made an alliance with the Hyksos. Kamose, "a mighty king in Thebes," writes: "I should like to know what serves this strength of mine, when a chieftain is in Avaris, and another in Kush, and I sit united with an Asiatic and a Nubian each man in possession of his slice of this Egypt, and I cannot pass by him as far as Memphis."

Kamose decided to deliver Egypt from Asian power and set out to crush the Hyksos, along the way meting out ruthless destruction to the towns that had "forsaken Egypt, their mistress." He also captured a messenger traveling southward to the chieftain of Kush. The letter he was carrying from Apopi, the chieftain of Avaris, makes clear the alliance between the two: "Why have you arisen as chieftain without letting me know? Have you [not] beheld what Egypt has done against me, the Chieftain who is in it, Kamose the Mighty, ousting me from my soil . . . come, fare north at once, do not be timid. . . . Then will we divide the towns of this Egypt between us."

Kamose did not live to see the final destruction of Hyksos' rule. His younger brother, Ahmose, carried on the war, eventually bringing about the fall of Avaris and the expulsion of the Asian invaders. He also killed the king of Kush, thereby regaining control of Upper Egypt. By about 1570 B.C., through these successes, Egypt had regained its strength and Ahmose I became the founder of the Eighteenth Dynasty and the New Kingdom—in many ways the most glorious period of Egyptian history. The result of the Hyksos invasion was not a total loss to Egypt in that new ideas and techniques had come with it, among the most important of which was the horse-drawn chariot. The Thebans adopted not only the chariot but the Hyksos designs in armor and weapons in clashes with the enemy.

Ahmose I set to work to re-establish his kingdom and secure it from further invasion. The subduing of the states of the Levant as far as the Euphrates was to continue under his successors. The states of Palestine and Syria were formed into dependencies through treaties with the rulers, whose sons were removed to Egypt as hostages for guarantee of good behavior. On the whole, this was a policy of indirect rule rather than one of colonization, and it was quite different from the treatment meted out to Kush.

Once again in power, the pharaohs waxed supreme and complacent. By 1370 B.C., however, the Hittites of the Anatolian plateau had become strong enough to present a direct challenge to Egypt. No effective answer was given, and Akhenaten, a somewhat eccentric pharaoh who was on the throne at the time, was entirely abstracted by his new religious ideas, which were apparently monotheistic. As a result, Egyptian influence in Syria waned.

Early in the twelfth century B.C. masses of peoples, known in Egyptian texts as the Peoples of the Sea, migrated through the Levant in search of land; they spread destruction wherever they passed, causing further loss of Egyptian power and prestige. Though Egypt did manage to protect its own borders, all its possessions to the northeast had to be sacrificed. Egypt remained a conservative element in the fast-developing world of the Mediterranean. Throughout the New Kingdom the power of the pharaoh was identified with military conquest and the preservation of Egypt's borders, a concept that could not be satisfied once strong enemies and new iron weapons successfully challenged its supremacy.

On the western borders of Egypt the Libyans became troublesome, and on more than one occasion attempted to settle on the rich Delta lands. Driven out of their territory by the incursions of Sea Peoples, and possibly also by increasing aridity of their own lands, the Libyans were so harried that they were difficult to repel. Even after Pharaoh Ramses III of the Twentieth Dynasty crushed them finally, parties of Libyans still infiltrated Egypt. Many became mercenaries in the army, later forming a special military caste that grew strong enough to provide two dynasties among the rulers of Egypt.

The abundance of archeological discoveries from the New Kingdom makes its civilization seem very real—even the shrunken forms of dead kings can be seen, their names known, their possessions studied. The splendor of the tomb of Tutankhamon—rich in alabaster, gold, and pre-

The Eighteenth Dynasty "Heretic King," Akhenaten, worshiped only the sun god, Aten. In the relief above, he is seen at left, seated with Nefertiti and their daughters under the sun disc.
STATE MUSEUM, BERLIN · F. L. KENETT

cious ornaments—gives an idea of the luxury and art of the period, as do the fine temples and sculpture. This was a time of massive architecture and colossal statues, much of which still stand as testimony to the power of the pharaoh. But the basic wealth of Egypt was in agriculture, and the tomb paintings frequently depict agricultural pursuits. The wealthy occupant of the tomb is shown inspecting his fields, vineyards, and gardens. But there were also fishing trips and wild fowl hunts or picnics and entertainments in his house, accompanied by his servants and slaves or on appropriate occasions by his family. The gulf that separated the rich from the poor, the landlord from the peasant, is very clear.

After the Twentieth Dynasty, about 1075 B.C., Egypt again fell into lawlessness and decay. Over the centuries Libyans, Kushites, Persians, Greeks, and Romans dominated, each group holding power for as long as it could. The Libyans form the Twenty-second and the Twenty-third Dynasties. Having been soldiers in the army, they set up a form of military dictatorship; but it ended in dissension and instability, to be succeeded in time by a line of Kushite kings.

The pharaohs of the New Kingdom had brought Kush under direct government control. The territory was put into the charge of a governor, "King's Son of Kush," residing

probably at modern Amarna, a town on the east bank of the Nile well above the Second Cataract. He was appointed by the pharaoh and was directly responsible to him. The frontier was extended beyond the area of the Middle Kingdom forts to a point south of the Fourth Cataract. Towns and temples and military garrisons were established, and the names of many of the rulers are to be found carved on temple walls and columns in the land of Kush. Frequent raids by Egyptian forces were needed to keep the population under control, both the riverain people, with whom they were mainly in contact, and the desert tribesmen, who never became imbued with Egyptian influences. In time the riverain Kushites became completely Egyptianized, adopting Egyptian religious practices and becoming part of the land of the pharaohs. Kush supplied many products that added greatly to the wealth and luxury of Egypt, in particular gold, ebony, ivory, cattle, and slaves.

Under the New Kingdom Kush prospered and became culturally and economically part of Egypt, their people serving in the army and government. Many Egyptian priests, traders, and officials settled in Kush and gave the Kushites a lasting flavor of their culture. At Jebel Barkal a religious center devoted to Egyptian theological beliefs was probably controlled by an Egyptian priesthood.

But by the end of the Twenty-second Dynasty, profiting

Though King Tutankhamon was a man of peace, Egyptian custom dictated that a pharaoh be shown also as a brave and mighty warrior. This feather holder depicts him as an archer in a chariot drawn by caparisoned horses.
EGYPTIAN MUSEUM, CAIRO

from the weakness that had overcome Egypt, Kush became effectively independent, although maintaining its traditions and orthodoxy. Napata, on the east bank of the Nile just downstream from the Fourth Cataract, was the great city of Kushite-Egyptian culture and became the capital of the independent state of Kush. About 750 B.C. a Kushite king, Kashta, felt himself powerful enough to gain control of Upper Egypt, and his son Piankhi (751–716 B.C.) completed the conquest of the country, though this was not accomplished lightly and the Kushite armies had to penetrate Egypt on more than one occasion to achieve their objective. Piankhi made the mistake of withdrawing to Napata, having, as he thought, subdued the Egyptian princes. As a result, it was left to his brother and successor, Shabako (707–696 B.C.), to establish power over the whole of Egypt and assert Kushite administration. Shabako became known throughout the ancient world as King of Kush and Misr (Egypt), and he and his successors form the Twenty-fifth Dynasty.

The Kushite kings, imbued with an orthodox, slightly old-fashioned view of Egyptian life, a reflection of their remoteness from the sources of their adopted culture, were probably welcomed by some in Egypt: by the Theban priests, who saw the possibility of re-establishing their own power under the piety of the conquerors; by those who foresaw a return to the good old days of law and order under the traditionalist usurpers. Indeed, the Kushite kings

proved themselves to be pharaohs in the old manner, larger-than-life majesties who left a fine record, both in Egypt and in Kush. They, too, were responsible for temples, colossal statues, inscriptions in Egyptian hieroglyphs—extremely valuable in relating the events of the period—and they were able to establish a measure of law and order that gained them the respect of other rulers.

In time the Assyrians replaced the Hittites as the dominant power in western Asia. In the reign of Pharaoh Taharqa, in 671 B.C., the Assyrians descended on Egypt. The king was forced to retreat to Thebes from the residence he had established at Tanis (Avaris) in the Delta. A second invasion in the reign of Taharqa's successor, Tanwetamani (664–653 B.C.), drove the pharaoh out of Egypt and back to his own domains. The descendants of these Kushite kings were to rule in their own land for nearly a thousand years, maintaining a state with its own complex culture.

The Kushite capital was moved from Napata to Meroë, located above the Atbara River, probably in the sixth century B.C., perhaps because of the sack in 591 B.C. of Napata by the Greek mercenaries of an Egyptian pharaoh, Psammetik II. An equally likely reason for the move was the fact that Meroë lies in an area of annual rainfall (approximately 4 inches), and grazing for the huge herds of Kushite cattle was more certain.

The Greeks called the Kushites "Ethiopians," which means "burnt faces," implying a darker skin color than that to which they were accustomed. The term does not denote any connection with the modern state of Ethiopia. The Kushites were probably much like modern Sudanese, a varying mixture of the light brown-skinned people of North Africa and the more Negroid people from farther south. In Egyptian tomb paintings they are always shown as darker than the Egyptians themselves. Kushite art, too, makes it clear that there was a difference; the royal ladies of Kush are shown as markedly plump women, and both male and female portrait subjects often are characterized by tightly curled Negroid hair. The culture of Kush, though always overlaid with characteristic Egyptian influences, became more individual after the removal of the capital to Meroë, partly because links with Egypt were more tenuous and partly because lively and more essentially African influences were at work. At one time the Kushites were literate to some extent in Egyptian language and hieroglyphs (though this may have been the prerogative of the priesthood only), but lack of close contact with Egypt caused this skill to decline. The shapes of signs were altered and sometimes given different phonetic values, and finally a new script was developed. While the phonetic values of the new signs are known, they express a language that cannot as yet be interpreted. Except when Meroë is mentioned in the writings of other peoples, knowledge of its culture has to be inferred from material remains.

Many standing monuments of the Kushites can be seen today: the ruins of the city of Meroë; the pyramids where members of the royal family were buried both near Napata and near Meroë; temples; reservoirs for catching water during the rainy season. The greatest concentration of monuments is in the "Island of Meroë," not actually an island but the stretch of country between the Nile and Atbara rivers that was the heartland of the state. Southwest of Meroë is the famous site at Musawwarat-es-Sufra—a complex of temples built, altered, and rebuilt over a period of a thousand years. It is a most spectacular place, where temples, once plastered with sparkling white gypsum, were set in a small plain surrounded by black hills, and it is thought to have been a place of pilgrimage, for there are no dwellings other than a single house, presumably that of a priest.

Objects found in Meroitic pyramid tombs show the influences of pharaonic and Hellenistic Egypt, but also, especially in the pottery, the spirit of Africa. In the Egyptian fashion, objects both precious and useful were placed in the graves: gold and enameled jewelry, beads of all kinds, glass, silver and bronze vessels, bells that were buckled to the necks of cattle, both decorated and plain pottery, quiv-

Wooden models of a pharaoh's army include ranks of Nubians.

ers, arrowheads, spears, bronze and silver lamps, wooden and ivory boxes, furniture, wrappings of cotton cloth, and scatters of animal bones indicating the sacrifice of cattle and horses. The royal pyramid tombs, the majority looted before archeological excavation, must have been very rich in these objects. The mound graves of the common people, with a burial chamber cut deep into the ground, offered up pottery, beads of stone and glass, traces of basketware and fragments of cloth, a hunter's favorite weapon, or a child's toy. In the royal tombs many of the objects were ones that had been imported from Egypt and are some indication of the wealth of the royal personages and of the continuing trade with Hellenistic and Roman Egypt. But the presence of local ware also expresses their appreciation of their own, less sophisticated products, including their beautiful decorated pottery, both that showing Mediterranean influences and that more typically African—such as can be found in many parts of the continent still today.

Little is known of the social organization of Kush in Meroitic times. However, it is clear that royalty was revered, probably as divine beings as in Egypt. Also, there was possibly an elite priesthood, again in the tradition of Egypt. The importance of the royal ladies, as evidenced by temple reliefs and by reference to Candace, queen of the Ethiopians, in the Acts of the Apostles ("Candace" is a Meroitic word meaning "queen" or "queen mother"), suggests that it may have been a matrilineal society; in that case succes-

sion to the throne would have been through the female line, a not uncommon African practice. As in Egypt, there may also have been brother-sister marriages, though it is more likely that they were marriages of cousins, an arrangement still considered desirable in many parts of Africa today. Indeed, cousins are referred to and thought of as brothers and sisters in some African societies. Religion was obviously an important part of life, as shown by the devoted work, both architectural and artistic, in temples; they were all built of hewn sandstone blocks in contrast to the sun-dried brick dwellings, royal or common.

The greatest achievement of Meroë, however, was the practice of ironworking. Iron was first introduced into Egypt perhaps by Greeks who had settled there or perhaps by the Assyrians, who used iron weapons in war. As far as is at present known, the Kushites seem to be the first people of sub-Saharan Africa to have used iron, starting perhaps about 500 B.C., though this may be due simply to the accident of where excavation and study have taken place. The Kushites were fortunate in having iron-bearing sandstone in their hills and the wood for charcoal with which to smelt it. So precious was this metal reckoned that an iron spearhead, wrapped in gold foil, was buried in the tomb of King Taharqa. Mounds of iron slag abound at Meroë, and smelting as well as forging were practiced on a fairly large scale. Whether this knowledge passed from Meroë to other parts of Africa, as has often been argued, cannot yet be established.

Apart from raiding bands of desert dwellers, Kush was left largely alone and grew into a state that stretched from the borders of Egypt between the First and Second Cataracts to at least as far south as Sennar in the modern Sudan. Meanwhile, Egypt had fallen prey to yet another invader. The Persian conquest of Egypt in 525 B.C., when Cambyses defeated Psammetik III, hardly affected Kush, though the Persians made an unsuccessful attempt to invade the country.

Subsequently, the Greeks, led by Alexander the Great, occupied Egypt in 332 B.C. The Greeks were not strangers in Egypt, their forebears having lived and worked there for some centuries as merchants and soldiers, and having been allowed to establish a trading center of their own at Naukratis in the Delta. Ptolemy, one of their victorious generals, was left in charge of Egypt. When the Greek empire broke up at Alexander's death, Ptolemy became the ruler of an independent kingdom. Attempts at peaceful integration were made: the Greeks worshiped Egyptian gods, and upper-class Egyptians learned Greek. But the peasant population was oppressed and resentful at having to hand over to the foreign ruler half their produce as rent for their land. The ruling dynasty of the Ptolemies encouraged trading ventures, setting up new ports on the Red Sea coast and extending trade toward the east. (Ptolemy II completed the last link in a series of canals reaching from the Nile to the Red Sea.) They introduced currency into Egypt, where barter had been the common practice, and Alexandria, said to have been planned and laid out by Alexander himself, became a center of learning and crafts, among the greatest in the ancient world.

During the period of Hellenistic power in Egypt, Kush appears to have enjoyed particular prosperity. The Kushites maintained friendly relations with the Greeks, and one of the Kushite kings, Arkamani (about 218–200 B.C.), called Ergamenes by the Greeks, is said to have acquired a smattering of Greek learning. He is known to have joined Ptolemy IV in some temple building; and the number of buildings erected in Kush and the luxury of the objects found in the royal tombs illustrate the degree of security known. Somewhat later Netekamani and his queen, Amantari, also built extensively, including two temples at Naqa, a town some distance from the Nile. The first structure, the Lion Temple, shows Apedemek, an indigenous lion god or god of war, who, on this occasion at least, had three heads and four arms, causing speculation about possible contacts with India. (A number of local gods had been added to the Egyptian pantheon some time after the capital was moved to Meroë. Whether they were of long standing or not is unknown.) By contrast, the second temple, known as the

The Kushite kingdom of Meroë in northern Sudan was forgotten by the world for centuries until travelers and archeologists in recent times began to reveal evidences of its ancient glories. The Kiosk (opposite), a temple with both Egyptian and Roman influences, was built at Naqa, a Meroitic center, by Netekamani and his queen, Amantari, about the first century B.C. The colossal statue at right, several centuries older, was found on the site of the Temple of Isis at Meroë itself.

NY CARLSBERG GLYPTOTEK, COPENHAGEN

Kiosk, is strikingly Roman in style, and though decorated with Egyptian symbols, it seems very strange so far south in Africa.

Roman occupation at the death of Cleopatra in 30 B.C. brought no relief to the discontented peasantry of Egypt. Their country became merely a province of the Roman empire, exploited for its grain supplies and paying taxes to the colonial governors. The middle classes became poor, and the poor, destitute. It was not surprising that Alexandria's intellectuals and malcontents began to look at the teachings of a new religion. By A.D. 330, when Christianity was the religion of the Roman empire and the Christian capital was Constantinople, not Rome, most of Egypt had already been converted, and Alexandria had already been a great center of Eastern Christianity for almost two hundred years. Later, at the Council of Chalcedon in A.D. 451, the patriarch of Alexandria declined to subscribe to the orthodox doctrine. As will be explained more fully in Chapter Three, the Church was divided over doctrinal issues, and Egypt became more secluded from its neighbors, its indigenous Coptic Church no longer a participant in the mainstream of the Christian world. Kush, too, became more remote as its contacts with the northern neighbors declined. Further, it was harried by desert tribesmen and by a new power to the southeast, Axum, whose strength was already being felt.

To explain the rise of Axum, one must go back to 700 B.C., when bands of immigrants from the Yemen began to cross the Red Sea and settle among the people of the Ethiopian highlands. They mixed with the local population, and there is no evidence that they did so violently; their impact seems

to have been cultural. They were sophisticated farmers who understood terracing and the intricacies of irrigation, and employed such tools as the plow. They spoke a Semitic language, Sabean, and inscriptions in Sabean characters have been found, though there are enough departures from the language used in Saba (Sheba), to show its local development. The earliest inscriptions and monuments so far discovered date from about 500 B.C. By the third or second century B.C., one group of them, the Habashat (from which came the later name Abyssinia), established a strong kingdom with its capital at Axum and developed their own language, Ge'ez. This was one of the Ethiopian kingdoms that grew out of the synthesis of Yemenite and local endeavor. There is not much information about its early days, yet we know that their religion was analagous with that of southern Arabia: worship of the divinities Astar, Mahrem, and Beher, the divine symbol being a disc resting on a crescent, the Sabean moon god's symbol.

When the Ptolemies began to extend their trade empire, the Axumite state became of immediate importance, being well placed to take advantage of the new commercial development. Its main port was Adulis. The Ptolemies wanted to acquire elephants for war purposes, and among other trade goods were rhinoceros horn, tortoise shell, and the various perfumes, incense, and spices for which this area had been famous as the probable Land of Punt to which Hatshepsut sent ships. Much of this trading activity was in the hands of Greeks, and Greek became the language of commerce and diplomacy in Axum. Greek and Jewish traders from the Levant settled there from about the first century A.D., and, later, inscriptions on coins and monuments were in Greek. By the fifth century A.D. the state of Axum had probably become the main trading center for the Mediterranean-Indian Ocean routes. It may have been the Greeks who first brought Christianity to Axum; sometime in the fourth century it had become the official religion of the country, as it still is, being retained with great tenacity in the fastnesses of Ethiopia.

The culture of Axum was largely south Arabian in character, modified by local tradition, but uninfluenced by contacts with Egypt or Meroë. The buildings of Axum, of which there are remnants visible today, were characterized by stepped walls. Stone thrones or their pedestals, column bases and capitals, and fragments of columns, all testify to architectural achievement. Most impressive of all are the tall steles, some sixty feet high, which recreate in stone many-storied wooden buildings typical of Axumite architecture; these were probably funerary monuments.

Ambition led the rulers of Axum to extend the boundaries of their new kingdom and to regain the land of their ancestors. About the first century B.C. their agents are found in the Yemen, making alliances with various tribes in an attempt to regain control in southern Arabia, though it is not clear whether they achieved a position of direct rule there. At later times invasions were made culminating in that of King Afilas toward the end of the third century A.D. (see Chapter Four). The Axumites also sought to subdue their immediate neighbors and claimed to have taken their power to the borders of Egypt by the third century A.D.

An inscription found on a stele of one Axumite king, Ezana, relates that about A.D. 350 he and his army invaded the kingdom of Kush, which had been a source of perpetual annoyance to him. He burned and destroyed their cities, "both those built of bricks and those built of reeds," causing as much devastation as possible and chasing the Kushites for twenty-three days. The nomads, called the Red and the Black Noba according to Ezana, had been particularly troublesome, interfering with his officials and messengers and fighting among themselves, which they had promised not to do. "Twice and thrice they had broken their solemn oaths," Ezana says. So, he claims, he attacked and scattered them also. This may be an overboastful account of the event, especially as recent excavations at Meroë show no sign, so far, of sudden destruction or burning; but, equally, there is no doubt that the power of Kush waned at about this time, and it was no longer a viable kingdom.

Once Meroë had ceased to be a power, wandering bands of tribesmen, the Noba and the Blemmyes, both from the desert areas beyond the Nile, mingled with the Kushites and assimilated their culture. From Roman accounts they seem to have been a rather intractable people, and at a time when Egypt was already virtually a Christian country, they won special dispensation from the Romans to worship the Egyptian goddess Isis at the temple at Philae, the last remnant of pharaonic religion in the Nile Valley.

Rich tombs of their rulers at Ballana and Qustul in Egyptian Nubia were filled with amazing objects showing a strong flavor of pharaonic culture allied to Byzantine splendor: jewel-studded crowns of Byzantine style, decorated with pharaonic religious symbols such as the uraeus, or sacred serpent, the ram's head and plumes of Amon, the eye of Horus; iron furniture and inlaid wooden boxes, bronze vessels and hanging lamps, vessels of silver and glass, elaborate and beautiful horse trappings, pottery, linen shrouds, and fragments of rugs on which the dead had rested. Many were luxury imports from Egypt; indeed, the decoration of a cross on some of them implies their manufacture at Byzantine hands. To accompany him in death, the king's retinue, his queen, slaves, and guards, his dogs and horses, were sacrificed with him. This was not an Egyptian or Meroitic custom in which the necessity of providing servants for the afterlife had been circumvented by placing in the tomb little figures called *shawabtis*, which were thought to come to life to perform their services. The people of Ballana and Qustul, known to archeologists as the X-Group, had acquired a marked overlay of Egyptian-Meroitic culture, but certainly retained features of their own culture. Eventually, they and the peoples of the Sudan as far south as modern Khartoum became Christian under the teachings of the Byzantine Church.

Egypt made little attempt to influence other parts of Africa beyond Kush; rather, it held them at arm's length, concentrating all its effort in its own domain. Whether this was equally true of Kush cannot yet be seen. Except at Axum, where three undoubtedly Meroitic bronze bowls were found, and in the kingdom of Darfur in the western Sudan, where a Meroitic stone thumb ring is thought to have been found, almost nothing of certain Egyptian or Sudanese origin has so far been discovered in any other part of Africa. (A single faience bead in the Coryndon Museum in Nairobi could be Egyptian, but it is of doubtful provenance.)

As yet there is little archeological evidence for the passage of ideas, either for their actual passage or for the direction in which they flowed. The Nile Valley may have sent knowledge of agricultural and metallurgical techniques upstream and out across the deserts and savannas, or they may equally well have been independent inventions elsewhere.

It is not known when agriculture started in West Africa, for example, either in the Sudanic belt or in the forest areas to the south. Agricultural techniques were transmitted slowly—it appears to have taken about a thousand years for the practices in use in the Fayum to reach Shaheinab. Moreover, the crops which grew well in Egypt—wheat and barley—were not suited to climates farther south, so that different grains, mostly sorghum and other millets, had to be cultivated, and these are still the main crops of the Sudanic belt. Farther south in West Africa yam cultivation took the place of grain, calling for different tools and techniques, and there, particularly, agriculture may have been a separate invention; but because it leaves no traces—no grains, no bins, no grinding stones—knowledge of when it started may never be discovered.

Information about events and human development west of the Nile is much more limited, partly because the societies there were illiterate and partly because less investigation has been undertaken. Such cultural traits as are common between the Nile civilizations and those to the west of them may be a product of common African thought, as divine kingship for example, or may have been transmitted by the Saharan peoples over a long period of time. Although it has frequently been suggested that Meroë was the center from which the knowledge of ironworking spread throughout Africa, this skill might more easily have reached West Africa by trans-Saharan routes from Phoeni-

cian Carthage, where ironworking was well known, or it could have been independently discovered. The earliest iron-using communities yet discovered in West Africa are those of the Nok culture, named after a village on the Jos Plateau of north Nigeria. In the course of open-cast mining operations at Nok were found some remarkable terra-cotta heads of men and animals, together with iron and stone tools. A second site of the same people, at Taruga, produced an iron-smelting furnace. There is no doubt that iron was smelted and worked there from about 300 B.C., a date obtained by radiocarbon methods.

The working of iron gave to its users improved weapons, more control over their environment, and was instrumental in enabling them to establish the trading centers, which in time developed into an important feature of the western Sudan. The basis of trade was the gold, produced in an area to the southwest of the Sahara and transported by desert caravan to North Africa. The middlemen in this operation—those who met the caravans, brought the gold from the producers to them, and arranged an exchange of goods—were the ones who set up the trading centers that later became the great medieval states of the western Sudan. The earliest of these was Ghana, a state that grew up in southern Mauritania; its connection with the present Republic of Ghana is only indirect. Nothing is known of its beginnings as yet, and it is first mentioned by Arab travelers about A.D. 800; but according to local tradition, which was written down in the sixteenth and seventeenth centuries, it was already flourishing by the seventh century, and its early days may well reach further back into history.

While a great deal is known about ancient Egypt, the history of the civilizations of the rest of Africa is only now emerging. There are many tantalizing threads to follow, though they may never be fitted into the tapestry: the possibly Indian influences in Kush; the stone terracing that transformed the agriculture of Ethiopia and is seen also at Zimbabwe in southern Rhodesia; the bronze casting by the lost-wax process known in ancient Egypt and used again, much later, by the West African artists of Ife and Benin; the facts behind the statement by the medieval Arab geographer Al-Masudi that the sons of Kush, having crossed the Nile, separated, and some "very numerous, marched toward the setting sun," to mention but a few of them. Little is known of the comings and goings of peoples or of the interchange of ideas and techniques across this vast continent. Literate Egypt, with all its achievements, overshadows the rest of Africa; but more research, exploration, and excavation may help to redress the balance.

OF MEN AND MYTHS

Figures from a vase made by a predynastic Egyptian farmer

THE SOURCE

Ancient Europeans' knowledge of the Nile was mostly based on hearsay, and that remarkably inaccurate. It was commonly accepted that the river rose somewhere in Mauretania (Morocco and part of Algeria), and not until the Greek geographer Strabo made a visit to Egypt did these misconceptions begin to be replaced with observed data. The world's longest river actually rises in equatorial Africa, from whence it flows some 4,160 miles to the Delta and the Mediterranean. It is fed by two principal courses: the White Nile and the Blue Nile. The former originates in Lakes Victoria and Albert, and then sweeps briskly into the Sudan, where it becomes choked in the sudd, 50,000 square miles of almost impassable swamp. At Khartoum it is joined by the Blue Nile, which, especially during the monsoon season, comes flooding down from the Ethiopian highlands. Then, after being met by another Ethiopian tributary, the Atbara, the Nile enters a region of six rapids, the last at Aswan. From there to the sea it runs some 750 miles through a narrow valley, never more than twelve miles in width, until it reaches the Delta, whose seven branches run to the sea. Strabo's commentary on his own discoveries, made around A.D. 19, and his professional criticism of earlier geographers' assertions is excerpted in the passage below.

The Nile flows from the Aethiopian boundaries toward the north in a straight line to the district called "Delta," and then, being "split at the head," as Plato says, the Nile makes this place as it were the vertex of a triangle, the sides of the triangle being formed by the streams that split in either direction and extend to the sea. . . . An island, therefore, has been formed by the sea and the two streams of the river; and it is called Delta on ac-count of the similarity of its shape; and the district at the vertex has been given the same name because it is the beginning of the above-mentioned figure; and the village there is also called Delta. Now these are two mouths of the Nile, of which one is called Pelusiac and the other Canobic or Heracleiotic; but between these there are five other outlets, those at least that are worth mentioning, and several that are smaller; for, beginning with the first parts of the Delta, many branches of the river have been split off throughout the whole island and have formed many streams and islands, so that the whole Delta has become navigable—canals on canals having been cut, which are navigated with such ease that some people even use earthenware ferry-boats. Now the island as a whole is as much as three thousand stadia in perimeter; and they also call it, together with the opposite river-lands of the Delta, Lower Egypt; but at the rising of the Nile the whole country is under water and becomes a lake, except the settlements; and these are situated on natural hills or on artificial mounds, and contain cities of considerable size and villages, which, when viewed from afar, resemble islands. The water stays more than forty days in summer and then goes down gradually just as it rose; and in sixty days the plain is completely bared and begins to dry out; and the sooner the drying takes place, the sooner the ploughing and the sowing; and the drying takes place sooner in those parts where the heat is greater. . . . Aegypt consists of only the river-land, I mean the last stretch of river-land on either side of the Nile, which, beginning at the boundaries of Aethiopia and extending to the vertex of the Delta, scarcely anywhere occupies a continuous habitable space as broad as three hundred stadia. Accordingly, when it is dried, it resembles lengthwise a girdle-band, the greater diversions of the river being excepted. . . .

Now the ancients depended mostly on conjecture, but the men of later times, having become eye-witnesses, perceived that the Nile was filled by summer rains, when Upper Aethiopia was flooded, and particularly in the region of its farthermost mountains, and that when the rains ceased the inundation gradually ceased. This fact was particularly clear to those who navigated the Arabian Gulf as far as the Cinnamon-bearing country [of the Somali], and to those who were sent out to hunt elephants or upon any other business which may have prompted the Ptolemaic kings of Aegypt to dispatch men thither. . . . When Cambyses took possession of Aegypt, he advanced with the Aegyptians even as far as Meroë; and indeed this name was given by him to both the island and the city, it is said, because his sister Meroë—some say his wife—died there. The name, at any rate, he bestowed upon the place in honor of the woman. It is surprising, therefore, that the men of that time, having such knowledge to begin with, did not possess a perfectly clear knowledge of the rains. . . . They should have investigated, if they made any investigations at all, the question, which even to this day is still being investigated, I mean why in the world rains fall in summer but not in winter, and in the southernmost parts but not in Thebais and the country round Syene; but the fact that the rising of the river results from rains should not have been investigated, nor yet should this matter have needed such witnesses as Poseidonius mentions; for instance, he says that it was Callisthenes who states that the summer rains are the cause of the risings, though Callisthenes took the assertion from Aristotle, and Aristotle from Thrasyalces the Thasian [one of the early physicists], and Thrasyalces from someone else, and he from Homer, who calls the Nile "heaven-fed": "And back again to the land of Aegyptus, heaven-fed river."

HYMN TO THE NILE

Adoration of the Nile is as old as Egyptian civilization itself. This paean was probably written around 1600 B.C. for the annual Theban festival marking the river's rise.

Praise to thee, O Nile, that issuest forth from the earth and comest to nourish the dwellers in Egypt. Secret of movement, a darkness in the daytime.

That waterest the meadows which Re hath created to nourish all cattle.

That givest drink to the desert places which are far from water; his dew it is that falleth from heaven.

Beloved of the Earth-God, controller of the Corn-God, that maketh every workshop of Ptah to flourish.

Lord of fish, that maketh the water fowl to go upstream, without a bird falling.

That maketh barley and createth wheat, that maketh the temples to keep festival.

If he is sluggish the nostrils are stopped up, and all men are brought low;

The offerings of the gods are diminished, and millions perish from among mankind.

When he arises earth rejoices and all men are glad; every jaw laughs and every tooth is uncovered.

Bringer of nourishment, plenteous of sustenance, creating all things good.

Lord of reverence, sweet of savor, appeasing evil.

Creating herbage for the cattle, causing sacrifice to be made to every god.

He is in the Underworld, in heaven, and upon earth,

Filling the barns and widening the granaries; giving to the poor.

Causing trees to grow according to the uttermost desire,

So that men go not in lack of them.

MEMPHIS, THE FAIR ONE

This love song, written during the Nineteenth Dynasty (1320–1200 B.C.), is dedicated to Memphis. According to historical tradition, Narmer created the city as part of his plan to unite Upper and Lower Egypt into a single nation. The brilliant capital, built near the apex of the Delta, the ancient division between the Two Lands, remained an economic and religious center throughout Egypt's dynastic history, losing its influence only when Alexandria was established in 332 B.C.

My boat sails downstream
In time to the strokes of the oarsmen.

A bunch of reeds is on my shoulder,
And I am traveling to Memphis, "Life of the Two Lands."

And I shall say to the god Ptah, Lord of Truth:

"Give me my fair one tonight."
The god Ptah is her tuft of reeds,

Riverine paradise as seen by the Egyptians
EGYPTIAN MUSEUM, CAIRO

The goddess Sekhmet is her posy of blossoms,

The goddess Earit is her budding lotus,
The god Nefertum is her blooming flower.

My love will be happy!
The dawn irradiates her beauty.

Memphis is a crop of pomegranates,
Placed before the god with the handsome countenance.

KING ZOSER'S MAGICIAN

Imhotep, a universal genius of pharaonic times, was counselor and architect to King Zoser, constructing for him the famous Step Pyramid of Saqqara around 2650 B.C. In the following modern biography, the English physician and historical writer Jamieson B. Hurry outlines Imhotep's feats in medicine, magic, literature, and building, and also describes his deification as god of medicine.

Imhotep devoted his life to various activities . . . [including] A. Vizier, B. Architect, C. Chief Lector Priest or Ritualist, D. Sage and Scribe, E. Astronomer, F. Magician-Physician.

The office of vizier to the ruling Pharaoh was one of high dignity and responsibility. The occupant of the post . . . [had] jurisdiction . . . over the various departments of state. . . . The following list of titles in itself indicates the multitudinous responsibilities: "chief judge," "overseer of the King's records," "bearer of the royal seal," "chief of all works of the King," "supervisor of that which Heaven brings, the Earth creates and the Nile brings," "supervisor of everything in this entire land." Amongst some of the departments of his office are enumerated the Judiciary, the Treasury, War [Army and Navy], the Interior, Agriculture, and the General Executive. . . .

As architect, Imhotep [was called] "the chief of all the works of the King of Upper and Lower Egypt". . . . [He] doubtless owed some of his architectural knowledge to his father Kanofer, a man of some distinction who was known as the "Architect of South and North Egypt."

In all probability Imhotep designed for his royal master the well-known Step-Pyramid of Sakkarah near Memphis. . . .

Imhotep [was] chief lector priest or ritualist. The Egyptian priesthood included two main classes of priests, the higher class being designated prophets . . . or servants of the gods, and the lower class ordinary priests. . . . Some priests were permanent officials of a temple, others served in rotation and enjoyed an interval of three months' leave between two periods of service. The chief lector priest or ritualist belonged to the higher class and was a permanent functionary entrusted with important duties. One of these was to attend the daily cult of the temple, where he sprinkled the god with water, fumigated him with incense, clothed and anointed him, applied cosmetics to his eyes and arrayed him with various ornaments. He also had to recite prayers from the holy books during the temple liturgy, and since according to the Egyptian faith these religious texts possessed magical powers, the common people regarded this priest as a magician.

The chief lector priest also assisted at the ritual of embalmment and recited spells while the manipulations were in progress. Further, he officiated at the ceremonies connected with the presentation of offerings in the mortuary cult, which has been called the "Liturgy of Funerary Offerings." The formula which was pronounced over each element in that liturgy was intended to impart to the mummy after restoration of its faculties offerings of food and drink to sustain its renewed physical life. . . .

Another series of ceremonies was known as "The Opening the Mouth," the object being to restore to the inert corpse the functions of which it had been deprived by death and embalmment. The mouth was symbolically opened that the mummy might speak, and the eyes touched that they might see. . . .

Imhotep

As regards his literary activities, [he] is said to have produced works on medicine and architecture, as well as on more general subjects, and some of his works were extant at the dawn of the Christian era. His proverbs, embodying the philosophy of life which experience had taught, were handed down from generation to generation, and were noted for their grace and poetic diction, their author being described as a "master of poetry."

A remarkable song, or rather dirge, known as the "Song of the Harper," has survived in which the names of Imhotep and Hardedef [another wise man] are linked together and in which these two sages dilate on the uncertainty and brevity of life, and enforce the doctrine that since man is so soon gone and forgotten, he should enjoy his life to the full. . . .

Although Imhotep was a noted magician, it appears that medicine was the mistress he most zealously wooed; it is his eminence as a healer of the sick that has given him imperishable fame, and that led eventually to his deification. For

a time he was probably both court physician and vizier to King Zoser; he evidently moved in the highest social circles. . . . Magic and medicine were closely associated in therapeutics. . . . Magical papyri are leavened with medical prescriptions, while medical papyri . . . are constantly interspersed with incantations and invocations. . . . The fact that he later on received divine honors—a most unusual event except in the case of a Pharaoh—proves him to have been a man of rare distinction. . . .

The worship of the demigod Imhotep doubtless originated at his tomb, which was probably not far removed from the Step-Pyramid which had been erected, probably by Imhotep himself, for his royal master Zoser. The mastaba of the famous magician-physician by degrees became a place of pilgrimage, especially for sick and suffering persons, and apparently . . . some temples were erected in his honor. . . . The custom arose amongst Egyptian scribes of pouring a libation out of their water-bowl to Imhotep "that most famous of scribes." This custom . . . doubtless arose from the scribe's desire to prosper his own task, and the words of invocation "Water from the water-bowl of every scribe to thy *Ka*, O Imhotep!" were frequently inscribed on the roll of papyrus which so often lies on the knees of the statuettes of the demigod. . . .

Well-nigh twenty-five centuries elapsed between the time Imhotep held office under the Pharaoh Zoser and the time he was raised to the rank of full deity of medicine. His apotheosis appears to have taken place somewhere about 525 B.C., the year in which Egypt was conquered by Cambyses and became a Persian province.

The preceding period in Egyptian history, lasting from the expulsion of the Assyrians in 654 B.C. to the Persian Conquest in 525 B.C. and corresponding with the XXVIth Dynasty, is known as the Saitic Restoration. . . . With the return of ordered government a great national revival took place resulting in increased economic prosperity. Industry flourished, art revived, a veneration for the glorious history of the Pyramid Age impressed itself on the soul of the nation. The worship of the early Pharaohs who had ruled at Memphis was restored and the ritual of their mortuary services was resuscitated and endowed. Even the pyramids were repaired on an extensive scale.

As further indication of the desire to pay honor to those who in former days had brought glory to the nation, the famous Imhotep . . . was now advanced to the status of full deity of medicine with the title of son of Ptah, one of the oldest of all Egyptian deities, and also god of healing. . . .

An interesting story has survived which illustrates the practice of incubation at Imhotep's temples. . . . The story relates to a man named Satmi Khamuas, the son of the Pharaoh Usermares, who had no man-child by his wife Mahituaskhit; this troubled him greatly in his heart, and his wife Mahituaskhit was greatly afflicted with him. One day, when Satmi was more depressed than usual, his wife Mahituaskhit went to the temple of Imhotep, son of Ptah, and uttered this prayer before him, saying: "Turn thy face towards me, my lord Imhotep, son of Ptah: it is thou who dost work miracles, and who are beneficent in all thy deeds; it is thou who givest a son to her who has none. Listen to my lamentation and give me conception of a man-child."

That same night Mahituaskhit, the wife of Satmi, slept in the temple and dreamed a dream in which one spake with her, "Art thou not Mahituaskhit, the wife of Satmi, who dost sleep in the temple to receive a remedy for thy sterility from the hands of the god? When to-morrow morning comes, go to the bath-room of Satmi thy husband, and thou wilt find a root of colocasia that is growing there. The colocasia that thou meetest with thou shalt gather with its leaves; thou shalt make of it a remedy that thou shalt give to thy husband, then thou shalt lie by his side, and thou shalt

conceive by him the same night."

When Mahituaskhit awoke from her dream after seeing the vision, she at once carried out the instructions given her in her dream; then she lay by the side of Satmi, her husband, and conceived by him. . . .

Religious festivals played a prominent part in the life of the Egyptians and were celebrated by vociferous demonstrations of joy. Great processions were organized in which took part the priests with shaven heads, clad in linen of spotless white, as well as throngs of devotees, all eager to do honor to their deities. Music, singing, dancing, floral decorations, banquets all added to the gaiety of the ceremonies, while at night numerous torches illuminated the streets with flickering lights and prolonged the feasting far into the night. Important festivals might extend over several days or even weeks. . . . Under the Ptolemies regular festivals were celebrated at Memphis in honor of the god Imhotep.

METROPOLITAN MUSEUM OF ART, ROGERS FUND, 1946

Thoth

THE SILENT MAN

For the ancient Egyptians, who believed that the universe was essentially static, life was a constant striving to maintain a perfect integration with the established order, or maat.

Anyone who broke the existing equilibrium was a wrongdoer acting out of ignorance or lack of self-control. This prayer to Thoth, god of wisdom and patron of scribes, was written in the thirteenth century B.C. and was used as a school text. The supplicant, proclaiming himself a "silent man," hence the master of his impulses and in harmony with the divine order, seeks to gain Thoth's support at the last judgment. Conversely, the "noisy man" could expect no solace in the afterlife.

O Thoth, take me to Hermopolis, to thy
    city, where it is pleasant to live.
Thou suppliest what I need in bread and
    beer and thou keepest watch over
    my mouth when I speak.

Would that I had Thoth behind me to-
    morrow (when I shall die)!
Come to me when I enter before the
    Lords of Maat (the judges in the
    hereafter)
And so shall I come forth justified.
Thou great dom palm, sixty cubits high,
    whereon are fruits;
Stones are in the fruits and water is in the
    stones.
Thou who bringest water to a distant
    place, come deliver me, the silent
    man.
Thoth, thou sweet well for one who
    thirsts in the desert;
It is closed for one who argues but open
    for him who keeps silence.
The silent one comes and finds the well.
The hot-headed comes and thou art
    [choked].

THE AMARNA HERESY

The Hymn to Aten, which follows, is one of ancient Egypt's literary masterpieces. It was written during the reign of Amenhotep IV (1370–1353 B.C.), who initiated a religious and artistic revolution, which was short-lived. He discredited Egypt's innumerable deities and substituted a faith based on the worship of the Aten, the "One God," whose symbol was the sun disc. The "Heretic King" even changed his name to Akhenaten, "he who is serviceable to the Aten," and moved his capital from Thebes to Amarna in Middle Egypt. He also encouraged realism in art. Akhenaten's religion never gained followers among the masses of people; after his death Egypt returned to its ancient polytheism.

Thou appearest beautifully on the horizon of heaven,
Thou living Aten, the beginning of life!
When thou art risen on the eastern horizon,
Thou hast filled every land with thy beauty.
Thou art gracious, great, glistening, and high over every land;
Thy rays encompass the lands to ... all that thou hast made:
As thou art Re, thou reachest to the end of them;
(Thou) subduest them (for) thy beloved son.
Though thou art far away, thy rays are on earth;
Though thou art in their faces, no one knows thy going.

When thou settest in the western horizon,
The land is in darkness, in the manner of death.
They sleep in a room, with heads wrapped up,
Nor sees one eye the other.
All their goods which are under their heads might be stolen,
(But) they would not perceive (it).
Every lion is come forth from his den;
All creeping things, they sting.
Darkness is a shroud, and the earth is in stillness.
For he who made them rests in his horizon.

At daybreak, when thou arisest on the horizon,
When thou shinest as the Aten by day,
Thou drivest away the darkness and givest thy rays.
The Two Lands are in festivity every day,
Awake and standing upon (their) feet,
For thou hast raised them up.
Washing their bodies, taking (their) clothing,

Their arms are (raised) in praise at thy appearance.
All the world, they do their work.

All beasts are content with their pasturage;
Trees and plants are flourishing.
The birds which fly from their nests,
Their wings are (stretched out) in praise to thy *ka.*
All beasts spring upon (their) feet.
Whatever flies and alights,
They live when thou hast risen (for) them.
The ships are sailing north and south as well,
For every way is open at thy appearance.
The fish in the river dart before thy face;
Thy rays are in the midst of the great green sea.

Creator of seed in woman,
Thou who makest fluid into man,
Who maintainest the son in the womb of his mother,
Who soothest him with that which stills his weeping,
Thou nurse (even) in the womb,
Who givest breath to sustain all that he has made!
When he descends from the womb to breathe
On the day when he is born,
Thou openest his mouth completely,
Thou suppliest his necessities.
When the chick in the egg speaks within the shell,
Thou givest him breath within it to maintain him.
When thou hast made him his fulfillment within the egg, to break it,
He comes forth from the egg to speak at his completed (time);
He walks upon his legs when he comes forth from it.

How manifold it is, what thou has made!
They are hidden from the face (of man).
O sole god, like whom there is no other!
Thou didst create the world according to thy desire,
Whilst thou wert alone.

All men, cattle, and wild beasts,
Whatever is on earth, going upon (its) feet,
And what is on high, flying with its wings.

Thy rays suckle every meadow.
When thou risest, they live, they grow for thee.
Thou makest the seasons in order to rear all that thou hast made,
The winter to cool them,
And the heat that they may taste thee.
Thou has made the distant sky in order to rise therein,
In order to see all that thou dost make.
Whilst thou wert alone,
Rising in thy form as the living Aten,
Appearing, shining, withdrawing, or approaching,
Thou madest millions of forms of thyself alone.
Cities, towns, fields, road, and river—
Every eye beholds thee over against them ...

Thou art in my heart,
And there is no other that knows thee
Save thy son Neferkheperure Waenre,
For thou hast made him well-versed in thy plans and in thy strength.
The world came into being by thy hand,
According as thou has made them.
When thou hast risen they live,
When thou settest they die.
Thou art lifetime thy own self,
For one lives (only) through thee.
Eyes are (fixed) on beauty until thou settest.
All work is laid aside when thou settest in the west.
(But) when (thou) rises (again),
[Everything is] made to flourish for the king ...
Since thou didst found the earth
And raise them up for thy son,
Who came forth from thy body:
the King of Upper and Lower Egypt ...
Akhenaten ...
and the Chief Wife of the King ...
Nefertiti, living and
youthful forever and ever.

EGYPTIAN WAY OF DEATH

The fight for immortality gave rise to two abiding symbols of Egyptian civilization: pyramids and mummies. The Greek historian Herodotus, who visited the Nile Valley in the fifth century B.C., *has left us a fairly accurate account of Egyptian burial customs. The following passage, from his* Histories, *fails to mention the one foe against whom even a pharaoh was not secure: the tomb robber.*

The following is the way in which they conduct their mournings and their funerals:—On the death in any house of a man of consequence, forthwith the women of the family beplaster their heads, and sometimes even their faces, with mud; and then, leaving the body indoors, sally forth and wander through the city, with their dress fastened by a band, and their bosoms bare, beating themselves as they walk. All the female relations join them and do the same. The men, too, similarly begirt, beat their breasts separately. When these ceremonies are over, the body is carried away to be embalmed.

There are a set of men in Egypt who practice the art of embalming, and make it their proper business. These persons, when a body is brought to them, show the bearers various models of corpses, made in wood, and painted so as to resemble nature. The most perfect is said to be after the manner of [Osiris] whom I do not think it religious to name in connection with such a matter; the second sort is inferior to the first, and less costly; the third is the cheapest of all. All this the embalmers explain, and then ask in which way it is wished that the corpse should be prepared. The bearers tell them, and having concluded their bargain, take their departure, while the embalmers, left to themselves, proceed to their task. The mode of embalming, according to the most perfect process, is the following:— They take first a crooked piece of iron, and with it draw out the brain through the nostrils, thus getting rid of a portion, while the skull is cleared of the rest by rinsing with drugs; next they make a cut along the flank with a sharp Ethiopian

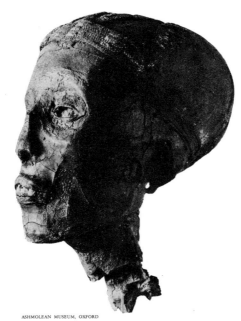

ASHMOLEAN MUSEUM, OXFORD
Mummified head of young king Tutankhamon, discovered in his royal tomb at Thebes

stone, and take out the whole contents of the abdomen, which they then cleanse, washing it thoroughly with palm wine, and again frequently with an infusion of pounded aromatics. After this they fill the cavity with the purest bruised myrrh, with cassia, and every sort of spicery except frankincense, and sew up the opening. Then the body is placed in natron for seventy days, and covered entirely over. After the expiration of that space of time, which must not be exceeded, the body is washed, and wrapped round, from head to foot, with bandages of fine linen cloth, smeared over with gum which is used generally by the Egyptians in the place of glue, and in this state it is given back to the relations, who enclose it in a wooden case which they have made for the purpose, shaped into the figure of a man. Then fastening the case, they place it in a sepulchral chamber upright against the wall. Such is the most costly way of embalming the dead.

If the persons wish to avoid expense, and choose the second process, the following is the method pursued:—Syringes are filled with oil made from the cedar tree, which is then, without any incision or disemboweling, injected into the abdomen. The passage by which it might be likely to return is stopped, and the body laid in natron the prescribed

number of days. At the end of the time the cedar oil is allowed to make its escape; and such is its power that it brings with it the whole stomach and intestines in a liquid state. The natron meanwhile has dissolved the flesh, and so nothing is left of the dead body but the skin and the bones. It is returned in this condition to the relatives, without any further trouble being bestowed upon it.

The third method of embalming, which is practiced in the case of the poorer classes, is to clear out the intestines with a clyster, and let the body lie in natron the seventy days, after which it is at once given to those who come to fetch it away.

The wives of men of rank are not given to be embalmed immediately after death, nor indeed are any of the more beautiful and valued women. It is not till they have been dead three or four days that they are carried to the embalmers. This is done to prevent indignities from being offered then. It is said that once a case of this kind occurred; the man was detected by the information of his fellow workman.

SONG OF THE HARPER

During troubled times the ancient Egyptians often cast off their characteristic self-controlled, positive outlook and became hedonistic and agnostic. The poem, whose oldest version dates from either the First or Second Intermediate Periods—two anarchic times—probably stems from a widespread pessimism. It exhorts the living to follow the advice of the renowned sages Imhotep and Hordedef, and to eat, drink and be merry, for man has no certainty that earthly propriety will lead to eternal bliss. The song's great beauty made it popular with the scribes of the Eighteenth and Nineteenth Dynasties, relatively stable times.

All hail to the prince, the good Man,
Whose body must pass away,
While his children remain for aye.

The gods of old rest in their tombs,
And the mummies of men long dead;

Bas-relief of a harper of the New Kingdom

The Same for both rich and poor.

The words of Imhotep I hear
The words of Hordedef, which say:
"What is prosperity? tell!"

Their fences and walls are destroyed
Their houses exist no more;
And no man cometh again from the tomb
To tell of what passeth below.

Ye go to the place of the mourners,
To the bourne whence none return:
Strengthen your hearts to forget your
    joys,
Yet fulfill your desires while ye live.

Anoint yourselves, clothe yourselves
    well,
Use the gifts which the gods bestow,
Fulfill your desires upon earth.

For the days will come to you all
When ye hear not the voice of friends,
When weeping avails you no more;

So feast in tranquillity now,
For none taketh his goods below to the
    tomb
And none cometh thence back again.

PEPI'S LEGIONS

*An Old Kingdom military campaign against
an agricultural people, most probably in Palestine, is the subject of the following selection.
It is taken from the fragmented cenotaph inscription of a career officer named Uni, who
describes his exploits under Pepi I (around
2350 B.C.). Uni derides the enemy as "Sand-
Dwellers," in reference to their habitations,
and he exaggerates the size of his army.*

When his majesty imposed punishment
upon the Asiatics Who-are-Upon-the-
Sands, his majesty made an army of
many ten-thousands, in the entire Upper
Egypt . . . in Lower Egypt . . . among the
Nubians . . . and from the land of the
Temeh-Libyans. His majesty sent me at
the head of this army, while the counts,
while the Seal-Bearers of the King of
Lower Egypt, while the Sole Companions of the Palace, while the nomarchs
and mayors of Upper and Lower Egypt,
the companions and chief dragomans,
the chief prophets of Upper and Lower
Egypt, and the chief bureaucrats were
[each] at the head of a troop of Upper
or Lower Egypt, or of the villages and
towns which they might rule, or of the
Nubians of these foreign countries. I was
the one who used to make the plan for
them, although my office was [only that
of] Chief Domain Supervisor of the Palace, because I was [so] fitted for the post
that not one of them [so much as] laid a
hand upon his fellow, that not one of
them appropriated [so much as] a lump
of dough or a pair of sandals from a way-
farer, that not one of them carried off [so
much as] a loincloth from any town, that
not one of them carried off any goat from
anybody. . . .
This army returned in safety,
    After it had hacked up the land of the
    [Sand]-Dwellers.
This army returned in safety,
    After it had crushed the land of the
    Sand-Dwellers.
This army returned in safety,
    After it had thrown down [the land's]
    enclosures.
This army returned in safety,
    After it had cut down its fig trees and
    its vines.
This army returned in safety,
    After it had cast fire into all its dwell-
    ings.

This army returned in safety,
    After it had killed troops in it by many
    ten-thousands.
This army returned in safety,
    [After it had taken troops] in it, a great
        multitude as living captives.
    His majesty praised me for it more than
anything.

    His majesty sent me to lead [this] army
five times, in order to repel the land of
the Sand-Dwellers each time that they
rebelled, with these troops.

THE BROKEN REED

*The Hyksos domination of Egypt from 1730
to 1570 B.C. completely shattered Egyptian morale. The following passage is one of
the few extant accounts of the invasion. It
comes from the writings of Josephus, a Jewish
historian of the first century A.D. He claims to
be quoting the Egyptian historian Manetho,
who lived in the third century B.C. The record probably exaggerates the savagery of the
onslaught and misinterprets the term* hyksos,
*which actually comes from the Egyptian
words* hikau khasut, *meaning "rulers of
foreign countries." Modern scholarship has
revealed that the Hyksos were a composite
people of preponderantly Semitic origin who
were once settled in the uplands of Palestine, Lebanon, Syria, and farther Asia.*

Tutimaios. In his reign, for what cause I
know not, a blast of God smote us; and
unexpectedly from the regions of the
East invaders of obscure race marched in
confidence of victory against our land.
By main force they easily seized it without striking a blow; and having overpowered the rulers of the land, they then
burned our cities ruthlessly, razed to the
ground the temples of the gods, and
treated all the natives with a cruel hostility, massacring some and leading into
slavery the wives and children of others.
Finally, they appointed as king one of
their number whose name was Salitis. He
had his seat at Memphis, levying tribute
from Upper and Lower Egypt, and always leaving garrisons behind in the
most advantageous places. . . . In the

Sethroite nome [province] he found a city very favorably situated on the east of the Bubastite branch of the Nile [Delta], and called Avaris after an ancient religious tradition. This place he rebuilt and fortified with massive walls. . . . After reigning for 19 years Salitis died; and a second king Bnon succeeded and reigned for 44 years. Next to him came Apachnan, who ruled for 36 years and 7 months; then Apophis for 61, and Iannas for 50 years and 1 month; then finally Assis for 49 years and 2 months. These six kings, their first rulers, were ever more and more eager to extirpate the Egyptian stock. Their race as a whole was called Hyksos, that is "king-shepherds"; for *hyk* in the sacred language means "king" and *sos* in common speech is "shepherd."

THE QUEEN'S PEACE

The Hyksos were finally driven out of Egypt around 1570 B.C. In an inscription written almost a century later, Queen Hatshepsut expresses her nation's lingering outrage. Her remarks, quoted in part below, are carved on the façade of Istabl Antar temple, Middle Egypt.

Hear ye, all people and the folk as many as they may be, I have done these things through the counsel of my heart. I have not slept forgetfully, [but] I have restored that which had been ruined. I have raised up that which had gone to pieces formerly, since the Asiatics were in the midst of Avaris of the Northland [the Hyksos capital], and vagabonds were in the midst of them, overthrowing that which had been made. They ruled without Re, and he did not act by divine command down to [the reign of] my majesty. [Now] I am established upon the thrones of Re. I was foretold for the limits of the years as a born conqueror. I

am come as the uraeus-serpent of Horus, flaming against my enemies. I have made distant those whom the gods abominate, and earth has carried off their foot[prints]. This is the precept of the father of [my] fathers, who comes at his [appointed] times, Re, and there shall not occur damage to what Amon has commanded. My [own] command endures like the mountains, [while] the sun disc shines forth and spreads rays over the formal titles of my majesty and my falcon is high above [my] name-standard for the duration of eternity.

THE FABLED LAND OF PUNT

Hatshepsut's greatest economic triumph—the revival of trade with the remote regions of Punt—is told in reliefs and hieroglyphs on the walls of her magnificent funerary temple at Deir el Bahri. Scholars differ as to the precise location of Punt, but it was probably on the Somali coast along the Gulf of Aden; "God's Land" was perhaps across the gulf in southwest Arabia. The objective of her mission to the land of myrrh trees was the exchange of Egyptian weapons, beads, rings, and the like for the coveted riches of Punt: apes and incense, ivory and gold, slaves, ebony, greyhounds, leopard skins. In the following account, she exalts herself as the daughter of the god Amon-Re (Thothmes I was her mortal father) and tells how the god directed her in fulfilling his desires.

A command was heard from the great throne, an oracle of the god himself [Amon-Re], that the ways to Punt should be searched out, that the highways to the Myrrh-terraces should be penetrated: "I [said the oracle] will lead the army on water and on land, to bring marvels from God's-Land for this god [Hatshepsut], for the fashioner of her beauty." It was done, according to all that the majesty of this revered god commanded, according to the desire of her majesty, in order that

she might be given life, stability, and satisfaction, like Re, forever. . . .

"I [Hatshepsut] shine forever in your faces through that which my father hath desired. Truly, it was greatly my desire in doing, that I should make great him that begat me; and in assigning to my father, that I should make splendid for him all his offerings; that which my fathers, the ancestors knew not, I am doing as the Great One [did] to the Lord of Eternity; I am adding increase to that which was formerly done. I will cause it to be said to posterity: 'How beautiful is she, through whom this has happened,' because I have been so very excellent to him, and the heart of my heart has been replete with that which is due to him. I am his splendor [on high, and in the nether world.] I have entered into the qualities of the august god. . . . He hath recognized my excellence. . . . I am the god, the beginning of being, nothing fails that goes out of my mouth. . . . I have given a command of my majesty that the offerings of him who begat me should be made splendid. . . ."

"[I Hatshepsut commanded] to send to the Myrrh-terraces, to explore his ways [for him,] to learn his circuit, to open his highways, according to the command of my father, Amon. . . . Trees were taken up in God's Land, and set in the ground in [Egypt]—— for the king of the gods. They were brought bearing myrrh therein for expressing ointment for the divine limbs, which I owed to the lord of Gods."

Said my majesty. "I will cause you to know that which is commanded me, I have hearkened to my father . . . commanding me to establish for him a Punt in his house, to plant the trees of God's-

Scarabs, used for protective amulets and seals, incised with appropriate hieroglyphs

Land beside his temple, in his garden, according as he commanded. It was done, in order to endow the offerings which I owed.——I was [not] neglectful of that which he needed. . . . He hath desired me as his favorite; I know all that he loveth. . . . I have made for him a Punt in his garden, just as he commanded me, for Thebes. It is large for him, he walks abroad in it."

IN SEARCH OF PEACE

When Ramses II became pharaoh, Egypt resumed its war with the Hittites of Asia Minor for possession of Syria and Palestine. By about 1280 B.C. both empires, exhausted after eighty years of conflict, were ready to make peace. Portions of the resultant treaty between Ramses and Hattusilis, king of the Hatti, or Hittites, are quoted below. Aside from a mutual nonaggression pact and provisions for a defensive alliance against a third enemy, the agreement also calls for the extradition of political refugees—both great and humble. Elsewhere in the document is included a list of the gods who witnessed it, thus combining the ancient concept of divinity with a sophisticated code of international law. The Egyptian version, used here, was carved on the walls of the Temple of Amon at Karnak and the Ramesseum at Thebes. Predictably, it makes Hattusilis the first to cry for peace; the roles are reversed in the Hittite version. Thus each side preserved its dignity.

Year 21, 1st month of the second season, day 21 [late November, 1280 B.C.]. . . . On this day, while his majesty was in the town of Per-Ramses Meri-Amon [the capital city of Ramses in the Delta], doing the pleasure of his father Amon-Re [and other gods] . . . there came the Royal Envoy and Deputy . . . and Messenger of Hatti . . . carrying [the tablet of silver which] the Great Prince of Hatti, Hattusilis [caused] to be brought to Pharaoh—life, prosperity, health!—in order to beg [peace from the majesty of (Ramses)], Son of Re . . . bull of rulers, who has made his frontier where he wished. . . .

Behold, Hattusilis, the Great Prince of Hatti, has set himself in regulation

with [Ramses], the great ruler of Egypt, beginning from this day, to cause that good peace and brotherhood occur between us forever, while he is in brotherhood with me and he is at peace with me, and I am in brotherhood with him and I am at peace with him forever. . . . [The land of Egypt], with the land of Hatti, [shall be] at peace and in brotherhood like unto us forever. Hostilities shall not occur between them forever. . . .

If another enemy come against the lands of [Ramses II] . . . and he send to the Great Prince of Hatti, saying: "Come with me as reinforcement against him," the Great Prince of Hatti shall [come to him and] the Great Prince of Hatti shall slay his enemy. However, if it is not the desire of the Great Prince of Hatti to go [himself], he shall send his infantry and his chariotry, and he shall slay his enemy. Or, if . . . [the great ruler of Egypt], is enraged against servants belonging to him, and they commit another offense against him, and he go to slay them, the Great Prince of Hatti shall act with him [to slay] everyone [against whom] they shall be enraged.

But [if] another enemy [come] against the Great Prince [of Hatti] . . . [the great ruler of Egypt, shall] come to him as reinforcement to slay his enemy. . . .

If a man flee from the land of Egypt—or two or three—and they come to the Great Prince of Hatti, the Great Prince of Hatti shall lay hold of them, and he shall cause that they be brought back to [Ramses II], the great ruler of Egypt. But, as for the man . . . do not cause that his crime be raised against him; do not cause that his house or his wives or his children be destroyed; [do not cause that] he be [slain]; do not cause that injury be done to his eyes, to his ears, to his mouth, or to his legs; do not let any [crime be raised] against him.

Similarly, if men flee from the land of the Hatti . . . let Ramses . . . lay hold [of them and cause] that they be brought to the Great Prince of Hatti, and the Great Prince of Hatti shall not raise their crime against them. . . .

MISSION TO BYBLOS

By about 1100 B.C. pharaonic power was illusory and the real rulers of Egypt were Heri-Hor, the high priest of Amon-Re at Thebes, and Ne-su-Ba-neb-Ded, the prince at Tanis in the Delta. Egypt was in a state of chaos, and its prestige in Asia had waned. This sorry state of affairs is elucidated in one of the most famous Egyptian historical papyruses, The Journey of Wen-Amon to Phoenicia. It tells of Wen-Amon, an official at Amon-Re's temple at Thebes, who journeys to the Phoenician port of Byblos to buy cedar wood for the god's ceremonial barge. In past generations emissaries of Wen-Amon's position set forth in a grand style befitting their rulers' status and were always courteously received by the princes of Byblos. But Wen-Amon traveled unescorted and could offer only paltry amounts of gold and silver as royal gifts. He is so reduced, in fact, that he does not even have his own vessel, but stops first at Tanis, where Ne-su-Ba-neb-Ded and his wife, Ta-net-Amon, find a passage for him on a Syrian ship. When he finally arrives at Byblos, he is humbled by its prince, as this excerpt indicates. Only after much persuasion does he succeed in his mission.

I [set myself up in] a tent [on] the shore of the [sea], [in] the harbor of Byblos. And [I hid] Amon-of-the-Road [a portable idol of Amon-Re]. . . .

And the [Prince] of Byblos sent to me, saying: "Get [out of my] harbor!" And I sent to him, saying: "Where should [I go to]? . . . If [you have a ship] to carry me, have me taken to Egypt again!" So I spent twenty-nine days in his [harbor, while] he [spent] the time sending to me every day to say: "Get out [of] my harbor!"

Now while he was making offering to his gods, the god seized one of his youths and made him possessed. And he said to him: "Bring up [the] god! Bring the messenger who is carrying him! Amon is the one who sent him out! . . .

When morning came, [the Prince of Byblos] sent and brought me up, but the god stayed in the tent where he was, [on] the shore of the sea. And I found him sitting [in] his upper room, with his back

The temple of the god Amon at Karnak

turned to a window, so that the waves of the great Syrian sea broke against the back of his head.

So I said to him: "May Amon favor you!" But he said to me "How long, up to today, since you came from the place where Amon is?" So I said to him: "Five months and one day up to now." And he said to me: "Well, you're truthful! Where is the letter of Amon which [should be] in your hand? Where is the dispatch of the High Priest of Amon which [should be] in your hand?" And I told him: "I gave them to Ne-su-Ba-neb-Ded and Ta-net-Amon." And he was very, very angry, and he said to me: "Now see—neither letters nor dispatches are in your hand! Where is the cedar ship which Ne-su-Ba-neb-Ded gave to you? Where is its Syrian crew? Didn't he turn you over to this foreign ship captain to have him kill you and throw you into the sea? . . . And I was silent in this great time.

And he . . . said to me: "On what business have you come?" So I told him: "I have come after the woodwork for the great and august barque of Amon-Re, King of the Gods. Your father did [it], your grandfather did [it], and you will

do it too!" So I spoke to him. But he said to me: "To be sure, they did it! And if you give me [something] for doing it, I will do it! Why, when my people carried out this commission, Pharaoh—life, prosperity, health!—sent six ships loaded with Egyptian goods, and they unloaded them into their storehouses! You—what is it that you're bringing me—me also?" And he had the journal rolls of his fathers brought, and he had them read out in my presence, and they found a thousand *deben* of silver and all kinds of things in his scrolls.

So he said to me: "If the ruler of Egypt were the lord of mine, and I were his servant also, he would not have to send silver and gold, saying: 'Carry out the commission of Amon!' There would be no carrying of a royal-gift, such as they used to do for my father. As for me—me also—I am not your servant! I am not the servant of him who sent you either! . . . What are these silly trips which they have had you make?"

And I said to him: "[That's] not true! What I am on are no 'silly trips' at all! There is no ship upon the River which does not belong to Amon! The sea is his, and the Lebanon is his, of which you say: 'It is mine!' . . . Why, he spoke—Amon-Re, King of the Gods—said to Heri-Hor, my master: 'Send me forth!' So he had me come, carrying this great god [Amon-of-the-Road]. But see, you have made this great god spend these twenty-nine days moored [in] your harbor, although you did not know [it]. Isn't he here? Isn't he the [same] as he was? You are stationed [here] to carry on the commerce of the Lebanon with Amon, its lord. As for your saying that the former kings sent silver and gold—suppose that they had life and health; [then] they would not have had such things sent! [But] they had such things sent to your fathers in place of life and health! Now as for Amon-Re, King of the Gods—he is the lord of this life and health, and he was the lord of your fathers. They spent their lifetimes making offering to Amon. And you also—you are the servant of

Amon! If you say to Amon: 'Yes, I will do [it]!' and you carry out his commission, you will live, you will be prosperous, you will be healthy, and you will be good to your entire land and your people! [But] don't wish for yourself anything belonging to Amon-Re, [King of] the Gods. Why, a lion wants his own property! Have your secretary brought to me, so that I may send him to Ne-su-Ba-neb-Ded and Ta-net-Amon, the officers whom Amon put in the north of his land, and they will have all kinds of things sent. . . ."

So he entrusted my letter to his messenger, and he loaded on the keel, the bow-post, the stern-post, along with four other hewn timbers—seven in all—and he had them taken to Egypt. And in the first month of the second season his messenger who had gone to Egypt came back to me in Syria. And Ne-su-Ba-neb-Ded and Ta-net-Amon sent: 4 jars and 1 *kak-men* of gold; 5 jars of silver, 10 pieces of clothing in royal linen; 10 *kherd* of good Upper Egyptian linen; 500 [rolls of] finished papyrus; 500 cowhides; 500 ropes; 20 sacks of lentils; and 30 baskets of fish. And she sent to me [personally]: 5 pieces of clothing in good Upper Egyptian linen; 5 *kherd* of good Upper Egyptian linen; 1 sack of lentils; and 5 baskets of fish.

And the Prince was glad, and he detailed three hundred men and three hundred cattle, and he put supervisors at their head, to have them cut down the timber. So they cut them down, and they spent the second season lying there.

THE KUSHITE TAKEOVER

By the second half of the eighth century B.C. Egypt was ripe for conquest. The final assault came around 730 B.C. under the command of Piankhi, king of Kush. His father, Kashta, had invaded Upper Egypt, conquering the temple city of Thebes. Piankhi's military campaign won him control over Egypt; it was so successful that he recorded its progress on a granite stele, which he erected at Jebel Barkal, near his capital of Napata at the Nile's

Fourth Cataract. The inscription tells of his journey down the river and how he forced all of Egypt's gods and rulers into submission. The selection below opens with Piankhi's swaggering account of himself. Then follows a report on the brilliant strategy that won him Memphis, gateway to the domination of Lower Egypt. Lastly, having laid the foundation for seventy years of Kushite rule, Piankhi loads his ships and sails for home.

"Hear of what I did, more than the ancestors. I am a king, divine emanation, living image of Atum [an aspect of the god of Creation], who came forth from the womb, adorned as a ruler, of whom those greater than he were afraid; whose father knew, and whose mother recognized that he would rule in the egg, the Good God, beloved of the gods, achieving with his hands, Meriamon-Piankhi." . . .

Then [the soldiers] threw themselves upon their bellies before his majesty [saying]: "It is thy name which endues us with might, and thy counsel is the mooring-post of thy army; thy bread is in our bellies on every march, thy beer quenches our thirst. It is thy valor that giveth us might, and there is strength at the remembrance of thy name; [for] no army prevails whose commander is a coward. Who is they equal therein? Thou art a victorious king, achieving with his hands, chief of the work of war." . . .

[His majesty sailed north to] Memphis; then he sent to them, saying: "Shut not up, fight not. . . . As for him that would go in, let him go in; as for him that would come out, let him come out; and let not them that would leave be hindered. . . . [The people] of Memphis [shall be] safe and sound; not [even] a child shall weep. Look ye to the nomes of the South; not a single one has been slain therein, except the enemies who blasphemed against the god, who were dispatched as rebels."

Then they closed their stronghold; they sent forth an army against some of the soldiers of his majesty, being artisans, chief builders and sailors. . . .

Lo, that chief of Sais [Tefnakhte] arrived at Memphis in the night, charging his infantry and his sailors, all the best of his army, a total of 8,000 men, charging them very earnestly: "Behold, Memphis is filled with troops of all the best of the Northland; [with] barley and spelt and all kinds of grain, the granaries are running over; [with] all weapons of [war. It is fortified with] a wall; a great battlement has been built, executed with skillful workmanship. The river flows around the east side, and no [opportunity of] attack is found there. Cattle yards are there, filled with oxen; the treasury is supplied with everything: silver, gold, copper, clothing, incense, honey, oil." . . .

When day broke, at early morning, his majesty [Pianki] reached Memphis. When he had landed on the north of it, he found that the water had approached to the walls, the ships mooring at [the walls of] Memphis. Then his majesty saw that it was strong, and that the wall was raised by a new rampart, and battlements manned with mighty men. There was found no way of attacking it. Every man told his opinion among the army of his majesty, according to every rule of war. Every man said: "Let us besiege [it] —; lo, its troops are numerous." Others said: "Let a causeway be made against it; let us elevate the ground to its walls. Let us bind together a tower; let us erect masts and make the spars into a bridge to it. We will divide it on this [plan] on every side of it, on the high ground and —on the north of it, in order to elevate the ground at its walls, that we may find a way for our feet."

Then his majesty was enraged against [Memphis' defences] like a panther; he said: "I swear, as Re loves me, as my father, Amon [who fashioned me], favors me, this shall befall [the city], according to the command of Amon. . . . I will take it like a flood of water. . . .

Then he sent forth his fleet and his army to assault the harbor of Memphis; they brought him every ferry-boat, every [cargo]-boat, every [transport], and the ships, as many as there were, which had moored in the harbor of Memphis, with the bow-rope fastened among its houses. [There was not] a citizen who wept, among all the soldiers of his majesty. [Either all were considered in the distribution of the spoil, or no man was injured in the assault.]

His majesty himself came to line up the ships, as many as there were. His majesty commanded his army [saying]: "Foward against it! Mount the walls! Penetrate the houses over the river. If one of you gets through upon the wall, let him not halt before it, [so that] the [hostile] troops may not repulse you. . . .

Then Memphis was taken as [by] a flood of water, a multitude of people were slain therein, and brought as living captives to the place where his majesty was. . . .

Then the ships were laden with silver, gold, copper, clothing, and everything of the Northland, every product of Syria, and all sweet woods of God's-Land. His majesty sailed up-stream, with glad heart, the shores on his either side were jubilating. West and east . . . [the people were] jubilating in the presence of his majesty; singing and jubilating as they said: "O mighty, mighty Ruler, Piankhi, O mighty Ruler; thou comest, having gained the dominion of the Northland. Thou makest bulls into women. Happy the heart of the mother who bore thee, and the man who begat thee. Those who are in the valley give to her praise, the cow that hath borne a bull. Thou art unto eternity, thy might endureth, O Ruler, beloved of Thebes."

KING OF PURE MOUNTAIN

Even after they lost control of Egypt around 660 B.C., the kings of Kush (or Cush) styled themselves kings of Upper and Lower Egypt. The Kushites, whose civilization was strongly influenced by Egypt, believed that their rulers, like the pharaohs, were divinely chosen. The following excerpt comes from one of the steles found at the holy site of Jebel Barkal, "Pure Mountain." It describes the nomination, in 593 B.C., of Aspalta as king of

Kush and concludes when Aspalta steps forward to receive the crown and scepter.

Year 1, 2nd month of the second season, day 15, under the majesty of the Horus: Beautiful of Appearances; the Two Goddesses: Beautiful of Appearances; the Horus of Gold: Mighty of Heart; the King of Upper and Lower Egypt, Lord of the Two Lands: [Merka-Re]; the Son of Re, Lord of Diadems: [Aspalta], beloved of Amon-Re, Lord of the Thrones of the Two Lands, Resident in the Pure Mountain.

Now the entire army of his majesty was in the town named Pure Mountain, in which Dedwen, Who Presides over Nubia, is the god—he is [also] the god of Cush—after the death of the Falcon [previous Kushite King] upon his throne. Now then, the trusted commanders from the midst of the army of his majesty were six men, while the trusted commanders and overseers of fortresses were six men. Now then, the trusted chief secretaries were six men, while the officials and chief treasurers of the palace were seven men. Then they said to the entire army: "Come, let us cause our lord to appear, [for we are] like a herd which has no herdsman!" Thereupon this army was very greatly concerned, saying: "Our lord is here with us, [but] we do not know him! Would that we might know him. . . ."

Then the army of his majesty all said with one voice: "Still there is this god Amon-Re, Lord of the Thrones of the Two Lands, Resident in the Pure Mountain. He is [also] a god of Cush. Come, let us go to him. We cannot do a thing without him; nothing is good which is done without him, [but] a good fortune [comes] from the god. He is the god of the kings of Cush since the time of Re. It is he who will guide us. In his hands is the kingship of Cush, which he has given to the son whom he loves. . . ."

So the commanders of his majesty and the courtiers of the palace went to the Temple of Amon. They found the prophets and the major priests waiting. . . .

Then the prophets and the major priests entered into the temple, that they might perform every rite of his purification and his censing. Then the commanders of his majesty and the officials of the palace entered into the temple and put themselves upon their bellies before this god. They said: "We have come to thee, O Amon-Re, Lord of the Thrones of the Two Lands, Resident in the Pure Mountain, that thou might give [to] us a lord, to revive us, to build the temples of the gods of Upper and Lower Egypt, and to present divine offerings. That beneficent office is in thy hands—mayest thou give it to thy son whom thou lovest!"

Then they offered the King's Brothers before this god, [but] he did not take one of them. For a second time there was offered the King's Brother, Son of Amon, and Child of Mut, Lady of Heaven, the Son of Re: [Aspalta], living forever. Then this god, Amon-Re, Lord of the Thrones of the Two Lands, said: "He is your king. It is he who will revive you. It is he who will build every temple of Upper and Lower Egypt. It is he who will present their divine offerings. His father was my son, the Son of Re: [Inle-Amon], the triumphant. His mother is the King's Sister, King's Mother, Mistress of Cush and Daughter of Re: [Nenselsa], living forever. . . ."

THE "ISLAND OF MEROE"

The Kushites most probably shifted their capital from Napata to Meroë after 591 B.C. Meroitic civilization began to bloom about 350 B.C., and by 100 B.C. the city-state had become a large and powerful empire. This first-century A.D. account of Meroë from Pliny the Elder's Natural History *is largely based on the findings of a Roman exploratory expedition—one of the few in ancient times—ordered by Nero to discover the source of the Nile. The river's mystery was not solved, and the naturalist's fantastic description of the peoples of the "extremity" of Ethiopia is a vivid example of how ignorance could spread suspicion among different peoples.*

The persons sent by Nero for the purposes of discovery have reported that . . . from [Napata] to the island of Meroë the distance is three hundred and sixty miles. They also state that the grass in the vicinity of Meroë becomes of a greener and fresher color, and that there is some slight appearance of forests, as also traces of the rhinoceros and elephant. They reported also that the city of Meroë stands at a distance of seventy miles from the first entrance of the island of Meroë, and that close to it is another island, Tadu by name, which forms a harbor facing those who enter the right-hand channel of the river. The buildings in the city, they said, were but few in number, and they stated that a female, whose name was Candace, ruled over the district, that name having passed from queen to queen for many years. They related also that there was a temple of Jupiter Hammon there, held in great veneration, besides smaller shrines erected in honor of him throughout all the country. In addition to these particulars, they were informed that in the days of the Aethiopian dominion, the island of Meroë enjoyed great renown, and that, according to tradition, it was in the habit of maintaining two hundred thousand armed men, and four thousand artisans. The kings of Aethiopia are said even at the present day to be forty-five in number.

The whole of this country has successively had the names of Aetheria, Atlantia, and last of all, Aethiopia, from Aethiops, the son of Vulcan. It is not at all surprising that towards the extremity of this region the men and animals assume a monstrous form, when we consider the changeableness and volubility of fire, the heat of which is the great agent in imparting various forms and shapes to bodies. Indeed, it is reported that in the interior, on the eastern side, there is a people that have no noses, the whole face presenting a plane surface; that others again are destitute of the upper lip, and others are without tongues. Others again, have the mouth grown together, and being destitute of nostrils, breathe through one passage only, imbibing their drink through it by means of the hollow stalk of the oat, which there grows spontaneously and supplies them with its grain for food. Some of these nations have to employ gestures by nodding the head and moving the limbs, instead of speech. Others again were unacquainted with the use of fire before the time of Ptolemy Lathyrus, king of Egypt.

MAKEDA'S EDUCATION

Axum—the forerunner of modern Ethiopia —arose in the fourth century B.C., at about the same time as Meroë was beginning to develop. Historical tradition and archeological evidence indicate that its appearance was preceded by the migration of peoples from southern Arabia. This merging of Arabians and Africans perhaps forms the basis for one of Christian Ethiopia's most popular traditions, a variation on the biblical story of Solomon and Sheba. The Ethiopian version holds that the Queen of Sheba was an Ethiopian sovereign named Makeda (Magda) and that she returned from her celebrated journey to the court of Solomon in Jerusalem bearing the king's son, David, who became first king of Ethiopia, ruling as Menelik I.

Ethiopian early miniature of King Solomon

Makeda's tale is told in an ancient Ethiopian book, the Kebra Negast, *or Glory of Kings, from which this romance is taken.*

"Let my voice be heard by all of you, my people. I am going in quest of Wisdom and Learning. My spirit impels me to go and find them out where they are to be had, for I am smitten with the love of Wisdom and I feel myself drawn as tho by a leash toward Learning. Learning is better than treasures of silver and gold, better than all that has been created upon earth. And afterward what can be compared to Learning here below? . . . ."

Thereupon the Queen set out with much state and majesty and gladness, for by the will of the Lord, she wished in her heart to make this journey to Jerusalem, to rejoice in the Wisdom of Solomon. They had loaded seven hundred and ninety boats, and mules without number. And the Queen set forth, her trust in God. . . .

After Queen Magda had remained six months in Jerusalem, she desired to return to her own country.

She sent unto Solomon messengers who said to him as follows: "My wish would be to stay with you; but because of those I have brought with me, I must return into my kingdom. God will grant that all I have learned from you may bear fruit in my soul and in the soul of those of my people who, like me, have heard you."

When the King received this message, he meditated in his heart, and he thought: "This woman full of beauty has come to me from the uttermost parts of the earth. Who knows if it be not the will of God that I should have seed of her?"

And so he sent unto the Queen this response: "Since you have done as much as to come hither, will you leave without seeing the glory of my kingdom, the workings of my government, without admiring how my soldiers maneuver, and how I honor the dignitaries of my kingdom? I treat them like saints in Paradise. In each of these things you will find

much Wisdom. So I beg of you that you will come and be present at these spectacles. You shall remain behind me, hidden by a curtain. I will show you the things which I tell you of now. You shall become acquainted with all the customs of my kingdom and this Learning which has pleased you shall remain with you until the end of your days."

Magda sent another messenger who brought back this response: "I was ignorant, and through you I have learned Wisdom. . . . That which you now ask of me is only so that my knowledge and my honor may increase. I will come as you desire."

Then was King Solomon satisfied. He bade his dignitaries array themselves in fine apparel. He made his table twice as large as it was. He ordered that the banquet hall and all the palace be got ready in splendor.

The supper of the King was as formal as the Law of the Kingdom. The Queen entered after the King, she was seated behind him with much honor and pomp. She witnessed all that was going on during the repast. She was amazed at what she saw and at what she heard, and in her heart she gave thanks to the God of Israel.

Solomon had raised for her a throne covered with silken carpets bound with fringes of gold, of silver, of pearls, and of brilliants. He had had his servants scatter about the palace all sorts of perfumes. . . . When one entered one was satisfied without eating, because of these perfumes.

Now Solomon caused them to serve unto Magda a repast prepared expressly for her so that she might become very thirsty. . . . She partook of this repast and when Solomon had presided over the banquet until the guests, the stewards, the councilors, the great chiefs, the servitors had been seven times renewed, and had departed, the King rose.

He went in unto the Queen and finding her alone he said: "I beg you to rest here until to-morrow, out of love for me."

She answered: "Swear to me by your God, by the God of Israel, that you will not use of your strength against me? If in any way whatever I transgress from the law of my country, I shall be plunged into sorrow, into sickness and suffering. . . ."

Solomon answered: "I swear to you that my force shall make no attack upon your honor. But now you in turn must swear that you will touch nothing within this palace." . . .

She answered: "Then swear that you will not lay hold with violence upon my honor, and I will promise with all my heart to touch nothing of what belongs to you."

He swore, and he made her swear.

Then he got upon his bed which was made ready in the next room to this one. And she remained where she was.

Immediately he gave orders to the servants in attendance to wash a vase and to fill it with very pure water, and to put it where it might be seen in the room of the Queen. Then the man was to close the doors and the outside windows. The servant did as Solomon had ordered him in a language which the Queen did not understand.

Solomon did not go to sleep but he feigned unconsciousness. As for the Queen, she dozed a little, then she roused herself, got up, and found that her mouth was dry, for the King had with malice given her food which creates a thirst. She was tormented by this thirst. She tried to bring saliva to her lips to moisten them. But she found none. Then she wished to drink the water she had seen before she had fallen asleep. She looked toward Solomon, and she could see him. . . .

The King pretended to sleep heavily but he was awake and he was watching until the Queen should rouse herself to drink the water.

She got down from her bed, she walked stealthily, she lifted with her hands the vase of pure water. But before she could drink he had seized her by the arm.

He said: "Why have you broken your vow? You promised that you would touch nothing in my palace."

She was trembling, she answered: "Is it breaking my vow to drink a little water?"

"And what more precious treasure than water have you known under the sun?"

She said: "I have sinned against myself. But you, you will be faithful to your vow and you will permit me to drink?"

He asked: "Do you free me of the oath which I have given?"

She said: "Be free of it but let me drink. . . ."

He let fall her arm, she drank. And after she had drunk he did as he would with her, and they slept together.

Now as the King was sleeping he had a vision. He saw a dazzling sun which came down from the heavens and shed its rays upon Israel. This brilliancy endured a certain length of time, then the sun moved away. It stopt in its course over Ethiopia and it seemed that it was shining there for centuries. The King waited for the return of this star to Israel, but it did not come back. And again he saw a second sun which came down from the heavens and which shone upon Judaea. It was brighter than the sun which had preceded it, but the Israelites blasphemed it because of its ardor. They raised against it their hands with sticks and with swords. They wished to extinguish it, so that the earth trembled and clouds darkened the world. Those of Israel thought that this star would not rise a second time. They had put out its light. They had buried it. But in spite of their watchfulness the buried sun rose up again. It lighted the world. Its light illuminated the sea, the two rivers of Ethiopia, and the Empire of Rome. Further than ever it withdrew from Israel and it mounted upon its former throne.

While this vision was descending upon King Solomon in his sleep, his soul was troubled and his mind worked like lightning. He awoke trembling. Then he admired the courage, the force, the beauty, the innocence and the virginity of the Queen, for she had governed her country since her earliest youth and during this delightful time she had kept her body in purity.

Then Queen Magda said to King Solomon: "Send me back to my country."

He went within his palace, he opened his treasure, he gave splendid presents for Ethiopia and important riches, dazzling raiment, and everything that is good. Then he got ready the caravan of the Queen: chariots, animals. The chariots numbered six thousand. They were laden with precious things. Some of them rolled upon the ground, others moved by the aid of the wind. The King had built them according to the learning which God had given him.

The Queen went away satisfied. She departed, and set out upon her way. Now Solomon accompanied her with much pomp and majesty.

When they had gone a certain distance he wished to speak alone with Queen Magda. He took from his finger a ring. He gave it to her and said: "Take this ring and keep it as a token of my love. If thou shouldst ever bear a child this ring will be the sign of recognition. If it should be a son send him to me. And in any case may the peace of God be with thee. While I was sleeping by thy side I had a vision. The sun which before my eyes was shining upon Israel, moved away. It went and soared above Ethiopia. It remained there. Who knows but that thy country may be blessed because of thee? Above all keep the truth which I have brought thee. Worship God. . . . May thy journey be a safe one."

SHOPPERS' GUIDE TO AXUM

The Periplus of the Erythrean Sea *was written by an unknown Greek in the second half of the first century* A.D. *The document is a sailors' and commercial travelers' guide to the Indian Ocean, the Aden and Persian gulfs, and the bustling ports along the way. The following selection describes the Axumite city of Adulis, the chief entrepôt for goods from the Ethiopian interior and such far places as India and the Mediterranean world.*

Adulis [is] a port established by law, lying at the inner end of a bay that runs in toward the south. Before the harbor lies the so-called Mountain Island, about two hundred stadia seaward from the very head of the bay, with the shores of the mainland close to it on both sides. Ships bound for this port now anchor here because of attacks from the land. They used formerly to anchor at the very head of the bay, by an island called Diodorus, close to the shore, which could be reached on foot from the land; by which means the barbarous natives attacked the island. Opposite Mountain Island, on the mainland twenty stadia from the shore, lies Adulis, a fair-sized village, from which there is a three days' journey to Coloe, an inland town and the first market for ivory. From that place to [Axum] the city of the people called Auxumites there is a five days' journey more, to that place all the ivory is brought from the country beyond the Nile through the district called Cyeneum [probably modern Sennaar, in the Eastern Sudan], and thence to Adulis. Practically the whole number of elephants and rhinoceros that are killed live in the places inland, although at rare intervals they are hunted on the seacoast even near Adulis.

There are imported into these places, undressed cloth made in Egypt for the Berbers; robes from Arsinoë [modern Suez]; cloaks of poor quality dyed in colors; double-fringed linen mantles; many articles of flint glass, and others of murrhine [probably agate or carnelian], made in Diospolis [probably Thebes]; and brass, which is used for ornament and in cut pieces instead of coin; sheets of soft copper, used for cooking utensils and cut up for bracelets and anklets for the women; iron, which is made into spears used against the elephants and other wild beasts, and in their wars. Besides these, small axes are imported, and adzes and swords; copper drinking-cups, round and large; a little coin for those coming to the market; wine of Laodicea [on the Syrian coast] and Italy, not much; olive oil, not much; for the King,

gold and silver plate made after the fashion of the country, and for clothing, military cloaks, and thin coats of skin, of no great value. Likewise from the district of Ariaca [on northwest coast of India around Gulf of Cambay] across this sea, there are imported Indian cloth called *monaché* [fine quality cotton] and that called *sagmotogene* [probably tree cotton], and girdles, and coats of skin and mallow-colored cloth, and a few muslins, and colored lac. There are exported from these places ivory, and tortoise-shell and rhinoceros-horn. The most from Egypt is brought to this market [Adulis] from the month of January to September, that is from Tylei to Thoth; but seasonably they put to sea about the month of September.

KING EZANA'S CRUSADE

Trade between Meroë and Axum flourished until the early centuries of Christianity. Then the Noba, or Nubians, gradually began to infiltrate Meroë, taking over some of its cities, where they built their characteristic straw huts amongst the Meroitic brick buildings. By the early fourth century the Noba had become the dominant power. Around A.D. 350 Ezana, the first Christian king of Axum, who also claimed sovereignty over Meroë, set out to crush the Noba, who were making frequent attacks on his kingdom and its dependencies. His campaign most probably dealt a death blow to Meroitic Kush, which subsequently vanished from history. Ezana left a lively description of this memorable military expedition on a stele, from which the following is taken. The Noba eventually adopted much of Meroitic culture, and in 543 they converted to Christianity, building a literate Nubian civilization that lasted until it was slowly engulfed by the faith of Islam between 1275 and the end of the fifteenth century.

"I, 'Ezana, the son of 'Ella 'Amida, a native of Halen, king of Axum and of Himyar and Raydan and of Saba, and of Salhen, and of Seyamo and of Beja [Blemmyes] and of Kasu [Kush-Meroë], king of kings . . . made war upon Noba, for the peoples had rebelled and had boasted of

it . . . "They [the Axumites] will not cross the river Takkaze [the River Atbara]," said the peoples of Noba. And they were in the habit of attacking the peoples of Mangurto and Khasa and Barya and the blacks and of making war upon the red peoples [citizens of Axum]. Twice and thrice they had broken their solemn oaths, and had killed their neighbors without mercy, and they had stripped our deputies and messengers whom I sent to enquire into their raids, and had stolen their weapons and belongings. And as I had warned them, and they would not listen but refused to cease from their evil deeds and betook themselves to flight, I made war on them . . . and fought with them on the Takkaze, at the ford of Kemalke. They fled without making a stand, and I pursued them for 23 days, killing some and capturing others . . . I burnt their towns, both those built of bricks and those built of reeds, and my army carried off their food and copper and iron . . . and destroyed the statues in their temples, their granaries, and cotton trees and cast them into the river Seda [Nile]. And I came to Kasu [Kush, where indigenous Meroitic peoples still lived] and fought a battle and captured prisoners at the junction of the rivers Seda and Takkaze. And the next day I dispatched the army Mahaza, and the army Hara, and Damawa and Falha and Sera up the Seda to raid the country and the cities built of bricks and of reeds. The cities built of brick were 'Alwa [possibly Meroë] and Daro [possibly Kadaro north of Khartoum] . . . and after that I sent the army of Halen and the army of Laken down the Seda against the four towns of the Noba which are made of reeds. . . . The towns built of bricks which the Noba had taken were Tabito and Fertoti. And my peoples reached the frontier of the Red Noba [presumably Napata] and they returned in safety, having defeated the Noba and spoiled them by the might of the Lord of Heaven. And I planted a throne in that country at the place where the rivers Seda and Takkaze join. . . .

The Step Pyramid at Saqqara, near Cairo, constructed around 2650 B.C.

AFRICA'S
RADIANT
DAWN

The joyous season of harvest is celebrated above, in a drawing after a wall painting in an Eighteenth Dynasty Theban tomb. Menna, the pharaoh's "field scribe," oversees activities from his canopied stool, receiving a report from one of his stewards, while another encourages reapers to greater efforts. The detail opposite above, from an Eleventh Dynasty relief, shows a cow being milked.

Canals to drain the land in wet seasons and irrigate crops in the dry are among Egypt's oldest technological achievements. As shown at left, these ancient waterways have helped to support a mixed economy, including cattle, grains, and fruit-bearing trees. Since early times river water has been raised to fill them by a device known as a shadoof, the counterpoised sweep pictured opposite.

THE GREAT PROVIDER

The agricultural revolution probably came to the hunters and gatherers of the Lower Nile around 5000 B.C. The two basic techniques of food production—plant cultivation and animal husbandry—were introduced most likely from western Asia, but their development in Egypt's arid lands depended upon a highly organized system of water control and conservation. Each year after the harvest season armies of peasants were impressed to repair and extend the kingdom's canals, and through these efforts a belt of some 12,000 square miles was made cultivable along the Nile's banks. Planting began after the annual floods receded, generally in December, and most crops were harvested in late spring. Barley and wheat were cereals essential to the making of bread and beer, and orchards, vegetable gardens, beehives, and vineyards yielded in abundance. It was said of the royal grapes at Luxor that their juice was "more plentiful than the water of the Nile at its highest mark."

BLACK STAR - TOR EIGELAND

HASSIA

The votive Palette of Narmer dates from the Archaic Period. On the front of the slate (left) King Narmer wears the White Crown of Upper Egypt and smites a captive. On the reverse (opposite) he has assumed the Red Crown of conquered Lower Egypt and, in triumph, inspects the headless bodies of his victims; below him, slaves snare two long-necked panthers.

BOTH: EGYPTIAN MUSEUM, CAIRO

The political unification of Upper and Lower Egypt, around 3100 B.C., brought to an end centuries of strife between the powerful kings of the Nile Valley and the Delta. Narmer, one of the chieftains of Upper Egypt, is generally credited with the inauguration of the dynastic period, which was to continue, despite foreign invasion and internal disruption, until Egypt fell into the hands of the Romans. As the first of the pharoahs, Narmer seems to have formalized the concept of the divine king, and in recognition of the dual source of his temporal power, he began the building of a new capital, Memphis, near the meeting point of the two ancient kingdoms. Greater political organization followed: a growing corps of ministers was entrusted with overseeing Egypt's agricultural, mining, trade, public works, and military interests, and the state was divided into nomes, or districts, to see that the work was carried out efficiently.

BUILDERS OF CIVILIZATION

Fluted columns above, in imitation of papyrus reeds, once supported Zoser's temple at Saqqara. The ruins stand adjacent to his Step Pyramid, which in form and construction was the precursor of the pyramids at Giza. Pharoah Menkaure, pictured below with his wife, followed Cheops and Chephren in building these incomparable monuments to immortality.

THE KING AND HIS PEOPLE

According to the most ancient African concept of kingship, the ruler was not mortal, but a god in the guise of man; he was the bridge between the divine forces of nature and his subjects. The efficacy of his powers maintained his people while he ruled, and also helped to sustain them from his tomb. These attributes were adopted by Egypt's kings at the beginning of the Archaic Period, around 3100 B.C. Specifically Egyptian, however, was the identification of the living king with the falcon-headed god Horus, and in death with the god Osiris, ruler of the underworld. The pharoah stood at the apex of society. He was hailed as "the beautiful silver hawk, who protects Egypt with his wings . . . the castle of strength and of victory." He was responsible for the flooding of the Nile, the bounty of the harvest, and his nation's success in peace and war. Egyptian society, from the highest noble to the lowliest peasant, willingly expedited his commands to gain his blessings in the afterlife and to ensure the nation's well-being.

The pharaoh's majesty is symbolically represented in the massive portrait of Zoser opposite. The realm was run by a multitude of officials. Mitri, a Fifth Dynasty provincial administrator, is shown with his staff and scepter in the wooden statue at lower left. His contemporary, a scribe, is portrayed in the painted limestone statue (detail, below right); also a civil servant, he kept accounts and copied documents. But life was not all work, and reminders of its pleasures, like the Old Kingdom sculpture at right of children playing leapfrog, often accompanied rulers to the next world.

OVERLEAF: *Many different races helped forge the splendid civilization of dynastic Egypt. Some are depicted in this copy of a wall painting that decorates the tomb of Seti I, who was buried in the Valley of the Kings at Thebes around 1300 B.C. Reading from the top row right, the parade shows white-skinned people of Libya; black-skinned people of Kush, or Nubia; and brown-skinned people of Canaan in the Levant. The four figures at bottom center are Egyptians; they have a reddish skin tone, in keeping with an artistic convention that men be painted red, and women yellow. Horus, symbol of the living king, ends the procession.*

LEPSIUS, *Denkmäler . . . ., 1860*

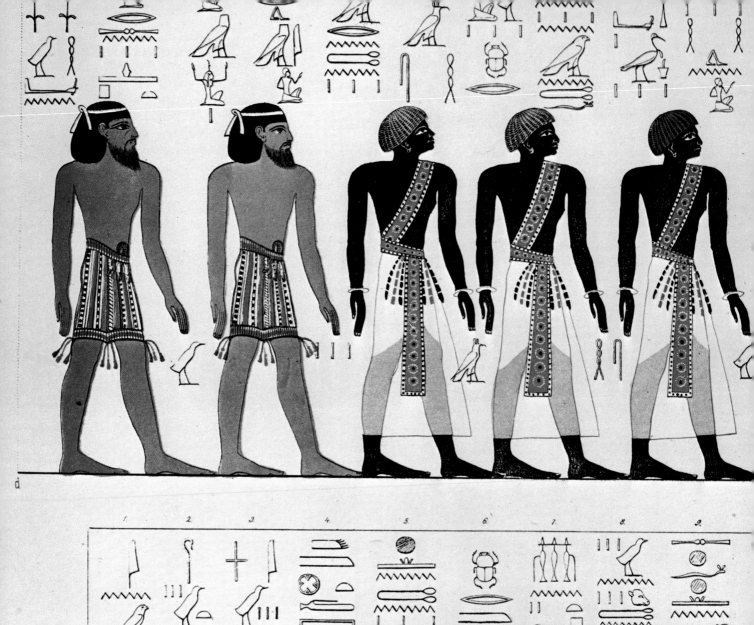

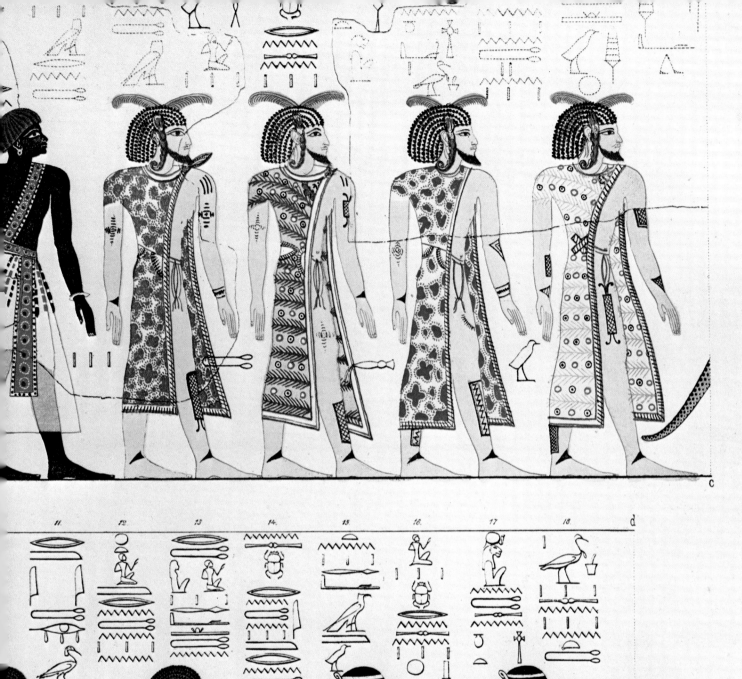

The horse-drawn chariot, like the one seen above, was a means of transportation developed chiefly for warfare. It was introduced by the Hyksos, who invaded in the eighteenth century B.C. Egyptian ships, however, were of indigenous invention. Vessels, such as the one below in the copy of a Sixth Dynasty tomb painting, were constructed of wood and papyrus and propelled by linen sails and a team of rowers. As technology advanced, ships up to one hundred feet in length and able to carry eighty tons of cargo, were put into service on rivers and seas.

A MERGING OF IDEAS

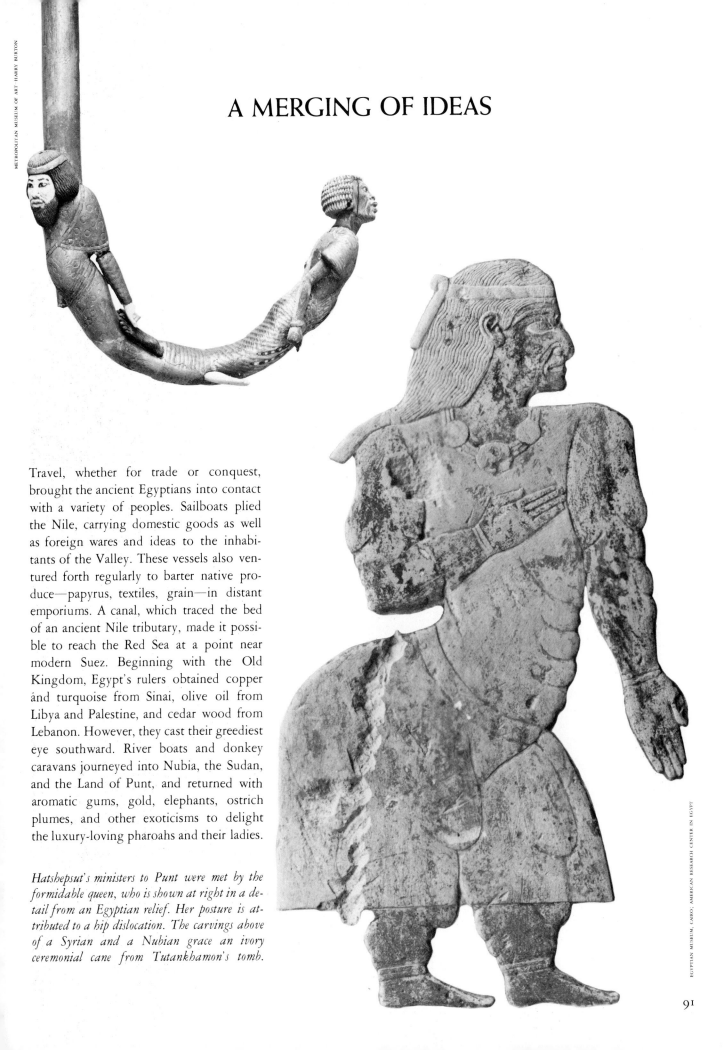

Travel, whether for trade or conquest, brought the ancient Egyptians into contact with a variety of peoples. Sailboats plied the Nile, carrying domestic goods as well as foreign wares and ideas to the inhabitants of the Valley. These vessels also ventured forth regularly to barter native produce—papyrus, textiles, grain—in distant emporiums. A canal, which traced the bed of an ancient Nile tributary, made it possible to reach the Red Sea at a point near modern Suez. Beginning with the Old Kingdom, Egypt's rulers obtained copper and turquoise from Sinai, olive oil from Libya and Palestine, and cedar wood from Lebanon. However, they cast their greediest eye southward. River boats and donkey caravans journeyed into Nubia, the Sudan, and the Land of Punt, and returned with aromatic gums, gold, elephants, ostrich plumes, and other exoticisms to delight the luxury-loving pharoahs and their ladies.

Hatshepsut's ministers to Punt were met by the formidable queen, who is shown at right in a detail from an Egyptian relief. Her posture is attributed to a hip dislocation. The carvings above of a Syrian and a Nubian grace an ivory ceremonial cane from Tutankhamon's tomb.

GATEWAY
TO
THE SOUTH

Nubians, like the one in the relief opposite, swelled the ranks of Egypt's armies and left a strong mark on its culture. Their close ties are also manifest in such objects as the New Kingdom razor handle at right, topped with a Negro lutist. The site above is the north wall of the newly excavated fort at Buhen.

From the third millennium B.C., if not earlier, Nubia and the northern Sudan were a vital crossroads for cultural interchange between the peoples of Egypt and those farther south and west. Various pottery-making techniques and weapons may have come into Egypt from the Sudan. Egypt's kings coveted the land of Kush, rich in gold and copper and the gateway to the south. During the Middle Kingdom they built a series of fortresses, including one at Buhen just below the Second Cataract. These strongholds gave them control of Kush as far as Semna. Then, during the New Kingdom, Egypt advanced its frontiers to the "Horns of the World," probably below the Fourth Cataract. The late tenth and ninth centuries B.C. saw a resurgence of Kushite independence. From 751 to 656 B.C. a line of Kushites ruled Egypt as the Twenty-fifth Dynasty.

93

The giant steles of Axum, like those pictured here, evoke the city's triumphal past. Hewn from granitelike stone, they rise skyward up to one hundred ten feet. Most likely they were erected between the second century B.C. and the fourth century A.D. Some may have been funerary monuments or religious symbols. Others, carved with windows and doorways to resemble multistoried houses, and having richly decorated sacrificial altars at their bases, were used in pagan rites. However, since the precise purpose of these monuments is still shrouded in mystery, they offer the archeologist an intriguing field for study.

WERNER FORMAN

Pyramids of the Kushite kings, as depicted in an 1833 engraving
AMERICAN MUSEUM OF NATURAL HISTORY

MEROE AND AXUM

The two greatest African empires to rise in the lands beyond Egypt were Meroë, an outgrowth of Kush, and Axum, parent of modern Ethiopia. After 591 B.C. the Kushites shifted their capital from Napata to Meroë, near the Sixth Cataract. Thenceforth the city-state developed a distinctive style of art and architecture. Meroë also gained renown as an important iron-working center, and was probably instrumental in the spread of iron technology to more southerly parts of Africa. It traded in distant Asia and on the continent, and may have had contacts with peoples as far west as Lake Chad. However, after the first century A.D. Meroë was gradually eclipsed by Axum, its neighbor to the east. Axum became the foremost commercial power of the southern Red Sea area—the center for trade between the Mediterranean, Central and East Africa, Arabia, and the lands of the Indian Ocean. In the fourth century it delivered the final blow to Meroë, adopted Christianity, and began forging the unique, and still existing culture of Christian Ethiopia.

A painted pot from Kush
WERNER FORMAN

Chapter Three

THE

BARBARY COAST

(c. 500 B.C.–A.D. 639)

by

Stuart Schaar

TWO DISTINCT GEOGRAPHICAL REGIONS are found in North Africa: in the east Egypt and Cyrenaica (eastern Libya); in the west Tripolitania (western Libya), Tunisia, Algeria, and Morocco. The western region juts out of the Sahara, forming an erratic quadrilateral surrounded by water on three sides. To medieval Arab geographers, who saw the Sahara as a vast sea of sand, the western portion of North Africa, with its many oases, seemed an island of refuge, and so they named the region *jazirat al-maghreb*, "the island of the west." Egypt and its geological appendage Cyrenaica, separated from the Maghreb by one of the most desolate stretches of the Sahara, more often than not shared a common history. Yet, though sand and sea have at times acted as barriers isolating the Maghreb from sub-Saharan Africa, Egypt, and Europe, these same barriers also served as bridges for the diffusion of new ideas and technology and as highways for invaders, traders, and missionaries.

The western Sahara, the massive Atlas Mountains, and the Mediterranean Sea have molded the Maghreb into a unit. The Sahara is more than just sand; it comprises high, arid mountains reaching to ten thousand feet, deep depressions similar in appearance to those on the surface of the moon, salt flats, high steppelands, moving dunes, and fertile oases that support large settlements. Life depends on underground rivers and natural springs scattered throughout the vast desert, and sudden rains, at times followed by flash floods, make even the most arid regions bloom.

To the north of the Sahara the Atlas Mountains, called by different names from west to east, stretch out between Morocco and Tripolitania and keep the desert sands from invading the fertile, densely settled coastal plains. (The Jebel Akhdar range in Cyrenaica, though geologically distinct from the Atlas range, also serves the same protec-

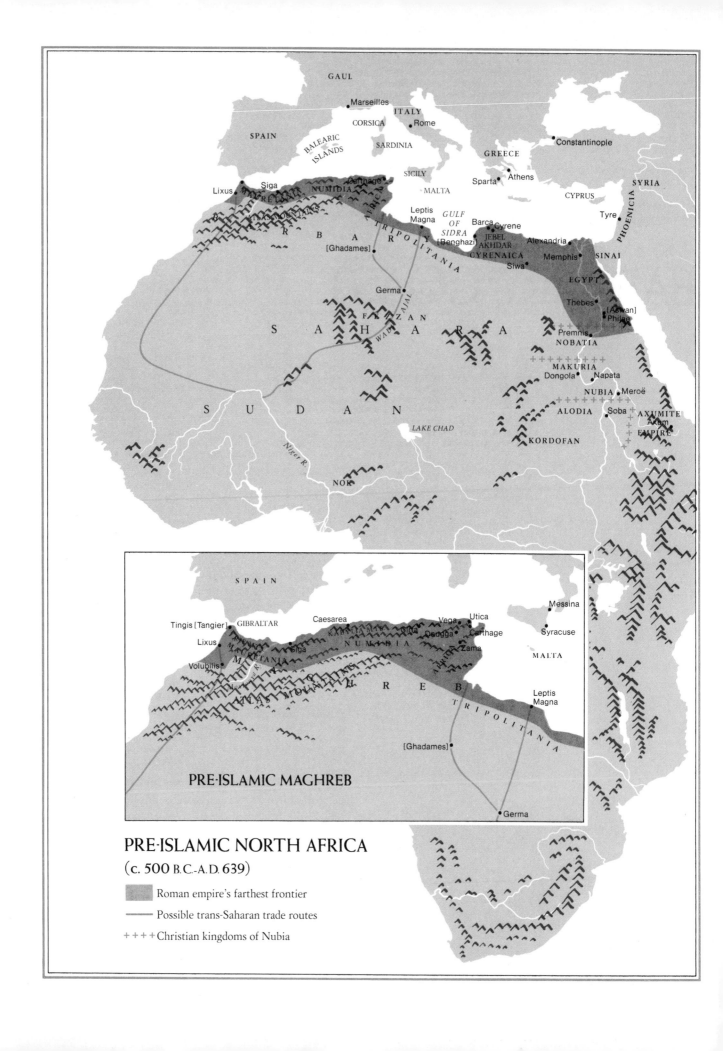

PRE-ISLAMIC NORTH AFRICA

(c. 500 B.C.-A.D. 639)

Roman empire's farthest frontier

Possible trans-Saharan trade routes

++++ Christian kingdoms of Nubia

PRE-ISLAMIC MAGHREB

tive function.) The Atlas peaks are highest in Morocco, reaching 13,600 feet. Their maximum elevation in Algeria is 7,600 feet, less than 4,500 feet in Tunisia, and 2,500 feet in Tripolitania, becoming hills. The coastal plains start out as a very narrow strip in Tripolitania and widen to between fifty and one hundred miles as they extend westward, reaching their widest expanse on the Atlantic coast of Morocco, an area of abundant rainfall.

Rainfall in North Africa becomes irregular and unpredictable in duration and intensity as one moves from west to east, and water sources become less plentiful. Cyrenaica consists of oases surrounded by desert, and other than the Nile Valley, the Suez region, and some scattered oases, Egypt is all desert. Most of the North African population has therefore lived in dispersed plains or oases, separated from one another by gorgelike valleys or inhospitable deserts. Internal communications have been especially difficult in Morocco and Algeria because of the ruggedness of the mountains and the hazards of crossing valleys.

As large portions of the Sahara, Morocco, and Algeria have traditionally been inaccessible, especially the Atlas chain and the more northerly Rif and Kabylia mountains, the Berber peoples of North Africa tended over the centuries to seek safety from foreign conquests in mountainous and desert zones. As they escaped from conquerors, they trekked westward so that, according to one recent estimate, 45 per cent of the Moroccan population speak Berber, 30 per cent do so in Algeria, and less than 2 per cent do in Tunisia. Other Berber-speaking people live in the Siwa oasis in Egypt near the Libyan frontier and throughout the Sahara, and some are located south of the Niger River.

Notable among the desert dwellers are the Tuareg, who are the only modern Berber people known to have an alphabet. When other Berbers wish to write their language, they have on rare occasions in recent centuries composed their works in Arabic script. The language used in antiquity by the ancestors of the Berbers, containing an alphabet of twenty-three consonants, has long been forgotten, and although the Tuareg have partly derived their own dialect and writing system from it, knowledge of the Tuareg alphabet does not help them to decipher hundreds of Berber inscriptions that date from Roman times.

Where the Berbers originated and how they got to North Africa remain mysteries. Ancient inscriptions, which seem to have been written by the ancestors of the modern Berbers, have been discovered in the Sinai peninsula and in the Nile Delta, leading some scholars to conclude that these people migrated into Africa from southwest Asia. Recent

analysis of African languages lends some credence to this view. Linguists, notably Joseph Greenberg, have grouped the numerous Berber dialects, which vary from region to region, with the larger Afro-Asiatic family of languages, along with old Egyptian, Somali, Galla, Hebrew, and Arabic.

Whatever the outcome of future research into the problems of when and if these intruders conquered North Africa from other people, it is known that by the fifth century before the Christian era, when written sources were available for the Maghreb, the Berbers had already spread throughout the northern third of the continent. There they had come into contact with a darker-skinned population. According to numerous Greek and Latin texts, these dark-skinned people, known generically as Ethiopians in antiquity, occupied the majority of the oases in the Sahara until the first few centuries of the Christian era. Supposedly they formed nations and moved about as they pleased.

These Negroid people shared a common culture; they traced their earlier history to Neolithic fishing-and-hunting communities located along rivers near marshes and dominating the Sahara. It seems that these people migrated after a wet phase, between approximately 5500 and 3000 B.C., when the Sahara began drying up. Those moving south would have mixed with the Sudanese population. Migrants to the north and those remaining on oases presumably later intermarried with the ancestors of the Berbers and Egyptians of North Africa and the Galla, Somali, and Beja of the East African Horn. Such migrations and communications over once-navigable rivers probably aided in the diffusion into surrounding areas of social and cultural institutions.

The most powerful of the ancient desert dwellers, the Garamantes, whose skin color is still a matter of controversy, lived on the Wadi Ajal, a populous hundred-mile-long chain of oases located south of the Tripolitanian coast in the desert region known as the Fezzan. As Herodotus noted, from at least the fifth century B.C. commercial relations between the Tripolitanian coast and the Fezzan flourished. The intervening routes offered few obstacles to communication; thus the Garamantes were placed at the heart of an important crossroads that connected Egypt, the coast, and the south. Their commercial empire, with its center at the town of Germa, extended westward to the town of Ghadames and possibly reached southward to the central Sudan around Lake Chad. Their forts protected trade routes, and the horses that they bred were used to police the desert. United into a kingdom since at least Roman times, they served as the chief middlemen in the central Saharan trade.

The Sahara, meaning "desert" in Arabic, covers more than 3,000,000 square miles, much of it windswept, barely passable dunes like these.

Just as some Saharans mixed with the Berbers, so did other peoples, for in antiquity Phoenicians, Greeks, Egyptians, Persians, Romans, Vandals, and Byzantines controlled parts of the Maghreb. Yet, despite these contacts, the Berbers remained aloof from external controls and influences. Long distances and the difficulty of the terrain limited communications and restricted the number of permanent settlers who came to the Maghreb. Although oxen and horses crossed the Sahara during the first millennium B.C., the desert ceased to be an impenetrable barrier in the Maghreb only after the second century A.D., when the use of camels became widespread.

The stereotyped prejudices that classical writers developed about the North Africans tended to heighten Berber isolation even more. Many authors viewed them scornfully as uncivilized, violent, and passionate people who lacked subtlety. Although some Greek and Latin literary sources at times portrayed them as courageous, sober, and persevering, most writers reproached them for sensuality, apparent cruelty, turbulence, laziness, love of raiding and pillaging, and double standards of truth. Since the Berbers lived outside the pale of classical civilization, the Greeks and Romans considered them barbarians, from which the name "Berber" evolved to designate the light-skinned inhabitants of North Africa. The Arabs later called the area they inhabited Barbary. (Alternatively, the area was known by the Greek name "Libya," after the Lebu Berbers.)

Barbary entered written history about 1100 B.C. The first foreign settlements were made by Phoenicians from the city-state of Tyre in present-day Lebanon, who were drawn west by the prospects of gaining access to silver, copper, tin, and lead in the Iberian Peninsula. In the last quarter of the ninth century B.C. these Middle Easterners founded Carthage (*Kart Hadasht*, or "New City"), and within three centuries this tiny settlement had grown into a city-state, asserted its independence from Tyre, and organized the other Phoenician colonies in the western Mediterranean into a powerful Punic empire under its leadership.

Toward the start of the fifth century B.C. Carthage became the first maritime and commercial power in the western Mediterranean. It had set the limits to the expansion of the Greeks, restricting their activity in southern Spain and sweeping them out of Sardinia and the African coast west of Cyrenaica. Despite gigantic efforts and the establishment of several strongholds in western Sicily, Carthage had failed to destroy Greek colonies in the eastern regions of the island. This enemy presence was a threat to the whole system of Carthaginian dominance: Sicily served as an ideal staging base to launch invasions against North Africa and as a gateway to both Spain, with its metal production, and Sardinia, where African Berbers had settled. The Sicilian and Sardinian colonies also provided Carthage with precious wheat supplies, which they exacted as a tithe on produce, and soldiers. Both were critically needed during African revolts and invasions, when the city-state was deprived of local agricultural resources and manpower. All attempts by Greeks and Romans to drive the Carthaginians from Sicily were therefore resisted fiercely; it became a cornerstone of Punic foreign policy to maintain a foothold there.

Carthage had escaped the westward onslaught of Iranians when the Phoenicians, vassals of Persia between 538 and 332 B.C., refused to join in the invasion of Carthage because, in the words of Herodotus, "of the close bond which connected Phoenicia and Carthage, and the wickedness of making war against their own children." King Cambyses of Persia conquered Egypt in 525 B.C., but failed to conquer both the Nubian country to the south and the site of the oracle of Amon-Re at the Siwa oasis in Egypt's western desert. It fell to Darius I (521–486 B.C.) to pacify the sprawling Persian empire, torn by revolt, and to organize Egypt into one of twenty satrapies ruled from the Middle East. Darius, after extending his realm beyond the Indus River in India, sent his troops as far as Euesperides (Benghazi) on the Cyrenaican coast and annexed Cyrenaica in 515 B.C. The Greek towns of Cyrene and Barca were joined to the Egyptian satrapy and helped pay the seven hundred talents in tribute offered annually. Neighboring Libyans added gifts, and the Nubians were required to bring to the Persians every second year two quarts of gold, two hundred ebony logs, five young boys, and twenty elephant tusks.

The combination of Persian power to the east and Greek hostility in Sicily forced various Phoenician settlements in North Africa to unite with others in southern Spain, western Sicily, Sardinia, the Balearic Islands, and Corsica, all under Carthaginian leadership. Carthage also sought to protect itself through alliance with the Etruscans of Italy in the sixth century B.C., but in 474 the Greeks defeated these allies. Earlier they had repelled an invasion of the Greek mainland by King Xerxes of Persia (485–465 B.C.) and the Carthaginian attempt to conquer Sicily. Also, the Greeks of Marseilles closed ports of Gaul and Spain to Punic ships. Athens even attacked the Phoenician coast in 459 B.C., but its ambitions were soon checked when it supported an unsuccessful rising in Egypt. The Greek historian Thucydides in his *History of the Peloponnesian War* describes the events that followed:

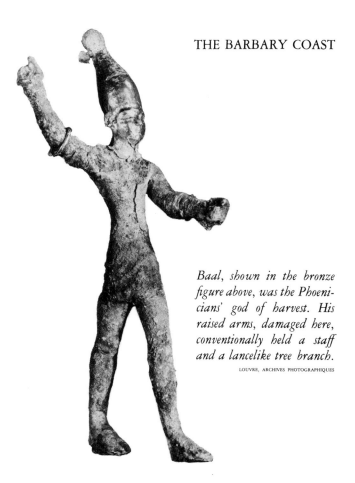

Baal, shown in the bronze figure above, was the Phoenicians' god of harvest. His raised arms, damaged here, conventionally held a staff and a lancelike tree branch.
LOUVRE, ARCHIVES PHOTOGRAPHIQUES

. . . a Libyan king . . . on the Egyptian border . . . caused a revolt of almost the whole of Egypt from King Artaxerxes [Persian ruler from 465–424 B.C.], and placing himself at its head, invited the Athenians to his assistance. Abandoning a Cyprien expedition upon which they happened to be engaged with two hundred ships . . . they arrived in Egypt and sailed from the sea into the Nile . . . making themselves masters of the river and two-thirds of Memphis . . . and the king sent . . . a Persian to Lacedaemon [Sparta] with money to bribe the Pelopennesians to invade Attica and so draw off the Athenians from Egypt. Finding that the matter made no progress, and that the money was only being wasted, he . . . sent . . . a Persian with a large army to Egypt. Arriving by land he defeated the Egyptians and their allies in a battle, and drove the Hellenes out of Memphis. . . . the Libyan king, the sole author of the Egyptian revolt, was betrayed, taken and crucified.

Thenceforth until 332 B.C., the moment of Alexander the Great's invasion, Egypt remained under nominal Persian control; but periodic revolts broke out, and as early as 404 B.C. rulers of the satrapy asserted their independence.

Throughout the fifth and fourth centuries B.C. Carthage

fought the Greeks for control of Sicily. By 375 Carthage had won control over the western third of the island, which it retained more or less for a century. But continual wars weakened both belligerents, benefiting an expanding Rome.

However, the wars served to accelerate the introduction into Barbary of Hellenic influences—to a slight degree in religion, but significantly in the arts, military science, and weaponry. A large number of rich Carthaginians settled in Syracuse; many members of the Punic aristocracy served in the army or in Sicilian diplomatic posts and came into direct contact with Greek civilization. In the fourth century splendid works of art were brought as booty to Africa from Sicily. An important Hellenic colony settled at Carthage, Greek cults spread, and Greek mercenaries joined the Punic army. Carthage could no longer remain aloof.

During the turbulent first half of the fifth century B.C. Carthage's trade with the Mediterranean world had declined, and outlets for selling raw materials and precious metals dried up. This commercial depression, combined with the necessity to use its silver and gold to pay for mercenary troops and its initial stalemate in Sicily, had also turned Carthage inward to Africa. By the middle of the fifth century it had built a land empire so that fifty years later, despite numerous Berber revolts against Punic expansionism, the new territory (corresponding to northeastern Tunisia) provided the bulk of army recruits; by the early third century, with the assistance of Numidia (corresponding to parts of present-day Algeria and western Tunisia) it raised adequate grain to feed Carthage's population of about 400,000, including slaves and foreigners.

In the century after its founding, Carthage had paid an annual tribute to the neighboring Berbers as a form of rent for the soil it occupied. During a part of the sixth century it had freed itself of this burden and ceased to pay anything for many years. But toward the end of the century it had to submit once again. Sometime around 475 to 450 B.C. Carthage permanently revoked the obligation. This was accompanied or followed by the growth of a sizable settlement beyond the city so that by 400 B.C. Carthage reached its greatest extent. At the same time the Carthaginians settled sites along the Barbary coast between Cyrenaica and the Atlantic and established regular commercial relations with the Berbers.

In the western Mediterranean Carthage sought to reserve for itself the exclusive exploitation of vast markets and supplies of raw materials. From the fourth century its dependencies save Sicily were closed to all but Punic merchants. The Punic fleet even sank ships that navigated toward the Strait of Gibraltar, and to discourage foreign exploration, sailors or merchants invented imaginative tales of the dangers and obstacles in the Atlantic Ocean, including encounters with gigantic sand bars, impassable fields of algae, enormous sea monsters, and thick fogs. Herodotus, taking his information from Carthaginian sources, describes how Punic traders bartered merchandise for gold along the same Atlantic coast:

> The Carthaginians also tell us that they trade with a race of men who live in a part of Libya beyond the Pillars of Heracles. On reaching this country, they unload their goods, arrange them tidily along the beach, and then, returning to their boats, raise a smoke. Seeing the smoke, the natives come down to the beach, place on the ground a certain quantity of gold in exchange for the goods, and go off again to a distance. The Carthaginians then come ashore and take a look at the gold; and if they think it represents a fair price for their wares, they collect it and go away; if, on the other hand, it seems too little, they go back aboard and wait, and the natives come and add to the gold until they are satisfied. There is perfect honesty on both sides; the Carthaginians never touch the gold until it equals in value what they have offered for sale, and the natives never touch the goods until the gold has been taken away.

About 470 B.C. Hanno, a member of the Carthaginian ruling class, supposedly led a group of settlers on a voyage of colonization along Africa's Atlantic coast, ostensibly to consolidate the gold trade, a major Punic enterprise. It now seems well established that Hanno's description of his voyage was not, as has long been thought, a Greek translation of an inscription on a Carthaginian temple; rather, it was the product of pure fantasy mixed with some facts drawn from earlier authors and was composed perhaps as a school exercise in the first century B.C. A Greek geographer of Asia, known as the Pseudo-Scylax, writing about 338 B.C., also reports that Phoenicians exchanged perfume, Egyptian stones, and Athenian pottery for animal skins, hides, and tusks, all of which could have been found in the region corresponding to present-day Morocco. He, like the author of the document describing Hanno's voyage, omitted to mention the gold trade, which the Carthaginians did not readily publicize. Doubtless some Punic colonies beyond the Strait of Gibraltar traded in gold on a small scale until Roman times. According to a source that the Greek geographer Strabo mistrusted, this trade ended prior to the first century A.D., when the Pharusians and the Nigrites attacked. (They were nomadic horsemen and archers about whom we know little more than that they lived south of Morocco.) Strabo relates that they destroyed more than three hundred trading posts on the Atlantic coast.

Punic merchants rarely, if at all, had direct commercial relations with the Sudan. Instead, as previously stated, the Garamantes played the role of middlemen, supplying Carthage with precious stones known as carbuncles and possibly slaves, whom, according to Herodotus, they "hunted" in horse-drawn chariots in the Sahara south of the Tripolitanian coast. One series of rock drawings shows these chariots were in use from the Fezzan to the Niger Bend, but nothing indicates that Carthage received gold from the Fezzan. Rather, the weight of evidence suggests that Carthaginian gold came entirely from the Atlantic coast, and even this source seemingly ceased to be active by Roman times.

Finds of tomb jewelry attest that Carthage had gold objects in quantity during the seventh and sixth centuries B.C. Although they had stopped burying such valuable commodities in their graves by the fifth century, the reliable historian Thucydides informs us that the enemies of Carthage believed that they possessed a great deal of gold and silver. But supplies of these metals did not suffice to underwrite the Sicilian wars of the fourth century B.C. During this period and in the following century Carthage passed through a financial crisis. During the First Punic War against Rome (264–241 B.C.) the North African state lacked money to the point that it had to double taxes on Berber subjects, taking from them fifty per cent of their harvests, and even then could not pay its mercenaries. Only the conquest of the entire Iberian Peninsula, beginning in 237 B.C., provided large amounts of silver to pay off the Roman indemnity and later to fight the Second Punic War (219–201 B.C.).

With commerce as the main source of Carthaginian riches, land never became a major concern of the ruling class, whose members remained basically wholesale merchants and shipping magnates. Commercial needs therefore dictated foreign policy. By force or by treaties or by founding colonies the state opened up new markets for the merchants and, where possible, organized monopolies and negotiated reciprocal trade agreements. It also assured the liberty of navigation against pirate attacks.

By the fifth century B.C. about three hundred of the wealthiest Carthaginians shared in the control of the state through the agency of the senate. Although they were divided into rival clans, they came to terms with each other in order to maintain stability for trade. Short wars increased the senators' fortunes and filled the treasury with booty. Conquests also benefited the ruling families by expanding markets, eliminating competitors, producing new administrative posts, and, in Africa, extending their private property. However, senators disdained long wars. Besides being costly, such drawn-out struggles disrupted trade and fortified the position of ambitious generals.

In addition to two *sufets*, executive officers who held office for a year and presided over the senate and an assembly of citizens, the Carthaginians appointed generals as commanders in chief on extraordinary occasions, usually for the duration of a war. They, too, were traditionally chosen from the upper class. Fearing that popular commanders might usurp their power and establish tyrannies, the senators generally chose mediocre men for these posts. By the middle of the fifth century B.C. a court of one hundred four judges, chosen from the senate, supervised and oversaw the activities of the generals. In the third century a few members out of an executive body of at least thirty senators accompanied officers overseas to exercise control over political decisions. The fear of sentences passed by the high court dissuaded the best men from assuming a command, and more than one incapable or unlucky general was fined, had his property confiscated, lost his life, or faced exile, as a result of senatorial action.

Below the senate was an assembly of citizens composed of retail merchants, manufacturers, administrators, and employees of large firms, who depended on the senatorial aristocracy for their jobs and livelihood. We do not know the exact number of citizens within the capital of Carthage (estimates range in the area of eighty thousand) or how many among them qualified for membership in the assembly. Citizenship could be granted to foreigners whom the state judged worthy of the honor, and Phoenicians from the Middle East and citizens of other Phoenician or Carthaginian colonies also probably enjoyed rights of citizenship in Carthage.

Until the late third century the citizen assembly scarcely affected government. If the senate and the *sufets* agreed on policies, there was no need to submit issues to any other body. At times a popular vote took place in the assembly even when the two executives and the senators agreed in order to obtain general support for hazardous ventures. This procedure gave citizens the illusion of participation. In return for their collaboration, citizens paid no taxes in peacetime, and after the sixth century B.C., did not have to serve in the army. Contingents were then drawn from among Carthage's disfranchised subjects and government-financed mercenaries. It had become cheaper to use precious metals to hire mercenaries than to withdraw a large number of citizens from wealth-producing trade. Moreover, there were far too few citizens in Carthage to provide for the defense of the empire. Two serious army defeats would have wiped out their forces, so that if Carthage had relied on a citizen army, it might have disappeared long before 146 B.C., when Rome ulitmately defeated Carthage because of its greater manpower reserves.

Besides the citizens, the population of Carthage included Libyans, who had migrated to the city from surrounding rural areas to find work, and also slaves, who were imported from all over the Mediterranean, the Sahara, and farther south. Most Libyans and all slaves had no political rights in Carthage. Merchants, commercial agents, and artisans also flocked to the city-state from Sicily, Italy, and Greece. Fusion with the citizenry was not easy, but Carthaginians did intermarry with other peoples. Mixed marriages were especially frequent with Libyans, less perhaps in the capital than in the coastal colonies. No source indicates how many Libyans became Carthaginian citizens.

In urban centers slaves were employed by the Carthaginians as servants in rich families or as workers in artisanal shops, commercial houses, and state arsenals. On the sea they manned merchant and war galleys. A few Negroes served as slaves in the cities or regions of Barbary close to the coasts, but it does not seem that at this time they furnished enough manpower to play an important role in the working of the agrarian estates of the aristocracy. North Africa was well enough populated with poor Berbers to provide a cheap local supply of farm labor, and rich Carthaginians certainly used war prisoners and victims of piracy to cultivate their fields. We do not know, however, if these captives were purchased by their masters or loaned out by the state. The rural Berber population rarely had slaves. They were too poor to buy them, and if any were acquired in warfare, the Berbers were better off selling their captives than feeding them. Besides, women did most of the hard labor among the Berbers. It is possible that Punic merchants sold Negro slaves to Greeks and Italians, but in smaller numbers than those that reached the Mediterranean by way of Egypt.

The slaves who cultivated the suburban estates of the rich had little to lose by revolting against their masters, and there were periodic uprisings in the fourth century B.C. They therefore had to be watched carefully. Also, a part of the free Libyan population that had migrated to the cities joined urban riots in rare periods of crisis, often just for the chance to raid the homes of the rich. To offset rebellious reactions, the ruling class responded with utmost ferocity and cruelty when threatened.

Meanwhile, Rome was regarding Carthage with increasing jealousy. The potential for a clash between the two had become evident in 268 B.C., when Carthage took over the Sicilian seaport of Messina, across the channel from the Italian coast. Between 264 and 241 B.C. the two powers fought the First Punic War, which ended in the destruction of the Carthaginian fleet. Carthage finally had to evacuate Sicily and pay Rome a heavy indemnity. To compensate for the loss of Sicily, Sardinia, and Corsica, the Carthaginian general Hamilcar Barca led a campaign to conquer Spain beginning in 237 B.C. The booty and the precious metals sent back to Carthage from the Iberian Peninsula enriched the treasury, and the conquest opened new Spanish markets to Carthaginian commerce and industry. His son, Hannibal, became the most famous of the Barcids. While in his mid-twenties he provoked the Second Punic War with Rome. With the vast silver mines and manpower of Spain at his disposal, and backed by the popular support of the Carthaginians, he crossed the Alps in 218 B.C., leading his soldiers and elephants into Italy. In order to prevent revolts during these war years, he sent Spanish soldiers to Africa and Berbers to Spain. These men did not get along with the population among whom they lived, but while serving as hostages they kept the peace.

Hannibal's fortunes were reversed in 203 B.C. when, after fifteen years of military campaigns on the Italian peninsula, he was forced to return to Carthage to oppose the Roman legions of Publius Cornelius Scipio, thereafter known as Scipio Africanus. Hannibal was defeated and ultimately forced to flee Carthage when he attempted to reform its government structure. He then served several Hellenistic princes, among them Antiochus III of Syria in his unsuccessful resistance to Rome. Finally, to avoid being handed over to the Romans, he committed suicide in 183 B.C., apparently by taking poison.

His career has been immortalized in the following description by the less than objective Roman satirist Juvenal:

> Put Hannibal in the scales: how many pounds will that peerless
> General mark up today? This is the man for whom Africa
> Was too small a continent, though it stretched from the surf-beaten
> Ocean shores of Morocco east to the steamy Nile,

To Ethiopian tribesmen, and new elephants'
    habitats.
Now Spain swells his empire, now he surmounts
The Pyrenees. Nature throws in his path
High Alpine passes, blizzards of snow: but he
    splits
The very rocks asunder, moves mountains with
    vinegar.
Now Italy is his, yet he still forces on:
"We have accomplished nothing," he cries, "till we
    have stormed
The gates of Rome, till our Carthaginian standard
Is set in the City's heart." A fine sight it must have
    been,
Fit subject for caricature, the one-eyed commander
Perched on his monstrous beast! Alas, alas for
    glory,
What an end was here: the defeat, the ignominious
Flight into exile, everyone crowding to see
The once-mighty Hannibal turned humble hanger-
    on,
Sitting outside the door of a petty Eastern despot
Till his Majesty deign to awake. No sword, no
    spear,
No battle-flung stone was to snuff the fiery spirit
That once had wrecked a world: those crushing
    defeats,
Those rivers of spilt blood were all wiped out by a
    Ring, a poisoned ring. Oh, on, you madman,
    drive
Over your savage Alps, to thrill young schoolboys
And supply a theme for speech-day recitations!

Thus, despite Hannibal's efforts, Carthage lost the war.
It gave up Spain and its colonies along the North African
coast and had to pay Rome another heavy indemnity. By
200 B.C. Rome had become the center of the Mediterranean
world, and Carthage was relegated to the status of a weak
dependency of the Latin state. Fifty years later Rome,
jealous of Carthage's continued commercial success, provoked the state's leaders into violating the peace treaty and
sent its army to enforce stiffer demands. The Carthaginians
surrendered, but when the Romans insisted as a condition
of future peace that they raze their city and build a new one
inland, the Carthaginians locked the city's gates. This was
the beginning of the Third Punic War. Legionnaires destroyed Carthage in 146 B.C., and the people who survived, an estimated fifty thousand, were sold into slavery,
bringing a once-powerful state to an ignoble end.

Hannibal, as shown on a Punic shekel

Like later North African conquerors in antiquity, the
Carthaginians had settled in urban clusters located mainly
along the Mediterranean. Such cities as Carthage, Utica,
and Lebda (Leptis Magna) served as pockets of cosmopoli-
tan influence, but being artificial, albeit glorious, creations,
they scarcely affected the way of life in the hinterland.
Moreover, as stated earlier, from the fifth to the mid-third
century B.C. Carthage prohibited outsiders from sailing into
the western Mediterranean, so the chances to renew and
enrich the culture through foreign contacts were restricted.
Adaptation to external influences took place only gradually;
and it was most successful when Berber dynasties molded
foreign practices and beliefs to local conditions. Mediterranean civilization reached the Berbers largely through the
efforts of Berber kings, who ruled over large, loosely administered states in the shadow of Carthage and Rome.

Since the end of the second millennium B.C. kingship
was hereditary among the Lebu, a Berber people living west
of Egypt in an area that is now part of modern Libya. In
the next millennium iron and the horse were introduced
into North Africa, two innovations that enhanced the military and technological strength of those who possessed
them. Most probably Berber states were formed by the unification under one authority of diverse lineage groups.
Originally, chieftains were necessary only in time of war.
When circumstances warranted it, an assembly of family
elders met and decided on common action. In case of external threat, they would choose a chief for the duration of
the hostilities or for a year. But such a chief might abuse
his authority or refuse to give up his office once peace was
restored. If a loyal following grouped around him or if he
amassed allies, he became a prince, though he would still
have to respect the autonomy of the lineages that supported
his authority and consult with their representatives. Once
he consolidated his personal power through victorious war-

A five-part Berber drinking vessel with ritual ornamentation

MUSEUM FUR VOLKERKUNDE, HAMBURG

fare, a prince could impose himself on others, making his territory and his lineage the center of a rudimentary state. The chief would have then become a king and would, in all likelihood, establish a dynasty.

Kingly rule was constantly challenged in antiquity. Berbers in the mountains, who in their inaccessibility were almost immune to nomadic raids, periodically pillaged the kingdoms of the plains. Also, internal rivalries among ambitious chiefs and pretenders abounded. To limit treason and rebellion, kings held members of powerful families as hostages in their retinues. They also chose wives from among the daughters of the chiefs and kept the sons of rural notables in their bodyguard. When a ruler died or was deposed, crises erupted, and the interregnums were marked by civil wars. Being menaced from all sides, these kings had to work diligently to maintain authority over their subjects. Ultimately, sovereigns sought ways to enhance their legitimacy and celebrated the "divinity" of former kings.

The main wealth of Berber kingdoms came from the agricultural produce of the sedentary population living on the plains. Monarchs therefore favored agriculture in order to increase tax yields, and whenever possible, they forced nomads to settle. A primary function of the kings was to protect farmers against nomadic raids and town dwellers against foreign invasions. They needed at their disposal both mobile forces to police their territory and regular troops to man strategic garrisons and to fight in wars for and against Carthage or Rome. These forces watched over nomadic displacements and helped to collect taxes on transhumant livestock. Even when they could not enter turbulent areas, Berber princes could control dissidents by threatening to close down regional markets, where the

population came to buy and sell. The rulers developed commercial relations and guaranteed the flow of goods within their realms. Sales and market taxes as well as custom dues probably helped to fill the treasury. Since rural taxes were paid in kind, kings served as the greatest merchants of their states. They exported wheat, wool, skins, livestock, horses, wild animals, carbuncles, ivory, wood, marble, and some slaves.

In the third century B.C. three large kingdoms dominated the Moroccan, Algerian, and Tunisian hinterland. To the extreme west (corresponding to modern Morocco) were the Moors (*Mauri* in Latin), who lived in the kingdom of Mauretania. Moving eastward from the Moulouya River, there were at least two Numidian kingdoms, that of the Massaesylins, centering on the province of Oran, and that of the Massylins, smaller in size and bordering on Carthage.

The Massaesylin king Syphax, who died in 201 B.C., was the first Berber monarch about whom we have any detailed historical information. According to the Roman historian Titus Livy, he was the "wealthiest of the African princes," and before the Romans defeated him in 203 B.C., he controlled all but the Saharan regions of the country that is now called Algeria. He had two capitals: Siga in the extreme west of Oran province; Cirta (modern Constantine) in the east. Both Rome and Carthage tried to make Syphax an ally, but for a time the king believed that he could play the arbiter between these adversaries. He imitated Hellenistic monarchs by wearing a crown and minting coins engraved with his image. Recognizing his importance, one of the most powerful Carthaginian families gave him a daughter to marry.

Syphax lost his territories to Masinissa, an heir to the Massylin throne and an ally of Rome. Masinissa, who died in 148 B.C., was one of the greatest Berber personalities in history. This intelligent, fearless, and subtle man is shown on contemporary coins as a king in his forties or fifties, with sharp features, wide eyes, thick eyebrows, long hair, and a pointed beard. He led an extraordinarily vigorous life, so that at eighty he still could jump on his horse without aid and ride bareback. At the age of eighty-six one of his wives bore him a son, bringing the total of his male progeny to at least forty-four. Several of them survived him when he died at the age of ninety. His kingdom was divided among three of his sons, and his dynasty ruled Numidia for a century, then transferred to Mauretania to reign for sixty years more.

In Spain Masinissa had seen Roman legions in action, and he predicted that the Latins would reign over all of Libya. He wisely allied his kingdom with Rome against

Carthage and King Syphax, who was at this time aligned with the Punic state. In return Rome allowed Masinissa slowly to absorb the maritime colonies that had once belonged to Carthage, leaving him a free hand to conquer Berber subjects. In this way he extended his kingdom from the frontiers of Cyrenaica to the Moulouya River. Conveniently, this expansion into Carthaginian territory also provided Rome with the pretext to destroy Carthage in the Third Punic War.

Masinissa possessed a palace at Cirta, where in the manner of the Carthaginians he gave lavish banquets complete with silver dishes, gold baskets, and Greek musicians to entertain his guests. Although he was raised in the tradition of the Berbers—indeed, his mother had been a popular Berber prophetess—he knew the refined culture of Carthage, where he perhaps spent some of his early years. He married the daughter of a leading Carthaginian and gave his sons a Greek education. The Carthaginians of high rank so respected kings such as Syphax and Masinissa that they did not believe they were lowering their social status by giving their children as wives or sons-in-law.

Berber kings helped to diffuse Carthaginian religious practices throughout Barbary. From earliest times the Berbers were nature worshipers; they had developed cults venerating the sun, mountains, water, trees, and other natural phenomena. Phoenicians, who worshiped nature gods, probably contributed elements to these cults, and certainly Berber influences entered Punic beliefs when Carthage expanded into North African territory in the fifth century B.C. Even after Rome conquered Barbary, the Carthaginian deities of Baal Hammon, the lord of harvests, and Tanit, goddess of life and fertility, still had a large number of devotees, though their names were Romanized respectively as Saturn and Caelestis. Inscriptions discovered at Constantine and its suburbs, in the heart of Numidia, prove that the Berbers, like the Carthaginians, at times sacrificed their first-born children before the Romans prohibited the practice. Rationale for this custom lay in the belief that the virtue of the gods must be maintained by a continual supply of blood. The practice fit into the general character of the Punic religion, which accepted the premise that man was weak and had to submit to capricious and powerful gods who demanded to be appeased.

A large number of Berbers, especially women, still follow magical rites that apparently have their origins in antiquity. These include ceremonies invoking the gods of fertility and incantations to produce rain. Others accompany birth, marriage, and death. Women still tie rags to trees and gather stones, only to throw them away, thus transferring evil to other objects. From the Stone Age, Berbers have worn amulets, which they believe give protection through a genie, or jinni, who deposited some of his power in the object. The fear of the evil eye, the practice of anthropolatry (the worship of men), the belief in genies, and the ritual sacrifice of animals are also holdovers from pre-Islamic times.

In the maritime colonies and over a large part of Tunisia and eastern Algeria the population spoke Punic. Army veterans and merchants gradually spread the language throughout the Maghreb, beyond the towns and regions under direct Carthaginian control. To Berber princes Punic was the lingua franca, since the people they ruled spoke a multitude of Berber dialects. Under Rome, neo-Punic, a development of the old Carthaginian language, was gradually replaced by Latin in the cities, but in some rural areas it died out very slowly and was not extinguished until the beginning of the third century A.D.

The Berbers adopted new agricultural and stockbreeding techniques from their Carthaginian mentors. However, outside Punic Tunisia olive-tree cultivation, grain farming, and viticulture hardly spread before Roman times; most other North Africans continued to raise livestock. The Phoenicians also taught the Berbers how to use bronze and iron in the manufacture of tools and other objects. Exploitation of a copper mine in Numidia only began under the Phoenicians, and Barbary lacked tin to make bronze.

Carthaginians brought Greek and Italian ceramics and Egyptian glassware into Barbary; however, most of these goods were probably beyond the purchasing power of the Berbers, who manufactured their own pottery. They also produced clothes of wool and leather, and ambulant or local blacksmiths supplied them with their iron weapons, plows, utensils, and tools. It was most likely that Carthage furnished Berber princes and chiefs with luxury goods such as ornamented weapons, fine textiles, jewels, perfume, and rugs. Less expensive merchandise was probably sold to veterans who had served in Carthaginian armies. Goods supplied to the general populace in the interior were handled through the intermediary of Berber princes.

Direct relations were established between Carthage and Egypt after Alexander the Great's conquest of the East and the founding of Alexandria in 332 B.C. Alexandria was made the capital of Egypt by Ptolemy, one of Alexander's Macedonian generals and founder of the Ptolemaic dynasty. From the end of the fourth century Carthage competed with Alexandria as Africa's chief trade center, exporting to the burgeoning Hellenistic centers.

Egypt also challenged Carthage on the political front. In 310 B.C. an independent Ptolemaic governor of the Greek cities of Cyrenaica plotted with a tyrant of Syracuse to annihilate the Punic capital. In return for his aid the governor was promised all of Carthage's North African possessions, but the Syracusan killed his co-plotter and the scheme never materialized. During the first war against Rome (264–241 B.C.) Carthage, lacking money to pay its mercenaries, asked King Ptolemy II of Egypt (285–246 B.C.) for a loan of two thousand talents. Although the monarch refused, the fact that Carthage could approach him for such a large sum attests to the close ties between the Nile Valley and the Maghreb.

Other evidence of these connections can be seen in Egyptian styles of architecture and art, which entered the Maghreb with the Phoenicians, who themselves had borrowed heavily from the older civilization of the Nile Valley. The Phoenicians introduced such Egyptian construction procedures as placing blocks of stone on one another without mortar, baking large bricks in the sun, and making stucco. The Carthaginians also borrowed Egyptian weights and measures, including the cubit—a linear measure based on the length of the arm from the elbow to the fingertip. Phoenician merchants who had commercial establishments on the Nile Delta and formed an important colony at Memphis initially imported Egyptian pottery, statuettes, ritual razors decorated with Egyptian divinities, gold work, seals, scarabs used as amulets, and small pendant masks, many of which later Maghrebin artisans copied locally. The cult of the Egyptian sun god Amon-Re spread from Thebes into the Siwa oasis. The Greeks of Cyrenaica knew him under the name of Zeus, and Berbers accepted him as a great nature god.

The Roman emperors, however, regarded Egypt as their private domain, and except for its trade, attempted to keep the Nile Valley isolated from the rest of the empire. An experienced businessman known for his loyalty to the emperor was usually chosen as the Egyptian prefect and acted as the personal representative of the imperial household. To ensure Egypt's isolation, no member of the Roman senate could enter the province without the permission of the emperor.

Under Roman rule the senate was entrusted with administering a truncated version of the old Carthaginian empire—a political unit known by the Latin name "Africa" and encompassing an area of some five thousand square miles. Initially, the senators showed little interest in "Af-

rica." Masinissa's heirs controlled and policed that part of Barbary bordering on the new possession, and some coastal cities enjoyed for a time autonomy and exemption from taxation. Very few Romans settled in the province; those that did, viewed their sojourn as an opportunity to make a quick fortune, which they hoped to spend in Rome.

After surveying its newly conquered lands, Rome allowed small holders to continue farming, but compelled them to pay taxes. The province barely brought in as much revenue as was needed to pay the cost of administration. Rome confiscated estates belonging to the Carthaginian aristocracy and distributed some of them to Roman war veterans and other deserving citizens, who mostly had to work their plots by themselves or with the aid of a few slaves. Rich absentee landlords employed overseers to supervise slaves or freemen to cultivate their property.

Berber kings were at first allowed considerable independence by the Romans since the central government wanted rulers at their disposal who facilitated commands, organized contingents to fight in wars, and co-operated readily in selling wheat to Latin merchants. These kings policed also frontiers and facilitated the penetration of Roman commerce into their territory. But they were allies who had to be treated well and were not humble or docile vassals.

Masinissa's grandson, Jugurtha, broke with dynastic tradition and opposed Rome in the Jugurthine Wars (111–105 B.C.). In an attempt to wrest all of Numidia from Rome, he bribed a number of Roman senators. When the plot was revealed, Jugurtha was summoned to the capital, where he is quoted as saying, "Rome is a city for sale, and doomed to perish if it can find a purchaser." The Roman historian and politician Sallust provides some clues to Jugurtha's charisma. He writes:

As soon as Jugurtha grew up, endowed as he was with great strength and handsome looks, but above all with a powerful intellect, he did not let himself be spoiled by luxury or idleness, but took part in the national pursuits of riding and javelin-throwing and competed with other young men in running; and though he outshone them all he was universally beloved. He also devoted much time to hunting; and was always to the fore at the killing of lions and other wild beasts. His energy was equaled by his modesty: he never boasted of his exploits . . . [later, when fighting in Spain] by dint of hard work and careful attention to duty, by unquestioning obedience and the readiness with which he exposed himself to

Cleopatra, shown in this temple relief, was the last of the Ptolemies and Egypt's last native ruler.

risk, he won such renown as to become the idol of the Roman soldiers and the terror of the enemy. He was in fact both a tough fighter and a wise counselor—qualities extremely hard to combine. . . .

Another Berber king, Juba II, who died in A.D. 23 or 24, married Cleopatra Silene, the daughter of Antony and Cleopatra. This legendary couple, who really lacked the proper administrative ability to make Egypt a profitable province, had provided Rome with the pretext for annexing Egypt. Juba, although an Algerian, had been raised in Rome and was given the best Greek education possible; he became an art connoisseur, and wrote or compiled at least fifty works in Greek, none of which, unfortunately, has survived. Pliny the Elder wrote that during the forty-eight years Juba was king of Mauretania his "glory as a scholar was greater than his reputation as a sovereign." Indeed, he had great difficulty in maintaining the loyalty of his subjects and was confronted with a series of Berber revolts that ultimately were crushed through Roman intervention. Apparently, he carried his cultural affinities and friendship with Rome to extremes, antagonizing his subjects. Even when he attempted to establish himself as a living god, he failed to enhance his legitimacy adequately enough to prevent rebellions.

It was his wife, Cleopatra Silene, who probably intro-

duced the Egyptian cult of Isis, the mother goddess of fertility, into Mauretania. The same cult also spread to Tripolitania. Latin soldiers introduced the popular Egyptian god Sarapis (the Ptolemaic amalgam of the two male fertility symbols, Osiris and Apis the bull) into the Berber pantheon. The success of these cults stemmed from the vagueness of Egyptian doctrines. Since Egyptians viewed their gods as mere symbols of cosmic or ethical forces, they could be easily syncretized with the most popular local deities. Ornate Egyptian rituals and mysterious ceremonies must have intrigued initiates, but at the same time the Osirin influence injected optimism into their religion and promised the faithful immortality and life after death. The Berbers easily associated Sarapis with Baal Hammon or Saturn, and Isis with the Punic goddess Tanit. Under Christianity, statues of Isis would readily become identified with the Virgin Mary, and some Isiac rituals would find their correlatives in Christian practice.

By A.D. 40 Rome had extended its control over Numidia and Mauretania and extinguished the Berber dynasties. The Roman senatorial aristocracy, sometimes by means of small payments and with the connivance of the state, carved for themselves vast holdings out of former Berber crown lands.

In the majority of cases the new owners lived in Italy and leased their land to companies; these in turn sublet plots to North Africans, who at first became hereditary occupants, and by the fourth century, serfs. The Berbers paid rent to the companies, and both master and farmer paid taxes to the state. The chief exception to this pattern was the domains of the emperor, acquired through bequests, purchases, or confiscations. Those who leased estates from the Crown paid as rent one third of their produce, usually wheat. However, if they were slaves, they worked the imperial domains without compensation. Over the centuries more and more acreage would come under these latter systems.

By A.D. 50 Rome faced the problem of depopulation at home and could not spare settlers for Africa. The emperors therefore had to send experts to teach Africans how to administer their holdings. They had to depend on the local population to run the bureaucracy and serve in the army. To garrison the province of "Africa" after A.D. 150, the Romans recruited the Third Legion from 5,500 locally born sons of legionnaires. In addition, until about the end of the fourth century, they used about 7,500 Berber auxiliaries in Numidia and 15,000 in Mauretania to keep the peace. During revolts locally conscripted irregulars swelled these ranks. Much earlier Rome had fortified its North African cities and allowed the people to arm themselves in case of

Berber or pirate attacks. Large farms also had their citadels.

Under the empire not only did Roman Africa contain several large and beautiful cities, among them Carthage, Leptis Magna, Volubilis, and Dougga, but the Romans created a special municipal spirit. This cosmopolitanism permeated several hundred small towns (numbering more than 450 in the fourth century) each with 3,000 to 10,000 people, who prospered and possessed municipal councils, forums, temples, and baths and other amenities. Town dwellers, including merchants, artisans, and farmers, came to believe that municipal life was the highest and, ultimately, the only form of civilization. This ideology, stemming from the practice of granting citizenship to urbanites, made city dwellers feel superior to that part of the rural population that lived in the remote regions, and set them apart as an elite. Although most townsmen had some Berber ancestry by the fourth century and although the most famous of their countrymen, Septimius Severus of Leptis Magna, reigned over the Roman empire from A.D. 193 to 211, the Romans only had a limited success in incorporating large numbers of Berbers into urban civilization. They succeeded most in those areas where Carthaginian and Numidian cities had previously flourished.

By organizing the imperial cult, Rome won the support of the urban aristocracy and, through their influence, a majority of the subject population. Every town elected delegates from among the upper class, who celebrated the cult at the provincial capital once a year. At that time every province chose a single priest from those delegates who, among other things, presented local grievances to the governor and could, if he had a complaint against this high official, carry his case directly to the emperor.

The closer a peasant lived to a municipal center, the more fully Roman magistrates protected his legal rights. In isolated regions the rural population was forced to submit to local lords, though at times, when their grievances went unanswered, sharecroppers would stage a strike by remaining at home and refusing to work. This put pressure on imperial or private landlords to come to terms, improve conditions, reduce the number of corvées, or lower taxes.

Rome preferred that taxes and rents be paid in kind, and collectors assembled revenues in warehouses throughout Barbary. After the African garrisons received their rations and collectors removed their share as salaries from these stores, the remaining stocks were dispatched to ports and transported to Rome. From 125 B.C. to the time of Julius Caesar, who died in 44 B.C., a sector of the population of Rome received a monthly allotment of five free bushels of wheat per man from the state. Shortly after 63 B.C. about 320,000 citizens were receiving a dole. In 46 B.C. Caesar reduced the number to 150,000, but in the time of Augustus (63 B.C.–A.D. 14) the number had risen to 200,000. In addition to distributing these handouts, the state sold cereals at reduced prices. At the beginning of the empire the Maghreb and Egypt each provided one third of Rome's wheat supplies while other provinces such as Sicily and Sardinia produced the rest. When Sicilian and Italian agricultural yields declined, Barbary's surplus provided enough grain to feed the entire city of Rome, including those receiving free food, for eight months out of a year; the Egyptians contributed enough to cover the remaining four months. After the foundation of Constantinople in A.D. 330 and the takeover of Egypt by eastern emperors, Rome depended on grain from the Maghreb alone.

When oil became scarce in Italy during the second century, the people of the Maghreb increased the acreage devoted to olive trees. Initially, Romans disliked the strong taste of African oil, but as production methods improved, both Romans and Egyptians imported large quantities for cooking, bathing, and fueling their lamps. Although the grain trade, mining, and marble quarrying had all been Roman state monopolies, commerce in oil remained in private hands. Not only did peasants in eastern Barbary become rich from their olive trees, but a large number of middlemen thrived as never before. In the second and third centuries these businessmen invested their wealth in numerous public monuments. By the second century a local ceramic industry had developed in the olive-producing areas so that Roman Africans, instead of importing luxury-quality pottery, as they formerly had done, were able not only to satisfy their own needs but to become exporters of pottery.

As the Romans developed techniques for growing olives in dry country, they extended cultivation into semiarid zones. They planted trees several feet apart, destroyed all weeds near them, kept the ground clean, and painstakingly worked the soil so that it would absorb all available moisture. (At the end of the nineteenth century the French in southern Tunisia, learning from the archeologists, applied these techniques with gratifying results to land that had reverted to scrub over the centuries following Roman occupation.) The Romans also employed engineering specialists called *aquilegi*, whose task was to seek out water sources. Hydraulic devices allowed them to take full advantage of rain and spring water, and to conserve water use. They erected dams, and dug wells and cisterns. Dikes diverted water to the plains, where canals and trenches carried it to

Septimus Severus, shown above with his family, was born near Leptis Magna. He rose by military coup to become Rome's emperor in A.D. 193. His successor, Caracalla, is seen beside the blurred image of his murdered brother. The portrait at left depicts a Romanized citizen of third-century A.D. Fayum.

fields, while aqueducts supplied the towns.

The Roman expansion of agriculture into southern zones far from the Barbary coast provoked serious clashes with the nomadic population of the Maghrebin steppe and desert. Their constant movement and pillaging brought them into contact with their neighbors to the north and south, and, like the strongest Berber kings before the Christian era, imperial Rome tried unsuccessfully to extend its domination over them.

By the first century A.D. the political situation between the Romans and the Maghrebin nomads had become critical. Forced into restricted areas, somewhat like reservations, they demanded more and better pasturage for their goats and sheep. Between A.D. 17 and 24 the southern part of North Africa from Roman Mauretania to Tripolitania rose up under the leadership of the Numidian Tacfarinas. His defeat signaled the temporary victory of the sedentary population over the nomads.

The Garamantes, too, caused Rome much trouble in the Fezzan. In addition to raiding "Ethiopians" in the south, they attacked coastal settlements along the Gulf of Sidra, aided Tacfarinas, and offered a haven to other fugitives. For these acts the Romans punished them several times. Short of permanently occupying the Fezzan, Roman governors stopped the Garamantes from further pillaging and, to en-

sure communications in the Sahara, formed a protectorate over them. Evidence of Roman presence on the Fezzan oases has been unearthed: traces of Roman-style irrigation and remains of Roman merchandise. Rome certainly received tusks from the Garamantes by way of the overland Saharan route to compensate for dwindling supplies of ivory in Barbary by the fourth century A.D. Toward the end of the first century a king of the Garamantes had led some Roman officers into a Sudanese region that he dominated. However, this and another expedition were exceptional.

The official limits of Roman occupation in the Maghreb stopped at the northern boundaries of the Sahara. In southern Numidia Romans hardly entered the desert areas, and in Mauretania they stayed away from it completely. From A.D. 24, and for more than two hundred years thereafter, Rome either settled colonies of veterans in the south and the far west or founded military posts on the edge of the desert to control the nomads. Their frontier defenses, or *limes*, which extended through Numidia from Tripolitania, consisted of ditches, walls, camps, forts, lookout towers, and road networks.

Beginning in the second century, Rome also imported as guards Syrian nomads with camels. Known for their speed and their ability to go without water for up to ten days, the *mehari*, or riding camel, made it possible to cover greater distances between wells than horses or oxen could, thereby adding to the mobility of the nomads. Besides rendering the chariot obsolete in the Sahara, these camels facilitated the disruptive raids of nomadic fugitives, whose migrations and conquests would continue into the Islamic period.

For a long time before the Roman conquest, ancestors of the Berbers living in the Libyan region of the Sahara had dominated the habitable oases. From the end of the second millennium B.C., if not earlier, they had attempted to settle in Egypt, but they never presented major threats to the inhabitants of the Nile Valley. In the Roman period, as the following passage from Strabo's *Geography* shows, Egypt lived in peace with its neighbors to the west and south.

> Now Aegypt was generally inclined to peace from the outset, because of the self-sufficiency of the country and the difficulty of invasion by outsiders, being protected on the north by a harborless coast and by the Aegyptian Sea, and on the east and west by the desert mountains of Libya and Arabia . . . and the remaining parts, those towards the south, are inhabited by the Troglodytes, Blemmyes, Nubae [Noba], and Megabari, those Aethiopians who live above Syene. These are nomads, and not numerous, or warlike either, though they were thought to be so by the ancients, because often, like brigands, they would attack defenseless persons. As for those Aethiopians who extend towards the south of Meroë, they are not numerous either, nor do they collect in one mass, inasmuch as they inhabit a long, narrow, and winding stretch of riverland . . . neither are they well equipped either for warfare or for any other kind of life. And now, too, the whole country is similarly disposed to peace.

Strabo, however, refers to incidents following Rome's conquest of Egypt in 30 B.C., when Kushites revolted and raided Syene (Aswan) in a series of attempts to seize lower Nubia. Rome retaliated and sacked Napata near the Fourth Cataract in 23 B.C., but moved no farther south. Instead, a garrison was stationed at Premnis (Qsar Ibrim). According to a papyrus dating from the second half of the first century A.D., Romans and "Ethiopians" clashed somewhere in the eastern desert, but no other sources recorded the specific incident. Was there a connection between this skirmish and the decision of the Roman emperor Nero to send the Praetorian Guard on a mission to Meroë about A.D. 61? Perhaps future archeological finds will provide an answer to this question.

In Hellenistic times, when the Ptolemies established the Nile Delta as the hub of an international commercial network, contacts between Egypt and Nubia had been the rule. The Egyptians received through Nubia gold, ivory, ebony, panther skins, incense, gums, slaves, and wild animals in exchange for manufactured goods, wine, corn, and olive oil.

Under Rome, commerce and travel between Egyptian rule and Meroë continued, but gradually slackened. The Meroites sent some ambassadors to the Romans, and occasional envoys probably returned these visits. Meroite pilgrims mixed with Romanized Egyptians at Philae, the site of the temple to Isis, and Egyptian artisans had a hand in temple building in the south. However, by the third century Meroitic rulers were no longer being buried with imported luxury goods, and pyramid construction had deteriorated—signs of the decline in Meroë's power.

At the end of that century, when Roman control over Egypt weakened, the Blemmyes, mounted on camels, began to infiltrate the Upper Nile Valley. Their raids forced Rome to evacuate Nubia in A.D. 289 and to relocate its southern border at the First Cataract. Seven years later Emperor Diocletian called in a people known as the Nobatae (perhaps the same people as the Noba mentioned by Strabo) to protect the southern frontier from further Blemmye incursions. Early in the fourth century Meroë collapsed as a result of conflicts with the Nobatae, and Axumite raids under King Ezana (about 320–360) would help to extinguish the dying kingdom. During his reign Axum converted to Christianity and established close links with the Alexandrine patriarchate and the Byzantine empire. Meanwhile, Axum also had indirect commercial ties with India and must have competed successfully with Meroë for control of the caravan routes to Central Africa.

Following the destruction of Meroë, Nubia experienced a period of political fragmentation. The former enemies, Blemmyes and Nobatae, united forces and toward A.D. 450 attacked the temple site of Philae. Rome, in turn, defeated them by 453, forcing them to give up Roman prisoners and pay an indemnity for the damage they committed. In return, the nomads were allowed to visit the Isis sanctuary and even carry her statue back periodically to Nubia. When these nomads broke the peace a few years later, another Roman expedition punished them, and Rome agreed to pay them a subsidy for a period of one hundred years to keep the peace.

The Roman territories in North Africa, excluding Egypt and Cyrenaica, covered only about 140,000 square miles during the period of its strength. This relatively small area,

The temple to Isis at Aswan, today submerged in the Nile, was a durable symbol of ancient Egyptian religion. Built to honor the wife of Osiris, it attracted not only Egyptians and Nubians but Roman schismatics who preferred her mysteries to their own militant state creed.

mainly the fertile, "useful" zone in the north, represented less than ten per cent of the present-day Maghreb, but it contained most of the Maghrebin population of approximately 6,500,000 people. The region was divided into four provinces during the high empire: Africa Proconsularis (Tunisia and coastal Tripolitania), Numidia (eastern Algeria), Mauretania Caesariensis (western Algeria), and Mauretania Tingitana (northern Morocco). But even this proved too large an area to control effectively. At the end of the third century Rome amputated about one third of its territory around Tripolitania and in the west, leaving intact a region relatively safe from the nomads. Rome also regrouped the provinces: it joined Egypt and Cyrenaica with other eastern holdings, and for administrative convenience, attached Mauretania Tingitana to Spain and divided the rest of the Maghreb into seven smaller provinces.

Numerous revolts in the far west taxed the Romans dur-

ing much of the third and fourth centuries, but the emperors never attempted to restrict the movement of nomads in and out of the Mauretanias. Most mountainous zones also escaped Roman control. By A.D. 253 mountaineers began raiding their lowland neighbors; they continued their attacks on and off until the end of the century. About A.D. 370 the Berber prince Firmus, based in the mountainous region of Kabylia, a perennial stronghold for dissidents, led a destructive revolt that spread through Numidia, and the Romans imported troops from Europe to crush the rebellion in 375. A revolt that lasted from 396 to 398, led by Firmus' brother Gildo, proved to be less serious and was easily put down. Both, however, represented Berber aspirations for autonomy and their desire for revenge against the rich masters. They had the sympathy of North Africa's growing Christian community, especially the Donatist heretics, who themselves led a revolt against official Christianity from their remote rural settlements in Numidia.

Before the end of the first century, Christianity had spread into Egypt, to the Greek-speaking educated urban population, who increasingly were moving toward a monotheistic belief. Important Church fathers, among them Clement and Origen, helped establish this initial Greek predominance, with Alexandria as the most significant theological center of the empire, vying with Rome for pre-eminence. When large numbers of Copts, as the indigenous Egyptians were known, converted in the last years of the third century, Church leaders produced a corpus of Coptic literature written in the Greek alphabet, helping to fuse Greek and Coptic elements of the population into a new unity. Hermits, who withdrew alone or in groups into the Egyptian desert, where the demons of temptation were believed to dwell, helped organize the first monasteries in Christendom. As monks, they spread the faith among most of the rural folk during the fourth century. Attempts were also made to convert the Nubians, but they had little effect before the sixth century, when new Nubian states arose.

Christianity took root in the Maghreb during the second century among slaves, Berber agricultural laborers, and lower-class urbanites. By the third and fourth centuries, when the faith had spread throughout the country, the Maghreb, with its many towns, contained six hundred bishops, more than Gaul and Egypt combined, and produced such great Church fathers as Tertullian, Cyprian, and Augustine. Christian missionaries attempted to convert the Jewish minority, some of whom dated back to the Phoenician settlement and others to the destruction of the Temple in Jerusalem in A.D. 70.

Starting in the third century, North Africa, from Egypt to Morocco, became the scene of furious religious controversies, denunciations, and persecutions, which led to the establishment of local or national Christian churches such as those at the Monophysites in the Nile Valley and of the Donatists and Arians in Barbary. Doctrinal and partisan issues confused the illiterate, who often blindly followed their bishops in or out of the orthodox Church.

The affinity for rebellion or rejection of submission and orthodoxy shielded the technologically weak, and therefore vulnerable, Berbers and other North African peoples from total assimilation and loss of identity despite centuries of alien rule. It eased North African integration into a wider ecumene, for by passing over the heretical road, segments of the population assimilated the basic ideas of their overlords without having to sacrifice their local heritages.

Donatism began as a simple heresy within a puritanical tradition; it emphasized martyrdom, unremitting faith, morality, and poverty. However, Donatism became the vehicle of a great social revolt of agricultural laborers whose situation had deteriorated by the fourth century. The Donatist heresy centered around the issue of whether or not members of the clergy who had yielded to Rome during its persecution of North African Christians should be restored to communion with the Church. Besides making Christianity palatable to the population of the central Maghreb, it acted as a convenient substitute for armed rebellion. It reached extremes by equating martyrdom with suicide and in allying itself with violent bands of migrant workers, the Circumcellions, who refused to be tied to the land. Until the Donatist sect was outlawed in A.D. 412, and even afterward, it won many adherents, especially in Numidia, and split the Church into an orthodox wing loyal to Rome and a puritanical African branch supported by many Berbers.

The Monophysite movement developed out of complicated theological disputes over the nature of God (whether he had one or two natures as the Father and the Son), with the Egyptians, led by the Alexandrine patriarchs, championing a strict unitary position. Until A.D. 451 the Alexandrines prevailed in Church councils, and their views were considered orthodox; but at the Council of Chalcedon the bishops, led by the Constantinople hierarchy, rejected the Monophysite creed and declared that Christ had two natures. Those who supported the council came to be known as Melchites, or royalist followers of Constantinople, whereas the others, the Monophysites, were branded as heretics.

The partisan roots of this controversy dated back to A.D. 381, when Constantinople was declared the second city in Christendom, thereby pre-empting Alexandria's position as a rival to Rome. Alexandrine leaders fought this decision and used the Monophysite doctrine as a vehicle to outmaneuver Constantinople and maintain their dominance in the Church. The issue became an Egyptian cause, and the doctrine served as an ideology of national unity. When the bishops of Alexandria lost their majority at the Council of Chalcedon, the Egyptians broke away from the Roman-Byzantine Church, though Egypt still remained part of the empire until 616, when the Persians conquered the country.

With the doctrinal split between the Orthodox and Coptic sects well defined, the two competed for converts in the region of the Upper Nile. By A.D. 540 there were three separate Nubian kingdoms: the northernmost, Nobatae, or Nobatia, between the First and Third Cataracts; Makuria, with its royal city at Dongola; and farther south, Alodia, with its capital at Soba. After A.D. 640 Nobatia and Makuria were united into a single kingdom, with its capital at Dongola, and Monophysite Christianity became the state religion. Sometime early in the seventh century Alodia also converted to the same sect. Greek became the liturgical language of all Nubia and was later supplemented by Coptic and Nubian, including Greek loan-words and written in the Greek alphabet.

After A.D. 410 the Maghreb was the only part of the western Mediterranean not seriously disrupted by Germanic hordes. The relative prosperity of Barbary, even though in decline, certainly must have attracted their attention. By this time the Roman army in Africa consisted mainly of Goth mercenaries who constantly fought desert marauders. In A.D. 429 cousins of the Goths, the Vandals, crossed over from Spain to North Africa in Roman ships, after their king Genseric received an invitation from Bonifacius, the Roman governor of Africa, to join his mercenary forces. Within the next ten years the Vandals, numbering some 80,000 and including 15,000 soldiers, had become ambitious in their own behalf and in A.D. 439 went on unopposed to conquer Carthage, nominally held by Rome.

All of Morocco and most of Algeria were untouched by the Vandal conquerors, who concentrated their rule on Tunisia and a small part of Algeria. Most of the Tunisian laborers who worked the large Roman domains stood by and watched one landlord replace another. The wealthy fled when they could to the Italian peninsula or Constantinople. Vandal governors won the support of non-Romanized pagan Berbers, and with their aid Genseric formed a powerful fleet, which he used for piracy.

The conquest allowed independent Berber mountain republics to develop, and mountaineers raided Numidia and Mauretania. These desert invasions further hastened the disintegration of urban life. The Vandals respected the Roman civilization that they found there and did not ruin the country through "vandalism"—a term first coined in eighteenth-century France. They returned most of it to nomads and mountaineers, who brought to a standstill the slow assimilation processes that had characterized Carthaginian and Roman rule for a millennium.

The Vandal army, weakened by constant struggles against marauding Berbers and, more significantly, against invading Tripolitanian nomads, crumbled when the Byzantines launched their seaborne invasion in A.D. 533. The eastern Roman army contained trained archers who had perfected their warlike skills in battles with the Persians. The Vandals, accustomed to fighting with swords and spears, were tech-

nologically overwhelmed. The conquerors shipped the majority of Vandal male captives to Constantinople, where they were integrated into the imperial army. A small number remained in Barbary as slaves or artisans, and Vandal women married Byzantine soldiers.

The Byzantines conquered Vandal territories with the aid of Berber chiefs, to whom they promised autonomy after victory. Instead, eastern administrators and lawyers attempted to re-establish Barbary as it was prior to the coming of the Vandals. Vandal proprietors were dislodged, and land was returned to descendants of former owners or turned over to the Church, the imperial Crown, or the conquering officers. The Byzantines also disestablished Arianism, the Christian heresy adopted by the Vandals. Because the eastern Romans did not fulfill their part of the bargain, they had to fight off continual revolts. Although the Garamantes converted to Christianity after signing a treaty of alliance with the Byzantines in A.D. 569, such alliances hardly sufficed to prevent nomads from raiding up to the walls of Carthage.

The Vandals had appointed new Arian bishops, who championed yet another heresy to weaken Christianity as a whole in Africa. People became confused even further when the Byzantines attempted to re-establish orthodoxy after ejecting the descendants of Genseric from Barbary and the Persians from Egypt in A.D. 626. In addition to the general corruption of the Eastern empire and Church, the newcomers persecuted Arians, Donatists, Monophysites, pagans, and Jews alike, and succeeded in alienating the population that they had hoped to win over. A general atmosphere of disillusionment prevailed. Social solidarity, already strained by late Roman and Vandal times, was taxed even further, and resistance to foreign conquest crumbled. The way was opened to a syncretic religion like Islam, which in one prodigious sweep would render doctrinal controversies meaningless.

The new followers of Islam, invading from the East, took Egypt and Cyrenaica from A.D. 641 to 642. Tripolitania fell in 643, setting the stage for the first raids to the west, which began in 647. Although the new invaders faced little opposition from the Byzantine army, their initial conquests proved superficial. The real battles of establishing political control over the North Africans and winning them over first to Islam and then to Arabic culture still lay ahead. They accomplished these tasks in the Maghreb over centuries filled with rebellion, mass migrations, new heresies, and much political bargaining, and only, finally, on terms acceptable to the North Africans.

Mythological figure; detail of a frieze
COLLECTION OF MR. AND MRS. JAN MITCHELL

THE COPTIC VISION

Egypt's Coptic art was born of the peasant. It was the plastic expression of a people's adherence to their own folk traditions in the face of major efforts by others to impose foreign—Greek, Roman, Byzantine—traditions upon the land. The art was modest, reflecting the fundamentalist creed that inspired it. Produced in monasteries far from such sophisticated urban centers as Alexandria, its practitioners had neither the means nor the instinct to produce monumentality, and the materials used were commonplace—limestone, wood, linen, wool—rather than the porphyry, granite, gold, and silks, with which others glorified their gods. The Coptic artists also maintained a distinct personality in the subject matter of their work, honoring a galaxy of local saints, many of them martyred by the Romans for their doctrinal intransigence.

Christ presenting a saint, possibly an abbot of the Apollo Monastery at El Bawiti, source of this sixth-century icon
LOUVRE

Above, an obscure personage, perhaps a military hero, being received into Heaven, in a bas-relief of the fourth to sixth centuries

Below, an architectural frieze, combining the cross with such pagan motifs as birds and grapevines, from a Christian site near Thebes

Above, the three Wise Men and the Virgin, as shown in a twelfth-century manuscript

Left, a rare example of Coptic scultpure-in-the-round, showing Hellenistic influences

BETWEEN SEA AND SAND

BERBER BELIEFS

North Africa has been host to numerous colonizers—including the Phoenicians, Romans, Vandals, Byzantines, and Arabs. Most have come and gone, but Barbary's indigenous Berber culture has persisted. Edward Westermarck, the author of the next two selections, is a noted expert on Morocco, where the greatest number of Berber-speaking people live today. The passages are from Ritual and Belief in Morocco *(1926).*

Owing to our very defective knowledge of the early Berbers it is to a large extent impossible to decide what elements in the demonology of Morocco are indigenous and what not, though a more minute comparison between Moorish and Eastern practices and beliefs than could be undertaken at present might throw some new light on the subject. The extreme prevalence of fowl sacrifices in the cult of *jnun* as well as of saints is a North African peculiarity. Al-Bakri speaks of a Berber tribe called Ursifan, who never went to war without previously sacrificing a black cow to the *semarih*, as they named their demons. The idea that butchers and slaughtering-places are haunted seems to have a Berber origin, to judge by the dread which the aborigines of Gran Canaria had of butchers and the present Tuareg have of slaughtering-places; but similar ideas may of course have prevailed among the Arab invaders. The occult "science" which enables the magician to call up *jinn* and make them do his bidding by invoking them by name and by writing down mysteriously arranged letters, figures, words, and numbers, is widespread in the East, but the Maghrebins are reputed the most learned

and skillful in it. . . . Both in Arabia and Egypt Maghrebins excell in the art of discovering hidden treasures, and Barbary sends there "whole troops of adventurers, who have no other means of living than the arts of magic." Thus the *jinn-cult* of the West has also influenced that of the East, and not only been influenced by it. Klunzinger observes in his book on Upper Egypt that the names of the *jinn* summoned "generally sound unlike Arabic, and may afford the philologist not uninteresting hints regarding the origin of this 'science'." In Morocco some names of *jnun* are expressly said to be Sudanese; and it is notable that the chief magicians, who practice their art by the instrumentality of the *jnun*, come from Sus, the southernmost part of Morocco, where the negro influence is considerable.

The *jinn* are usually invisible, but they are capable of assuming various shapes. They may appear in the shape of human beings, sometimes of the stature of men and sometimes of a size enormously gigantic. . . . In the *Arabian Nights* they are often represented as appearing, first of all, in a monstrous undefined shape, like an enormous pillar, and as only gradually assuming a human shape.

Even today some Berbers cling to their age-old superstitions. The omnipresent menace of the evil eye is a continual threat to a happy life.

Besides the *jnun* the evil eye is a very frequent cause of misfortune. It is said that "the evil eye owns two-thirds of the graveyards" . . . or that "one half of mankind dies from the evil eye" . . . or that

at any rate one-third of all living beings are killed by the same enemy. There is another saying, that "the evil eye empties the castles [or 'houses'] and fills the graves." . . . So firmly is the evil eye believed in, that if some accident happens at a wedding or any other feast where a person reputed to have an evil eye is present, it is attributed to him and he may have to pay damages; and if such a person looks at another's animal and it shortly afterwards dies, he is likewise held responsible for the loss. . . .

The belief in the evil eye is obviously rooted both in the expressiveness and the uncanniness of the look, which makes the eye appear on the one hand as an instrument of transmitting evil wishes, and on the other hand also as an original source of injurious energy emanating from it involuntarily. [Francis] Bacon said, "There seemeth to be acknowledged, in the act of envy, an ejaculation, or irradiation of the eye." In Morocco the danger is considered to be particularly great when the look is accompanied with speech. There is not only an evil eye, but an evil mouth; in many cases, as we shall see, magic influence is attributed to the spoken word. . . . The worst of all persons is he who has a black heart and a joking mouth. But jocular, allegorical, or laudatory speech, when combined with a look, is feared even though there is no feeling of ill-will or envy. As instances of this may be quoted the following stories, which I heard among the Jbala of Andjra.

A party of men were sitting together near a place where black lambs belonging to one of them were playing. A man of the party who had the evil eye said to the others, "Look at those ravens, how they have pounced upon corpses." This was said merely as a joke, without any evil intention. Nevertheless on the following night the lambs began to die, and after some time not one of them was left. Their owner, who also possessed the evil eye, decided to take revenge. One afternoon, when he saw the other man riding on a white mare, he said to the people, "Look, that funeral is coming alone and there is nobody with it." On the same night the mare got stomach-ache, and on the next day she was dead. The owner thought of accusing the man who had caused the death of his mare, but he refrained from doing so because, if he did, the other man might accuse him of killing his lambs.

A man had an enemy in his village, whom he tried to injure by his look, but without success. He then went to a neighboring village to fetch another man, who was known to have very dangerous eyes, so as to achieve his aim with his assistance. When they came near the enemy's village the other man said, "Now I am going to shut my eyes, tell me when we arrive at the house of your enemy." By closing his eyes he wanted

to give greater efficacy to his evil look, the first glance always being the most powerful. When they came to the house the man who had fetched him said jokingly, "Now set loose those greyhounds," meaning that he should open his eyes and cast an evil look upon the enemy, just as a greyhound is let loose on its prey. But as the man who uttered these words also possessed an evil eye, the result was that the eyes of the other one fell out. "You are worse than I am," the latter said; "you brought me here and caused my eyes to fall out." There was a man whose eyes were so terrible that he killed all his children by looking at them.

THE TONGUE

This delightful legend is typical of the morality tales cherished by the Berbers of Morocco.

One day, a man, at the hour of his death, sent for his son and said to him: "Go to the sacrificer and ask him to give you the best part of an animal he has sacrificed."

The son went immediately to a butcher, who gave him a tongue and he took it to his father and said to him "See, this is the best part." The father again said to him, "Go now and find for me the worst part."

And the son returned to the butcher. This time he gave him another tongue, which he took immediately to his father.

Then the father said to him: "It is for you to understand, before I die, that the tongue can be the best and it can be the worst. The reason for this, is because through it comes equally the good and the bad."

HANNIBAL'S OATH

Rome became increasingly jealous of Carthage's wealth, and conflict between the two powers led to the three Punic Wars (264–146 B.C.). One of the chief protagonists was the Carthaginian general Hannibal. Polybius, writing about the Punic Wars, said of this hero: "Of all that befell the Romans and Carthaginians, good or bad, the cause was one man and one mind—Hannibal." Polybius, who lived from about 202 to 120 B.C., was a diligent Greek scholar, whose work is accorded a high degree of credibility. In this excerpt from his Histories, *Hannibal addresses his ally, Antiochus* III, *king of Syria.*

When my father [Hamilcar Barca] was about to go on his Iberian expedition I was nine years old: and as he was offering the sacrifice to Zeus I stood near the altar. The sacrifice successfully performed, my father poured the libation and went through the usual ritual. He then bade all the other worshipers stand a little back, and calling me to him asked me affectionately whether I wished to go with him on his expedition. Upon my eagerly assenting, and begging with boyish enthusiasm to be allowed to go, he took me by the right hand and led me to the altar, and bade me lay my hand upon the victim and swear that I would never be friends with Rome. So long, then, Antiochus, as your policy is one of hostility to Rome, you may feel quite secure of having in me a most thoroughgoing supporter. But if ever you make terms or friendship with her, then you need not wait for any slander to make you distrust me and be on your guard against me; for there is nothing in my power that I would not do against her.

RULE IN CARTHAGE

By the end of the fifth century B.C. *the city-state of Carthage had become the dominant power in the western Mediterranean. It was the only non-Greek state whose constitution was admired by Greek political writers. However, the document itself is now lost. All that survives are scattered comments by classical authors, among them this analysis given in the fourth century* B.C. *in Aristotle's* Politics. *Aristotle's chief criticism of the Carthaginian political system was that it was oligarchical, by which he meant a government by a class whose qualification was wealth not virtue. Indeed, the Carthaginians' principal interest was commerce and trade.*

A group of young Berber goatherds

The Carthaginians are also considered to have an excellent form of government, which differs from that of any other state in several respects, though it is in some very like the Lacedaemonian. Indeed, all three states—the Lacedaemonian, the Cretan, and the Carthaginian—nearly resemble one another, and are very different from any others. Many of the Carthaginian institutions are excellent. The superiority of their constitution is proved by the fact that the common people remain loyal to the constitution; the Carthaginians have never had any rebellion worth speaking of, and have never been under the rule of a tyrant.

Among the points in which the Carthaginian constitution resembles the Lacedaemonian are the following:—The common tables of the clubs answer to the Spartan phiditia, and their magistracy of the 104 to the Ephors; but, whereas the Ephors are any chance persons, the magistrates of the Carthaginians are elected according to merit—this is an improvement. They have also their kings and their gerusia, or council of elders, who correspond to the kings and elders of Sparta. Their kings, unlike the Spartan, are not always of the same family, nor that an ordinary one, but if there is some distinguished family they are selected out of it and not appointed by seniority—this is far better. Such officers have great power, and therefore, if they are persons of little worth, do a great deal of harm, and they have already done harm at Lacedaemon.

Most of the defects or deviations from the perfect state, for which the Carthaginian constitution would be censured, apply equally to all the forms of government which we have mentioned. But of the deflections from aristocracy and constitutional government, some incline more to democracy and some to oligarchy. The kings and elders, if unanimous, may determine whether they will or will not bring a matter before the people, but when they are not unanimous, the people decide on such matters as well. And ·whatever the kings and elders bring before the people is not only heard but also determined by them, and any one who likes may oppose it; now this is not permitted in Sparta and Crete. That the magistracies of five who have under them many important matters should be co-opted, that they should choose the supreme council of 100, and should hold office longer than other magistrates (for they are virtually rulers both before and after they hold office)— these are oligarchical features; their being without salary and not elected by lot, and any similar points, such as the practice of having all suits tried by the magistrates, and not some by one class of judges or jurors and some by another, as at Lacedaemon, are characteristic of aristocracy. The Carthaginian constitution deviates from aristocracy and inclines to oligarchy, chiefly on a point where popular opinion is on their side. For men in general think that magistrates should be chosen not only for their merit, but for their wealth: a man, they say, who is poor cannot rule well—he has not the leisure. If, then, election of magistrates for their wealth be characteristic of oligarchy, and election for merit of aristocracy, there will be a third form under which the constitution of Carthage is comprehended; for the Carthaginians choose their magistrates, and particularly the highest of them—their kings and generals—with an eye both to merit and to wealth.

But we must acknowledge that, in thus deviating from aristocracy, the legislator has committed an error. Nothing is more absolutely necessary than to provide that the highest class, not only when in office, but when out of office, should have leisure and not disgrace themselves in any way; and to this his attention should be first directed. Even if you must have regard to wealth, in order to secure leisure, yet it is surely a bad thing that the greatest offices, such as those of kings and generals, should be bought. The law which allows this abuse makes wealth of more account than virtue, and the whole state becomes avaricious. For, whenever the chiefs of the state deem anything honorable, the other citizens are sure to follow their example; and, where virtue has not the first place, there aristocracy cannot be firmly established. Those who have been at the expense of purchasing their places will be in the habit of repaying themselves; and it is absurd to suppose that a poor and honest man will be wanting to make gains, and that a lower stamp of man who has incurred a great expense will not. Wherefore they should rule who are able to rule best. And even if the legislator does not care to protect the good from poverty, he should at any rate secure leisure for them when in office.

It would seem also to be a bad principle that the same person should hold many offices, which is a favorite practice among the Carthaginians, for one business is better done by one man. The legislator should see to this and should not appoint the same person to be a flute-player and a shoemaker. Hence, where the state is large, it is more in accordance both with constitutional and with democratic principles that the offices of state should be distributed among many persons. For, as I said, this arrangement is fairer to all, and any action familiarized by repetition is better and sooner performed. We have a proof in military and naval matters; the duties of command

A Punic coin honors the steadfast elephants that followed Hannibal to Italy in 218 B.C.

GEORGES VIOLLON

Numidian Berbers, influenced by the Romans, built this second-century B.C. *royal tomb.*

and of obedience in both these services extend to all.

The government of the Carthaginians is oligarchical, but they successfully escape the evils of oligarchy by enriching one portion of the people after another by sending them to their colonies. This is their panacea and the means by which they give stability to the state. Accident favors them, but the legislator should be able to provide against revolution without trusting to accidents. As things are, if any misfortune occurred, and the bulk of the subjects revolted, there would be no way of restoring peace by legal methods.

THE WEALTH OF CARTHAGE

One of Carthage's early accessions was the fertile Cape Bon peninsula, which lay east of the great city-state. It is described in the following selection by Diodorus Siculus, a first-century B.C. *Greek historian. His account presents a vivid picture of the region as it was around* 310 B.C., *some years before the Punic Wars, when Carthage was at its zenith.*

It was divided into market gardens and orchards of all sorts of fruit trees, with many streams of water flowing in channels irrigating every part. There were country houses everywhere, lavishly built and covered with stucco which testified to the wealth of their owners. The barns were filled with all that was needed to maintain a luxurious standard of living,

as the inhabitants had been able to store up an abundance of everything in a long period of peace. Part of the land was planted with vines, part with olives and other productive trees. Beyond these, cattle and sheep were pastured on the plains, and there were meadows filled with grazing horses. Such were the signs of prosperity of these regions where leading Carthaginians had their estates.

ARBITER OF DESTINY

Masinissa's "divine achievement" is set forth in the following excerpt from the Histories *of Polybius. This monarch became so powerful that the Romans determined to destroy Carthage rather than see him gain the prize.*

Masinissa, king of the Numidians in Africa, was the best man of all the kings of our time, and the most completely fortunate; for he reigned more than sixty years in the soundest health and to extreme old age,—for he was ninety when he died. He was, besides, the most powerful man physically of all his contemporaries; for instance, when it was necessary to stand, he would do so without moving a foot all day long; and again, when he had once sat down to business he remained there the whole day; nor did it distress him the least to remain in the saddle day and night continuously; and at ninety years old, at which age he died, he left a son only four years old, called Sthembanus, who was afterwards adopted by Micipses, and four sons besides. Owing, again, to the affection existing between these sons, he kept his whole life free from any treasonable plot and his kingdom unpolluted by any family tragedy. But his greatest and most divine achievement was this: Numidia had been before his time universally unproductive, and was looked upon as incapable of producing any cultivated fruits. He was the first and only man who showed that it could produce cultivated fruits just as well as any other country whatever. . . .

UNWELCOME MIRACLE

For many Berbers, the Roman conquest of North Africa signified the exchanging of one adversary for another. This Tunisian legend reflects the pride of the indigenous population.

When the Romans undertook the conquest of the country it was governed by a wise Berber monarch. But its armies could not resist the shock of the invaders and our monarch finally had to yield. However this ruler had a daughter who was said to be astonishingly beautiful. As soon as the Roman leader saw her he fell deeply in love and asked for her hand. The Berber princess who had a proud and noble soul refused to become the wife of the man who had enslaved her country. "Ask me for whatever you wish and I shall deposit it at your feet, but consent to share my life," said the Roman leader. And the princess replied, "Let the united waters of the Zaghouan and the Djouggar be brought to Carthage without touching the earth, and I shall then consent." She believed, poor child, that her consent would depend on an impossible condition. But for the Romans nothing was impossible and their leader ordered the construction of the most remarkable aqueduct anyone had ever seen.

One by one the arches, of which the ruins are still visible, rose towards the sky. At last the day came when, through the conduits they supported, flowed the waters of the Zaghouan and the Djouggar conjugated by the forces of men. The Roman leader then led the princess to this wonder of the world built for her. In order to admire fully the Roman masterpiece the princess asked if she could climb to the top of one of the arches. As soon as she reached that height she looked over the country of her birth, flung herself into space and was killed.

TACFARINAS' REVOLT

The nomadic peoples of the interior posed a continuous threat to the governance of Africa

Romana. Attempts by the emperors' armies to occupy the vast desert proved impossible, and periodic shows of force at oases settlements had only short-term effect. This excerpt, from the Annals of Tacitus, a first-century A.D. Roman historian, gives a partisan view of such an uprising. Led by Tacfarinas, these nomads harassed Roman legions for seven years before being defeated.

In this same year [A.D. 17] a war broke out in Africa, where the enemy was led by Tacfarinas. A Numidian by birth, he had served as an auxiliary in the Roman camp, then becoming a deserter, he at first gathered round him a roving band familiar with robbery, for plunder and for rapine. After a while, he marshaled them like regular soldiers, under standards and in troops, till at last he was regarded as the leader, not of an undisciplined rabble, but of the Musulamian people. This powerful tribe, bordering on the deserts of Africa, and even then with none of the civilization of cities, took up arms and drew their Moorish neighbors into the war. These too had a leader, Mazippa. The army was so divided that Tacfarinas kept the picked men who were armed in Roman fashion within a camp, and familiarized them with a commander's authority, while Mazippa, with light troops, spread around him fire, slaughter, and consternation. They had forced the Ciniphii, a far from contemptible tribe, into their cause, when Furius Camillus, proconsul of Africa, united in one force a legion and all the regularly enlisted allies, and, with an army insignificant indeed compared with the multitude of the Numidians and Moors, marched against the enemy. There was nothing however which he strove so much to avoid as their eluding an engagement out of fear. It was by the hope of victory that they were lured on only to be defeated. The legion was in the army's center; the light cohorts and two cavalry squadrons on its wings. Nor did Tacfarinas refuse battle. The Numidians were routed, and after a number of years the name of Furius won military renown.

A PATERNAL SCOLDING

The tribulations of a citizen of Roman Egypt are reflected in this lively letter. It was written from the Fayum during the first century A.D.

Hermocrates to his son Chaeras greetings. First of all I hope that you are well. [I have often begged you] to write about your health and your needs, and at other times I have written you about the property at Psya, but you never answered nor came. And now, if you do not come, I am likely to abandon the place. My partner did not give any help. The well was not even cleaned out. Besides the irrigation ditch was choked with sand, and the estate is unfit for cultivation. Not a single tenant wanted to take it. I am merely paying taxes without any return. There is hardly water enough for a single garden plot. So come without fail, for the trees are in danger of dying. Your sister sends greetings. Your mother is angry with you because you never answered her letters; besides she is bothered enough with the tax-collectors because you did not send them to yourself. So now send to her [the amount due on taxes?]. Farewell.

CARACALLA'S EDICT

This decree was issued by Emperor Caracalla in A.D. 215, a census year. However, it is less concerned with ascertaining the population of Alexandria than with forcing the peasants to return to the countryside, from where they had fled to avoid taxation.

All Egyptians who are in Alexandria, especially peasants, whoever have fled from elsewhere and can easily be found, must in every possible way be driven out, except, however, the traders in pigs, rivermen, and those who bring down reeds for heating the baths. Drive out the rest, whoever by mere numbers and for no good bring the city into an uproar. I learn that at the festival of Sarapis and on certain other feast days, or even on other days, the Egyptians are accustomed to bring down bulls or other beasts for sacrifice. In this matter they are not to be restrained. Those ought to be banned who have fled from their native place to avoid their farm duties, not however those who gather here to see the sights of the most glorious city of Alexandria or who come down for the sake of more urbane life or occasional business. After other matters: In regard to the linen-weavers, the real Egyptians may easily be recognized by their dialect or else their features and built reveal [them to be different] from others. Besides their way of living shows that the peasants are alien to city life.

UP FROM POVERTY

The following selection, a translation of an inscription found at the Roman colony of Mactaris in central Tunisia, recounts a rare instance of peasant success. It is written by a third-century Berber farmer who gained wealth and honor through hard labor.

I was born of poor parents, my father had neither an income nor his own house. From the day of my birth I always cultivated my field; neither my land nor I

Bust of a satyr found off the Tunisian coast
MAGNUM

ever had any rest. When the season of ripened harvests came I was the first to cut my thatch; and in the country when you would see the groups of harvesters who hire themselves out around Cirta, the Numidian capital, or in the plain dominated by the mountain of Jupiter, I was first to harvest my field. Then I left my country and for twelve years I harvested for another under a fiery sun; for eleven years I was head of a harvesting team and mowed the wheat in the Numidian fields. Thanks to my labors and since I was content with little, I finally became owner of a house and land: today I live at ease. I have even obtained honor, I was named to sit in the senate of my city: the modest peasant became censor. I have seen my children and grandchildren grow up; my life had been occupied, peaceful, and honored by all.

SERMONS AT HIPPO REGIUS

Saint Augustine, one of the foremost theologians of all time, was born at Tagaste near Hippo Regius (modern Bone, Algeria) in A.D. *354 and was in all probability a Berber. He is ranked as one of the original Doctors of the Church—a title given since the Middle Ages to outstanding theologians of acknowledged saintliness. He became coadjutor bishop of Hippo in 395, and soon after, its sole bishop, a position he held until his death in August, 430, when the Vandals were besieging the town. During his episcopate Augustine was obliged to deal with the many schisms that were dividing the African Church. He was especially avid in combatting the Donatists and in eradicating the remnants of paganism, which still colored the thinking of most North African Christians. The following selection, comprised of excerpts from his sermons, provides a glimpse of the life of rich and poor on the eve of the Vandal conquest.*

Brethren, let us imagine some rich dwelling. What a magnificent display of wealth there is! What luxury! How many gold and silver vases there are! What a great number of slaves, of beasts of burden and other animals! Finally, what delight the house itself gives, with its paintings, its marble, its paneled ceilings, its pillars, its courts and chambers.

Can it be said that these things are good: gold, silver, a beautiful estate, marble walls, and gilded ceilings? God forbid. . . . For the starry skies are more pleasing to the poor man than gilded ceilings are to the rich. . . .

Just as the term *house* is used to signify the inhabitants of a house; so, in this sense, we say that a marble house is bad and a smoky house is good. You find a smoky house in which good people dwell, and you say: "This is a good house." You find a marble house with decorated ceilings, in which the wicked dwell, and you say: "This is a bad house,"—calling the occupants, not the walls and rooms, a house. . . .

When men engage in the most unjust lawsuits for the right of sunshine and light in their buildings so that the rays of the sun may penetrate more fully through their windows, they often strive to demolish the houses of others and, with the most implacable enmity, they attack those who with unquestionable right oppose them. If, for the sake of the enjoyment of sunlight, a powerful person unjustly and wickedly oppresses one who is weaker; if he robs him and forces him into exile, or even death; is this the crime of the sun?

You accuse the miser and he, in turn, accuses God because He made gold. "God should not have made gold," [he says]. It now remains that because you cannot restrain yourselves from evil deeds, you blame the good works of God. The Creator of the universe displeases you. Then He should not have made the sun, because many dispute with regard to the openings for light and they drag one another into court.

You love silver because it is better than iron and copper; you love gold more, because it is better than silver; you love precious stones more, because they surpass even gold in their value; finally, you love that light which everyone who fears death fears to lose; you love that light, I say, with that intense love of the blind man who, following Jesus, cried out: "Have pity on me, Son of David."

For you are not rich, and the angel poor, who has not [as you have] horses and traveling carriages and numerous slaves. . . .

"When shall I bless God?" Is it when he is kind to you? when worldly possessions abound? when there is a great abundance of grain, oil, wine, gold, silver, slaves, and cattle? . . .

Is it not happiness to possess robust sons, well-dressed daughters, well-filled store-houses, numerous cattle; to have no broken wall and not even a broken hedge; to have no tumult nor clamor in the streets, but peace, repose, and an abundance of wealth, in homes and in cities? . . .

And in order that you may know that not money but avarice is condemned in the rich, give attention to what I say. You see this rich man standing next to you: perchance, he has wealth without avarice, whereas you have avarice without wealth.

But perhaps you have been reduced to extreme poverty and indigence because you had some sort of an inheritance or other to support you, and some calumny on the part of a rival took it from you. I hear you groan; you accuse the times; and if you could, you would do that which you deplore. Do we not see it? Are there not many daily examples of this? Yesterday, he was murmuring because he lost his fortune; today, attaching himself to a more powerful man, he robs others.

What is this patrimony? Is it gold, or silver, or precious stones, or estates and beautiful farms?

He is rich either from his parents, or from gifts and inheritances. . . .

As we enter and leave the church, the poor accost us and beg that we exhort you, that they may receive something from you. They have asked us to speak to you, and when they see that they do not receive from you, they think that we are laboring among you in vain. They expect something from us also. We give as much as we have; we give as much as we can; nevertheless, are we not powerless to provide for all their needs? Since, therefore, we are incapable of providing for their needs, we are their ambassadors to you. You have understood; you have applauded. Thanks be to God! . . .

Avarice commands not only "set forth," but also, "cross the seas and seek unknown lands." You must transport your merchandise to India. You do not know the Indic language, but the language of avarice is everywhere understood. You land among a people of whom you have never heard; you give and receive things in exchange; you buy articles which you carry back with you. The dangers which attended you on your oversea voyage to India also attend your return, and you cry to God amidst the tempest which tosses your vessel: "O God deliver me!" But do you not hear Him answer, "Did I send you hither? It is Avarice who bade you acquire that which you did not possess; whereas I have commanded you to give, without any labor on your part, to the poor man at your door. Avarice sent you as far as India to bring back gold. I placed Christ at your door so that you might purchase from Him the kingdom of heaven. You do everything to serve Avarice and nothing to obey Me". . . .

What do not merchants endure to satisfy their avarice? They cross the seas, subject their bodies and souls to winds and storms, forsake their own country and seek unknown lands. . . . And what will be the result when you will have obeyed the orders of Avarice? Your house will overflow with gold and silver.

JUSTINIAN'S AFRICA

In A.D. 533 the Byzantine army, led by Belisarius, the greatest general of the age, wrested Barbary from the Vandals. One of Byzantium's most vivid historians was Procopius, who accompanied the general and wrote the supportive Histories *of his campaigns. By*

contrast, Procopius' vituperative Secret History, *or* Anecdota, *from which this excerpt is taken, was composed in 550 for posthumous publication. "What I shall write," declares Procopius in his introduction, "now follows a different plan, supplementing the previous formal chronicle with a disclosure of what really happened." This account of North Africa under Justinian is highly exaggerated; nevertheless, it gives an idea of the ruin, social upheaval, and general disillusionment that helped to set the stage for the spread of Islam in the seventh century.*

That Justinian was not a man, but a demon, as I have said, in human form, one might prove by considering the enormity of the evils he brought upon mankind. For in the monstrousness of his actions the power of a fiend is manifest. Certainly an accurate reckoning of all those whom he destroyed would be impossible, I think, for anyone but God to make. Sooner could one number, I fancy, the sands of the sea than the men this Emperor murdered. Examining the countries that he made desolate of inhabitants, I would say he slew a trillion people. For Libya [North Africa], vast as it is, he so devastated that you would have to go a long way to find a single man, and he would be remarkable. Yet eighty thousand Vandals capable of bearing arms had dwelt there, and as for their wives and children and servants, who could guess their number? Yet still more numerous than these were the Mauretanians, who with their wives and children were all exterminated. And again, many Roman soldiers and those who followed them to Constantinople, the earth now covers; so that if one should venture to say that five million men perished in Libya alone, he would not, I imagine, be telling the half of it.

The reason for this was that after the Vandals were defeated, Justinian planned, not how he might best strengthen his hold on the country, nor how by safeguarding the interests of those who were loyal to him he might have the goodwill of his subjects: but instead he foolishly recalled Belisarius at once, on

the charge that the latter intended to make himself King (an idea of which Belisarius was utterly incapable), and so that he might manage affairs there himself and be able to plunder the whole of Libya. Sending commissioners to value the province, he imposed grievous taxes where before there had been none. Whatever lands were most valuable, he seized, and prohibited the Arians from observing their religious ceremonies. Negligent toward sending necessary supplies to the soldiers, he was overstrict with them in other ways; wherefore mutinies arose resulting in the deaths of many. For he was never able to abide by established customs, but naturally threw everything into confusion and disturbance. . . .

So while he was Emperor, the whole earth ran red with . . . blood. . . .

THE FIRST HERMIT

Christian monasticism originated among the indigenous Coptic population of Upper Egypt. Acting independently, a number of Christians abandoned the world and sought refuge in the desert, where they lived solitary and ascetic lives. According to tradition, the first Christian hermit was Saint Paul of Thebes, whose life reputedly spanned some one hundred thirteen years of the third and fourth centuries A.D. His story is told by Saint Jerome in a biography, from which the excerpt below is taken. Saint Anthony, another famous anchorite, is discussed in the next selection.

During the reign of Decius [A.D. 249–251] and Valerian [A.D. 253–260], the persecutors, about the time when Cornelius at Rome, Cyprian at Carthage, spilt their glorious blood, a fierce tempest made havoc of many churches in Egypt and the Thebaid. It was the Christian's prayer in those days that he might, for Christ's sake, die by the sword. But their crafty enemy sought out torments wherein death came slowly: desiring rather to slaughter the soul than the body. And as Cyprian wrote, who was himself to suffer: *They long for death, and dying is denied them.* . . .

Now at this very time, while such deeds as these were being done, the death of both parents left Paul heir to great wealth in the Lower Thebaid: his sister was already married. He was then about fifteen years of age, excellently versed alike in Greek and Egyptian letters, of a gentle spirit, and a strong lover of God. When the storm of persecution began its thunder, he betook himself to a farm in the country, for the sake of its remoteness and secrecy. But

"What wilt thou not drive mortal hearts to do,

O thou dread thirst for gold?"

His sister's husband began to meditate the betrayal of the lad whom it was his duty to conceal. Neither the tears of his wife, nor the bond of blood, nor God looking down upon it all from on high, could call him back from the crime, spurred on by a cruelty that seemed to ape religion. The boy, far-sighted as he was, had the wit to discern it, and took flight to the mountains, there to wait while the persecution ran its course. What had been his necessity became his free choice. Little by little he made his way, sometimes turning back and again returning, till at length he came upon a rocky mountain, and at its foot, at no great distance, a huge cave, its mouth closed by a stone. There is a thirst in men to pry into the unknown: he moved the stone, and eagerly exploring came within on a spacious courtyard open to the sky, roofed by the wide-spreading branches of an ancient palm, and with a spring of clear shining water. . . .

So then, in this beloved habitation, offered to him as it were by God himself, he lived his life through in prayer and solitude: the palm-tree provided him with food and clothing. [This is] incredible to those who believe not that all things are possible to him that believeth.

Paul, aged one hundred thirteen years, received a visit from Saint Anthony of Egypt.

And as they talked they perceived that a crow had settled on a branch of the tree, and softly flying down, deposited a whole loaf before their wondering eyes. And when he had withdrawn, "Behold," said Paul, "God hath sent us our dinner, God the merciful, God the compassionate. It is now sixty years since I have had each day a half loaf of bread: but at thy coming, Christ hath doubled His soldiers' rations." And when they had given thanks to God, they sat down beside the margin of the crystal spring. . . . Then they drank a little water, holding their mouths to the spring: and offering to God the sacrifice of praise, they passed the night in vigil.

But as day returned to the earth, the Blessed Paul spoke to Antony. "From old time, my brother, I have known that thou wert a dweller in these parts: from old time God had promised that thou, my fellow-servant, wouldst come to me. But since the time has come for sleeping, and (for I have ever desired to be dissolved and to be with Christ) the race is run, there remaineth for me a crown of righteousness; thou hast been sent by God to shelter this poor body in the ground, returning earth to earth."

At this Antony, weeping and groaning, began pleading with him not to leave him but take him with him as a fellow-traveler on that journey. . . .

Paul, knowing that he was about to die, asked Anthony to fetch him a cloak in which he could be buried. Anthony complied, and traversed the desert to procure the garment. He then recrossed the dry terrain and returned to Paul, only to find him dead.

Entering the cave, he saw on its bent knees, the head erect and the hands stretched out to heaven, the lifeless body: yet first, thinking he yet lived, he knelt and prayed beside him. Yet no accustomed sigh of prayer came to him: he kissed him, weeping, and then knew that the dead body of the holy man still knelt and prayed to God, to whom all things live.

So then he wrapped the body round and carried it outside, chanting the hymns and psalms of Christian tradition. But sadness came on Antony, because he had no spade to dig the ground. His mind was shaken, turning this way and that. For if I should go back to the monastery, he said, it is a three days' journey: if I stay here, there is no more that I can do. Let me die, therefore, as is meet: and falling beside thy soldier, Christ, let me draw my last breath.

But even as he pondered, behold two lions came coursing, their manes flying, from the inner desert, and made towards him. At sight of them, he was at first in dread: then, turning his mind to God, he waited undismayed, as though he looked on doves. They came straight to the body of the holy dead, and halted by it wagging their tails, then couched themselves at his feet, roaring mightily; and Antony well knew they were lamenting him, as best they could. Then, going a little way off, they began to scratch up the ground with their paws, vying with one another in throwing up the sand, till they had dug a grave roomy enough for a man: and thereupon, as though to ask the reward of their work, they came up to Antony, with drooping ears and down-bent heads, licking his hands and his feet. He saw that they were begging for his blessing; and pouring out his soul in praise to Christ for that even the dumb beasts feel that there is God, "Lord," he said, "without whom no leaf lights from the tree, nor a single sparrow falls upon the ground, give unto these even as Thou knowest."

Then, motioning with his hand, he signed to them to depart. And when they had gone away, he bowed his aged shoulders under the weight of the holy body: and laying it in the grave, he gathered the earth above it, and made the wonted mound. Another day broke: and then, lest the pious heir should receive none of the goods of the intestate, he claimed for himself the tunic which the saint had woven out of palm-leaves as one weaves baskets. And so returning to the monastery, he told the whole story to his disciples in order as it befell: and on the solemn feasts of Easter and Pentecost, he wore the tunic of Paul.

A choir boy pauses before one of the ten monolithic churches built by Ethiopia's King Lalibela.

SAINT ANTHONY OF EGYPT

Saint Anthony, the most famous of the early hermits, was born around A.D. 251 at Koma in central Egypt. He came from a prosperous family. His biography, a small section of which follows, was written by a contemporary, Saint Athanasius, bishop of Alexandria. Anthony devoted himself to asceticism when he was about eighteen and later became a desert hermit. When he was middle aged he abandoned solitude and organized his disciples into a loosely knit community, whose members shared a minimal common life. This modification of the eremitical life would mark the first significant step toward the development of Christian monastic orders.

And again as . . . [Anthony] went into the church, hearing the Lord say in the Gospel, "be not anxious for the morrow," he could stay no longer, but went out and gave those things also to the poor. Having committed his sister to known and faithful virgins, and put her into a convent to be brought up, he henceforth devoted himself outside his house to discipline, taking heed to himself and training himself with patience. For there were not yet so many monasteries in Egypt, and no monk at all knew of the distant desert; but all who wished to give heed to themselves practiced the discipline in solitude near their own village. Now there was then in the next village an old man who had lived the life of a hermit from his youth up. Antony, after he had seen this man, imitated him in piety. And at first he began to abide in places outside the village; then if he heard of a good man anywhere, like the prudent bee, he went forth and sought him, nor turned back to his own place until he had seen him; and he returned, having got from the good man as it were supplies for his journey in the way of virtue. So dwelling there at first, he confirmed his purpose not to return to the abode of his fathers nor to the remembrance of his kinsfolk; but to keep all his desire and energy for perfecting his discipline. He worked, however, with his hands, having heard, "he who is idle let

him not eat," and part he spent on bread and part he gave to the needy. And he was constant in prayer, knowing that a man ought to pray in secret unceasingly. For he had given such heed to what was read that none of the things that were written fell from him to the ground, but he remembered all, and afterwards his memory served him for books.

GOD'S "SAUCY SERVANTS"

The first code of monastic behavior was drawn up by another venerable Copt, Saint Pachomius (c. A.D. 290–346). Born in Upper Egypt of heathen parents, he served in the imperial army before converting to Christianity. He then lived as a hermit until about A.D. 320, when he built a monastery north of Luxor, at Tabennisi. There the inmates enjoyed a common life under an abbot. The Rule of Pachomius, now lost, gradually spread all over Christendom. The following passage was written by Palladius (c. A.D. 365–425), the most illustrious historian of early monasticism. It purports to give an approximate idea of the abbot's original rules.

There is a place in the Thebaid called Tabenna, in which lived a certain monk Pachomius, one of those men who have attained the highest form of life, so that he was granted predictions of the future and angelic visions. He was a great lover of the poor, and had great love to men. When, therefore, he was sitting in a cave an angel of the Lord came in and appeared to him and said: Pachomius you have done well those things which pertain to your own affairs; therefore sit no

longer idle in this cave. Up, therefore, go forth and gather all the younger monks and dwell with them and give them laws according to the form which I give thee. And he gave him a brass tablet on which the following things were written:

1. Give to each to eat and drink according to his strength; and give labors according to the powers of those eating, and forbid neither fasting nor eating. Thus appoint difficult labors to the stronger and those who eat, but the lighter and easy tasks to those who discipline themselves more and are weaker.

2. Make separate cells in the same place; and let three remain in a cell. But let the food of all be prepared in one house.

3. They may not sleep lying down, but having made seats built inclining backward let them place their bedding on them and sleep seated.

4. But by night let them wear linen tunics, being girded about. Let each of them have a shaggy goatskin, made white. Without this let them neither eat nor sleep. When they go in unto the communion of the mysteries of Christ every Sabbath and Lord's Day, let them loose their girdles and put off the goatskin, and enter with only their cuculla. . . . But he made the cuculla for them without any fleece, as for boys; and he commanded to place upon them certain branding marks of a purple cross.

5. He commanded that there be twenty-four groups of the brethren, according to the number of the twenty-four letters. And he prescribed that to

each group should be given as a name a letter of the Greek alphabet, from Alpha and Beta, one after another, to Omega, in order that when the archimandrite [the superior general] asked for any one in so great a company, that one may be asked who is the second in each, how group Alpha is, or how the group Beta; again let him salute the group Rho; the name of the letters following its own proper sign. And upon the simpler and more guileless place the name Iota; and upon those who are more ill-tempered and less righteous the letter Xi. And thus in harmony with the principles and the life and manners of them arrange the names of the letters, only the spiritual understanding the meaning.

6. There was written on the tablet that if there come a stranger of another monastery, having a different form of life, he shall not eat nor drink with them, nor go in with them into the monastery, unless he shall be found in the way outside of the monastery.

7. But do not receive for three years into the contest of proficients him who has entered once for all to remain with them; but when he has performed the more difficult tasks, then let him after a period of three years enter the stadium.

8. When they eat let them veil their faces, that one brother may not see another brother eating. They are not to speak while they eat; nor outside of their dish or off the table shall they turn their eyes toward anything else.

9. And he made it a rule that during the whole day they should offer twelve prayers; and at the time of lighting the lamps, twelve; and in the course of the night, twelve; and at the ninth hour, three; but when it seemed good for the whole company to eat, he directed that each group should first sing a psalm at each prayer.

But when the great Pachomius replied to the angel that the prayers were few, the angel said to him: I have appointed these that the little ones may advance and fulfill the law and not be distressed; but the perfect do not need to have laws given to them. For being by themselves in their cells, they have dedicated their entire life to contemplation on God. But to these, as many as do not have an intelligent mind, I will give a law that as saucy servants out of fear for the Master they may fulfil the whole order of life and direct it properly. When the angel had given these directions and fulfilled his ministry he departed from the great Pachomius. There are monasteries observing this rule, composed of seven thousand men, but the first and great monastery, wherein the blessed Pachomius dwelt, and which gave birth to the other places of asceticism, has one thousand three hundred men.

THE DESERT FATHERS

The following selection is from the History of the Monks in Egypt, *originally written in Latin by Rufinus, the fourth-century presbyter of Aquileia in northern Italy. He visited Egypt about* A.D. 371, *where he observed both cenobitic and eremitical monasticism.*

In the country around about Arsinoë, we saw a certain Serapion, priest and father of many monasteries: under his care he had more than ten thousand monks, in many and diverse congregations, and all of them earned their bread by the work of their hands, and the great part of what they earned, especially at harvest time, they brought to this Father, for the use of the poor. For it was the custom not only among these, but almost all the Egyptian monks, to hire themselves out at harvest time as harvesters, and each one among them would earn eighty measures of corn, more or less, and offer the greater part of it to the poor, so that not only were the hungry folk of that countryside fed, but ships were sent to Alexandria, laden with corn, to be divided among such as were prisoners in gaols, or as were foreigners and in need. For there was not poverty enough in Egypt to consume the fruit of their compassion and their lavishness.

So we came to Nitria [now Wadi el-Natrun]; the place most famous among all the monasteries of Egypt, about thirty-seven miles distant from Alexandria, and named after the neighboring town in which nitre is collected, as though in the providence of God it was foreseen that in these parts the sins of men would be washed and utterly effaced, even as stains by nitre are cleansed. In this place there are about fifty (or not many less) habitations, set near together and under one father, in some of which many brethren live together, in some a few, in some a brother lives alone: but though they be divided in their dwelling, yet do they abide bound and inseparable in spirit and faith and loving-kindness. . . .

Beyond this [Mount Nitria] there is another place in the inner desert, about nine miles distant: and this place, by reason of the multitude of cells dispersed through the desert, they call Cellia, The Cells. To this place those who have had their first initiation and who desire to live a remoter life, stripped of all its trappings, withdraw themselves: for the desert is vast, and the cells are sundered from one another by so wide a space, that none is in sight of his neighbor, nor can any voice be heard.

One by one they abide in their cells, a mighty silence and a great quiet among them: only on the Saturday and the Sunday do they come together to church, and there they see each other face to face as folk restored in heaven. If by chance any one is missing in that gathering, straightway they understand that he has been detained by some unevenness of his body and they all go to visit him, not indeed all of them together but at different times, and each carrying with him whatever he may have by him at home that might seem grateful to the sick. But for no other cause dare any disturb the silence of his neighbor, unless perchance to strengthen by a good word, or as it might be to anoint with the comfort of counsel the athletes set for the struggle. Many of them go three and four miles to church, and the distance dividing one cell from another is no less great: but so great is the love that is in them and by so strong affection are they bound towards one another and towards all brethren that they be an example and a wonder to all. So that if any one by chance should desire to dwell with them, as soon as they perceive it, each man offers his own cell.

BYZANTINE INTRIGUE

The conversion of the peoples of Nubia to Christianity in the sixth century has been picturesquely told by a contemporary Syrian, John, bishop of Ephesus. At that time Nubia was divided into the three kingdoms of Nobatia, Makuria, and Alodia. The following selection is from the bishop's Ecclesiastical History, *which is probably fairly accurate. It describes the court intrigue between the Monophysite empress Theodora and her Melchite husband, Emperor Justinian, over sending a missionary to Nobatia in* A.D. 543.

Among the clergy in attendance upon pope Theodosius, was a presbyter named Julianus, an old man of great worth, who conceived an earnest spiritual desire to christianize the wandering people who dwell on the eastern borders of the Thebais beyond Egypt, and who are not only not subject to the authority of the Roman empire, but even receive a subsidy on condition that they do not enter nor pillage Egypt. The blessed Julianus, therefore, being full of anxiety for his people, went and spoke about them to the late queen Theodora, in the hope of awakening in her a similar desire for their conversion; and as the queen was fervent in zeal for God, she received the proposal with joy, and promised . . . . and anxiously desired to send the blessed Julian thither. But when the king [Justinian] heard that the person she intended to send was opposed to the council of Chalcedon [i.e., a Monophysite], he was not pleased, and determined to write to the bishops of his own [Melchite] side in the Thebais, with orders for them to proceed

thither and instruct them, and plant among them the name of the synod. And as he entered upon the matter with great zeal, he sent thither, without a moment's delay, ambassadors with gold and baptismal robes, and gifts of honor for the king of that people, and letters for the duke of the Thebais [the Byzantine governor of Upper Egypt], enjoining him to take every care of the embassy, and escort them to the territories of the Nobadae [Nobatia]. When, however, the queen learnt these things, she quickly, with much cunning, wrote letters to the duke of the Thebais, and sent a mandatory of her court to carry them to him; and which were as follows: "Inasmuch as both his majesty and myself have purposed to send an embassy to the people of the Nobadae, and I am now despatching a blessed man named Julian; and further my will is, that my ambassador should arrive at the aforesaid people before his majesty's; be warned, that if you permit his ambassador to arrive there before mine, and do not hinder him by various pretexts until mine shall have reached you, and have passed through your province, and arrived at his destination, your life shall answer for it; for I will immediately send and take off your head." Soon after the receipt of this letter the king's ambassador also came, and the duke said to him, "You must wait a little, while we look out and procure beasts of burden, and men who know the deserts; and then you will be able to proceed." And thus he delayed him until the arrival of the merciful queen's embassy, who found horses and guides in waiting, and the same day, without loss of time, under a show of doing it by violence, they laid hands upon them, and were the first to proceed. As for the duke, he made his excuses to the king's ambassador, saying, "Lo! when I had made my preparations, and was desirous of sending you onward, ambassadors from the queen arrived, and fell upon me with violence, and took away the beasts of burden I had got ready, and have passed onward. And I am too well acquainted with the fear in

which the queen is held, to venture to oppose them. But abide still with me, until I can make fresh preparations for you, and then you also shall go in peace." And when he heard these things, he rent his garments, and threatened him terribly, and reviled him; and after some time he also was able to proceed, and followed the other's track, without being aware of the fraud which had been practiced upon him.

The blessed Julian, meanwhile, and the ambassadors who accompanied him, had arrived at the confines of the Nobadae, whence they sent to the king and his princes, informing him of their coming: upon which an armed escort set out, who received them joyfully, and brought them into their land unto the king. And he too received them with pleasure, and her majesty's letter was presented, and read to him, and the purport of it explained. They accepted also the magnificent honors sent them, and the numerous baptismal robes, and every thing else richly provided for their use. And immediately with joy they yielded themselves up, and utterly abjured the error of their forefathers, and confessed the God of the Christians, saying, "that He is the one true God, and there is no other beside Him." . . . As for the blessed Julian, he remained with them for two years, though suffering greatly from the extreme heat. For he used to say that from nine o'clock until four in the afternoon he was obliged to take refuge in caverns, full of water, where he sat undressed and girt with a linen garment, such as the people of the country wear. And if he left the water his skin, he said, was blistered by the heat. Nevertheless, he endured it patiently, and taught them, and baptized both the king and his nobles, and much people also. He had with him also a bishop from the Thebais, an old man, named Theodore, and after giving them instruction and setting things in order, he delivered them over to his charge and himself departed, and arrived in safety at Constantinople, where he was most honorably received by the queen.

A Roman aqueduct casts its shadow on a road in Tunisia, once part of Africa Proconsularis.

THE
NORTHERN
RIM

THE INSIDERS

Since late paleolithic times North Africa and parts of the Sahara have been inhabited by peoples of different skin colors and physical types. The Greeks dubbed them "Libyans," a term derived from the Lebu nomads, a group native to what is now Libya; the Romans called them *barbari*, meaning "foreigners" and thus rude; and in time the name was corrupted to "Berber." Their place of origin and the manner by which they came to Barbary is one of the great mysteries of African history. Possibly they migrated from southwest Asia. Since ancient times the Berbers have called themselves *imazighen*, or "freemen," their distinguishing characteristic being a fierce love of individual and group liberty. They have always been the true overlords of Barbary's mountain regions, their "homeland," and of many Saharan oases, where they were forced to adapt to desert conditions. Wherever they settled, they combined farming and animal husbandry with extensive trading enterprises. None of North Africa's colonizers ever managed to subjugate them completely. With the coming of the Arabs after the seventh century, numerous Berbers migrated or were pushed into the central or southern Sahara and even into the Sudan. A small number in the remoter areas retained their Berber dialects, but eventually most became Arabized, adopting the language, customs, religion, and dress of the Muslim conquerors.

The once-verdant Sahara is now reduced to an arid waste, relieved only by scattered oases, such as the Algerian site below. Cave paintings of horse-drawn war chariots dating from the second millennium B.C., like the one from the Fezzan shown above, attest to trans-Saharan contacts in ancient times. Similar depictions are distributed across the desert along ancient trade routes. The Berber girls opposite clap to the rhythm of village musicians at a festival in the Atlas Mountains. The distinctively striped wool shawls they wear identify their clan affiliation.

THE OUTSIDERS

Throughout antiquity prospects of trade lured outsiders to the northern shores of Africa. The Phoenicians, who arrived about 1200 B.C., founded the maritime-based Punic empire, which dominated the coast for the next millennium. Next, the Latins transformed Barbary, "arid nurse of the lions," into the granary of Rome, supplying the empire's cities with abundant cereals. In addition, galleys returning to Ostia were laden with fruits, ivory, wine, olive oil, horses, and even wild beasts (an estimated 3,500 were killed for sport at one twenty-six-day celebration in the reign of Augustus). Then, in the seventh century A.D., after two centuries of persecution and corruption—first by the Vandals and then the Byzantines—Europe lost control of North Africa.

A broad-beamed Phoenician cargo ship, as shown in a tomb relief

Cyrenaic exports readied for shipping, from a vase painted about 568 B.C.

Recalling the glory of Africa Romana, this crumbling head of Jupiter now lies before a temple built to him at Dougga in Tunisia.

RAPHO-GUILLUMETTE—BRIAN BRAKE

A king of Ethiopia, head of Church and state, receives a ceremonial blessing from his bishop before Axum's Cathedral of St. Mary of Zion.

"ATHLETES OF GOD"

Aside from various pagan cults, Christianity is Africa's oldest living religion. It spread to Egypt and the Maghreb during the first and second centuries A.D., becoming the official religion of Axumite Ethiopia in the fourth century and reaching Nubia in the sixth. It was accompanied by bitter schisms. Hundreds of martyrs, or "athletes of god," as one theologian called them, died for their faith and inspired myriad conversions. Some Christians sought refuge in the Egyptian desert, where they founded prototypes of eremetical and monastic communities. Doctrinal disputes so weakened Maghrebin Christianity that it eventually lost its following to the militant new creed of Islam. However, the Arabs tolerated Egypt's Monophysite Coptic Church, which survives as a minority faith today. Nubia, having fallen to the Muslims in 1504, also adopted Monophysitism, as did Ethiopia. The Ethiopian Orthodox Church, a blend of Jewish, traditional animist, and Coptic elements, is a truly indigenous Christian institution in the heart of Africa.

The most ambitious of Ethiopia's architectural undertakings was the building in the 1200's of the rock-hewn
edifices at Lalibela. Some are dug inside caverns; others,
like that above, are carved into the sides of cliffs.
Still others are freestanding, cut from a single rock.

Reverence for the Egyptian goddess Isis and her son
Horus, shown at left in an Egyptian statuette of the
Ptolemaic period, was easily converted to veneration of
Mary and Jesus. The fourth-century fresco at far left
of the Madonna and Child adorns a Coptic monastery.

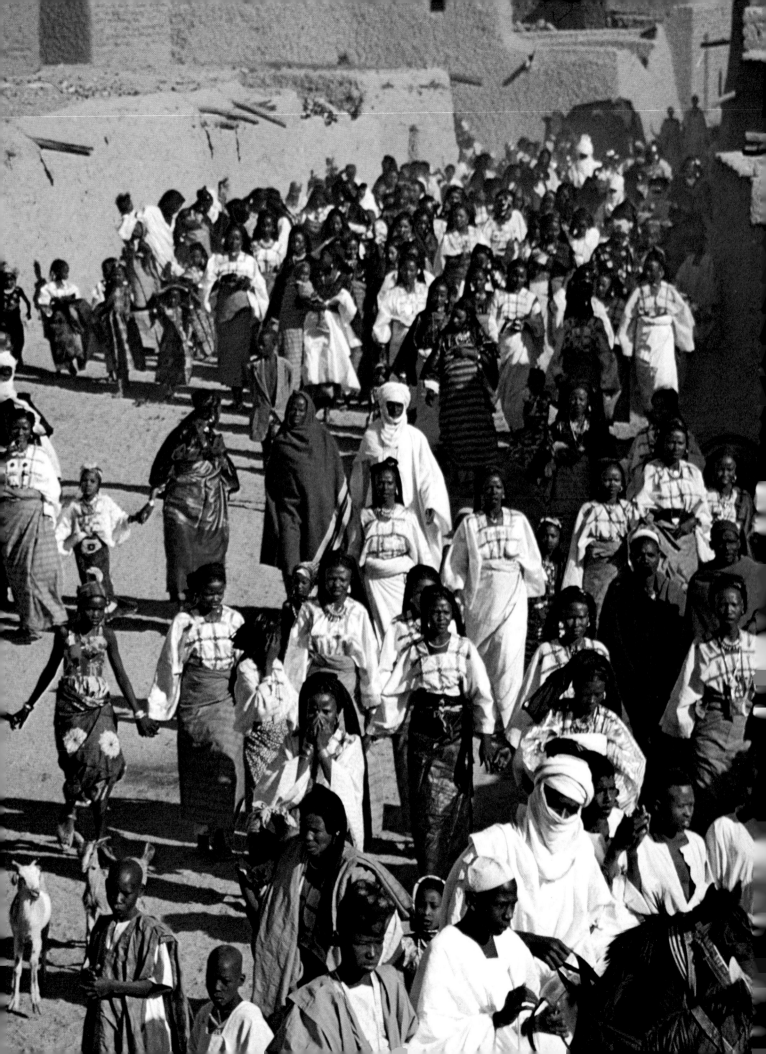

Chapter Four

THE SPREAD OF ISLAM

(c. A.D. 500-1500)

by

John Ralph Willis

THE MILLENNIUM BETWEEN A.D. 500 and 1500 witnessed significant changes in the historical evolution of Abyssinia (Ethiopia), Arabia, and the East African littoral. At the commencement of this epoch the Christian civilization of Axum was at its apogee. In the fourth century, somewhere between A.D. 320 and 350, Axumite warriors had successfully overthrown the power of Kush, invading its once-celebrated capital at Meroë. The final collapse of Meroë, which seems already to have been in decline, shifted the focal point of Nile Valley culture from ancient Kush to its successor states, the Christian kingdoms of Nubia. The prosperity of Axum derived from the strategic location of its chief port, Adulis, a favorite emporium for Greek ships frequenting the Red Sea routes and other vessels participating in the east-west trade between the Yemen and the Nile Valley.

With the rise of Islam and the development of Arab power, however, came the disruption of the lucrative Red Sea trade and the eclipse of Abyssinian influence in this region. Henceforth, until the appearance of the Portuguese toward the end of the millennium, Arab culture and influence became the dominating force in the trading communities that sprang up along the East African coast. The rise of Arab power brought forth a rapid and wide-ranging diffusion of Islam into significant portions of East Africa (including parts of Abyssinia itself), and as far as North and northwest Africa, where it took root among Berber and Sudanic peoples. The chapter begins with a discussion of relations between Abyssinia and Arabia at the dawn of the Islamic period. Later sections trace the development of Arab culture on the East African coast and in the region of northwest and West Africa, where Islam emerged the dominant religion.

The sixth century seems to mark the apogee of Abyssinian

[P]ious Muslims stream through Agadès in the Niger Republic during the fast month of Ramadan.

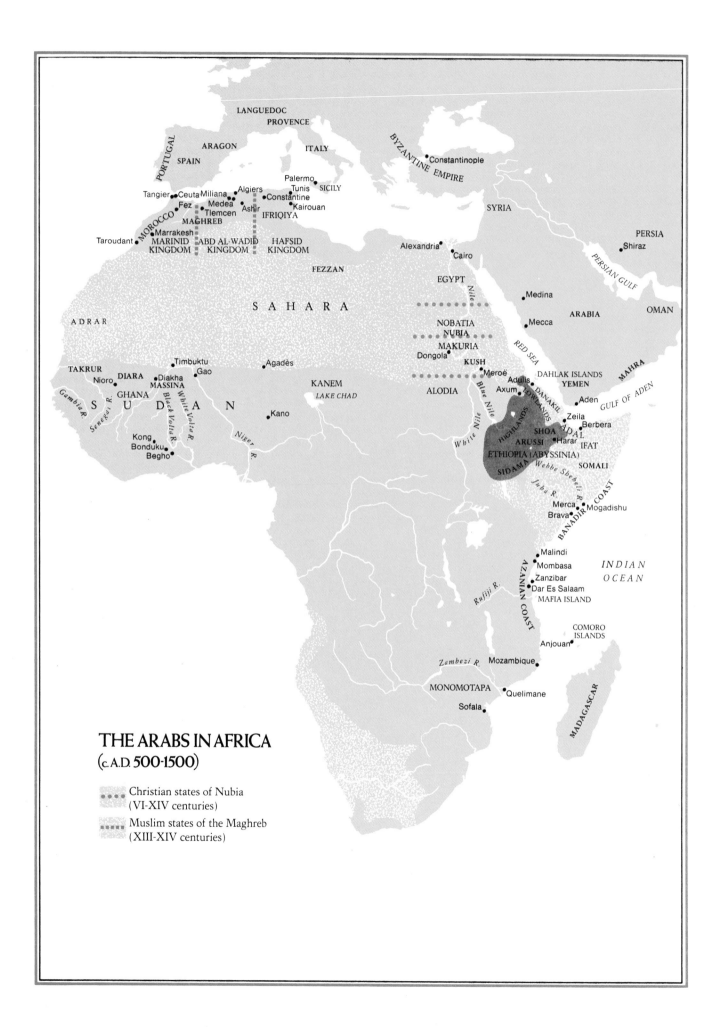

LANGUEDOC
PROVENCE

ARAGON
PORTUGAL
SPAIN
ITALY
Constantinople
BYZANTINE EMPIRE

Palermo
Tangier Ceuta Miliana Algiers Tunis SICILY
Fez Medea Constantine
Tlemcen Ashir Kairouan
MOROCCO MAGHREB
Marrakesh IFRIQIYA
Taroudant MARINID ABD AL-WADID HAFSID
KINGDOM KINGDOM KINGDOM

SYRIA

PERSIA
Shiraz

PERSIAN GULF

Alexandria
Cairo

FEZZAN

EGYPT
Medina
ARABIA
OMAN
Mecca

SAHARA

ADRAR

NOBATIA
NUBIA
MAKURIA
Dongola
KUSH
Meroë
RED SEA

MAHRA

TAKRUR
Timbuktu
Agadès
Nioro DIARA Gao
Diakha
GHANA MASSINA
KANEM
LAKE CHAD
SUDAN
ALODIA
Adulis DAHLAK ISLANDS
YEMEN
Axum DANAKIL
Aden GULF OF ADEN
Zeila
LOWLANDS Berbera
HIGHLANDS SHOA ADAL
ARUSSI Harar IFAT
ETHIOPIA (ABYSSINIA)
SIDAMA SOMALI

Gambia R.
Senegal R.
White Volta R.
Black Volta R.
Kong
Bonduku
Begho
Niger R.
Kano

White Nile
Blue Nile

Webbe Shebeli R.
Juba R.
Merca
Brava Mogadishu
BANADIR COAST

Malindi
Mombasa
INDIAN
OCEAN
Zanzibar
AZANIAN COAST
Dar Es Salaam
MAFIA ISLAND

Rufiji R.

COMORO
ISLANDS
Anjouan

Zambezi R. Mozambique

MADAGASCAR

MONOMOTAPA
Quelimane

Sofala

THE ARABS IN AFRICA
(c. A.D. 500-1500)

Christian states of Nubia
(VI-XIV centuries)

Muslim states of the Maghreb
(XIII-XIV centuries)

influence in the Red Sea region. In A.D. 531 the Abyssinians succeeded in establishing their authority in southern Arabia. Subsequently, however, Abyssinians who had ruled in south Arabia at the pleasure of the Christian Negus broke away from Abyssinian control and set up an independent regime in the Yemen. The leader of this new state was a Christian Abyssinian called Abraha, formerly the slave of a Byzantine merchant of Adulis. The creation of a government in south Arabia, which fell outside the sphere of Abyssinia, caused difficulties for the latter as well as Byzantium, which together were at that time attempting to counteract Persian influence in the Red Sea zone. It was also in A.D. 530–531 that Justinian entered into negotiations with the Abyssinians, proposing that they attempt to purchase silk from the Indians and resell it to the Romans, thus circumventing their common competitor, the Persians. This scheme proved untenable, however, because Persian merchants had succeeded in taking control of the key harbors frequented by Indian ships and, in addition, had occupied the adjoining areas. By purchasing the entire cargoes of these ships, the Persians were able to monopolize Indian trade in the Red Sea region.

Toward the end of the sixth century the Christian Yemenite leader Abraha is said to have launched an attack on Mecca, which was to result in the unification of the Arabs and the sealing off of their country against Abyssinian influence for all time. This was the beginning of the so-called War of the Elephant, romanticized in Arab history and mentioned in the following verses of the Holy Qur'an (Koran):

In the name of Allah, the
      Beneficent, the Merciful.
Hast thou not seen how thy
      Lord dealt with the pos-
      sessors of the elephant?
Did He not cause their war
      to end in confusion?
And send against them birds
      in flocks?
Casting at them decreed
      stones—
So he rendered them like
      straw eaten up?

Legend recalls that Abraha wished to undermine the attraction of the Kaaba, the ancient pagan shrine in Mecca to which pilgrims flocked from all over Arabia. According to Muslim tradition, Abraha set out to destroy the Kaaba, accompanied by a large number of troops and one (some sources say more than one) elephant. But upon entering the vicinity of the Meccan territory, the elephant is said to have kneeled down and refused to advance farther toward the city of Mecca, though when his head was turned in any other direction his movement went unrestricted. Flights of birds are said to have dropped stones upon the invading troops, as mentioned in the Qur'an, who all died. A rationalizing explanation of this phenomenon held that the invading troops were in actuality smitten with smallpox. Abraha himself, it is claimed, was afflicted with the loathsome disease and repatriated to the Yemen, where he soon died.

Some authorities contend, however, that the legendary story of Abraha the Christian Yemenite is in reality a conflation of two records of south Arabian attacks on Mecca: that by Abraha and a much earlier one led by the Axumite king Afilas, whom numismatic evidence places at about A.D. 300. It was during this period that the kingdom of Axum exercised a brief hegemony over south Arabia, and it is thought that a military enterprise farther north was not an impossibility. According to these authorities, the word "Afilas," the Abyssinian, and al-fil, the "elephant" in Arabic, became confused as the two legends merged into one. A modern interpretation hazards that if Abraha had actually undertaken such an expedition, a more likely explanation of his aims is that the rapprochement between Abraha and his former Abyssinian superiors against Persian intrusions allowed Abraha to adopt a more aggressive policy toward Persia. According to this interpretation, the expedition was the first move in a projected attack on Persian dominions. In Islamic history the main relevance of the episode of the "Elephant" was that tradition ascribes the birth of the Prophet Muhammad to this period, known historically as the Year of the Elephant (about A.D. 570).

In the Muslim view, the Islamic Dispensation constitutes the last in a series of Covenants between Allah and His people. Muslims readily recognize that other peoples, notably Jews and Christians, have entered into Covenants with the Almighty. Indeed, the Islamic revelations continue the Judaic and Christian traditions insofar as Islam accepts the authenticity of previous prophets and messengers through whom Allah communicated His Will. But the Qur'an is seen as the ultimate communication of the Divine Will, and Muhammad is looked upon as the final prophet of Allah. The followers of Muhammad are called Muslims because by embracing the message that Allah revealed to Muhammad, as contained in the Qur'an, they thereby "submit" themselves to the Divine Will. Hence the words "Islam" and "Muslim," derived from

As the Islamic legend of the "Year of the Elephant" indicates, the elephant is regarded by Muslims as a creature of remarkable wisdom and is treated with due respect. A versatile beast, it is able to exist in a variety of climates and consequently has played a major part in the local and trading economy of many African peoples. Unlike the Indian elephant, it is rarely domesticated; rather it is hunted with great ritual for its meat, ivory, bristle, and hide. Even the ear has its use—as the skin of royal drums. This miniature is from The Description of Animals, *an Arab bestiary done before* 1258.

the same root, both stress the necessity of "submission" to what Allah commanded Muhammad to "recite" (the meaning of "Qur'an") to his people.

It was the genius of Muhammad that over a remarkably short period he was able to transform the basis of Arab society —to mold out of the anonymity of collective life a place for the individual. The ties of Islam and the community of faith were to supersede the bonds of kinship. The inauguration of the Islamic Dispensation was to herald a new relationship between men. "The white man was not to be above the black nor the black above the yellow," said the tradition, "all men were to be equal before their Maker," and equal before the Law. Among believers, superiority was to be marked only by priority in the faith or by stricter observance of its precepts.

The Islamic religion came to be premised upon five pillars. Believers were required to accept the Muslim faith, professed in the words, "there is no Deity but Allah, and Muhammad is the Prophet of Allah." Belief in the "oneness" of Allah remains a fundamental tenet in Islam. Second, Muslims were required to pray at five prescribed times of the day. A third duty obliged all believers to give alms to the needy, and a collection was taken up for this purpose at certain times of the year. Muslims were further under obligation to endure a thirty-day fast, called Ramadan, during which they could neither eat nor drink between sunrise and sunset. A fifth duty prescribed that all Muslims undertake the pilgrimage to

Mecca and Medina, the cherished cities of Islam, at least once in their lifetime, provided they had the means.

When Muhammad died in A.D. 632, he bequeathed a legacy of unity within his religious community. Four successors, who continued his work but did not inherit his gift of prophecy, were elected by the community, though not without opposition. Muhammad had been accepted by his people both as prophet and political leader. The Meccan and Medinan peoples through their *shaykhs*, or leaders, entered into a compact with Muhammad and recognized his authority. It became the task of his successors to maintain those treaties, and often they found it necessary to resort to force in order to secure the unity for which he had strived. Efforts to subdue opposition to the new leaders of Islam generated a movement that reached beyond Arabia and culminated in the expansion of Islam in many lands. The ancient provinces of the Roman empire, including Egypt and Syria, as well as the once-powerful Persian dominions, all fell within the sphere of the rising Crescent.

But the expansion of Islam can be attributed to another factor. Islam spread from the Arabian Peninsula by virtue of the jihad Muhammad's followers declared upon his enemies. Despite its popular conception, the jihad, another fundamental duty in Islam, involves much more than "holy war" waged to expand Islamic frontiers or to defend the faith against foreign intrusion. For the believer, jihad is a form of effort—"a struggle in the path of Allah"—that can be undertaken by peaceful or military means. In short, the diffusion of Islam was viewed by Muslims as a serious effort to be undertaken for Allah's sake, as indeed the Crusades were launched by Christians "for the glory of God" and the protection of His Church.

If the Persian intrusion had served to disrupt the sea and trade routes in the Red Sea to the detriment of Abyssinian interests, the expansion of Islam, which soon enveloped the whole of Arabia, had an equally damaging effect of severing Abyssinia, at least temporarily, from its spiritual source, the patriarchate of Alexandria. This was indeed the beginning of many centuries of isolation for Abyssinia, whose peoples retired within their impregnable mountain fastnesses. Moreover, the penetration of Islam led to the Islamization of the Abyssinian lowlands, as Muslim powers were able to establish sovereignty over the African Red Sea littoral. As the pace of conversion accelerated in Abyssinia, Islam reached as far as eastern Shoa and the Sidama country.

For Abyssinia, the period from the tenth century to the twelfth was a time of great internal weakness, as well as one that witnessed the continued penetration of Islam over a wide area. Early in the tenth century a people called Falasha, Hamitic-speaking peoples who practiced the Jewish religion, were able to dislodge the "Solomonian" dynasty of Abyssinia (so called because of the attempts of Abyssinian rulers to link themselves genealogically with King Solomon of biblical times) and establish their own power. The result of this change of dynasty was that the preservers of "Solomonian" claims took refuge in Shoa to the south, and Axum (the ancient capital) ceased to be the political capital, though it remained the principal religious center and the place where subsequent kings of the "Solomonian" line were installed.

Muslim traders and men of religion were instrumental in the spread of Islam throughout parts of Abyssinia and the adjoining regions. Islam took root in the Dahlak archipelago, the Danakil and Somali coasts, among the Bedja (Beja) in the north, in the Ifat imamate of eastern Shoa, at Harar in the east, and near Lake Zway in the west. The religion also made converts of the Sidama peoples in the south, whose ruling classes, through trading relations, are said to have adopted the new persuasion.

Moreover, the slave trade proved a powerful stimulant to the Islamization of the coastal plains. This was because trading in slaves, largely controlled by Muslim merchants, brought about a link with the Arab world and resulted in the creation and sustenance of such Muslim-controlled centers as Zeila and Mogadishu, which became linked with the Danakil and Somali hinterlands. It is further believed that slave raiding greatly aided in the diffusion of Islam among pagan peoples of the East African coast, as conversion would have been an expedient means of avoiding the difficulties of a slave existence. Islamic law forbade the enslavement of free Muslims, but tolerated the continued enslavement of peoples who converted after their capture. Finally, it is known that the slave-raiding activity itself generated a process of state-building, which culminated in the establishment of Muslim power in Harar, Arussi, and the lake district in the southwest. Powerful slave merchants used their slaves as a source of influence and military power, and ultimately, as a basis for the establishment of independent states.

The beginnings of the Muslim state in eastern Shoa date most probably from the late ninth century A.D. In 1285, however, the Shoan imamate was overthrown and absorbed into that of Ifat, the predominant Muslim state of Abyssinia and the *foyer* of Muslim expansion throughout that region. From the fourteenth until the sixteenth century a war of attrition ensued between the highlands of Christian Abyssinia and the swiftly developing Muslim imamates or communities that became entrenched all along the eastern and southern fringes of the Abyssinian plateau. It was during this period that the walled city of Harar to the south of Zeila became a Muslim city-state and a powerful center of Islamic commerce and cultural propagation.

Shortly after the rise of Islam, Muslim Arabs and Persians created a series of coastal settlements in the region that came to be called Somalia. In these towns Arab and Persian merchants settled as local aristocracies, initiated a process of Islamization, and by intermarrying with local women formed a mixed Somali-Arab culture—the Somali counterpart to the more extensive Swahili society of the East African coast to the south. The Somali traditionally set much store on alleged descent from noble Arab lineages and, indeed, from the family of Muhammad himself. Such claims commemorate the prolonged period of contact between the Somali and the civilization of the Arabian coasts—a contact that has brought Islam and many other elements of Muslim-Arab culture to Somaliland. Such cultural borrowings betray themselves in the Somali language, which contains numerous Arabic loan-words, and again are manifest in the widespread use of Arabic as a second language. Conversely, however, the Somali language retains its unique character as a separate and vigorous tongue possessing an unusually rich oral literature. Poetry among the Somali is not merely the private medium of the author, but frequently the collective tongue of a clan or other group.

The two warriors at left, depicted somewhat fancifully by a nineteenth-century Italian, belonged to Ethiopia's ancient professional army. The empire regularly kept one of the largest forces on the continent; it was estimated by one observer to number more than 200,000 men. But Ethiopia's geographical location, which placed the militant faith of Christianity in uneasy proximity to that of Islam, and the constant challenge of the pastoral Galla peoples of the south, permitted few peaceful years.

FERRARIO, *Costume Antico e Moderno*, 1815

Typical of those centers of Arab influence in northern Somalia were the seaports of Zeila and Berbera. The walled city of Zeila, after the decline of Axum in the sixth century A.D., became the most important port for the coffee trade of the Abyssinian highlands; it was described by Ibn al-Wardi (about 1340) as the "emporium of the Habash," or Abyssinians. It emerged also as one of the largest ports for the slave trade with Arabia. In ancient times goat skins were the chief export that the Yemen market absorbed in great quantities during the course of a rapid development of the leather industry under Persian rule. In the fourteenth century Zeila was visited by the celebrated Arab traveler Ibn Battuta, who died in 1377. While conceding its importance as a commercial center, Ibn Battuta described the town as "vile and evil-smelling." The infamous stench of Zeila rose from the great quantity of fish that was brought there, as well as from the blood of camels customarily slain in the streets. In the fifteenth century Zeila was occupied by the Turks; but in 1516 they gave way to the Portuguese, who burned the town.

Berbera, southeast of Zeila and opposite Aden, was identified by the *Periplus*, Ptolemy, and Cosmas Indicopleustes as the Land of Frankincense—a designation more properly ascribed to the Arabian region of Mahra, the most productive source of aromatic plants. Situated in the state of Ifat, Berbera formed part of the Muslim province of Adal, whose amir, or commander, was apparently strong enough to rule Ifat in the fifteenth century. Founded in the ninth or tenth century, Adal frequently served as a refuge for Muslims farther to the south, who sought to flee Abyssinian jurisdiction. Its rulers belonged to the ruling house of Zeila, and the history of the two areas was often linked. Adal reached its zenith in the fourteenth century, but declined precipitously during the Muslim struggles to conquer Abyssinia in the sixteenth century.

In later times, when the Somali began to expand, their relationship with the Arab cities of the Banadir coast—Mogadishu, Merca, and Brava—developed from that of a trading partnership to one of political domination. The Arab cities of the Banadir were commercial towns largely dependent for their prosperity upon the trade between Abyssinia, Arabia, and the markets of the East.

The foundation of Mogadishu (Maqdishu) as an Arabian colony is ascribed to the tenth century A.D. Evidence from certain inscriptions points as well to a Persian settlement, which took place at about the same time. João de Barros, writing in the sixteenth century, noted that the first people to export gold from Sofala were the merchants of Mogadishu. By the end of the twelfth century, however, the gold trade had passed into the hands of Kilwa traders. The original commercial treaty was made between Mogadishu and Sofala, but later this most favored treatment was acquired by Kilwa, and with it the gold trade of Sofala. The merchants of this Indian Ocean entrepôt were constrained at times to band together against the Somali threat, which seemed to be constant, and against other invaders who came by sea. They organized themselves into a confederation of thirty-nine clans. One of these clans, the *Muqri*, acquired a religious supremacy over the others who agreed that the *qadi*, or jurisconsul, in religious matters should be appointed from within its ranks. In the sixteenth century Mogadishu declined in commercial prosperity due to continued Somali intrusions. Archeological remains uncovered at Mogadishu reveal it as larger than and culturally superior to Kilwa, though the latter was more important as a commercial center.

Brava (Barawa), directly south of Mogadishu, was known to the Arab geographer Yaqut al-Rumi, who died in A.D. 1229, as an amber-exporting area. Tradition holds that it was founded shortly after Mogadishu, and the commercial fate of the two cities was always closely linked. The Bantu language "Chimbelazi" survives in the town of Brava and is probably derived from the common speech of the coastal cities in Somalia.

In the earlier period of its history African traders frequented the coast with slaves and ivory, which were conveniently stored in centers near the mouth of a river or on some offshore island until they could be gathered by dhows, which came south before the beginning of the monsoon season. Gold and ivory were brought from the region of what is today Rhodesia and exchanged at Sofala for Indian beads. The trade route down to Sofala and by sea along the coast of Kilwa was of crucial importance to the economic prosperity of East Africa. Other commodities that drew merchants to the coast were leopard skins, palm oil, copper and iron, tortoise shells, rhinoceros horns, and the more prosaic hides. In addition to beads, foreign traders used spears, knives, axes, and porcelain as items of exchange.

By the tenth century a striking change in the commercial character of the coast had taken place. No longer were the participants traders from the Yemen, as the East African trade was now separated from that of the Aden Gulf coast. In place of the Yemenites we find merchants from the Persian Gulf and Oman. And by this period the trade had extended itself as far as the Comoro Islands, the lands of the Zambezi, and the great island of Madagascar. The trade in ivory was probably the most important at this period. According to al-Masudi, who died in A.D. 956, ivory was seldom employed for indigenous use owing to its value as an export item. Although the slave trade is not specifically mentioned by this author, it doubtless continued to be of considerable importance.

Kilwa served as an entrepôt for gold traded from Mutapa (Mwenemutapa or Monomotapa) through Sofala. Its domains are said to have included the settlements that developed along the coast as far as Kilwa Kivinje, and possibly to the Rufiji River, the island of Mafia, and in the south, to the region of Mozambique and Sofala. It was probably at its apogee in the twelfth and thirteenth centuries, but regained some distinction after the rebuilding of the Great Mosque, the finest surviving monument in East Africa. It struck a copper coinage of a single denomination from the commencement of the thirteenth century, but it is conjectured that this might have been more a matter of prestige than of commercial convenience.

Vasco da Gama, who visited Kilwa (Quiloa) on his second voyage, left a detailed description of the town and its inhabitants (about 1502). He described the city as large, and being of "good buildings of stone and mortar with terraces, and . . . much wood works. The city comes down to the shore, and is entirely surrounded by a wall and towers, within which there may be 12,000 inhabitants. The country all round is very luxuriant with many trees and gardens of all sorts of vegetables, citrons, lemons, and the best sweet oranges that were ever seen, sugarcanes, figs, pomegranates, and a great abundance of flocks, especially sheep, which have fat in the tail, which is almost the size of the body, and very savory. The streets of the city are very narrow as the houses are very high, of three and four stories, and one can run along the tops of them upon the terraces, as the houses are very close together: and in the port there were many ships."

There is some evidence of an Umayyad-Abbasid tradition of architecture at Kilwa. According to the *Kitab al-Zanuj* (the Chronicle of the Zanj) and other late sources, all of which are difficult to assess as to their reliability, immigrants came to East Africa from Arab lands during the chronological period spanned by the Umayyad and Abbasid dynasties (A.D. 661-1258). One is tempted to associate this architectural tradition with these early immigrants, although there is an alternative hypothesis. The Kilwa Chronicle speaks of immigrants arriving from the Persian city of Shiraz and settling at Kilwa in about the tenth century A.D. Some authorities have suggested that these immigrants might have been responsible for the distinctly Umayyad-Abbasid type architecture at Kilwa. Recent archeological

In East Africa slavery remained legal until this century, as this early photo-
graph of a Dar es Salaam master and his obeisant servant records. Swahili
society recognized a hierarchy even within the slave class, based on length
of ancestral service, type of employment, reputation, and the owner's status.

findings in the region, however, point toward a much later
immigration of the Shiraz newcomers. These investigations
indicate that the Shiraz settlement took place some two
hundred years later than the date in the latter part of the
tenth century, which has hitherto been accepted. The arrival
of the Shirazi, as they are called, is related to the appearance of coins of Ali b. al-Hasan, who is identified with the
first ruler of the so-called Shirazi dynasty at Kilwa (about
A.D. 1200). From this change of dynasty is interpreted a
marked cultural break in the latter part of the thirteenth or
early fourteenth century. Subsequent to this event came a
fresh settlement of immigrants and the seizure of Sofala
and its gold trade. Finally, it is contended that the Shiraz
settlement consisted not of a migration of people from the
Persian Gulf directly to Kilwa and other places, as was formerly held, but rather a movement of settlers from the
Banadir coast.

The legendary Sofala, situated in the southern region of
Mozambique, was often called Sofala or Zanj or Golden
Sofala in order to differentiate it from another port by the
same name near Bombay in India. This medieval emporium was known to al-Masudi as a rich gold-producing

area possessing an agreeable climate and a fertile land. It
was also al-Masudi who pointed to Sofala as the place
wherein the Zanj built their capital—important evidence
that may lend support to the contention that the Bantu (if
we read "Bantu" for "Zanj") had already inhabited the
coast of Africa south of the equator by the tenth century.
(A full discussion of the Bantu migrations appears in
Chapter Seven.) The Bantu are known to have arrived
from the interior, and at their farthest northern extension,
they are said to have reached the Webbe Shebeli river,
which flows through Somalia, curving southward parallel
to Mogadishu and Brava.

Subsequently, however (probably about the eleventh
century), these Bantu speakers were driven south by the
Somali to the valley of the Juba River in southern Somaliland. Here they remained for another five hundred years.
The Bantu, however, cannot be considered a significant
factor in molding the culture of the East African coast during the period under discussion. Their impact was farther
south and in the interior, though they are known to have
forged important trading links with the Arab settlements
on the coast. Export to Kilwa from various Bantu-domi-

nated areas can be presumed for an earlier period, while more regular trade developed after the establishment of Sofala by the Arabs in the tenth century.

According to al-Idrisi, who died in A.D. 1166, Sofala was famous for its iron mines as well as its gold. Yaqut perpetuated Sofala's reputation as a land of gold; he mentions that commercial transactions were effected by means of "dumb barter" (that is, the participants made no actual contact with each other during the trade). During the time of the Arab geographer Ibn al-Wardi (about 1340), Sofala gained some distinction for its iron deposits. Iron from Sofala mines was considered purer and more malleable than that found in India. The Indians smelted the iron and made steel, from which tools and weapons with fine cutting edges were fashioned. De Barros spoke of a "tower" at Sofala over twelve stories high, as well as similar erections of stone, all of which the Zanj called *zimbabwe* (literally "stone house") in referring to the official residences of their leaders. Modern archeology has revealed the Zanj as a hunting and fishing people of the Bushman type—at least this designation would apply to those who inhabited the Azanian coast. The implements of these autochthonous inhabitants of the coast have been found in many places, and it is from their discovery that archeologists have been able to reconstruct something of their cultural characteristics.

In the sixteenth century the commerce of Sofala shifted to Quelimane in the region north of the Zambezi, and by the seventeenth century Sofala's exports were insignificant. When the Portuguese upset the balance of power and the pattern of trade in the Indian Ocean, Arab trading settlements such as Sofala were at their zenith. The results of the Portuguese intrusion were manifest in the interruption of the gold trade between the coast and India. The Portuguese sought to redirect this trade to their own advantage, and in the course of doing so, wrought much destruction upon the wealth of Arab trading cities, which had so long monopolized commercial transactions on the coast.

Islam and Arab civilization also took root in many parts of North and West Africa. In East Africa Islam failed to develop significantly in the hinterland, although Arabs were able to evolve a prosperous series of settlements along the coast. In contrast, Islam in North and West Africa was accepted by urban dwellers along the coast and in the interior, as well as by nomadic groups who inhabited the vast Saharan regions. The Islamization of North and West Africa, however, was a very long and uneven process. Although Islam made its first appearance in this area in the seventh century (as early as A.D. 639), the initial Arab venture was more a

reconnaissance mission than a settling migration. The first Arabs in North Africa came for the purpose of establishing a foothold. The military contingents used for this purpose were not extensive, and the soldiers were compelled to leave their families behind and bring only that which was necessary to accomplish a limited military objective. Hence it is highly unlikely that substantial conversions to Islam could have taken place much before the beginning of the eighth century on the coast and the tenth century in the interior. The diffusion of Islam before the eighth century would have taken a veritable army of specialized religious teachers to preach Islamic doctrines appropriately. Moreover, these teachers would have had to speak Berber, the language of the dominant group on the coast, and further, would have had to establish the necessary rapport among the people conducive to the spread of a new religion.

In North Africa as in East Africa, Muslim proselytizers achieved the more rapid success along the coast. Urban centers were created or revived by the Arab occupiers, and because of a larger Arab presence, the Islam that developed in metropolitan areas came to differ quite markedly from that which took root in the hinterland. Qairawan (Kairouan), the first Muslim military outpost (established in what is today Tunisia) also became an important religious center, with an important mosque and several places of religious instruction. Other cities, however, were slow to develop, a factor that seriously restricted the intensity of Islamic diffusion. Indeed, until the creation of Fez (A.D. 808), one can hardly speak of cities in Morocco, except for Tangier and Ceuta, which were quite atypical. Between Tlemcen and Constantine was a barren area almost totally devoid of settlement. It would not be until the second half of the tenth century that such cities as Ashir, Medea, Miliana, and Algiers would make their appearance or reappearance. Only Ifriqiya (Tunis) could demonstrate a relatively substantial urban density.

Qairawan, the capital of Ifriqiya, was built by Uqba b. Nafi, the Arab commander who led the initial reconnaissance expedition to North Africa. The city was established in A.D. 670 as a base of operations, supply depot, and a means of keeping in awe the numerous Berber groups that inhabited adjacent areas. "I intend," the historian al-Nuwairi makes him say, "to build a town which can serve as a depot of arms [Qairawan] for Islam to the end of time." The site of the new town, two days' journey from the shore, had been chosen to put the Muslims beyond the danger of an attack from the Byzantines, who still held the towns on the coast. The earlier part of its existence, to the mid-eleventh century, is commonly held to have been one of great economic prosperity, especially remarkable for its agriculture. A political, economic, and cultural metropolis, Qairawan seems also to have been a major commercial and industrial center.

Until very recently it was thought that the prosperity of Qairawan declined sharply as a result of the eleventh-century invasion of Ifriqiya by the nomadic Hilali Arabs. Unlike the first Arab intrusion in this region, described above as a reconnaissance mission, the Hilalian invasion was a veritable settling migration involving nomadic Arabs as well as their women and children. It differed further from the initial mission in that the Hilalians settled in the interior among the Berber peoples, who carried on a similar nomadic existence. The Hilalian appearance in this region was likened to a swarm of locusts swooping down upon the unattended agricultural plains of Ifriqiya and wreaking havoc and destruction in its wake. The Hilalians are further made responsible for a cessation of gold trade from the Sudanic lands of the deep interior to Qairawan on the coast.

Such traditional interpretations, which make the Hilalians the cause of Ifriqiya's woes, have fallen into disfavor. Recent research reasons that the effect of the Hilalis was perhaps more to precipitate a development already well advanced, to wit, the gradual weening away of Qairawan's satellite regions from the metropole. A final and crucial distinction that must be made between the initial reconnaissance mission and the Hilalian settling migration is that the latter was of great quantitative significance. Although figures advanced to reckon Hilalis in the millions are doubtlessly a gross exaggeration, one may conservatively hazard that their numbers must have been in the thousands, whereas the initial wave of the Arab quest numbered no more than a few hundred fighting men. In short, for the first time Arabs arrived in sufficient numbers to make a lasting impact on the culture and civilization of the North African hinterland and beyond.

In the thirteenth and fourteenth centuries Arab nomads arrived in the Maghreb in ever-increasing numbers, settling not so much along the coast, but rather in the interior, among Berber nomads. These series of nomadic Arab settlements culminated in the Arabization and Islamization of Berber peoples throughout the region. Arabic became a principal language among these people, and through its use they began to acquire the basic rudiments of Arab culture. At least initially, Islamic doctrine was poorly understood by those Berbers, as indeed it had been superficially held by their nomadic Arab counterparts. What is impor-

tant to remember, however, is that despite its unlearned character, rural Islam developed within a decidedly Muslim framework and attained a certain vigor that was to give rise to the two great Islamic revivalist movements of the period under discussion. The Almoravid and Almohad revolutions, as they were called, were generated from the rural hinterland by militant Berber groups seeking to diffuse Islam among unconverted pagan peoples. The Almoravid movement gained numerous adherents among the Sanhaja Berbers of the western Sahara. It began as a movement to implement stricter Islamic practices among various Berber groups that later formed the Sanhaja confederation. Its leader, Abd Allah b. Yasin, attempted to impose a rigid adherence to Islamic law upon those Berbers who were constrained to follow closely classical legal texts that interpreted Qur'anic dictates for the believers. The Almohad movement rose partly as a reaction to such rigidity, and its leader, Ibn Tumart, a Berber of the Masmuda clan, sought to allow a more direct access to Qur'anic teachings without total reliance upon classical Muslim exegetists. The Almoravid movement, begun in the middle of the eleventh century, was carried to Morocco, as far as Algiers, and then to Spain, where the ideology of the Muslim West and a part of Christian Europe merged in a new synthesis. Similarly, however, the Almohad efforts at Muslim revival were not restricted to the Maghreb, as the followers of the Ibn Tumart's teachings subjected much of Spain after A.D. 1145.

In the thirteenth century, after its temporary unification under the Almohads, the Maghreb was divided into three independent states: the Marinid regime prevailing at Fez, the Abd al-Wadid state with its capital at Tilimsan (Tlemcen), and the Hafsid state of Ifriqiya. The last was to become the most formidable of these states, ultimately bringing the others under its control. Hafsid power spread as far as Morocco and Spain, which fell under a token submission. The Hafsids entered into treaties with Provence, Languedoc, and the Italian republics, and from 1239 onward relations with Sicily became more intimate. At about the same time bonds of friendship were forged between the Hafsids and Aragon, and Christian merchant communities (notably Spanish, Provençal, and Italian) settled in the ports of Ifriqiya, each with its own consul. Moreover, during this period many Spanish Muslims, craftsmen, and men of letters emigrated to Hafsid domains, and before long constituted a powerful Andalusian political force. Hafsid rulers continued relations with Christian nations, especially with the kingdom of Aragon, which came to the assistance of the Hafsids during several internal crises.

The Great Mosque at Kairouan, Tunisia, is judged by Muslims to be so sublime in conception that the city itself is ranked with Mecca, Medina, and Jerusalem as one of the four gates of Paradise. Work on the mosque was begun around A.D. 836; it stands on the site of one constructed by Uqba ibn Nafi, who founded Kairouan in A.D. 670 as a base of operation against the Berbers. Shown at left is one of the galleries.

Tunis under the Hafsids developed into a thriving commercial state. Many markets were established under the direction of merchants trading in cereals (during times of good harvest), dates, wax, olive oil, salted fish, fabrics, tapestries, coral, armaments, items of leather, and above all, wool. In exchange for these export commodities, the Hafsids imported cereals, wild fowl, items made from wood, armaments, jewels, ironmongery, cotton, silk, flax, hemp, and various metals, perfumes, medicinal plants, and spices.

It was during the period from the thirteenth to the sixteenth centuries that Islamic culture attained maturity in North Africa. By the middle of the thirteenth century the Hafsids had already adopted the madrasa, a kind of religious boarding school, as a center of learning. The institution of the madrasa in Islam grew out of the older form of education associated with the mosque, which was at once a place of worship and religious study. In Muslim education students were encouraged to commit the Qur'an to memory and to master the corpus of Hadith, consisting of all the actions and sayings of Muhammad, which formed the basis of proper conduct for the believer. Within one hundred and fifty years, some ten major madrasas were founded, one of the more famous being al-Zaytuna, which is still extant in Tunis. From the beginning the madrasa was a state institution, enjoying the patronage of the sovereign. One of its functions was to defend Islamic orthodoxy against heretical doctrines, though it emerged also as a principal center for the exposition of legal texts.

Sufism, or Islamic mysticism, developed rapidly in the Maghreb from the thirteenth century onward. Originally, it was the expression of the devotional feeling of the townsmen—grinding a channel of its own that burst the bonds of orthodox discipline and found a new freedom in the ranges of mysticism. As early as the eleventh century Sufism enlisted in its service a large proportion of the vital spiritual energies of the Muslim community and created within Islam a fount of self-renewal, which maintained its spiritual vigor throughout the later period of political and economic decay.

The movement in its early stages was personal and individual, but late in the eleventh century it became organized, and confronted the opposition of the official Islamic clerisy and sometimes the leading political figures of the state. Simultaneously, however, the movement swelled beyond the ranks of the faithful and appealed to the popular imagination, supplying a spiritual satisfaction and vitality that militated against the rigidity of the law and its teachings—in short, it emphasized the inwardly felt spiritual needs of the believer, whereas the law, made somewhat sterile by the strict interpretations that prevailed, stressed the external or formal requirements of Islam. The earliest religious confraternity to rise from North African soil was the Shadhiliyya, based on the teachings of Nur al-Din al-Shadhili (1196-1258). Tunis provided a rich recruiting ground for the new order, but al-Shadhili later encountered hostility from political authorities and was forced to flee to Alexandria, where he was instantly successful in his teaching.

In the Maghreb, Islam had been, down to the end of the fourteenth century, a religion of towns and cities. Late in this century and early in the following this situation radically changed. Islam became primarily a rural phenomenon. The *zawiya*, the Sufi religious center, replaced the mosque and the madrasa as the chief center of learning, and the Sufis displaced the traditional clerisy as guardians and expounders of the faith.

The Islamization of the Sanhaja Berbers, which culminated in the Almoravid movement, meant the ultimate defeat and displacement of the Sarakholle (a Mande-speaking group also known as the Soninke) living in the Adrar in the early part of the ninth century. According to tradition, the desert (before the outbreak of the Almoravid movement) was inhabited by black peoples who led a sedentary existence. It was at the end of the eighth century that the Lamtuna, part of the large Sanhaja confederation, adopted the militant creed of the Almoravids, which espoused a purified version of Islam—to be spread by force if necessary. The result of their efforts was the partial Islamization of the Sarakholle, some of whom went on to take their place among the most avid agents of Islamic diffusion. Sarakholle proselytizing activity took place in Diara (a region of Nioro in the Sahel) and in some of their colonies in Massina (in Mali), notably Dia (Diakha). The cultivation of Islam by the Sarakholle also occurred in Galam (near Bakel in Senegal) and in Takrur (Futa Toro, Senegal) —an area which itself became synonymous in the eyes of Arab geographers and historians with West African Islam. Countless Takruris (or Sudanis, to cite another common term) made pilgrimage to the Muslim holy cities of Mecca and Medina.

Similarly, the Mande-Diula traders (who, according to their traditions, also emanated from Massina and merged

RAPHO-GUILLUMETTE—MARC AND EVELYNE BERNHEIM

with the Sarakholle of Dia) were greatly responsible for the diffusion of Islam around the Niger Bend as far as the limits of the dense forest region at Begho on the Black Volta. It was at this time, near the end of the fourteenth century and the beginning of the fifteenth, that the Muslim cities of Bonduku and Kong in present-day Ivory Coast were founded.

What was the impact of Islam on the western Sudan at this early date? Islam has been made responsible for far more than its implantation in this region would seem to warrant. Many authors have held that Islamic conversion brought with it a "higher culture" and the development of a unique trading system that arose along the trans-Saharan caravan trails. Such vigorous assertions must be regarded with considerable caution. The role of Islam in the development of the so-called Sudanese empires is still a subject of heated debate. (See also Chapter Five.) There is good reason to believe that Islam acted more as a stimulant than a catalyst in the evolution of these states. It is undeniable that the early Sudanese states of Ghana, Mali, and Songhai had already achieved a high degree of development before the adoption of Islam by their ruling aristocracies. What seems also irrefutable, however, is that Islam fertilized anew

PHOTO RESEARCHERS

Out of Mauritania's inhospitable Adrar massif (opposite) came the Almoravid zealots, whose jihad was to carry them south of the Sahara and north to the Atlas range. The traders above ride toward one of the towns they took, the Berber oasis of Taroudant.

the more ancient culture of the Sudan and stimulated new growth and new forms of government and institutions. But what is often lost sight of is that the old institutions formed the basis of these developments; that they were rarely completely abolished or overthrown; and that when change did take place, it was more in the guise of syncretistic developments, which owed their origin to the old as well as the new.

There is little basis, for example, for crediting Islam with the creation of a commercial network in the western Sudan. When Muslim merchants first entered the Sudan, they encountered a well-arranged system of commerce established everywhere, and conducted along roads well suited to their purpose. This is not to deprive the Muslims of specific innovations that brought about change within the network— it is simply to emphasize that such creations took place within an ancient framework.

The implantation of Islam among the common people was slow to take effect. To understand the reasons for this slow, albeit steady, development, it is necessary to say something of the nature of African society. To early authorities such as Maurice Delafosse and Jules Brévié, Islam had appeared in Black Africa as a religion of travelers and Berber

nomads, whereas the indigenous population (largely composed of sedentary cultivators) remained animist or "naturalist." "Naturalism" was a direct outgrowth of the communal needs and temperament of animist hunters and cultivators, whereas Islam corresponded more closely to the requirements of wandering nomads. The Arab, observed Brévié, condemned to travel eternally in solitude at the head of his flock, would not take easily to a *religion du foyer* —a faith that would attach him to the tomb of his ancestors. The nomad's conception of the deity was one of a "unique, omnipresent God, in whom the believer is immersed at every hour, and in every place, who will not abandon the believer during the course of his errancy, who may be invoked at each hour of the five daily prayers without recourse to priests, nor need of temples, and whose eyes are forever watchful over him." Hence, when the nomad perished in the wilderness, his comrades commended his spirit to Allah and his body to the desert, and departed. The religious life of the "naturalist," however, was seen as a successive link in a sequence of transformations: the "naturalist" was not his own master, he was but an element of the clan. While living, he dwelled beside his ancestors (interred at his bedside) and communed with them constantly for his very sustenance. At death, he entered the familial burial ground, where he awaited the moment of incarnation. As a consequence, neither peasants who pained over the soil nor artisans wedded to ancient methods of exploiting iron—to whom the land was the source of all their requirements— could conceive of a religion in which the earth, the rain, the rivers, and the stones were not the focal point of veneration.

In contrast to this rural majority was a minority of individuals who did not live off the land, either because they had left tillage to inferiors or because they had taken to a commercial existence of an itinerant nature. These town dwellers had lost contact with the land, and they had gained in the interim an important intangible: leisure. And it was precisely this sector among the African populace that emerged the most susceptible to Islamic conversion. Islam seemed to satisfy their pietist sentiments derived from preoccupation with an agrarian cult; it responded to their philistine instincts to differentiate themselves from their rural counterparts; it flattered their urge to instruct themselves and to occupy their leisure with theological and canonical discussions, the reading of sacred texts and famous secular works. They were to constitute the Islamic elite in Black Africa, and there would fall to them the task of convincing their ethnic counterparts of the superiority of this new dispensation.

IN THE NAME OF ALLAH

Allah's messenger to the Prophet Muhammad

GOD'S MESSENGER

Muhammad, Islam's holy prophet, was born at Mecca in A.D. 570. The first biography of this inspired leader, whose new faith and teachings had a vital impact on Africa as well as on Arabia, was written by Ibn Ishaq, who died at Baghdad about A.D. 767. Although the original is lost, the story is preserved in a ninth-century version by Ibn Hisham. This excerpt, from the Life of Muhammad, *describes the beginning of Muhammad's mission—his call from Allah.*

When Muhammad the apostle of God reached the age of forty God sent him in compassion to mankind, "as an evangelist to all men." . . . God said to Muhammad, "When God made a covenant with the prophets [He said] this is the scripture and wisdom which I have given you, afterwards an apostle will come confirming what you know that you may believe in him and help him." . . .

'Abdu'l-Malik b. 'Ubaydullah b. Abu Sufyan b. al-'Ala' b. Jariya the Thaqafite who had a retentive memory related to me [the author, Ibn Ishaq] from a certain scholar that the apostle at the time when Allah willed to bestow His grace upon him and endow him with prophethood would go forth for his affair and journey far afield until he reached the glens of Mecca and the beds of its valleys where no house was in sight; and not a stone or tree that he passed by but would say, "Peace unto thee, O apostle of Allah." And the apostle would turn to his right and left and look behind him and he would see naught but trees and stones. Thus he stayed seeing and hearing so long as it pleased Allah that he should

stay. Then Gabriel came to him with the gift of God's grace whilst he was on Hira' [a hill outside Mecca] in the month of Ramadan. . . . The apostle would pray in seclusion on Hira' every year for a month to practice *tahannuth* as was the custom of Quraysh [Muhammad's tribe] in heathen days. *Tahannuth* is religious devotion. . . .

Wahb b. Kaisan told me that 'Ubayd said to him: Every year during that month the apostle would pray in seclusion and give food to the poor that came to him. And when he completed the month and returned from his seclusion, first of all before entering his house he would go to the Ka'ba [Kaaba shrine] and walk round it seven times or as often as it pleased God; then he would go back to his house until in the year when God sent him, in the month of Ramadan in which God willed concerning him what He willed of His grace, the apostle set forth to Hira' as was his wont, and his family with him. When it was the night on which God honored him with his mission and showed mercy on His servants thereby, Gabriel brought him the command of God. "He came to me," said the apostle of God, "while I was asleep, with a coverlet of brocade whereon was some writing, and said, 'Read!' I said, 'What shall I read?' He pressed me with it so tightly that I thought it was death; then he let me go and said, 'Read!' I said, 'What shall I read?' He pressed me with it again so that I thought it was death; then he let me go and said 'Read!' I said, 'What shall I read?' He pressed me with it the third time so that I thought it was death and said 'Read!' I said, 'What then shall I read?'—and this I said only

to deliver myself from him, lest he should do the same to me again. He said:

'Read in the name of thy Lord
who created,
Who created man of blood
coagulated.
Read! Thy Lord is the most
beneficent,
Who taught by the pen,
Taught that which they knew
not unto men.'

So I read it, and he departed from me. And I awoke from my sleep, and it was as though these words were written on my heart. . . .

"When I was midway on the mountain, I heard a voice from heaven saying, 'O Muhammad! thou art the apostle of God and I am Gabriel.' I raised my head towards heaven to see [who was speaking], and lo, Gabriel in the form of a man with feet astride the horizon, saying, 'O Muhammad! thou art the apostle of God and I am Gabriel.' I stood gazing at him, moving neither forward nor backward; then I began to turn my face away from him, but towards whatever region of the sky I looked, I saw him as before. And I continued standing there, neither advancing nor turning back, until Khadija [Muhammad's wife] sent her messengers in search of me and they gained the high ground above Mecca and returned to her while I was standing in the same place; then he parted from me and I from him, returning to my family. And I came to Khadija and sat by her thigh and drew close to her. She said, 'O Abu'l-Qasim, where hast thou been? By God, I sent my messengers in search of thee, and they reached the high ground above Mecca and returned. . . .'"

Isma'il b. Abu Hakin, a freedman of the family of al-Zubayr, told me on Khadija's authority that she said to the apostle of God, "O son of my uncle, are you able to tell me about your visitant, when he comes to you?" He replied that he could, and she asked him to tell her when he came. So when Gabriel came to him, as he was wont, the apostle said to Khadija, "This is Gabriel who has just come to me." "Get up, O son of my uncle," she said, "and sit by my left thigh." The apostle did so, and she said, "Can you see him?" "Yes," he said. She said, "Then turn round and sit on my right thigh." He did so, and she said, "Can you see him?" When he said that he could she asked him to move and sit in her lap. When he had done this she again asked if he could see him, and when he said yes, she disclosed her form and cast aside her veil while the apostle was sitting in her lap. Then she said, "Can you see him?" And he replied "No." She said "O son of my uncle, rejoice and be of good heart, by God he is an angel and not a satan."

THE FIRST MUEZZIN

This selection, also from the copy of Ibn Ishaq's Life, *describes the origin of the call to worship—the same one that still resounds throughout the Islamic world five times a day, at daybreak, noon, midafternoon, after sunset, and in the early evening. Bilal, a tall, gaunt Ethiopian who had been brought to Arabia as a slave, became the first muezzin, or caller to prayer. In a stentorian voice he summoned Medina's faithful from a rooftop.*

When the apostle was firmly settled in Medina and his brethren the emigrants were gathered to him and the affairs of the helpers were arranged Islam became firmly established. Prayer was instituted, the alms tax and fasting were prescribed, legal punishments fixed, the forbidden and the permitted prescribed, and Islam took up its abode with them. It was this clan of the helpers who "have taken up their abode [in the city of the prophet]

and in the faith." When the apostle first came, the people gathered to him for prayer at the appointed times without being summoned. At first the apostle thought of using a trumpet like that of the Jews who used it to summon to prayer. Afterwards he disliked the idea and ordered a clapper to be made, so it was duly fashioned to be beaten when the Muslims should pray.

Meanwhile [a disciple] heard a voice in a dream, and came to the apostle saying: "A phantom visited me in the night. There passed by me a man wearing two green garments carrying a clapper in his hand, and I asked him to sell it to me. When he asked me what I wanted it for I told him that it was to summon people to prayer, whereupon he offered to show me a better way: it was to say thrice 'Allah Akbar. I bear witness that there is no God but Allah I bear witness that Muhammad is the apostle of God. Come to prayer. Come to prayer. Come to divine service. Come to divine service. Allah Akbar. Allah Akbar. There is no God but Allah.'" When the apostle was told of this he said that it was a true vision if God so willed it, and that he should go with Bilal and communicate it to him so

that he might call to prayer thus, for he had a more penetrating voice. When Bilal acted as muezzin 'Umar heard him in his house and came to the apostle dragging his cloak on the ground and saying that he had seen precisely the same vision. The apostle said, "God be praised for that!"...

Bilal used to give the call ... at dawn every day. He used to come before daybreak and would sit on the housetop waiting for the dawn. When he saw it he would stretch his arms and say, "O God, I praise thee and ask thy help for Quraysh that they may accept thy religion." I never knew him to omit these words for a single night.

THE WORD OF GOD

To African Muslims, as to all true children of Islam, the Koran is literally the word of God, revealed to Muhammad at various intervals during his lifetime through the angel Gabriel. The text, as we now know it, was fairly well established early in the eighth century, a hundred years after the beginning of the Muslim era. The book is divided into one hundred fourteen suras, or chapters. Ex-

According to Muslim tradition, the decision to use a muezzin to summon worshipers to the mosque was made upon the instruction of the angel Gabriel. That interview is depicted in the sixteenth-century Turkish miniature at right. Belief that portraying Muhammad's face was a sacrilege led the artist to shroud the Prophet in a veil.

cept for the first one, quoted below, the suras are arranged roughly in order of length, beginning with the longest and ending with the shortest. The first sura is recited daily at each of the five fixed times of prayer and before the completion of all solemn contracts and transactions. "The Opening of the Scripture" or "The Essence of the Koran", as it has been variously named, serves the same ritual function as the Lord's Prayer. The following version was translated by Marmaduke Pickthall.

In the name of Allah, the Beneficent, the Merciful.

1. Praise be to Allah, Lord of the Worlds,
2. The Beneficent, the Merciful.
3. Owner of the Day of Judgment,
4. Thee [alone] we worship; Thee [alone] we ask for help.
5. Show us the straight path,
6. The path of those whom Thou hast favored;
7. Not [the path] of those who earn Thine anger nor of those who go astray.

THE FIRST REVELATION

Each sura takes its name from a striking word or phrase contained within it, and all but one begin with the invocation: "In the name of Allah, the Beneficent, the Merciful." Sura XCVI, which follows in a translation by Marmaduke Pickthall, is entitled "The Clot." According to tradition, it was the first revelation. The prophet is said to have heard it before he received the call. In some English translations the words "blood coagulated" are used in place of "clot."

In the name of Allah, the Beneficent, the Merciful.

1. Read: In the name of thy Lord who createth,
2. Createth man from a clot.
3. Read: And thy Lord is the Most Bounteous,
4. Who teacheth by the pen,
5. Teacheth man that which he knew not.
6. Nay, but verily man is rebellious
7. That he thinketh himself independent!

8. Lo! unto thy Lord is the return.
9. Hast thou seen him who dissuadeth
10. A slave when he prayeth?
11. Hast thou seen if he [relieth] on the guidance [of Allah]
12. Or enjoineth piety?
13. Hast thou seen if he denieth [Allah's guidance] and is froward?
14. Is he then unaware that Allah seeth?
15. Nay, but if he cease not. We will seize him by the forelock—
16. The lying, sinful forelock—
17. Then let him call upon his henchmen!
18. We will call the guards of hell.
19. Nay! Obey not thou him. But prostrate thyself, and draw near [unto Allah].

"THE CITY"

The most humane portions of the Koran concern the treatment of slaves, orphans, and strangers. Manumission of slaves is deemed extremely pleasing to Allah and worthy expiation of many a sin. Sura XC, which follows, describes the two highways of life: the arduous path of virtue and the facile one of vice. Those who follow the path of charity and love will become "Companions of the Right Hand" and will attain salvation. "The City" is Mecca, Muhammad's birthplace.

In the name of Allah, the Beneficent, the Merciful.

1. Nay, I swear by this city—
2. And thou art an indweller of this city—
3. And the begetter and that which he begat,
4. We verily have created man in an atmosphere:
5. Thinketh he that none hath power over him?
6. And he saith: I have destroyed vast wealth:
7. Thinketh he that none beholdeth him?
8. Did We not assign unto him two eyes
9. And a tongue and two lips,
10. And guide him to the parting of the mountain ways?

11. But he hath not attempted the Ascent—
12. Ah, what will convey unto thee what the Ascent is!—
13. [It is] to free a slave,
14. And to feed in the day of hunger
15. An orphan near of kin,
16. Or some poor wretch in misery,
17. And to be of those who believe and exhort one another to perseverance and exhort one another to pity.
18. Their place will be on the right hand.
19. But those who disbelieve Our revelations, their place will be on the left hand.
20. Fire will be an awning over them.

ANTAR THE LION

The paragon of Arab chivalry is the warrior Antar, who was born in Arabia about the middle of the sixth century A.D. and who died around 615. His mother was a black Ethiopian slave; his father, a Bedouin chieftain. Antar's early youth was spent as a lowly camelkeeper. However, because of his great strength and leonine courage, he was soon promoted from his menial role to a fighting man. Eventually he won his freedom and became the leader of his tribe. His numerous exploits—both military and amorous—are the subject of one of the most popular anonymous works in Africa's Islamic literature, Sirat Antar, or The Romance of Antar, from which the subsequent selection is taken.

"What Arab art thou?" said he.

"My Lord," replied Antar, "I am of the tribe of the noble Abs."

"One of its warriors," demanded Monzar, "or one of its slaves?"

"Nobility, my lord," said Antar, "amongst liberal men, is the thrust of the spear, the blow of the sword, the patience beneath the battle dust. I am the physician of the tribe of Abs when they are in sickness, their protector in disgrace, the defender of their wives when they are in trouble, and their horseman when they are in glory, and their sword when they rush to arms."

Monzar was astonished at his fluency of speech, his magnanimity, and his in-

Transcribing the Koran was the supreme artistic challenge for a Muslim calligrapher. The page depicted is from an Andalusian copy executed in 1304 at a madrasa in Granada.

BIBLIOTHEQUE NATIONALE, SERVICE PHOTOGRAPHIQUE, MS. ARAB 385

trepidity, for he was then in the dishonorable state of a prisoner, and force had overpowered him. "What urged thee to this violence on my property," added Monzar, "and seizure of my camels?"

"My lord," said Antar, "the tyranny of my uncle obliged me to this act: for I was brought up with his daughter, and I had passed my life in her service. And when he saw me demand her in marriage, he asked of me as a marriage dower, a thousand Asafeer camels. I was ignorant, and knew nothing about them; so I consented to his demand, and set out in quest of them; I have outraged you, and am consequently reduced to this miserable state."

"Hast thou then," said Monzar, "with all this fortitude and eloquence, and propriety of manners, exposed thy life to the sea of death, and endangered thine existence for the sake of an Arab girl?"

"Yes, my lord," said Antar; "it is love that emboldens to encounter dangers and horrors; and no lover is excusable but he who tastes the bitterness of absence after the sweetness of enjoyment; and there is no peril to be apprehended, but from a look from beneath the corner of a veil; and what misfortune can drive man to his destruction, but a woman who is the root and branch of it!"

ANTAR THE POET

Antar was also a highly skilled poet, whose works combine an exaltation of war with sublime sentiments of love. One of his odes received the highest honor possible for a Muslim poet: it was chosen as one of the seven poems, known as the Mu Allakat, *that were written in gold and displayed in the Kaaba shrine at Mecca. His ode, from which the two following passages are excerpted, has moved generations of Arabs with its similes, stirring sensuality, and many dramatic battle scenes.*

Twas then her beauties first enslaved my
   heart—
Those glittering pearls and ruby lips,
   whose kiss
Was sweeter far than honey to the taste.
As when a merchant opes a precious box
Of perfume, such an odor from her
   breath
Came toward thee, harbinger of her
   approach;
Or like an untouched meadow, where the
   rain
Hath fallen freshly on the fragrant herbs
That carpet all its pure untrodden soil:
A meadow where the frequent rain-drops
   fall
Like coins of silver in the quiet pools,
And irrigate it with perpetual streams;
A meadow where the sportive insects
   hum
Like listless topers singing o'er their
   cups.

"As soon as I beheld the legions of our enemies advancing and animating one another to battle, I, too, rushed forward and acted without reproach.

"The troops called out, Antara! while javelins long as the cords of a well were forcibly thrust against the chest of my dark steed.

"I ceased not to charge the foe with the neck and breast of my horse until he was mantled in blood.

"My steed, bent aside with the strokes of the lances in his forehead, complained to me with gushing tears and tender sobbing.

"In the midst of the black dust the horses were impetuously rushing with disfiguring countenance every robust stallion and every strong-limbed mare.

"Then my soul was healed and all my anguish was dispersed by the cry of the warriors: 'Well done, charge again!'"

MUSLIM BATTLE CODE

Ibn Khaldun (1332–1406), the greatest historical philosopher of the Islamic world, was born in Tunis of a Spanish-Arab family. His Kitab al-Ibar, *or* Universal History, *deals with the Arabs, the Berbers, and the Muslim dynasties of North Africa. However, it is the* Muqaddimah, *meaning "introduction," that has won the author fame and the title "Father of Sociology." This exceptional work deals with the nature and principles of Islamic life and is the first interpretation of historical events to consider climate and geography as well as moral and spiritual forces. In the subsequent passage Ibn Khaldun prescribes some effective methods of warfare.*

Straighten out your lines like a strongly constructed building.

Place the armed men in front, and those who are not armed in the rear.

Bite on your molars. This makes it harder for sword blows to harm the head.

Keep [something] wrapped around [?] the tips of the spears. This preserves the sharpness of points.

Keep the eyes down. This keeps the soul more concentrated and gives greater peace to the heart.

Kill [all] noises. This drives vacillation away more effectively and is more becoming to dignity.

Do not hold your flags inclined and do not remove them. Place them in the hands only of those among you who are brave.

Call upon truth and endurance for aid, for "after endurance there is victory."

TARIK THE MOOR

Few heroes have been as splendidly immortalized as Tarik, for whom Gibraltar (from

*Moors take Christian captives, as shown in a thirteenth-century minia-
ture from the* Cantigas of Alfonso X, *a collection of Spanish poems.*

*Gebel Tarik, or "Mount of Tarik") is
named. The Muslim campaign on the Iberian
Peninsula was their most glorious military
operation in Europe. The initial reconnaissance was launched in July, 710, and its success inspired Musa, the Arab governor of the
Maghreb, to dispatch his Berber freedman,
Tarik ibn Zayyad, across the strait. The
story of Tarik's decisive victory over King
Roderick is retold below in an excerpt from
the* History of the Moors in Spain (1887),
by Stanley Lane-Poole, an Arabic scholar.

In 711, learning that Roderick was busy
in the north of his dominions, where
there was a rising of the Basques, Musa
despatched one of his generals, the Moor
[Berber] Tarik, with 7,000 troops, most
of whom were also Moors, to make another raid upon Andalusia. The raid
carried him further than he expected.
Tarik landed at the lion's rock, which has
ever since borne his name. . . , and after
capturing Carteya, advanced inland. He
had not proceeded far when he perceived
the whole force of the Goths under
Roderick advancing to encounter him.
The two armies met on the banks of a
little river. . . . The Prophet himself is
said to have appeared to Tarik, and to
have bidden him be of good courage, to
strike, and to conquer; and many like
fables are related. But whatever may have
been the dreams and visions of the armies

then encamped over against one another
near the river Guadalete, the result of the
combat was never doubtful. Tarik, indeed, although he had been reinforced
with 5,000 Berbers, commanded still but
a little army of 12,000 troops, and Roderick had six times as many men to his
back. But the invaders were bold and
hardy men, used to war, and led by a
hero; the Spaniards were a crowd of ill-
treated slaves, and among their commanders were treacherous nobles. The
kinsmen of Witiza [Roderick's prede-
cessor] were there, obedient to the summons of Roderick; but they intended to
desert to the enemy's side in the midst of
the battle and win the day for the Saracens. They had no idea that they were
betraying Spain. They thought that the
invaders were only in search of booty;
and that, the raid over and the booty secured, they would go back to Africa,
when the line of Witiza would be restored to its ancient seat. And thus they
lent a hand to the day's work which
placed the fairest provinces of Spain for
eight centuries under the Moslem domination.

When the Moors saw the mighty army
that Roderick had brought against them,
and beheld the king in his splendid armor
under a magnificent canopy, their hearts
for a moment sank within them. But

Tarik cried aloud, "Men, before you is
the enemy, and the sea is at your backs.
By Allah, there is no escape for you save
in valor and resolution." And they
plucked up courage and shouted, "We
will follow thee, O Tarik," and rushed
after their general into the fray. The battle lasted a whole week, and prodigies of
valor are recorded on both sides. Roderick rallied his army again and again; but
the desertion of the partisans of Witiza
turned the fortune of the field and it became the scene of a disastrous rout. . . .

"O Commander of the Faithful, these
are not common conquests; they are like
the meeting of the nations on the Day of
Judgment." Thus wrote Musa, the Governor of Africa, to the Khalif Welid, describing the victory of the Guadalete.
There is little wonder that the Saracens
stood amazed at the completeness of
their triumph. Leaving the regions of
myth, with which the Spanish chroniclers
have surrounded the fall of Roderick, it
is matter of sober history that the victory
of the Guadalete gave all Spain into the
hands of the Moors. Tarik and his twelve
thousand Berbers had by a single action
won the whole peninsula, and it needed
but ordinary energy and promptness to
reduce the feeble resistance which some
of the cities still offered. The victor lost
no time in following up his success. In
defiance of an order from Musa, who
was bitterly jealous of the unexpected
glory which had come to his Berber
lieutenant, and commanded him to advance no further, the fortunate general
pushed on without delay. Dividing his
forces into three brigades, he spread them
over the peninsula, and reduced city after
city with little difficulty. Mughith, one
of his officers, was despatched with seven
hundred horses to seize Cordova. Lying
hid till darkness came on, Mughith
stealthily approached the city. A storm
of hail, which the Moslems regarded as a
special favor of Providence, muffled the
clatter of their horses' hoofs. A shepherd
pointed out a breach in the walls, and
here the Moors determined to make the
assault. One of them, more active than

the rest, climbed a fig-tree which grew beneath the breach, and thence, springing on to the wall, flung the end of a long turban to the others, and pulled them up after him. They instantly surprised the guard, and threw open the gates to the main body of the invaders, and the town was captured with hardly a blow. The governor and garrison took refuge in a convent, where for three months they were closely beleaguered. When at length they surrendered, Cordova was left in the keeping of the Jews, who had proved themselves staunch allies of the Moslems in the campaign, and who ever afterwards enjoyed great consideration at the hands of the conquerors. The Moors admitted them to their intimacy, and, until very late times, never persecuted them as the Gothic priests had done. . . . When the fighting was over, Jew and Moor and Persian joined in that cultivation of learning and philosophy, arts and sciences, which pre-eminently distinguished the rule of the Saracens in the Middle Ages.

HOW TO GET RICH QUICKLY

The following excerpt, from the Muqaddimah, *contains Ibn Khaldun's shrewd guide to success in commerce. By the fourteenth century Morocco and a number of West African kingdoms were partners in an active trans-Saharan trade that enriched not only the principals but a host of desert-dwelling middlemen. Caravans transported such commodities as wheat, dried fruit, brass, clothing, horses, books, and salt southward, and gold, honey, rice, and kola nuts northward.*

The merchant who knows his business will travel only with such goods as are generally needed by rich and poor, rulers and commoners alike. [General need] makes for a large demand for his goods. If he restricts his good to those needed only by a few [people], it may be impossible for him to sell them, since these few may for some reason find it difficult to buy them. Then, his business would slump, and he would make no profit.

Also, a merchant who travels with needed goods should do so only with medium quality goods. The best quality of any type of goods is restricted to wealthy people and the entourage of the ruler. They are very few in number. As is well known, the medium quality of anything is what suits most people. This should by all means be kept in mind by the merchant, because it makes the difference between selling his goods and not selling them.

Likewise, it is more advantageous and more profitable for the merchant's enterprise, and a better guarantee [that he will be able to take advantage of] market fluctuations, if he brings goods from a country that is far away and where there is danger on the road. In such a case, the goods transported will be few and rare, because the place where they come from is far away or because the road over which they come is beset with perils, so that there are few who would bring them, and they are very rare. When goods are few and rare, their prices go up. On the other hand, when the country is near and the road safe for traveling, there will be many to transport the goods. Thus, they will be found in large quantities, and the prices will go down.

Therefore, the merchants who dare to enter the Sudan country are the most prosperous and wealthy of all people. The distance and the difficulty of the road they travel are great. They have to cross a difficult desert which is made [almost] inaccessible by fear [of danger] and beset by [the danger of] thirst. Water is found there only in a few well-known spots to which caravan guides lead the way. The distance of this road is braved only by a very few people. Therefore, the goods of the Sudan country are found only in small quantities among us, and they are particularly expensive. The same applies to our goods among them.

Thus, merchandise becomes more valuable when merchants transport it from one country to another. [Merchants who do so] quickly get rich and wealthy. The same applies to merchants who travel

from our country to the East, also because of the great distance to be traversed. On the other hand, those who travel back and forth between the cities and countries of one particular region earn little and make a very small profit, because their goods are available in large quantities and there is a great number of merchants who travel with them.

God "gives sustenance. He is strong and solid."

A POPE'S LETTER

During the Middle Ages relations between Christian Europe and Muslim North Africa were often marred by periods of bitter fighting. Nevertheless, the money-minded entrepreneurs and rulers of both continents often transcended moral and political differences in order to enjoy the profits of trade. Indeed, commercial activities existed between the Maghreb and such cities as Amalfi, Genoa, Pisa, and Venice. The following letter dates from the eleventh century. It was dispatched by Pope Gregory VII *to Al-Nasir (variously known as Anzir), sovereign of Mauretania. Al-Nasir had established diplomatic relations with the Vatican in an attempt to attract Christian merchants to his country.*

Gregory, bishop, servant of servants of god, to Anzir, King of Mauretania, of the province situated in Africa: greetings and papal blessings. Your Highness wrote to us this year to ask to consecrate as bishop, in accordance with the Christian principles, the priest Servand, which we are eager to do because your request is justified. At the same time you sent us presents; you have, in deference for the Blessed Peter, Prince of Apostles, and through love for us, ransomed the Christians who were captives in your land and promised to buy back those who are still to be found there. God, creator of all things, without whom we are nothing, has clearly instilled this goodness in you and has prompted your heart to this generous act. The Almighty God, who wants all men to be saved that no one may perish, sanctions in us the love of fellow man, after love which we owe to him, and the fulfillment of this rule: Do unto others as you would have others do unto you. We in particular, more than other people, must practice this virtue of charity, you and we, who, in different ways, adore the same, one God and each day must praise and worship the Creator of Centuries and the Master of the World. The nobles of the city of Rome, having learned through us of the act God inspired you to do, admire the loftiness of your heart and sing out your praises. Two among them, our habitual companions, Alberic and Ceucius, raised from their childhood with us at the palace of Rome, eagerly desire to make friends and trade favors with you. They will be happy to oblige you in this country. They will send you some of their men, who will tell you how much respect their masters have for your deed and your greatness, and how content they will be to serve you here. We recommend them to Your Magnificence, and we ask for them the same love and devotion that we will always have for you and all that concerns you. God knows that respect for the Almighty God inspires the friendship we have vowed to you, and how much we wish for your well being and your glory in this life and in the life to come. We pray from the bottom of our heart that you will be received after a long life in the breast of the blessedness of the saintly patriarch Abraham.

INSTRUCTION OF CHILDREN

The Arabs conferred great intellectual benefits on the cities and towns that were scattered throughout the Maghreb. The next excerpt, from the Muqaddimah, describes the manner in which Koranic study was transmitted.

It should be known that instructing children in the Qur'an [Koran] is a symbol of Islam. Muslims have, and practice, such instruction in all their cities, because it imbues hearts with a firm belief [in Islam] and its articles of faith, which

Young North Africans receiving instruction in the tenets of Islamic faith at an outdoor school

are [derived] from the verses of the Qur'an and certain Prophetic traditions. The Qur'an has become the basis of instruction, the foundation for all habits that may be acquired later on. . . . The methods of instructing children in the Qur'an differ according to differences of opinion as to the habits that are to result from that instruction.

The Maghribi method is to restrict the education of children to instruction in the Qur'an and to practice, during the course [of instruction], in Qur'an orthography and its problems and the differences among Qur'an experts on this score. The [Maghribis] do not bring up any other subjects in their classes, such as traditions, jurisprudence, poetry, or Arabic philology, until the pupil is skilled in [the Qur'an], or drops out before becoming skilled in it. . . .

The Spanish method is instruction in reading and writing as such. That is what they pay attention to in the instruction [of children]. However, since the Qur'an is the basis and foundation of [all] that and the source of Islam and [all] the sciences, they make it the basis of instruc-

tion, but they do not restrict their instruction of children exclusively to [the Qur'an]. They also bring in [other subjects], mainly poetry and composition, and they give the children an expert knowledge of Arabic. They do not stress teaching of the Qur'an more than the other subjects. . . .

The people of Ifriqiyah [Tunisia] combine the instruction of children in the Qur'an, usually, with the teaching of traditions. They also teach basic scientific norms and certain scientific problems. However, they stress giving their children a good knowledge of the Qur'an and acquainting them with its various recensions and readings more than anything else. Next they stress handwriting. In general, their method of instruction in the Qur'an is closer to the Spanish method [than to Maghribi or Eastern methods], because their [educational tradition] derives from the Spanish *shaykhs* who crossed over when the Christians conquered Spain. . . .

In his *Rihlah,* Judge Abu Bakr b. 'Arabi made a remarkable statement about instruction, which retains [the best of] the old, and presents [some good] new features. He placed instruction in Arabic and poetry ahead of all the other sciences, as in the Spanish method, since, he said, "poetry is the archive of the Arabs. Poetry and Arabic philology should be taught first because of the [existing] corruption of the language. From there, the [student] should go on to arithmetic and study it assiduously, until he knows its basic norms. He should then go on to the study of the Qur'an, because with his [previous] preparation, it will be easy for him." [Ibn al-'Arabi] continued: "How thoughtless are our compatriots in that they teach children the Qur'an when they are first starting out. They read things they do not understand and work hard at something that is not as important for them as other matters." He concluded: "The student should study successively the principles of Islam, the principles of jurisprudence, disputation, and then the Prophetic traditions and the sciences connected with them." He also forbade teaching two disciplines at the same time, save to the student with a good mind and sufficient energy. . . .

Severe punishment in the course of instruction does harm to the student, especially to little children, because it belongs among [the things that make for a] bad habit. Students, slaves, and servants who are brought up with injustice and [tyrannical] force are overcome by it. It makes them feel oppressed and causes them to lose their energy. It makes them lazy and induces them to lie and be insincere. That is, their outward behavior differs from what they are thinking, because they are afraid that they will have to suffer tyrannical treatment [if they tell the truth]. Thus, they are taught deceit and trickery. This becomes their custom and character.

WHAT TO WEAR TO MECCA

The Muqaddimah *also contains the following information on the crafts of weaving and tailoring, particularly as they apply to garments to be worn on the hadj, or pilgrimage, to Mecca. This journey is obligatory for all Muslims who have the strength and means to undertake it. It is an incentive to travel and fosters cultural exchanges between Africans and Muslims of many other lands.*

It should be known that people who are temperate in their humanity cannot avoid giving some thought to keeping warm, as they do to shelter. One manages to keep warm by using woven material as protective cover against both heat and cold. This requires the interlacing of yarn, until it turns out to be a complete garment. This is spinning and weaving.

Desert people restrict themselves to this. But people who are inclined toward sedentary culture cut the woven material into pieces of the right size to cover the form of the body and all of its numerous limbs in their various locations. They then put the different pieces together with thread, until they turn out to be a complete garment that fits the body and can be worn by people. The craft that makes things fit is tailoring.

These two crafts are necessary in civilization, because human beings must keep warm.

The purpose of [weaving] is to weave wool and cotton yarn in warp and woof and do it well, so that the texture will be strong. Pieces of cloth of certain measurements are thus produced. Some are garments of wool for covering. Others are garments of cotton and linen for wear.

The purpose of tailoring is to give the woven material a certain form in accordance with the many different shapes and customs [that may occur in this connection]. The material is first cut with scissors into pieces that fit the limbs of the body. The pieces are then joined together with the help of skillful tailoring according to the rules, either by the use of thread, or with bands, or [one] quilts [them], or cuts openings. This [craft] is restricted to sedentary culture, since the inhabitants of the desert can dispense with it. They merely cover themselves with cloth. The tailoring of clothes, the cutting, fitting, and sewing of the material, is one of the various methods and aspects of sedentary culture.

This should be understood, in order to understand the reason why the wearing of sewn garments is forbidden on the pilgrimage. According to the religious law, the pilgrimage requires, among other things, the discarding of all worldly attachments and the return to God as He created us in the beginning. Man should not set his heart upon any of his luxury customs, such as perfume, women, sewn garments, or boots. He should not go hunting or expose himself to any other of the customs with which his soul and character have become colored. When he dies, he will necessarily lose them [anyhow]. He should come [to the pilgrimage] as if he were going to the Last Judgment, humble in his heart, sincerely devoted to his Lord. If he is completely sincere in this respect, his reward will be that he will shed his sins [and be] like he was on the day when his mother gave birth to him. Praised be You! How kind have You been with Your servants and how compassionate have You been with them in their search for guidance toward You!

IBN YASIN'S JIHAD

The powerful Almoravid movement dominated North Africa and Spain from the middle of the eleventh to the middle of the twelfth century. Its fortunes are described in this excerpt from the Encyclopedia of Islam, *a mammoth compilation prepared in England early in this century by a team of leading Orientalists. Ibn Yasin, the founder of the movement, called on his disciples to join the jihad, or holy war, and urged them to "maintain the truth, to repress injustice, and to abolish all taxes not based on law."*

Almoravids is the name of a Muslim dynasty. This word has been derived from the Arabic *al-Murabitun*, a sort of warrior-monks inhabiting a *ribat* or convent more or less fortified. . . .

Under the name of Almoravids we understand especially the royal dynasty founded by several branches of the large Sahara-tribe of the Sanhadja [Sanhaja], which, grouped under the authority of a religious leader, invaded and conquered the Maghrib in the first half of the 5th [by the Christian calendar the middle of the 11th] century, afterwards breaking into Andalusia and mastering that as well.

In the first centuries of Islam the tribes forming the great group of the Sanhadja ... wearers of the *litham* (a veil covering the face below the eyes; hence also the name *mulaththamun* sometimes given to Almoravids) inhabited the vast wastes of the Sahara as far as the Sudan; they lived there as nomads, as their descendants, the Touaregs [Tuaregs], do to the present time.

Muslim writers, who do not always agree as to the dates of events of which we here give a résumé, are unanimous in tracing the origin of the Almoravid empire as follows:

In the first half of the 5th century of the Hidjra [Muhammad's flight to Medina] a chief of the Sanhadja, Yahya b. Ibrahim, of the branch of the Djaddala (or Gaddala) made the pilgrimage accompanied by men of distinction in his tribe. On his way back he met at Kairawan in Ifrikiya the professor of malikite law 'Abu 'Imiran al-Fasi. Yahya b. Ibrahim desirous of bringing among his uncultured compatriots a man able to direct them in true Muslim doctrine, asked the professor to entrust him with one of his disciples for this purpose. Not being able to find the man of letters he wanted at Kairawan, Yahya b. Ibrahim discovered him, on the recommendation of the professor Abu 'Imran, in the town of Nefis (now belonging to Morocco) among the followers of the professor Waggag, a disciple of Abu 'Imran, in the person of 'Abd Allah b. Yasin.

After having settled among the Sanhadja, Ibn Yasin, followed by seven or eight companions among whom were the two chiefs of the Lamtuna (a branch of the Sanhadja), Yahya b. 'Omar and his brother Abu Bekr b. 'Omar, constructed a hermitage for his companions and himself on an island in the Niger (or in the Senegal). This convent was a *ribat* and Ibn Yasin himself called his followers *Murabitun* (Almoravids). Soon the reputation of the sanctity of this spot and its pious inhabitants spread and a vast number of neophytes came to apply for admittance into this religious brotherhood. Ibn Yasin having gathered to his *ribat* about a thousand monks who were absolutely devoted to him and had all been recruited from among the warriors and the chiefs of the Lamtuna and of the Masufa, now thought of taking up a more active line. He sent forth his partisans, in the name of the true faith, against the different tribes of the Sanhadja, which had to submit one after the other. The victories and the booty soon persuaded those who had hesitated and the number of Almoravid warriors increased rapidly.

Ibn Yasin, keeping for himself the supreme direction of affairs and the political and financial administration of the brotherhood, entrusted his faithful disciple Yahya b. 'Omar with the leadership of the Almoravid army. After having brought the Saharean tribes under their authority Yahya b. 'Omar and Ibn Yasin advanced as far as the Wadi Dar'a where they made important raids. The sovereign of Sidjilmasa, Mas'ud b. Wanudin al-Maghrawi, offering opposition to the conquest of his kingdom, perished in a battle and his capital was taken [447 is 1055-1056 on the Christian calendar].

On the death of Yahya b. 'Omar which took place at about 447 or 448 (1055-1057), his brother Abu Bekr became commander in chief and marching northward continued the conquests begun in the south of the extreme Maghrib. The countries of Sus and their capital Tarudant were subjugated; next Aghmat and its province submitted to the power of the Almoravid conquerors. Abu Bekr married the widow of the king of Aghmat, the beautiful Zainab, of the tribe of the Nafzawa, who was destined to play a certain part in the establishment of the Almoravid empire.

Subsequently Abu Bekr and Ibn Yasin attacked the Berghwata Berbers, whose territories extended as far as the Atlantic Ocean. The Berghwata professed the subversive doctrines of their prophet Salih; it would be a good work to bring them to Islam. But these Berbers energetically resisted the attack of the Almoravids and Ibn Yasin, taking an active part in the military operations, found his death in a battle [in 1059]. Perhaps Ibn Yasin appointed a spiritual leader to take his place at the head of the Almoravids; Ibn Khaldun mentions as such Ibn 'Addu who, if he did exist at all, played a very subordinate part compared with Abu Bekr b. 'Omar. The latter appears as the real chief of the Almoravids and had coins struck in his name; he continued the war against Berghwata and subjugated them [in 1060]. Shortly afterwards he was informed that Bulugin, lord of the Kal'a of the Banu Hammad [who ruled Algeria], was marching with a large force against the countries of the extreme Maghrib, and at the same time that those portions of the Sanhadja who had remained in the desert were carrying on war with one another. He took advantage of the latter fact to leave the Maghrib for the time being and go back to the desert in order to re-establish peace among the Almoravids. Before leaving, Abu Bekr gave the command over the troops in the Maghrib and the direction of affairs to Yusuf b. Tashfin; he also abandoned to him, after divorcing her, his wife Zainab, who thus became the wife of Yusuf b. Tashfin. . . . This woman of remarkable intelligence, rare energy and great beauty acquired considerable ascendancy over her new husband's mind and had a happy influence on the fate of the young empire. Yusuf b. Tashfin continued the conquests in the extreme and in the central Maghrib. Abu Bekr, after having re-established order in the desert and having received the news of his lieutenant's

Travelers in the Algerian Sahara, their faces toward Mecca, kneeling to recite their prayers
LIBRARY OF CONGRESS, CARPENTER COLLECTION

success, returned to the North to take again command over the Almoravids. But following Zainab's advice Yusuf b. Tashfin loaded him with presents and made him understand clearly that he was not at all disposed to give up the supreme authority. Abu Bekr judged it wise not to insist; he retired to the Sahara and to the Sudan where he died in 480 (1087-1088).

In his quality of supreme chief of the Almoravids Yusuf b. Tashfin founded Marrakush which became his capital and that of his successors; then he went on with his conquests in the extreme and in the central Maghrib as far as Algiers. In 475 (1082-1083) he came back to Marrakush after having left Almoravid officers in the conquered countries as governors.

Urged by the Muslim princes of Andalusia (*reyes de Taifas*), and in particular by . . . [the] king of Sevilla, Yusuf decided to cross to Spain with a strong army in order to make war against the Christians under Alfonso VI, king of Leon and Castile; he gained over the Christian armies the great victory of Zallaka [12 Radjab 479, or October 23, 1086] which was for the Almoravides the prelude to the conquest of Spain. Certain authors maintain that from this day Yusuf took the title of *Amir al-Mu'minin.*

This assertion is doubtful, at least it does not appear that the great Almoravid conqueror long retained this title denoting temporal and spiritual authority at the same time. We even know as a fact beyond dispute that the Almoravid sovereigns, while reserving for themselves temporal authority with the title of *Amir al-Muslimin*, attributed supreme authority and suzerainty in matters spiritual to the 'Abbasids of the East with the title of *Amir al-Mu'minin*, given to the Caliph.

The petty Muslim kings of Andalusia, al-Mu'tamid included, soon found out that the risks, their authority and their riches ran through the Almoravid chief, were much more formidable than those they feared from the Christians. They were soon robbed of their dignities and banished by Yusuf b. Tashfin, who left in Spain Almoravid troops and governors, chosen from among his relatives.

When Yusuf b. Tashfin died in 500 (1106-1107) he bequeathed to his son 'Ali a vast empire, comprising the countries of the Maghrib, a part of Ifrikiya and Muslim Spain (extending to the north as far as Fraga). His descendants succeeded each other on the throne of Marrakush for less than half a century and the Almoravid dynasty was destroyed in Africa when the Almohades led by 'Abd al-Mu'min conquered Mar-

rakush [in 541, or 1146-1147] and killed the last Almoravid king of the house of Yusuf. . . . Soon after the Almohades conquered Spain . . . and at the death of the Almoravid governor of Spain [in 1148-1149], the authority of the Almoravids in the peninsula was at an end.

THE BOOK OF ROGER

The first Western notice of the East African coast occurs in the writings of Al-Idrisi, a twelfth-century Moroccan Muslim scholar who spent most of his life in Palermo at the court of Roger II, a Norman ruler of Sicily. There, Al-Idrisi compiled the history of the whole known world, relying entirely on the writings of other historians and on the reports of informants who traveled at Roger's expense. His work, the source of this colorful selection, is known as the Kitab Rujar, *or* Book of Roger. *Its alternate title,* Nuzhat al Mushtaq fi Ikhtiraq al-Afaq, *has been freely translated as "The Recreation of Him Who Yearns to Travel the Lands."*

The Zanj of the East African coast have no ships to voyage in, but use vessels from Oman and other countries which sail to the islands of Zanj which depend on the Indies. These foreigners sell their goods there, and buy the produce of the country. The people of the Djawaga islands go to Zanzibar in large and small ships, and use them for trading their goods, for they understand each others' language. Opposite the Zanj coasts are the Djawaga islands; they are numerous and vast; their inhabitants are very dark in color, and everything that is cultivated there, fruit, sorghum, sugar-cane and camphor trees, is black in color. Among the number of the islands is Sribuza, which is said to be 1,200 miles round; and pearl fisheries and various kinds of aromatic plants and perfumes are to be found there, which attract the merchants.

Among the islands of Djawaga included in the present section is Andjuba [Anjouan-Johanna], whose principal town is called Unguja in the language of Zanzibar, and whose people, although mixed, are actually mostly Muslims. The distance from it to Banas on the Zanj coast is 100 miles. The island is 400 miles round; bananas are the chief food. There are five kinds, as follows: the bananas called *kundi; fili* whose weight is sometimes twelve ounces; *omani, muriani, sukari.* It is a healthy, sweet, and pleasant food. The island is traversed by a mountain called Wabra. The vagabonds who are expelled from the town flee there, and form a brave and numerous company which frequently infests the surroundings of the town, and which lives at the top of the mountain in a state of defense against the ruler of the island. They are courageous, and feared for their arms and their number. The island is very populous; there are many villages and cattle. They grow rice. There is a great trade in it, and each year various products and goods are brought for exchange and consumption.

From Medouna [on the Somali coast] to Malindi, a town of the Zanj, one follows the coast for three days and three nights by sea. Malindi lies on the shore, at the mouth of a river of sweet water. It is a large town, whose people engage in hunting and fishing. On land they hunt the tiger and other wild beasts. They obtain various kinds of fish from the sea, which they cure and sell.

They own and exploit iron mines; for them iron is an article of trade and the source of their largest profits. They pretend to know how to bewitch the most poisonous snakes so as to make them harmless to everyone except those for whom they wish evil or on whom they wish to take vengeance. They also pretend that by means of these enchantments the tigers and lions cannot hurt them. These wizards are called *al-Musnafu* in the language of the people.

It is two days' journey along the coast to Mombasa. This is a small place and a dependency of the Zanj. Its inhabitants work in the iron mines and hunt tigers. They have red colored dogs which fight every kind of wild beast and even lions. This town lies on the sea shore near a large gulf up which ships travel two

days' journey; its banks are uninhabited because of the wild beasts that live in the forests where the Zanj go and hunt, as we have already said. In this town lives the King of Zanzibar. His guards go on foot because they have no mounts: horses cannot live there.

THE LAND OF THE ZANJ

Islam spread to Africa's east coast more as a result of commerce than religious zeal. The first Muslims to establish themselves in the "Land of the Zanj," as the Arabs called the coastal area south of the Horn, were probably lured by gold. The story of the first settlements in this area, at Mogadishu and Brava, is told by the sixteenth-century Portuguese historian João de Barros. His précis of the now lost Chronicle of the Kings of Kilwa, from which this excerpt is taken, is one of the two extant summaries of this important work. However, De Barros appears to have consulted other sources besides the Chronicle. If accurate, these immigrations from Arabia may have occurred as early as the eighth or as late as the eleventh century; scholars disagree.

As the land of Arabia is very close to these lands, the first foreign people who came to settle in the land of Zanzibar were a tribe of Arabs, who had been banished after adopting a sect of Muhammad. As we learn from a Chronicle of the Kings of Kilwa, of which we shall make mention, they were called Zaidites. The cause of the banishment was that they followed the doctrines of a Moor named Zaid, who was the grandson of Husain, the son of 'Ali, who was the nephew of Muhammad, and had married his daughter Axa. This Zaid held some opinions which were contrary to those of the Koran, and the Moors call all who follow his doctrine Zaidites, that is to say followers of Zaid, and consider them heretics. As these were the first to come from outside to dwell in this land, they did not make any notable settlements, but only gathered together in parts where they could live safe from the Kafirs [black Africans who were not Muslims].

After their arrival, they worked their way like a slow plague along the coast, taking possession of fresh settlements, until there arrived three ships with a large number of Arabs in the company of seven brothers. These belonged to a tribe near the city of al-Hasa, which is over forty leagues from the island of Bahrein, which is at the entrance to the Persian Sea, very close to the land of Arabia and its interior. The cause of their coming was that they were very much persecuted by the king of al-Hasa. The first settlement they made in this land of *Ajan* [a form of the word Zanj] was the city of Mogadishu, and the next at Barawa [Brava], which even at the present time is governed by twelve chiefs in the manner of a republic, and they are descendants of these brothers. Mogadishu so excelled in power and statesmanship that it became overlord and capital of all the Moors of this coast. As the first people to come, who were called Zaidites, held different opinions from the Arabs regarding their faith, they were not willing to submit to them, and withdrew to the interior, intermarrying with the Kafirs and adopting their customs so that they became in all respects half breeds. These are the people the Moors who live along the coast called Baduis, a common name, just as among ourselves we call the country folk Alarves.

The first foreign nation to trade by sailing ships with the Sofala mine was this city of Mogadishu; not that they went to explore the coast, but because a ship belonging to it was driven there in a storm and by the force of the currents.

THE GOLD OF SOFALA

João de Barros is our only authority concerning Kilwa's miraculous evolution from a series of unprestigious commercial settlements to the principal trader of gold in the western Indian Ocean. This change probably began in the first quarter of the twelfth century, when the sultan of Kilwa learned of gold-rich Sofala and promptly secured what amounted to a trade monopoly on the precious commodity. The first part of this excerpt comes from the same source as the preceding selection; the second part, from his history, De Asia, which was first published in 1552.

This settlement, which the Moors had made in this place called Sofala, was not made by force of arms, nor against the will of the natives of the land, but by their wish and that of the prince who ruled at that time; because, by reason of this intercourse they [the people of Sofala] obtained benefits as well as cloth and other things which they had never had before, and for which they gave gold and ivory, which was of no use to them, and which, until then, had never been exported from Sofala. And, although this barbarous race never left the village in which they were born, and were not given to navigation, nor to travel by land in pursuit of commerce, gold nevertheless has this quality, namely, that wherever it is found on earth, the report of it spreads from one person to another so that they go to find its place of origin.

However it happened, we learn from the Chronicle of the Kings of Kilwa, which we have already mentioned, that the first people on this coast who came to the land of Sofala in search of gold were inhabitants of the city of Mogadishu. How the kings of Kilwa came into possession was in this manner. A man was fishing in a canoe outside the bar of Kilwa near an island called Miza. He caught a fish on the hook of the line he had cast into the sea. Feeling from the struggles of the fish that it was very large and not wishing to lose it, he weighed anchor and left himself at the will of the fish. Sometimes the vessel went where the fish took it and sometimes where the currents, which are very strong there, so that when the fisherman wished to return to the port whence he had come, he could not reach it. At last, more dead than alive from hunger and thirst, he came to the port of Sofala, where he found a ship of Mogadishu, which had come there to trade. In this vessel he re-

turned to Kilwa and related what had occurred and what he had seen of the gold trade.

It was part of the agreement between these Gentiles and the Moors of Mogadishu that every year they should send some young Moors so that there should be some of this race there. When the King of Kilwa learnt this part of the contract and its conditions from the fisherman, he sent a ship there to arrange commerce with the Kafirs. With regard to the young Moors for whom they asked, he offered to give so many cloths a head in lieu of those they asked, or, if they wanted them so as to have a race of them there, he said some of the inhabitants of Kilwa would go and settle there in a factory for merchandise, and that they would be glad to take their daughters as wives, by which means the people would multiply. By means of this entry the Moors of Kilwa got possession of the trade.

In course of time by means of the trade which the Moors had with these Kafirs, the kings of Kilwa became absolute masters of the gold trade. Chief among them was a man named Daut [Daud ibn Sulaiman, c. 1311–1170] . . . who resided there for some time and afterwards went to rule in Kilwa. From that time onwards the kings of Kilwa sent their governors to Sofala, so that everything might be transacted through their factors. . . .

Daut reigned at Kilwa for forty years and was succeeded by his son Soleiman Hacen, who conquered the greater part of the [this?] coast. With his father's support he became master of the trade of Sofala and of the islands of Pemba, Momfia, Zanzibar and a large part of the mainland coast. Besides being a conqueror, he beautified the city of Quiloa [Kilwa], erecting there a fortress of stone and lime, with walls, towers and other houses, whereas up till that time nearly the whole of the dwellings in the city had been made of wood. All these things he accomplished during the eighteen years he reigned.

MOGADISHU IN 1331

The well-organized life style of the peoples of Mogadishu is the subject of this piece by Ibn Battuta, the great fourteenth-century Moroccan traveler. Aside from making four pilgrimages to Mecca, this tireless peregrinator was qadi, or judge, of Delhi in India and of the Maldive Islands; he also visited all the countries of the Middle East, as well as East and West Africa, Ceylon, and China. He is the only medieval Muslim to have left an eyewitness description of the towns of the East African littoral, which he visited in 1331.

From [Zeila] we sailed fifteen nights and arrived at Mogadishu, which is a very large town. The people have very many camels, and slaughter many hundreds every day. They have also many sheep. The merchants are wealthy, and manufacture a material which takes its name from the town and which is exported to Egypt and elsewhere.

Among the customs of the people of this town is the following: when a ship comes into port, it is boarded from *sanbuqs*, that is to say, little boats. Each *sanbuq* carries a crowd of young men, each carrying a covered dish, containing food. Each one of them presents his dish to a merchant on board, and calls out: "This man is my guest." And his fellows do the same. Not one of the merchants disembarks except to go to the house of his host among the young men, save frequent visitors to the country. In such a case they go where they like. When a merchant has settled in his host's house, the latter sells for him what he has brought and makes his purchases for him. Buying anything from a merchant below its market price or selling him anything except in his host's presence is disapproved of by the people of Mogadishu. They find it of advantage to keep to this rule.

When the young men came on board the ship on which I was, one of them approached me. My companions said to him: "He is not one of the merchants: he is a lawyer." Then the young man called his companions and said: "This man is a guest of the Qadi." One of the Qadi's friends came among them, and he told him of this. The Qadi came down to the beach with some of his pupils and sent one on board to fetch me. Then I disembarked with my companions, and greeted the Qadi and his followers. He said to me: "In the name of God, let us go and greet the Shaikh." "Who is the Shaikh?" I asked, and he replied: "The Sultan." For it is their custom here to call the Sultan "Shaikh." I answered the Qadi: "I will visit him as soon as I have found lodging." He replied: "It is the custom here, whenever a lawyer, or a Sharif or a holy man comes, that he should not go to his lodging until he has seen the Sultan." So I did what I was asked in accordance with their custom.

As we have said, the Sultan of Mogadishu is called Shaikh by his subjects. His name is Abu Bakr ibn Shaikh Omar, and by race he is a Berber. He talks in the dialect of Mogadishu, but knows Arabic. When a ship arrives, it is the custom for it to be boarded by the Sultan's *sanbuq*, to inquire whence it has come, who are the owners and who its captain is. They also inquire the nature of the cargo and what merchants or other persons are on board. All this is told to the Sultan, who invites as his guest anyone worthy of such honor.

When I arrived at the palace with the Qadi, whose name was Ibn Burhan al-Misri, a eunuch came out and greeted him. The Qadi said: "Go and do your duty, and inform our master the Shaikh that this man has arrived from the Hijaz." He delivered the message and returned with a dish of betel leaves and areca nuts. He gave me six leaves of betel and some nuts, and the same amount to the Qadi: the rest he divided among my companions and the pupils of the Qadi. Then he brought a bottle of Damascus rose-water, and sprinkled some on me and on the Qadi, and said: "Our master orders that he be lodged in the house of the pupils."

This house was built specially for them. The Qadi took me by the hand,

and we went to this house, which is near that of the Shaikh. It was decorated with carpets and contained everything needful. Later the same eunuch brought us food from the Shaikh's house. He was accompanied by one of the wazirs, whose particular duty it was to look after guests. He said to us: "Our master greets you and bids you welcome." After this the meal was served and we ate.

The food of these people is rice cooked with butter, served on a large wooden dish. With it they serve side-dishes, stews of chicken, meat, fish, and vegetables. They cook unripe bananas in fresh milk, and serve them as a sauce. They put curdled milk in another vessel with peppercorns, vinegar, and saffron, green ginger and mangoes, which look like apples but have a nut inside. Ripe mangoes are very sweet and are eaten like fruit; but unripe mangoes are as acid as lemons, and are cooked in vinegar. When the Mogadishu people have taken a mouthful of rice, they take some of these pickles. One of them eats as much as several of us: they are very fat and corpulent.

When we had eaten, the Qadi went away. We stayed there for three days, and each day they brought us food three times a day, as is their custom. The fourth day, which was a Friday, the Qadi, his pupils and one of the wazirs of the Shaikh came and brought me a suit of clothes. Their dress consists of a loin-cloth, which is fastened round the waist, instead of drawers, of which they are ignorant. There was a tunic of Egyptian linen with a border, a cloak of Jerusalem stuff, doubled, and a fringed turban of Egyptian material. They also brought my companions clothes suitable to their rank.

We went to the chief mosque, and prayed behind the *maqsurah*, the enclosure for the Shaikh. When he came out of the *maqsurah*, I greeted him with the Qadi. He replied with his good wishes for us both, and talked to the Qadi in the local language, and then said to me in Arabic: "You are welcome: you have

honored our country by coming and have rejoiced us." He went out into the courtyard of the mosque and stopped at the tomb of his son, which is there. He recited a passage from the Koran and prayed. Then came the wazirs, the amirs and military commanders and greeted him. In doing this they observed the same customs as are followed in the Yemen. The man who gives his greeting places his forefinger on the ground, and then on his head, and says: "May God make you glorious!"

After that the Shaikh went out of the door of the mosque and put his sandals on. He ordered the Qadi and myself to do likewise, and set off on foot to his house, which is near the mosque, everyone else following barefoot. Over his head they carried a silk canopy, its four poles topped with a golden bird. He wore a sweeping cloak of green Jerusalem stuff, over clothes of Egyptian linen. He had a silk girdle and a large turban. In front of him they beat drums and played trumpets and oboes. He was preceded by the amirs of the army, and followed by the Qadi, the lawyers and the Sharifs.

With this ceremony he entered his audience hall. The wazirs, amirs and military commanders took their places on a bench set for them. A special carpet was spread for the Qadi on which he sat alone. He was accompanied by the lawyers and Sharifs. There they all remained until the afternoon prayer, which they said together with the Shaikh. Then all the soldiers were drawn up in lines according to their rank, and the drums, oboes, trumpets, and flutes played. While they played, everyone stayed in his place, and anyone, who happened to be moving about, immediately stood still. When the band stopped playing, those present greeted the Shaikh with their fingers in the manner we have described and then went away. This is their custom every Friday.

On Saturday the people come to the door of the Shaikh's house and sit on benches outside. The Qadi, the lawyers, the Sharifs, the holy men, the shaikhs and those who have made the pilgrimage enter an outer room and sit on wooden benches arranged for that purpose. The Qadi sits on his bench alone, and each of these classes of person has its own bench, which is not shared with any other. The Shaikh then takes his place in his hall of audience, and sends for the Qadi. He takes his place on the Shaikh's left, and then the lawyers come in, and the chief of them sit in front of the Shaikh. The others greet the Shaikh and go back again. Then the Sharifs enter, and the chief of them sit before him: the remainder greet him and go back outside. But if they are guests of the Shaikh, they sit on his right hand. The same ceremonial is observed by persons of position and pilgrims, and then by the wazirs, the amirs and the military commanders, each rank by itself.

Then food is brought, and the Qadi, the Sharifs and those who are in the audience chamber eat in the presence of the Shaikh, and he with them. If he wishes to honor one of the chief amirs, he sends for him and has him eat with them. The rest eat in a refectory. There they observe the same precedence as that of their entering the Shaikh's audience chamber.

After this the Shaikh retires to his private apartments, and the Qadi, the wazirs, the private secretary and four of the chief amirs sit to hear causes and complaints. Questions of religious law are decided by the Qadi: other cases are judged by the council, that is, the wazirs and amirs. If a case requires the views of the Sultan, it is put in writing for him. He sends back an immediate reply, written on the back of the paper, as his discretion may decide. This has always been the custom among these people.

A GIRAFFE FOR THE EMPEROR

One of the most alluring chapters of East African history concerns that area's relations with China. Before the Ming dynasty (1368–1644) the regions traded indirectly, and no Chinese ever visited Africa. However, during the early 1400's the Chinese sponsored seven major expeditions to the ports of the Indian Ocean; two sailed all the way to Africa and visited Malindi, Brava, and Mogadishu. The undertakings were part of the Chinese government's effort to invigorate foreign trade and to strengthen its international prestige. The fleets were commanded by Cheng Ho, a court eunuch known as the "Three-jewel Eunuch." The following discussion of China's discovery of Africa is by J. J. L. Duyvendak, professor of Chinese at Leyden University. It is a lecture he gave in London in 1947.

It may be asked what was the motive that took the Chinese . . . as far as the east coast of Africa? This is a very peculiar one. It should be remembered that the

The first giraffe in China, the gift of an African ruler, arrived in 1414. A contemporary artist recorded the remarkable event.

expeditions, on their visit to the distant countries, collected as many rare and precious objects as possible. Among these objects strange animals always occupied an important place. . . . There was, in the capital, an Imperial Zoological Garden in which such rarities were kept, and when the expeditions returned they were regularly followed by a string of foreign ambassadors (including, on one occasion, even an ambassador from "Misr," Egypt) with their gifts of lions, tigers, oryxes, nilgaus, zebras, ostriches, etc. Now we learn that in 1414 a present arrived from Bengal (that had been visited by one of the secondary expeditions, detailed from the major fleet), consisting of a giraffe. Bengal, of course, is not a country where the giraffe is native, so it must have come from elsewhere. I think the riddle is solved by the fact that the following year suddenly the African country of Melinda [Malindi], with which China so far never had entertained any relations, came to Court presenting a giraffe. I believe that what happened is this: we know that in Bengal there just was a new king, Saifu'd-Din, who on ascending the throne, naturally received presents from the various Mohammedan, including African, countries. Among these presents must have been giraffes, one of which he passed on to the Chinese Emperor, and the Chinese must have met the Ambassadors from Melinda and given them a hint that such an animal would be a very welcome gift at Court. The result was that the following year Melinda came to present a giraffe. These ambassadors had to be conducted home, and so we see that on the fifth voyage (1417–1419) for the first time the itinerary is extended . . . to Melinda. It was the giraffe, therefore, that caused the Chinese to sail to Africa. . . .

It happens that in the Somali language the giraffe is called *girin* which, to Chinese ears, would sound like *ki-lin*. Now this sound is very close to that of the word *k'i-lin* (modern pronunciation *ch'i-lin*) the fabulous animal, which we equate generally with our "unicorn."

The appearance of the unicorn was always regarded as a happy portent; it was a sign of Heaven's favor and proof of the virtue of the Emperor. Under a perfect reign the cosmic forces could come to such complete development that from the surplus, as it were, such wonderful beings as dragons and giraffes could develop and exercise their beneficent influence. Now there was a superficial resemblance between the giraffe and the K'i-lin which was supposed to have "the body of a deer and the tail of an ox," to eat only herbs and to harm no living being. For the eunuchs, leaders of the expeditions, professional flatterers as they were, this resemblance of form and sound of the name was enough: the presentation of a K'i-lin would be a supreme flattery of the Emperor. In the previous years several supernatural appearances had already been reported, such as vegetarian tigers, extraordinarily large ears of grain, sweet dew, etc. A K'i-lin would cap this series in masterly fashion. Not knowing whether the giraffe from Bengal would stand the hardships of the transportation, they made sure that . . . the Melinda people would present another sample.

When the giraffe from Bengal arrived at Court on September 20, 1414, under the guise of a K'i-lin or unicorn, it caused quite a stir. The Board of Rites asked to be allowed to present a Memorial of Congratulation. The Emperor declined, saying: "Let the Ministers but early and late exert themselves in assisting the government for the welfare of the world. If the world is at peace, even without K'i-lins there is nothing that hinders good government. Let congratulations be omitted."

When, however, in the following year the giraffe from Melinda arrived, a similar request was made and, although the Emperor again declined, he went out to the Feng-t'ien gate to receive the animal in great state, together with a "celestial horse" (zebra) and a "celestial stag" (oryx?), and all the officials prostrated themselves and offered congratulations. The Emperor said: "This event is due to the abundant virtue of the late Emperor, my father, and also to the assistance rendered me by my Ministers. That is why distant people arrive in uninterrupted succession. From now on it behoves Us even more than in the past to cling to virtue and it behoves you to remonstrate with Us about Our shortcomings."

The members of the Imperial Academy, the Han-lin, as well as the Court painters did not miss the opportunity to immortalize the extraordinary event of the arrival of a K'i-lin at Court. . . . [One courtier wrote:] "Respectfully I consider that Your Majesty succeeded to the Emperor T'ai-tsu's Grand Heritage and that Your virtue transforms [the world] and causes the Three Luminaries to follow their regular course and all living souls to perform their duty. Consequently a Tsou-yü [vegetarian tiger] has appeared, Wonderful Ears are produced, Sweet Dew has descended, the Yellow River has been Clear and Savory Springs have gushed forth. All the creatures that spell good fortune arrive. In the 9th month of the year chia-wu of the Yung-lo period [1414] a K'i-lin [giraffe] came from the country of Bengal and was formally presented as tribute to the Court. The ministers and the people all gathered to gaze at it and their joy knows no end. I, Your servant, have heard that, when a Sage possesses the virtue of the utmost benevolence so that he illuminates the darkest places, then a K'i-lin appears. This shows that Your Majesty's virtue equals that of Heaven; its merciful blessings have spread far and wide so that its harmonious vapors have emanated a K'i-lin, as an endless bliss to the state for a myriad myriad years. . . ."

Thus it happened that the giraffe from the African wilderness, as it strode into the Emperor's Court, became the emblem of Perfect Virtue, Perfect Government, and Perfect Harmony in the Empire and in the Universe. Rarely have such extravagant cosmic claims been made in such refined language for any living animal. Surely it is the most sophisticated instance of therolatry in history, the apogee of the lore of the unicorn! This is what the discovery of Africa did for Chinese Confucian ideology.

CHINA LOOKS AT AFRICA

Admiral Cheng Ho's reports on his naval expeditions are not extant. However, Fei Hsin, a scholar who traveled with the fleet as a petty officer, kept the account from which the following description of Djubo, probably present-day Giumbo in Somalia, is taken.

The country of *Djubo:* "They live in solitary and dispersed villages. The country is situated in a remote corner of the west. The walls are made of piled up bricks, and the houses are masoned in high blocks. The customs are very simple. There grow neither herbs nor trees. Men and women wear their hair in rolls; when they go out, they wear a linen hood. The mountains are uncultivated and the land is wide; it rains very rarely. There are deep wells worked by means of cog-wheels. Fish are caught in the sea with nets. The products of the country are lions, gold-spotted leopards, and camel-birds which are six or seven feet tall. There are Dragon Saliva [ambergris], incense and golden amber. As merchandise are used vermilion, colored silks, gold, silver, porcelains, pepper, colored satins, rice, and other cereals."

THE PILLAR OF ZION

Medieval Ethiopia remained stalwartly Christian despite the many attempts made by its Muslim neighbors to conquer it. One of the most "perfect" Christian soldiers was Emperor Amda Seyon, or "Pillar of Zion." When this king came to the throne in 1313, his country was being seriously threatened by Muslim attacks. The first leader to campaign against him was Sabr ad-Din, the ruler of the Muslim principality of Ifat, to the east of Shoa. The Ethiopian monarch defeated Sabr as well as many other Arab leaders, and resolved not to cease fighting as long as the infidels continued to menace him.

He was everywhere victorious, and as related in the following passage from the reconstructed version of Ethiopian Royal Chronicles, many Muslim rulers joined forces against him. The translation is by Sir Wallace Ernest Alfred Budge, an archeologist.

The kings and governors made ready to throw off all allegiance to the king of Abyssinia, and banded themselves together to make war upon him. They were in number 2722 . . . and the number of their soldiers [?], not including those of Zalan and Gabal, was 12,048.

At this juncture Jamal ad-Din, whom 'Amda Seyon had made governor of the country in place of his brother Sabr ad-Din, revolted, and he sent a message to the king of 'Adal to this effect. "The king of Abyssinia is shut up in a mountain defile from which he cannot get out. Now you must do one of two things; either take gifts to him or do not. If you take gifts to him, before you do so sell your wife and children and all that you possess, for if you give him gifts you will make yourself and your posterity his servants for ever. If you wish to act wisely, send him no gifts, and gather together all your men who are able to fight with sword, bow, shield, javelin, lance and club, and I will join you with my cavalry and infantry and we will fall upon the king and his army and kill them with one blow." . . . The king of 'Adal and all the other kings collected their soldiers, and four months had elapsed before they had joined the army of Jamal ad-Din. When the host was ready for war this arrogant Arab began to boast what he would do to the Christians, and with the view of securing all the spoil of the Christians for himself he decided not to wait for the troops from Ifat, because the loot would not be sufficient for their king and himself.

Now at that moment it happened that 'Amda Seyon was alone, and he had none of his picked troops with him. His regiments of "Eyes of needles" and "Wolves" and the Korani horsemen, and the Barya, and the Harab Gonda, and many other great regiments were absent on duty elsewhere. When they fought they struck like eagles, and leaped like rams, their feet were like stone rollers and the noise of their feet was like that of the sea. And 'Amda Seyon lay sick in his tent, and for seven days and seven nights he had eaten and drunk nothing. He had sent out one of his men called Zana Yamanu with the dogs into the desert to hunt game for him, and whilst this man was hunting he came across the Arab army; he returned forthwith to the king and told him what he had seen, adding, "We have come back to die with you." The king sent out horsemen to reconnoitre, and they reported that the enemy were in numbers like a cloud of grasshoppers which had covered the earth. On hearing this he struggled up from his bed and tried to go outside the tent, but when he began to put on his war belt, his legs doubled up under him and he collapsed on his bed. His servants lifted him up and put on his belt, and he managed to go outside the tent, but he swayed from side to side through weakness. His two queens followed him and begged him to give up the idea of fighting, but he replied, "Am I to die like a woman? Certainly not. I know how to die like a soldier." Then he turned and ordered the queens to return to their tents. The elder of them, Djan Mangasha, prayed with tears to God to strengthen her lord, the priests prayed, and the king prayed, committing himself into the hands of God.

Meanwhile the Arab armies were advancing, every man armed, and in number they were as the stars of heaven and the sand of the sea-shore, and the rain clouds of the sky; as they marched the earth shook, and the wild beasts were so terrified that they ran before them and took refuge in the camp of 'Amda Seyon. And the queen sent to 'Amda Seyon a quantity of Jordan water and some dust from Golgotha. The king called the priest Takla Seyon and told him to baptize him with the water, as he stood there in full armor; and as the water fell upon him his weakness departed and the strength of God came upon him. And the king himself sprinkled his horses and his men with the water. The Arab army came on and in its van were a number of women who shrieked out curses. 'Amda Seyon sprinkled some of the water about to annul the effects of the curses, and sent on a detachment of horsemen to open the battle; these turned and fled, and entreated him to fight in his camp. When he refused, his friends kissed him and fled, leaving him alone to meet death as best he might. As they departed he hurled reproaches after them, and then being filled with rage, he sprang up like a tiger and leaped upon his horse . . . and ordered his chief officer of cavalry, called Zanasfare, to ride into the enemy's ranks on the right. Zanasfare, followed by five horsemen among whom was the king's son Saf-Sagad, did as he was bid. The king charged the enemy on the left, looking neither before him nor behind him, and at once became the target for arrows, javelins and spears, and the object of a shower of blows. Nothing stopped him, and when the enemy saw him spearing two men at a time they broke and fled. The soldiers who had forsaken him returned and joined Zanasfare and his men, and drove the fleeing enemy into a deep ditch which God seemed to have prepared for them. Then the king dismounted and attacked the enemy with his sword and smote them down until his strength failed. The enemy were men of huge stature and wore their hair hanging down to their waists like women, and though they tied themselves to each other by means of their clothes so that no man might flee, they were conquered by the king. 'Amda Seyon remounted his horse and set out with his soldiers to cut down those who were fleeing, and meanwhile the Abyssinian women came out and stripped the dead and carried their weapons back to their camp. The battle raged for six hours, until sunset, by which time the Muslims were either scattered or slain, and the king's arm was attached so tightly to his lance by the blood of the slain that force

had to be used to detach it. The dead lay round about in heaps, and the wounded could not be counted.

When the battle was over 'Amda Seyon returned to his camp, and entering his chapel gave thanks to God for the victory He had given him.

THE HILALIAN INVASION

In the middle of the eleventh century the Maghreb was invaded by Bedouin Arabs, the Beni Hilal and Beni Sulaim tribes. They were nomads who had moved from Arabia into Egypt. The Fatimid caliph of Cairo, anxious to rid his country of this troublesome element, urged them to invade Ifriqiya, where his authority had recently been repudiated. Cyrenaica, Tripolitania, the Fezzan, and much of Ifriqiya were overrun, and many of the Beni Hilal ultimately settled in Morocco. Historians are still weighing the degrees of destruction or enrichment the Arabs wrought in North Africa. Their legendary history and military exploits are described in a lengthy epic, Sira Beni Hilal, that was subsequently set down in Arabic. This work, still part of Arab Africa's oral tradition, is the source of the following selection, which describes the tribe's migration and conquest of Ifriqiya. The hero is Abu Zeid, and his adversary, the sultan of Ilam, is thought to be a Tuareg Berber chieftain.

Abu Zeid gathered his people together and addressed them saying:—

Make ready for war O! sons of the
    Beni Hilal.
I shall take you on a journey.
And you must not even ask why.
I shall encamp with you in the vast
    open spaces,
Fit for the galloping of horses.
I shall encamp with you by Amdizira
    and by Tiziriya.
By Kimar and Ligiya the Pleasant.
Three ponds, the pools of Abu Riz
Which have made you prosperous.
There will be camels like the moun-
    tain Abu Faja.
They march onwards and appear
    from behind to sway backward
    and forward,
I shall encamp with you by the lakes
    of Amseriha which make a chain
    of pools,
We shall catch the young of the
    hippopotamus,
And eat the young of the fish
    "Umm Sharib".

His people said to him, "This is to our own liking." Again he addressed them saying:—

O! sons of the Beni Hilal.
I shall take you on a journey.
Where there are neither gad flies nor
    sweat flies.
Nor mosquitoes to prevent one from
    sleeping.
But wave on wave of the seven fin-
    gered "Abu Asaba" grass,

And on the ant-hills
Where the hartbeeste is striped
Where you will eat and sleep.

His people were willing and said, "Take us away." He said to them:—

If we migrate on a Tuesday,
People will say that is a peculiar day.
If we start on a Wednesday,
They will say that is the fourth of
    the days.
If we start on a Thursday
They will say that is an unpropitious
    day.
If we start on a Friday,
They will say that bad luck will
    come our way:
Our horses will be captured,
Our leaders will die.
If we start on a Saturday,
They will say that we shall not see
    the next Saturday.
If we start on a Sunday,
They will say that Sunday is a divi-
    sion between the living and the
    many dead.
If we start on a Monday,
They will say that this is the day
    that will be propitious:
Its mornings may be ill-omened, but
    its afternoons are sweet indeed.

They said, "Thus it is. Let us migrate with him." So we set off with him.

We leave the old women on the
    highway,
And we let the slave-girl, wearer of

the loin-cloth,
Sleep and awake in her shoes.
We let the slow-marching Bazgi camel
Lie down and rise again with his loads.
We let the mare Umm Dar'an
Lie down and rise again in her bridle
We let the goats, long-eared and long-horned,
Lie down and rise again with binding on their teats.
Abu Zeid went again to his mother and said to her:—
Mother, O! my mother.
We shall journey as the Zerma,
And as a king,
And as the prophets journeyed.
When they set out in search of Mecca.
His mother said to him:—
Go take counsel with your men
And let them tie the food bags on their horses,
Twin son, whose father and grand-sire were both twins.
Do not undertake a night journey:
Let your wives travel in the day time,
And let the horses march behind them.
When your army lines up for battle
You take your stand between the lines of horses.
Like a rainbow
That shines from morn till night.
(Setting out on an expedition) is difficult for the man who has not seven young slave-girls,
With their bags of cumin seed,
And whose owner can take his repose near hanging draperies.
The horses of the strong and brave (Abu Zeid) assemble and line up in battle array,

The fat man dies and becomes food for birds.
Again Abu Zeid spoke and said:—
Hard for the man who has not seven newly-calved cows,
Their udders full of milk,
Hard for him who has not seven warriors
To shoulder the hardships of war.
Hard for him who has not seven concubines
To bring him edible fruits.
Hard for him who has not seven slaves
To carry the camel-bags.
We saddle our sleek steeds
Their well-kept bodies all covered with fat,
Our spears in our hands drawn ready for use, the long ones towering above the short ones.
Our followers mounted on barren mares which appeared like geldings,
Old men with beards, and youths the pride of maidens
Chewing the tobacco of prostitutes.
Saddle and mount for now the day of truth has come.
Again he said:—
I went out of my way to water and filled my water-skin,
And watered my steed,
Took up a short coat of mail and donned it,
And took up Al Jaz's coat and with it tied my loins.
The back of my head is as hard as nails,
Away on the outskirts of the town I heard people praising me.
So Abu Zeid went away with his tribesmen and came to Ilam [Tunis]. His men were so numerous that the wild animals came to the Sultan of Ilam's town, and the Sultan's wife said, "The whole of the bush is full of these wild animals." The Sultan of Ilam sent one of his men into the bush to bring them news of what was happening. He went off and found that the crowd was the tribesmen of Abu Zeid. He walked along their ranks for

about forty days, and even then he did not get to the end of them. So he went back to the Sultan of Ilam and gave him the news. The Sultan said, "Of what does their wealth consist?" The man said to the Sultan:—
Their wealth is beasts whose backs have humps,
And whose lips are split.
They call them "Bazgi,"
And we call them "Ibl."
I fear them, they will despoil our land.
Let us go out and meet them in the bush.
So they went out towards them, but before they came to them they found a slave-girl belonging to Abu Zeid, who was digging up ant-hills. They said to her, "Whose slave-girl are you?" She answered, "I am Abu Zeid's slave-girl." They said to her, "Where is the place in which Abu Zeid has encamped?" She answered, "Beneath that tree yonder, he and his tribesmen are there." They said to her, "Where is the tree that will seat him and all his tribesmen?" She said to them, "The tree has seven large branches from each of which shoot other seven branches, and beneath each branch there are seven wells, and by each well there are seven troughs, and at each trough there water seventy-seven horses and seventy-seven shield-bearers and seventy-seven herds of camels." Then the Sultan of Ilam said to his tribesmen, "Go back home. We cannot prevail against them. So they went back. Abu Zeid's slave-girl cried out and Abu Zeid heard and came to where the slave-girl was. Now the people of the Sultan of Ilam were carrying water in water-skins, and because they were so much afraid they poured the water on the ground and urinated, and the ground all turned to mud because of the dampness and prevented Abu Zeid from following them.

Now a slave of Abu Zeid was herding cattle, and he fell asleep. His name was Sa'id Zerbul, the son of Sa'idi Jugongot. This slave held his feet in the air [while he slept] and he had long legs. When the people of Ilam in the town saw this, they mounted their horses and came to where the slave was and found him asleep. They thrust him with a spear, and he thought that it was a mosquito which had bitten him. He touched the place where the spear had pierced him and said:—

Here there are neither gad flies,
Nor sweat flies,
Nor mosquitoes to hinder one from
sleeping,
What is it then that is biting me in
this place?

Then he opened his eyes and saw mounted men completely surrounding him. He said to them, "If you are hunters, away with you and hunt your game: and if you drive guinea-fowl, be off and chase them." They said to him,

Sa'id Zerbul
Son of a woman whose food is chaff,
Her favorite food,
Who will retrieve your herds when
the cattle raids come?

Sa'id answered them,

The man who retrieves our cattle
when we are harried
Is Abu Zeid, who keeps every one
right,
Abu Zeid the left-handed,
Who is like rain that falls from
morn till the afternoon,
He and his nephew, with the broad
chest and few bad qualities.

At that they frightened away the cattle, and he said to them, "Why have you driven off the cattle in the middle of the day?" He went off home, and Abu Zeid came out with his men against the Sultan of Ilam, and the Sultan, too, came out with his men against Abu Zeid. When they had drawn up in battle array the Sultan of Ilam said to his tribesmen, "To the man who kills Abu Zeid and brings his camel to me, I shall give wife upon wife and town upon town, and I shall give him my daughter Aze in marriage for him to live with her as his wife." Some of Abu Zeid's followers said of him:—

There is not amongst us or in our
tribe any one like him,
Whoever meets him [in battle] will

not live to rejoin his family.
As to meeting a maiden—
Food, even, he will not eat.
If Abu Zeid should charge at us
with his horse
Our mares would drop their foals;
And if he should slash at us with his
sword
Our spears would be twisted out of
shape.

Abu Zeid's followers said to him, "We are hungry, excuse us and allow us to go and eat and satisfy our hunger and then we shall fight." Abu Zeid excused them, but said to their women folk, "Your men will break faith with me. Laziness has taken hold of them."

Now the son of the Sultan of Ilam's sister was putting on his armor and was mounting his horse to come against Abu Zeid's people, saying, "O! sons of the Beni Hilal, who amongst you is my equal or my uncle's equal?" They said to him "There is no one amongst us like you or like your uncle." Abu Zeid took up his sword, and sharpening it, would go in amongst the people of Ilam: and he turned to the Sultan of Ilam's nephew and killed him. Then he came to the Sultan of Ilam and caught hold of him and said to Diyab "Stab him!" So Diyab stabbed him. When he caught hold of him, Abu Zeid said to him, "Who am I, O! Sultan of Ilam?" The Sultan of Ilam said to him, "You are indeed a jester, a son of mirth." Abu Zeid said to him, "I am not a jester nor one of humor's sons. My mother is a Sherif. My forbears were as the prophets." At that he killed him. When he came to them, his people said to Abu Zeid, "We have brought the white mare whose galloping is like the flapping of a bird's wings, and who can fly as a bird, and [Ilam] was on its back making a great shout." Abu Zeid said to them:—

Since we set out we have drunk only
fresh milk
And eaten prime meat.

Again Abu Zeid returned to the people of Ilam, and took prisoner the son of the Sultan of Ilam and said to him:—

We are brothers of yours
And your neighbors
Let us meet, and let a pact of peace
Be made between us and you:
You take our daughters in marriage
And we shall take yours,
And let us become related by mar-
riage.

The Sultan of Ilam's son refused, saying:—

Life did not last for ever for Cana'an
Whose house was of iron and silver
and gold and coral.

Abu Zeid's men said to him "Kill him." They said:—

Life did not last for ever for Thamra
Whose mother's children were nine
in number,
Whose father's children were eight,
And whose own numbered ten.
They all died. Her eyes came out,
Her legs broke,
She begged water to drink but got
not even that and she died.

So Abu Zeid killed him and his men despoiled their land.

FOLK WISDOM

These Moroccan proverbs, a commingling of Berber and Arabic cultures, were collected in this century by Edward Westermarck.

The pumpkin gives birth and the fence has the trouble.

A stone from the hand of a friend is an apple.

The tar of my country is better than the honey of others.

If you are a peg, endure the knocking; if you are a mallet, strike.

Among walnuts only the empty one speaks.

The world has not promised anything to anybody.

An old cat will not learn how to dance.

A pilgrim caravan is shown on its way to Mecca in this thirteenth-century Muslim painting.

OUT
OF
ARABIA

The Great Mosque at Kilwa, founded in the thirteenth century, is a silent reminder of the once-powerful trade center on Africa's east coast.

DOWN THE EAST COAST

Islam's penetration of East Africa was based on the development of maritime trade and was essentially peaceful. Difficult terrain and strong Christian states in Nubia and Ethiopia were obstacles to expansion from the north by land. However, by following sea routes long used by others, Muslims from Arabia and Persia settled along the East African coast, where towns already engaged in a trade that reached to China and Indonesia were discovered. Intermarrying with Africans and implanting Islamic religion and culture from the Red Sea coast to Mozambique, they created a string of city-states and sultanates like Kilwa in present-day Tanzania, whose wealth rested on the export of gold and ivory.

Evoking the image of Sinbad the Sailor, the Mombasa seaman at left combines Arab and African strains. Men like him, sailing Arab dhows (below), with their distinctive lateen sails, have conducted the commerce of East African coastal ports for centuries. A Ming Dynasty Chinese plate at right, probably from the fifteenth century, was discovered in an Arab burial ground in Dar es Salaam, evidence of the trade between Africa and far Asia.

171

Islamic armies of North Africa, like those seen at the left in a twelfth-century view of a naval assault on Spain, included Berbers as well as Muslims from the Sudanese states south of the Sahara. The Muslim standard shown below was carried on an expedition to the Iberian Peninsula and was captured by Christians at the siege of Salado.

ACROSS NORTH AFRICA

Unlike its gradual expansion in East Africa, Islam virtually exploded across North Africa. Armies of Bedouins, Arabian Desert dwellers, entered Egypt in A.D. 639 and by 711 were invading the Iberian Peninsula from the Maghreb, far in the west. Despite divisions and almost constant warfare among rival Muslim groups in the following centuries, the Islamic religion became firmly rooted. Everywhere in North Africa, save among a minority in Egypt, Christianity all but died out. Islam gave enduring cultural unity to the region, but competing factions kept it politically divided. As a result, several new capitals were built, including that of Fez below, founded in 808 by the Idrisids in the western Maghreb.

Swathed in a voluminous turban and colorful robes, this horseman of modern Kano in northern Nigeria reflects Arab influences of long ago.

INTO
THE DESERT

The map below, the first European depiction of the region of West Africa, was drawn in 1375 by Abraham Cresques. Relying on information from North African Muslim traders, the artist shows the Atlas range as a stone wall; he describes the Muslim ruler of Mali, Mansa Musa, shown lower right, as "the richest and most noble king in all the land."

The Arab armies that overran North Africa made little more than occasional raids into the Fezzan and trips of exploration in the desert south of their newly won territories. The trans-Saharan trade with the black peoples of the Sudan was left in the hands of Tuareg and other Berber tribesmen who had been plying the caravan routes across the desert for centuries. Only gradually, as these tribes became converted to Islam, was the Muslims' influence felt in the Sudanese states. But their involvement deepened early in the ninth century when Arabs, lured by the gold trade, established increasing contact with the rulers of Kanem, near Lake Chad, and of Ghana. By the eleventh century the kings of Kanem had converted to Islam, and mosques, like the one at left at Agadès in the present-day Niger Republic, arose across the savanna country of the sub-Sahara. In time all the principal states of the Sudan were Muslim, and Black cities such as Timbuktu and Gao had become centers of Islamic power and learning.

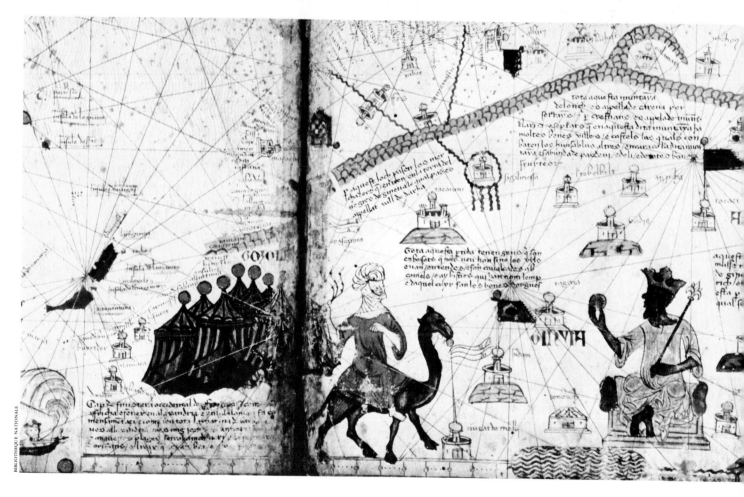

Chapter Five

KINGDOMS OF WEST AFRICA

(c. A.D. 500–1600)

by

A. Adu Boahen

IN WEST AFRICA, the area bounded to the north by the Sahara desert, to the south by the Atlantic Ocean, and to the east by Lake Chad and modern Cameroon, a number of independent states and empires evolved in the period between A.D. 500 and 1470. Among them were Ghana, Mali, Songhai, Kanem-Bornu, and the Hausa states, which were clustered along the southern frontier of the Sahara. Still farther south, between these states and the forest region, arose the Mole-Dagbane states and the Mossi states. Finally, in the forest and coastal zones of Guinea emerged the states of Takrur and Wolof in the region of the Senegal and Gambia rivers, or Senegambia; the Akan, Fante, and Ga states in the area of modern Ghana; and the states of Ife, Oyo, and Benin in Nigeria.

The questions that we shall attempt to answer here are: When did these states and empires crystallize and when did each attain its peak of greatness? How and why were they formed, and how were they governed? And what cultures and civilizations did they develop before the arrival of the Portuguese?

It is significant that the earliest of these states to grow into large kingdoms and empires were those in the savanna immediately to the south of the Sahara. Of these three, namely Ghana, Mali, and Songhai, the first to reach maturity was Ghana, peopled by the Soninke. It is not known for certain when it took form as a state. However, if there were as many as twenty-two kings before the rise of Islam in A.D. 622, as the oral traditions of Ghana tells, and if by the time the Persian geographer Al-Fazari was writing in A.D. 773–774 Ghana was already well known to North African and Middle Eastern traders as the Land of Gold, it is not unreasonable to suppose that it emerged as a full-fledged state in the fifth or sixth century A.D.

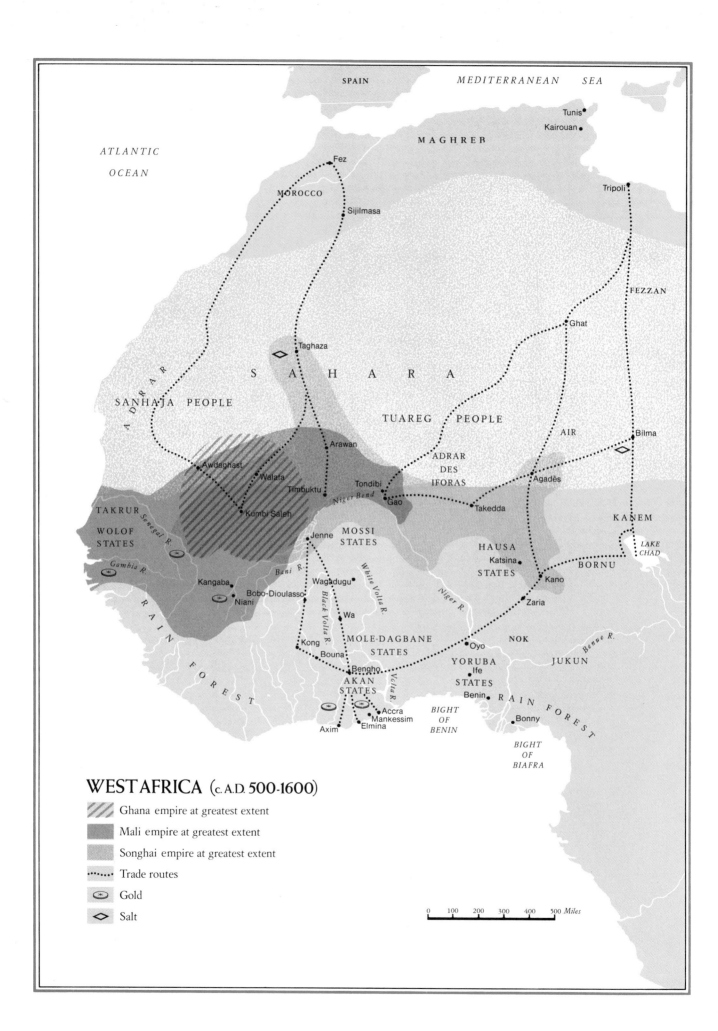

SPAIN   MEDITERRANEAN   SEA

Tunis
Kairouan

MAGHREB

ATLANTIC
OCEAN

Fez
MOROCCO
Sijilmasa

Tripoli

FEZZAN

S   A   H   A   R   A

Taghaza

A D R A R

SANHAJA PEOPLE

TUAREG   PEOPLE

Ghat

AIR

Bilma

Arawan

Awdaghast

Walata

Timbuktu

Tondibi

Gao

ADRAR
DES
IFORAS

Agadès

KANEM

Niger Bend

LAKE
CHAD

TAKRUR

Senegal R.

Kumbi Saleh

Takedda

Gambia R.

WOLOF
STATES

MOSSI
STATES

HAUSA
Katsina
STATES

BORNU

Kano

Kangaba

Bani R.

Jenne

Wagadugu

White Volta R.

Niger R.

Zaria

Bobo-Dioulasso

Niani

Black Volta R.

Wa

NOK

Benue R.

RAIN

Kong

MOLE-DAGBANE
STATES

Oyo

YORUBA

JUKUN

Bouna

Bengho

Ife
STATES

FOREST

AKAN
STATES

Volta R.

Benin

Accra
Mankessim

RAIN   FOREST

Axim

Elmina

BIGHT
OF
BENIN

Bonny

BIGHT
OF
BIAFRA

WEST AFRICA (c. A.D. 500-1600)

Ghana empire at greatest extent

Mali empire at greatest extent

Songhai empire at greatest extent

Trade routes

Gold

Salt

0   100   200   300   400   500 Miles

There is no doubt that by A.D. 1000 Ghana had attained the peak of its power, an empire ruling over a number of smaller tribute-paying states and monopolizing West Africa's enormous and valuable gold trade to North Africa and Europe. This meant that Ghana and its formidable armies also dominated the roads of the Sahara and the savanna. Ibn Hawqal, the first known Arab explorer of the western Sudan, offers in his tenth-century *Book of Ways and Provinces* his impression of the Ghanaian sovereign: "the wealthiest of all kings on the face of the earth on account of the riches he owns and the hoards of gold acquired by him and inherited from his predecessors since ancient times." He based his estimate on the quantity of goods he saw being shipped through the Moroccan entrepôt of Sijilmasa.

Ghana's capital city was then Kumbi Saleh, which the Arab writer Al-Bakri described in 1067 as consisting of "two towns situated on a plain, one principally inhabited by Muslim traders, the other settled by the emperor and the local populace." The Muslim town was "large and possessed twelve mosques; in one of these mosques they assembled for the prayers on Fridays. There were imams and muezzins as well as jurists and scholars."

Ghana, however, began to decline during the second half of the eleventh century. Saharan Berbers, driven by territorial ambitions and inspired by Almoravid zeal, succeeded in disorganizing trade and stirring up rebellion among Ghana's tributaries. The empire was overthrown in 1235 by one of its former vassal states, the Susu kingdom, under its ruler Sumanguru Kante.

Mali, which succeeded Ghana, had emerged as a rather small principality by the end of the ninth century A.D. Between the eleventh and the thirteenth centuries it was dominated first by Ghana and then by the Susu kingdom, and it was not until the reign of Sundiata (1230–1255) that Mali embarked on its career of conquest. Building upon the administrative model of Ghana, it extended its trading empire over large parts of the western Sudan, and through the leadership of Mansa Kankan Musa, who reigned from 1312 to 1337, it absorbed such centers as Timbuktu, Gao, and Walata. Ibn Battuta, visiting Mali two decades after Mansa Musa's death, was astounded by the peace, order, and racial tolerance that prevailed in the empire:

> The Negroes possess some admirable qualities. They are seldom unjust and have a greater abhorrence of injustice than any other people. Their Sultan shows no mercy to any one guilty of the least act of it. There is complete security in their country. Neither traveler nor inhabitant in it has any-

thing to fear from robbers or men of violence. They do not confiscate the property of any white man who dies in their country, even if it be uncounted wealth. On the contrary, they give it into the charge of some trust-worthy person among the whites, until the rightful heir takes possession of it.

Although the Portuguese, when they first came ashore in 1441, found that most of the states on the coast as well as in the immediate hinterland were still under the control of Mali, the state was already in a period of decline and Songhai was on the rise.

The Songhai people, with the city-state of Gao, or Al-Kawkaw, as their political center, had become active in the trans-Saharan trade by the end of the ninth century. Al-Yaqubi described Gao in 871 as "the greatest of the realms of the as-Sudan, the most important and most powerful, and all the other kingdoms obey its rulers." However, until the last quarter of the fourteenth century, it was controlled first by Ghana and then by Mali. Ibn Battuta, visiting Gao during the era of its vassalage to Mali, described it as "one of the finest towns in the Negroland. It is also one of their biggest and best provisioned towns with rice in plenty, milk and fish. . . ."

In 1375, however, Gao broke away from Mali, though it did not grow into an empire until the reign of Sunni Ali, the celebrated politician, soldier, and administrator who reigned from 1464 until 1492. The empire was consolidated and its frontiers further extended by the second of its most famous rulers, Askia Muhammad the Great. It was during his reign, which lasted from 1493 to 1528, that Songhai attained its peak, controlling the entire central region of the western Sudan.

Leo Africanus, a Christianized Arab geographer who visited Songhai in about 1510, has left us some vivid accounts of its intellectual and commercial life. For example, Gao was a town full of "exceeding rich merchants: and hither continually resort great store of Negroes which buy cloth here brought out of Barbarie and Europe. . . . It is a woonder to see what plentie of Merchandize is dayly brought hither, and how costly and sumptuous all things be."

However, during the last decade of that very century, for reasons to be discussed later, this sprawling and famous empire completely disintegrated. Its rulers were forced to retreat south along the Niger into their ancestral home in the region of Dendi.

In conformity with the Hamitic hypothesis, scholars of

the 1930's and 1940's attributed the foundation of these three states, as well as that of Kanem-Bornu and the Hausa states (which will be discussed in greater detail in Chapter Six), simply to some white-skinned invaders from the north. More recently, the introduction of the use of iron has been emphasized as the determining factor. To the present writer, their ascendance was the result of several major developments. The first was the rapid growth of population in the area immediately to the south of the Sahara and especially in the regions of the Niger Bend and the Senegambia. The second was the development of the caravan trade and the subsequent activities of wealthy and therefore powerful and ambitious families. The third was the spread of Islam.

The steady increase of the savanna's population between 1000 B.C. and A.D. 300 or 400 was caused in part by the Neolithic revolution (that is, the change from the hunting of wild animals and the collection of wild fruits to the cultivation of food crops and domestication of animals). Historians and ethnobotanists are still hotly debating whether or not there was an independent Neolithic revolution among the Mande peoples in the region of the Niger Bend in about 5000 B.C. But even if this revolution was introduced into Africa from Asia via Egypt, there is no doubt that the area between the Niger Bend and the middle Senegal River as well as the areas around Lake Chad proved a superior environment for the cereal crops, especially sorghum and millet, which were among the first crops to be cultivated. The Mande and the Kanuri peoples of those areas must, therefore, have obtained an early lead over all the others. Since they could also supplement their diet through fishing, these peoples must have been able to produce food in such quantities that their numbers multiplied. As the contemporary British Africanist J. D. Fage has pointed out, this Neolithic revolution must have also led to "the beginnings of urbanization and of organized government and administration, and, even, perhaps, the flourishing of the idea of a king as a god-like being supreme over all his subjects."

This increase in population must have been further accelerated by the steady desiccation of the Sahara from about 3000 B.C. onward. As the Sahara slowly assumed its barren look, a process that was complete by 1500 B.C., some of its inhabitants began to drift into the savanna belt.

The use of iron tools must also have had its effect on population growth in that it facilitated agriculture, but surely it was not, as some scholars have argued, the principal factor in the rise of the western Sudanese states. If this were so, it would follow that the states would have emerged

much earlier—nearer 300 B.C., when iron technology is thought to have reached the Nok culture on the lower Niger—and first in the east rather than in the west as, in fact, happened.

It would seem then to this writer that by about the last century B.C. or the first century A.D. the whole of the savanna in general, and the regions of Lake Chad, the Niger Bend, and Nok in particular, must have been occupied by large populations living in family, lineage, or clan groups, in villages bound together by kinship ties or even in city-states and small kingdoms ruled possibly by "divine" kings. Something else must have been needed to stimulate one or more of these nuclei to develop into larger kingdoms and, eventually, empires, and this stimulus must have been provided by the caravan trade. From rock paintings of two-wheeled horse-drawn war chariots and from other archeological data, it is clear that by 1000 B.C. the caravan trade was well established along two main routes. These were a western route through Morocco to the Niger Bend and a central route through the Fezzan, Ghat, and Adrar des Iforas, possibly to the region of Gao on the Niger. The main beasts of burden were bullocks and, after 1200 B.C., horses. It is equally clear from the fifth-century B.C. accounts of Herodotus and from other ancient Greek and Roman sources that both the Carthaginians and the Romans were trading with the people of the savanna belt through Berber intermediaries settled in the Fezzan and the western Sahara.

However, this trade could not have been very extensive until the introduction of the camel. The use of this singularly endowed beast of burden spread westward and then southward into the Sahara, and as a result, a complicated network of caravan routes across the Sahara was developed between about A.D. 200 and 500. To the Morocco-Niger route and the old Garamantes' route from Tripoli to Chad and to Gao was added a caravan route from Egypt to Gao by way of the Saharan oases, including Ghat and the future site of Agadès.

As trade expanded with the use of the camel, not only did more and more people grow wealthy but handicrafts, mining, and agriculture were stimulated. So, too, urban centers grew in size and influence. Wealth, of course, generates among individuals and families still greater ambition and the desire to control more and more trading activities and trade routes. It is the activities of the talented members of these families (especially of such men as Sundiata and Mansa Musa of Mali and Sunni Ali and Askia Muhammad of Songhai) and not the mere use of iron that bring about

The people of the Nok culture, in northern Nigeria, produced these sublime terra-cotta heads more than two thousand years ago. These and other artifacts offer a glimpse of an emerging agricultural society, which, further research may show, extended over hundreds of square miles. Material remains also indicate that the Nok were versed in ironworking and adept in making stone tools, not unlike those that are in use today.

ALL: F. L. KENETT

the creation of large states and empires.

The people who would be the first beneficiaries of this increasing trade would naturally be those living in the border zone between the Sahara and the savanna, an ideal position from which to play the lucrative role of the middleman. The Soninke of Ghana and the Kanuri of the old state of Kanem were the peoples at the crossroads of the Sahara and the savanna, and they were among the first to develop kingdoms and then empires. The fact that no large kingdoms emerged in Hausaland until the fourteenth century, when the north-south trade began there, provides a further indication of the importance of caravan trade in state-building.

The final factor, which did not cause, but rather accelerated or facilitated to some extent the growth of the empires of Mali and Songhai, as well as Kanem-Bornu and the Hausa states, must have been the introduction of Islām. This religion penetrated the Sahara via the caravan routes and reached the savanna in the ninth and tenth centuries.

Islam is not just a body of doctrines, but a complete way of life, having its own laws, its own system of taxation and administration of justice, its own statecraft, and its own language and traditions of scholarship. Islam's adoption by the rulers of Gao in the tenth century and of Mali and Kanem in the eleventh century must have given them access to all these sciences as well as the means by which to create an educated bureaucracy. A more intense exposure to Islam was gained by those who took the hadj, or pilgrimage, to the Islamic civilization of the Middle East.

It is known, for instance, that on Mansa Musa's celebrated pilgrimage to Mecca in 1324–1325, he met the Spanish scholar, poet, and architect As-Sahili, whom he successfully persuaded to go with him to Mali. It is also known

that not only did As-Sahili insist on a strict observance of Islam, but he revolutionized architecture of Mali and of the western Sudan in general by introducing brick as the building material for mosques and palaces. Similarly, during his equally famous hadj to Mecca in 1497 Askia Muhammad the Great also met and befriended great scholars such as Abd ar-Rahman as-Suyuti and Muhammad al-Majhili, with whom he began a lifelong correspondence. The latter actually visited him in Songhai and gave him as well as the king of Kano a great deal of advice on religion and politics.

Nevertheless, the governments of all these early Sudanese empires were of the divine-kingship type, a typically African conception, indicating that these states did not derive their political institutions from Islam, but possibly from ancient Ghana or, in any case, from indigenous Mande institutions. At the head of each was a hereditary monarch. He was assisted by a council of ministers, whose members, following the introduction of Islam, were mostly literate Muslims. Al-Bakri, writing in 1067, tells us that even though the king of Ghana held animistic beliefs, the official in charge of his treasury and the majority of his ministers were Muslims. Unfortunately, we do not have the titles of the ministers of Ghana, but they were probably similar to those of Songhai, whose cabinet included the *hi-koy* (the commander of the navy), *dyina-koy* (commander in chief of the army), *hari-farma* (minister in charge of navigation and fishing), *fari-mundyo* (minister of taxation), *waney-farma* (minister in charge of property), *korey-farma* (minister in charge of foreigners), and *sao-koy* (minister in charge of forests).

The divine-kingship nature of the government is further borne out by descriptions that we have of their court protocol and ceremonial. According to Al-Bakri:

A caravan approaching Timbuktu, the intellectual and trading center of the Songhai empire, as depicted in an 1853 German engraving

BARTH, *Travels in Central Africa*, 1857

The king [of Ghana] adorns himself like a woman wearing necklaces round his neck and bracelets on his forearms, and when he sits before the people he puts on a high cap decorated with gold and wrapped in a turban of fine cloth. The court of Appeal is held in a domed pavilion around which stand ten horses covered with gold-embroidered materials. Behind the king stand ten pages holding shields and swords decorated with gold and on his right are the sons of the vassal kings of his country wearing splendid garments and their hair plaited with gold. The governor of the city sits on the ground before the king and around are ministers seated likewise. At the door of the pavilion are dogs of excellent pedigree who hardly ever leave the place where the king is, guarding him. Round their necks, they wear collars of gold and silver studded with a number of balls of the same metal. The audience is announced by the beating of a drum which they call daba, made from a long hollow log. When the people who profess the same religion as the king approach him, they fall on their knees and sprinkle dust on their heads for this is their way of showing respect for him. As for the Muslims, they greet him only by clapping their hands.

Ibn Battuta, who visited and had an audience with Mansa Sulaiman, the brother and successor of Mansa Musa, describes another court ritual:

On certain days the Sultan holds audience in the palace yard.... The Sultan comes out of a door in a corner of the palace, carrying a bow in his hand and a quiver on his back. On his head he has a golden skull cap...[he] is preceded by his musicians.... As he takes his seat the drums, trumpets and bugles are sounded.... Two saddled and bridled horses are brought, along with two goats which they hold to serve as a protection against the evil eye.... The Negroes are of all people the most submissive to their king and the most abject in their behavior before him. They swear by his name.... If he summons any of them while he is holding an audience in his pavilion, the person summoned takes off his clothes and puts on worn garments, removes his turban and dons a dirty skull-cap, and enters with his garments and trousers raised knee-high. He goes forward in an attitude of humility and dejection, and knocks the ground hard with his elbows, then stands with bowed head and bent back listening to what he says. If any one addresses the king and receives a reply from him, he uncovers his back and throws dust over his head and back for all the world like a bather splashing himself with water. I used to wonder how it was they did not blind themselves.

And finally, from Leo Africanus' eyewitness account of the court of Songhai at Timbuktu:

> The rich king of Tombuto hath many plates and scepters of gold, some whereof weigh 1300 poundes . . . and he keeps a magnificent and well furnished court. When he travelleth any whither he rideth upon a camell, which is led by some of his noblemen; and so he doth likewise when hee goeth to warfar, and all his souldiers ride upon horses. Whosoever will speake unto this king must first fall downe before his feete, & then taking up earth must sprinkle it upon his owne head & shoulders: which custom is ordinarily observed by them that never saluted the king before, or come as ambassadors from other princes.

The drums, the linguists, the praise singers, the gold swords and caps, the prostrations and the removal of sandals in the presence of the king are closely observed to this very day in some courts of African kings (for example, among the Akan of modern Ghana). It is true that both Mali and Songhai added such Muslim trappings as banquets and Turkish and Egyptian bodyguards to their courts, while some of their symbols of investiture—the tunic, turban, and sword—were certainly Islamic. But the basic court ceremonial and protocol, and the position of the king in both Mali and Songhai, were definitely pre-Islamic and African in origin, most probably deriving from those of ancient Ghana.

However, some differences appear in the system of royal succession. It is clear from Al-Bakri's account that like the present practice among the Akan people, royal succession in Ghana was matrilineal, whereas in the later Mali and Songhai empires it was patrilineal. Al-Bakri was informed that Tunka Manin succeeded not his father but his maternal uncle. And as if to dispel any doubts, he added: "This is their custom and their habit, that the kingdom is inherited only by the son of the king's sister." He goes on to give an explanation of what appeared to him to be a most odd and non-Muslim practice: "He the king has no doubt that his successor is a son of his sister, while he is not certain that his son is in fact his own, and he does not rely on the genuineness of this relationship."

Although the fourteenth-century Tunisian historian Ibn Khaldun did report that one of the kings of Mali, Abu Bakr, was the son of a daughter of Sundiata, and although

it has been inferred from this that royal succession in Mali at times went through the female line, a recent authority has shown that this was an exception to the rule. It would appear then that royal succession in both Mali and Songhai generally followed the patrilineal rather than the matrilineal rule. This difference might well be due to the impact of Islam.

The systems of provincial government in these Sudanese empires show some differences, but in degree rather than in kind. In all three cases the kings were directly responsible for the administration of the core, or metropolitan part, of the empire, which they divided into provinces ruled by governors. In the case of both Mali and Songhai, these governors either were members of the royal family or former generals. The governors in turn appointed district chiefs to administer a number of villages, each of which was ruled by a village chief.

The other parts of the empire, consisting of states conquered and reduced to vassal or tributary status, were governed in a variety of ways. In Ghana it would appear that the states remained under their own rulers and that their main obligations were to pay annual tribute and to supply contingents to the king's army when called upon to do so. Sons of vassal rulers were occasionally kept at the king's court to ensure their fathers' continued allegiance. In Mali the same system prevailed, with some minor improvements: the sovereigns of the conquered states retained their right to rule, but only after being invested by the Mansa and given a Mande title; the swearing of allegiance and the payment of tribute were seen as proofs of loyalty.

The kings of Songhai, especially Askia Muhammad, made still greater improvements toward centralizing the administration of government. Askia Muhammad ruled metropolitan Gao directly, but he reduced the status of the conquered rulers further by placing governors and minor governors over them. As was the case in Mali, these were court favorites or members of the royal family. Above this structure he created four viceroyalties, or regions, each under a viceroy, or commissioner, who was in charge of a cluster of provinces. These viceroyalties were Dendi, Bal, Benga, and Kurmina. Since most of these administrative posts were appointive rather than hereditary, Songhai must have had a much more tightly controlled and more effective system of provincial administration than the other two.

Arabic sources do not throw much light on the system of justice in these states. For the most part, the kings were directly responsible for its administration. We are told by Al-Bakri that the kings of Ghana went out on horses every day to summon those people who had been wronged or had suffered any injustice to come and lodge a complaint. Trial by wood was also practiced in ancient Ghana. According to Al-Bakri, "When a man is accused of denying a debt or having shed blood or some other crime, a headman takes a thin piece of wood, which is sour and bitter to taste, and pours upon it some water which he then gives to the defendant to drink. If the man vomits, his innocence is recognized and he is congratulated. If he does not vomit and the drink remains in his stomach, the accusation is accepted as justified." The kings held what seem to have been courts of appeal in their palaces. Cases were initially heard, especially in the towns, by *qadis*, who obviously administered justice in accordance with the Koran and the Sharia (Muslim law). These judges also wielded great influence at the court of the kings. Ibn Battuta's main contact with the king of Mali was a *qadi*, whom he described as "a negro, a pilgrim, and a man of fine character." The chroniclers of the Timbuktu *Tarikh* indicate that the *qadis* of that town were all from the Aqit family and wielded considerable influence over the Askias. One of them, Al-Aqib, who died in 1583, was noted for his frankness. "He was of stout heart," wrote one of the chroniclers, "bold in the mighty affairs that others hesitate before, courageous in dealing with the ruler and those beneath him. He had many conflicts with them and they used to be submissive and obedient to him in every matter. If he saw something he thought reprehensible, he would suspend his activities as *qadi* and keep himself aloof. Then they would conciliate him until he returned."

These high-ranking officials appear to have been rewarded for their services. Most of them, certainly those of Mali and Songhai, were given fiefs, or serf domains, as well as valuable goods. According to Al-Umari, some of the provincial governors of Mali received as much as "1500 mithqals [a unitary measure equal to one eighth of an ounce] of gold every year besides which he the king keeps them in horses and clothes." To encourage civil servants and military men, the kings of Mali instituted various decorations, such as the award of golden bracelets, collars, and anklets. The highest of all the awards, presumably given to soldiers, was the Honor of the Trousers. An eyewitness told the fourteenth-century writer Al-Umari: "Whenever a hero adds to the list of his exploits, the King gives him a pair of wide trousers, and the greater the number of a knight's exploits the bigger the size of his trousers. These trousers are characterised by narrowness in the leg and ampleness in the seat."

It is interesting to note that the Scottish explorer Alexander Gordon Laing, who visited among the Mandingos of Solimana in 1822, observed: "The width of the trousers is a great mark of distinction." This is true of the Dagomba and Mamprusi of northern Ghana to this day.

For the maintenance of law and order, and for defensive as well as offensive purposes, each of these west Sudanese empires had an army. Mali and Ghana had no standing armies; they, like many African kingdoms, depended on contingents contributed upon demand by vassal states. According to Al-Bakri, the kings of Ghana could raise an army of 200,000, of whom 40,000 were archers; and Mansa Musa of Mali could call up 100,000, a tenth of whom were cavalrymen. Songhai also relied on levies until the reign of Askia Muhammad, who instituted a professional army. It was this new army that enabled him not only to ensure stability and order, but to extend the boundaries of the empire that he had inherited from Sunni Ali. The armies of all these empires used the same weapons and were organized in the same way. They were divided into cavalry and infantry, their main weapons being spears, swords, javelins, and bows and arrows. Firearms were completely unknown until the Moroccan invasion late in the sixteenth century.

It would appear that both Mali and Songhai established diplomatic relations with the Maghreb and Egypt and kept up regular contacts with the sultan of Morocco. Mansa Sulaiman, Mansa Musa's brother and successor as king of the Mali, exchanged deputations with Morocco's Marinid sultans, and on the occasion of a new sultan's enthronement, sent an embassy to do him honor. Sulaiman's successor is also known to have sent gifts to the new sultan of Morocco. Among them was a giraffe, which the Moroccans talked about for a long time "because of the various adornments and markings which it combined in its body and attributes."

The complex administrative machineries of these states must have been expensive to run. Three main sources filled the royal treasury: tribute from vassal states, import and export duties, and imperial domains. Details of the annual levies have not been preserved, but of the duties collected in Ghana, Al-Bakri writes, "for every donkey loaded with salt that enters the country, the king takes a duty of one gold dinar, and two dinars from every one that leaves. From a load of copper the king's due is five mithqals and from a load of other goods ten mithqals." We are also told that in Ghana any gold nugget found by anybody had to be surrendered to the king. Both Mali and Songhai imposed similar duties on goods coming to and fro. In fact, Songhai had a minister solely concerned with taxation.

The third, and probably the greatest, source of revenue was from the royal estates. Ghana's records are quite silent on this; but it is clear from the accounts of Mali and Songhai that the kings had royal domains—some hereditary and some acquired by war—in different parts of the empire. After his victory over Mali, Askia Muhammad is said to have added twenty-four fiefs to his holdings. These were occupied and worked by slaves whose overseers, or *fanfa*, were charged with raising a fixed quantity of produce every year for the kings.

"Some of these *fanfa*," says the chronicler of the Askia dynasty, "had under them 100 slaves employed in cultivation, whilst others had 60, 50, 40, or 20." Each estate had a special function: some had to provide such commodities as yams, grain, or fish; others had to manufacture such goods as bows and arrows. Before the reign of Askia Muhammad the Great, the quantity of articles or provisions to be produced by each fief was not fixed, but Askia the Great set rigid quotas. Thus the Abda estate in the province of Dendi had to produce 1,000 sunhas (6,500 bushels) of rice annually. A chronicler reported: "This was fixed, which could neither be increased nor reduced." The Dyam Tene and Dya Wali estates had to supply 100 iron spears and 100 arrows per family per year. As the personal property of the kings, the estates were often given away as presents to trusted courtiers and friends.

The principal exports of Ghana, Mali, and Songhai were gold, ivory, slaves, and later, from the thirteenth century onward, kola nuts, a stimulant highly prized among Muslims. Most of these commodities, especially gold and kola nuts, came from the forest regions along trade routes controlled mainly by the Diula, a Mande people. The chief imports from the north were salt, horses, textiles, linen, books, writing paper, swords, and knives.

Ghana, situated as it was in the borderlands between the Sahara and the savanna, was most dependent upon the caravan trade; its people played the leading role as middlemen between producers and merchants. Al-Yaqut says of thirteenth-century Ghana: "From here, one enters the arid waste when going to the land of gold, and without the town of Ghana, this journey would be impossible."

Elsewhere Al-Yaqut adds that merchants from the north took with them Ghanaians as interpreters and go-betweens in negotiating with gold miners to the south. (It would appear that only small amounts of gold were mined in Ghana itself.) Ghana was also able to control the crucial and very lucrative trade in salt imported from the Taghaza mines of the western Sahara, "the source of an enormous income,"

according to Al-Bakri.

Since both Mali and Songhai successively gained direct control over some of the southern gold-producing regions, Wangara in particular, and since they were able to establish peace and order along the caravan routes, they must have derived even more income from trade than had Ghana. It is quite clear from Maghrebin, Egyptian, and Sudanese sources that from the thirteenth to the fifteenth centuries, when Europe and the Muslim world were facing an acute shortage of precious metals, the western Sudan was their chief source of gold. The enormous quantities of gold that both Mansa Musa and Askia Muhammad took with them on their pilgrimages to Mecca, in 1324 and 1497 respectively, leaves no doubt about the wealth their states possessed in gold.

However, other commodities also contributed to the income of Mali and Songhai. Both were favorably situated to practice agriculture, cattle breeding, and fishing. Ibn Battuta and Leo Africanus indicate that a certain amount of rice and millet was exported great distances. Fishing was quite important among the Sorko clans of Songhai, and some of the royal estates had their quota of fish to catch. Numerous craftsmen, tailors, blacksmiths, and cloth weavers attracted traders, too. Leo Africanus reports that Timbuktu had "many shops of artificers and merchants and especially such as weave linen and cotton cloth." Another chronicler wrote that there were as many as twenty-six tailors' workshops in the crossroads city, each with between fifty and one hundred apprentices.

Society in the Sudanese states was highly stratified. At the top was the ruling aristocracy, consisting of the royal families, officials, and Muslim scholars. The second and major part of the population consisted of merchants, farmers, fishermen, and cattle breeders. At the bottom were the slaves, who constituted only a small percentage of the population. It should be emphasized that the status of a slave in these early states, as indeed in almost all African societies, was fundamentally different from that which would prevail in the Americas. Not only was the number relatively small but slaves were treated as human beings rather than as chattel.

Although Islam had remained essentially the religion of foreigners in ancient Ghana, superficial changes reflecting the influence of the new faith began to appear in Mali and Songhai. The administration of justice and the system of taxation in those states were based on the Koran. The architecture of the principal buildings, the mosques, and the palaces was Islamic, as was the attire of the town dwellers. Al-Umari wrote that "they wear turbans with ends tied under their chin like the Arabs, their cloth is white and made of cotton which they cultivate and weave in a most excellent fashion." Ibn Battuta was also impressed by the attention paid to religious worship. "They are careful to observe the hours of prayer," he noted, "and assiduous in attending them in congregations, and in bringing up their children to them."

By the late fifteenth century Timbuktu had developed into the educational and commercial metropolis of the western Sudan, or rather, as one writer called it, the Queen of the Sudan. Its university, in the Sankore district of the city, produced such scholars and historians as Mahmud al-Kati, author of the *Kitab al-Fattash*, a chronicle of Songhai's Askia dynasty, and Abd al-Rahman as-Sadi, author of the *Tarikh as-Sudan*, a chronicle of the Sudan. Even the West African historian J. Spencer Trimingham, who is rather skeptical about Sankore as a university, admits that there were as many as one hundred fifty Koranic schools in Timbuktu alone. Leo Africanus also talks of "the great store of doctors, judges, priests, and other learned men that are bountifully maintained at the King's cost and charges. And hither are brought diverse manuscripts or written books out of Barbarie which are sold for more money than any other merchandise."

Mahmud al-Kati pays tribute in the *Kitab al-Fattash* to his colleagues: "The scholars of this period were the most respected among the believers for their generosity, their force of character, and their discretion." We also have the names of scholars who went on lecture tours and set up schools in different parts of the western Sudan, and especially in Hausaland. Mahmud Ibn Umar, for instance, lectured in Kano in 1485 to large and reverent crowds of people. Indeed, the Timbuktu tradition of learning dominated the cities of the western and central Sudan until the beginning of the nineteenth century.

But if the towns in Mali and Songhai assumed an Islamic hue, it would appear that the rural areas of both empires stuck to their traditional ways. They maintained their animistic beliefs, their traditional cults and indigenous African way of life, their initiation rites, their sorcerers, and their family and clan heads and chiefs, who administered justice in accordance with customary law.

It should be obvious from the above that, in spite of the skepticisms of certain European writers, the early empires of the western Sudan were true states, with all the fundamental attributes of government that statehood implies. They had paid bureaucracies, strong economies based on

Using a hand hoe, the farmer at right prepares soil for cultivation along the banks of the Niger near Timbuktu. Africans of the western Sudan are credited among mankind's leading agricultural innovators, having developed a wide range of cereal grains such as fonio, acha grass, hungry rice, pearl millet, and sorghum. The cone-shaped structures opposite are granaries built by the Dogon people of Mali. Sun-dried bricks and thatch are the traditionally used construction materials.

BLACK STAR — C. TRIESCHMANN

trade, mining, agriculture, and political machinery capable of ensuring law, order, security, and diplomatic exchange.

The fall of all these states was due to both internal and external factors. The internal factors were usually the rivalries among members of the royal family. The external factors were for the most part foreign attacks. With the possible exception of Songhai, none of these empires had a really durable provincial administrative structure. As pointed out earlier, the conquered states and kingdoms within each empire were governed by their own rulers and were held to the central authority mainly by military might. Moreover, each empire was composed of different ethnic and linguistic groups, hence it lacked cultural and ethnic homogeneity. Some of the rulers of both Mali and Songhai did attempt to use Islam to provide cohesion, but only with very limited success. Both Ghana's central authority and its army were weakened as a result of the defeats they suffered between 1054 and 1076 by the adherents of the Almoravid movement. As described more fully in Chapter Four, this was an Islamic movement that arose in the eleventh century among the Sanhaja Berbers who occupied the western Sahara. Although Ghana did reconquer its capital from the Almoravids after 1087, it never really recovered from those earlier blows, and its vassal states broke away. The coup de grâce,

however, was delivered in 1203 by an external force, the rulers of the Susu kingdom to the south.

Mali fell victim principally to the internal breakdown of the central government, as a result of the inordinate ambition and frivolity of its royal family. The trouble began at the end of the reign of Mansa Sulaiman in 1359–1360. The history of the kings of Mali for the next several decades was a sordid record of regicides, civil wars, contested successions, and coups d'état. Indeed, within the brief period from 1360 to 1390 as many as seven people were enthroned, four of them between 1387 and 1390. Central authority collapsed, anarchy and instability came in its wake, and as in Ghana, the vassal states began to break away. The demise of the empire came after Mali had been attacked from three sides: the Tuareg attacked from the north, the Mossi from the south, and the Songhai from the east. By 1433 the Tuareg had captured Arawan, Walata, and Timbuktu, and in the 1460's and the 1470's the Mossi took arms against the southern and even the central regions of Mali. The rulers of Mali appealed to Portugal for assistance in the 1490's and again in the 1530's. The Portuguese could do nothing but send words of encouragement. The Songhai attacks delivered the final blow, and by the fourth decade of the sixteenth century Mali had shrunk again into the tiny Mande principality of Kangaba.

Songhai's glory lasted little more than a century after its victories over Mali. The establishment of the Askia dynasty in Songhai in 1493, a result of the military coup organized and led by Askia Muhammad, was the beginning of the internal division of the country. Being of the Soninke rather than the Songhai people, he tried to replace the animistic beliefs of the Songhai with Islam, as indeed Sunni Ali, his predecessor, had done in an effort to unify the empire. Though Askia Muhammad's attempts only alienated the Songhai people, he was shrewd and strong enough to contain these internal differences. His successors could not. As had been the case in Mali, a series of disputed successions, revolts, and usurpations broke out among members of his family. In the sixty years after his deposition as many as eight people mounted the throne. However, it would appear that at least one of the rulers, Askia Daud, was quite competent, and during his long reign from 1549 to 1582 the fortunes of Songhai improved. Although disputed successions broke out again after Daud, and as many as three rulers came to the throne between 1582 and 1591, the central authority would appear to have remained intact.

It was the decisive defeat inflicted by the forces of Sultan Al-Mansur of Morocco that precipitated the disintegration

187

of the empire. Led by Judar Pasha, a young Spanish eunuch, the sultan's army crushed the Songhai army at the battle of Tondibi in 1591 and marched south in search of Songhai's fabled riches. The Songhai army was estimated by Al-Kati to have been a huge one consisting of 18,000 cavalry and 9,700 infantry, while the Moroccans are said to have numbered only 4,000. The Moroccan victory was in some measure due to the fact that the Songhai fought with spears, swords, and bows and arrows, whereas the Moroccan army was equipped with harquebuses and cannon. When the advisers of Al-Mansur tried to dissuade him from undertaking what they considered to be a crazy enterprise, the sultan is said to have replied:

> You talk of the dangerous desert we have to cross, of the fatal solitudes, barren of water and pasture, but you forget the defenseless and ill-equipped merchants who, mounted or on foot, regularly cross these wastes which caravans have never ceased to traverse. I, who am so much better equipped than they, can surely do the same with an army which inspires terror wherever it goes. . . . Moreover, our predecessors would have found great difficulty if they had tried to do what I now propose, for their armies were composed only of horsemen armed with spears and of bowmen; gunpowder was unknown to them, and so were firearms and their terrifying effect. Today the Sudanese have only spears and swords, weapons which will be useless against modern arms. It will therefore be easy for us to wage a successful war against these people and prevail over them.

Following Al-Mansur's military success, however, anarchy broke out in the area of the Niger Bend, and it would continue intermittently until the late nineteenth century.

And what was happening in the regions to the south of the empires of Ghana, Mali, and Songhai? As has been already pointed out, a simultaneous process of state formation was at work. Arising just to the west in the regions of the Senegambia was the kingdom of Wolof; to the south emerged the Mole-Dagbane states and the Mossi kingdoms. Still farther south arose a number of forest and coastal states: Ife, Oyo, and Benin in Nigeria; the Ga kingdom and Akan states in modern Ghana. Their emergence was due to factors similar to those that gave birth to Ghana, Mali, and Songhai. Of first importance was the extension of the caravan trade routes southward into the savanna, the forest, and the coastal regions; of second was the the development within the region of trade among the coastal peo-

ples; and of third were the activities of the wealthy and ambitious families or clan groups who were stimulated by those commercial activities.

As has already been pointed out, the mainstays of the caravan trade—gold, kola nuts, ivory, and slaves—could all be obtained in the regions of the southern savanna and forest. From evidence rapidly accumulating today, it is certain that by the end of the fourteenth century, at the height of Mali's power, the trade routes from the Sahara, which had earlier stopped at the savanna cities of Walata, Timbuktu, Jenne, and Gao, had now been extended westward and southward.

The people who were responsible for the development of this trade between the forest regions and the states of Mali and Songhai were certainly the Diula group of the Mande people. They founded a number of caravan posts, including Bobo-Dioulasso (in modern Upper Volta), Kong and Bouna (in modern Ivory Coast), and Wa and Begho (in modern Ghana). Begho, the last of them, was established just north of the forest zone in about 1400. From Begho, routes radiated directly south to the coastal regions of Axim (in southwest Ghana) and southeastward through Asante to the coastal region of modern Cape Coast and Elmina.

Proof of the extension of northern trade routes to the coast can be taken from the fact that two items of clothing, *lanbens* (shawls) and *aljaravais* (dressing gowns) that were manufactured in Morocco and Tunis were in great demand on the coast of modern Ghana before the arrival of the Portuguese. Describing that trade in 1500, the Portuguese agent Pacheco Pereira also mentions peoples from the interior: "Boroes, Mandingoes, Cacres, Andeses, or Souzos." Here again, the "Boroes" are obviously the Bono of northern Asante, the "Cacres" are possibly the Kasena-Grusi of northern Ghana, and the "Mandingoes" and "Souzos" are readily identifiable as the Mandingos and the Susu of the larger family of Mande peoples.

The Portuguese and later the Dutch traders found the coastal peoples enjoying very lucrative salt and fish trade with the inland peoples. The Dutchman Pieter de Marees, writing in 1601 about one of the Akan settlements, states that "the inhabitants of the sea-side, come also to the markets with their . . . fish, which their husbands have gotten in the sea, whereof the women buy much and carry them to other townes within the land, to get some profit by them, so that the fish which is taken in the sea, is carried at least one hundred or two hundred miles up into the land, for a great present." William Bosman, an official of the Dutch West India Company who came to the coast during the second half of the seventeenth century, made a similar observation. There is no reason to think that trade in salt and fish was not going on prior to the arrival of the Portuguese. Salt has always been an indispensable commodity and has generated contact between people who produce it and those who do not, and we know that salt is not found in the forest region and can be produced only in very small quantities in the savanna regions to the north.

It also seems clear that the Mande were responsible for the extension of the routes eastward from Timbuktu and Gao into the Hausa states, probably in the fourteenth century. From these Hausa states, trade routes radiated southwestward across the Niger and through the Mole-Dagbane areas into the gold- and kola-producing areas of Asante in modern Ghana. The Kano Chronicle states that kola nuts reached Hausaland from northern Ghana during the first half of the fifteenth century. Other routes also led southward through the regions surrounding the confluence of the Benue and Niger rivers and into the Yoruba and Benin areas to the southwest. Ibn Battuta talks of copper from the Takedda mines being exported southward into Nigeria, and judging from the bronze works of Ife and Benin (to be discussed later), it is not unlikely, as the British ethnographer Frank Willett has suggested that "some of this Takedda ore eventually found its way even farther south."

Pre-European trade also existed between east and west via the sea, especially between the coasts of modern Ghana and Nigeria. Evidence for this conclusion is found in the oral tradition, very widely held among the Ga and the people of Asebu (one of the Akan states), that they migrated from Benin by sea into the coastal regions of modern Ghana and that the Ga kingdom was in fact a part of the empire of Benin. However, on the basis of linguistic and other ethnological data, it is exceedingly unlikely that the Ga and the Asebu did in fact originate from Benin. Rather, the oral tradition seems to be an echo of the old trading contacts between the people of Benin and those of the coast of modern Ghana. The fifteenth- and early sixteenth-century accounts of the Portuguese traders suggest that they merely exploited a pre-existing pattern of trade to their own advantage. Pacheco Pereira, who was there in the 1500's, says that they bought slaves at the port of Benin for "twelve or fifteen brass bracelets each, or for copper bracelets which they prize more; from there the slaves are brought to the castle of S. Jorze da Mina [the extant fortress of São Jorge at Elmina on the Ghana coast] where they are sold for gold." He also says that they traded on the Niger near the coast of the Bight of Benin, "principally in slaves,

in cotton stuff, some leopard skins, palm oil, and blue beads with red stripes which they call 'coris'—and other things which we are accustomed to buy here for brass and copper bracelets. All these commodities have value at the castle of S. Jorze da Mina. The Factor of our prince sells them to Negro traders in exchange for gold."

Pereira goes on to describe the local people's manner of travel: "At the mouth of the River Real [the Bonny River] . . . there is a very large village, consisting of about 2,000 souls. Much salt is made here, and in this country are to be found the largest canoes, made of a single trunk, that are known in the whole of Ethiopia of Guinea; some are so large that they hold 80 men. They travel distances of a hundred leagues and more down the river, and bring many yams, which are very good here and make a tolerable diet, many slaves, cows, goats and sheep."

Writing early in the next century, Pieter de Marees also describes the canoes in use on the coast of Ghana. He notes that the people of Accra had large canoes "to fish or go to sea withall," and that he saw one "cut out of a tree which was five and thirty foot long and five foot broad and three foot high, which was as big as a shallop, so that it would have held thirty men." In the same century Jean Barbot, agent general of the French Royal Africa Company, also saw canoes on the coast of Ghana of sizes ranging from fourteen to forty feet long, and he added that the largest of them could "carry above ten tons of goods with eighteen or twenty blacks to paddle them." He stated further that the best canoe men were the Elmina blacks, who "drive a great trade along the Gold Coast, and at Wida by Sea [Ovidah, a seaport in the area of modern Dahomey], and are the fittest and the most experienc'd men to manage and paddle the canoes over the bars and breakings, which render this coast, and that of Wida so perilous and toilsome to land either men, goods or provisions." One may conclude from these descriptions that going to sea in large canoes was already well established on the eve of the Portuguese arrival. Indeed, it probably dated as far back as the first millennium A.D., when the coastal areas began to be occupied by peoples from the interior, and commercial and cultural contacts were initiated.

As was the case farther north, the West African peoples who were geographically situated to play the role of middlemen would be those who could develop large states and kingdoms. To the south of Ghana and Mali, the first states to become sizable kingdoms were the Wolof kingdom to the west, the Mole-Dagbane and Mossi states to the south in the Volta River Basin, and the Ife, Oyo, and Benin kingdoms to the southeast. All except Benin were situated in the southern savanna belt. The Wolof people could control not only the lucrative salt trade from the sea, but could share in the gold trade with Morocco. The Mole-Dagbane states and the closely related Mossi states—all of which were founded during the first half of the fifteenth century—expanded mainly to establish a firm control over the trade routes linking the Niger Bend and Hausaland with the Akan's gold fields and kola-tree groves.

The oral traditions of the Akan peoples indicate that the first Akan states to emerge early in the fifteenth century were Bono-Manso in the region between the savanna and the forest and Adansi and Assin in the region where gold was obtained. Later on, different groups migrated northward to establish city-states, which were all within a few miles of where the routes that led from the Niger Bend terminated. It was these states that would later form the nucleus of the famous Asante empire.

The other Akan states of Aguafo, Fetu, Asebu, Fante, Agona, and the Ga kingdom—the so-called Gold Coast states—were created mainly in response to the demands of the transoceanic as well as the overland north-south trade. Their failure to develop into powerful kingdoms prior to the arrival of the Portuguese can be explained by the fact that they were one step further removed from the source of gold, trading through the intermediary of their sister Akan states in the interior. The Gold Coast states were also hampered by being crowded into a relatively short stretch of coast—the five Akan states occupied no more than one hundred miles.

Primarily by virtue of its geographical position, Benin became a center of both overland and sea trade, the latter by way of Ghana. Of the Yoruba states that later developed to the northwest of Benin, between 1380 and 1420, the first to develop into a sizable kingdom was Oyo. This northernmost Yoruba state was situated in the savanna region just below the Niger and, by the end of the fifteenth century, was able to claim the dominant share of trade between Hausaland and the Niger Bend and the other Yoruba states to the south. However, since Oyo had as rivals other centralized states to the south and west, its expansion could not be as rapid as that of Benin. Indeed, it was not until the seventeenth and eighteenth centuries that, using guns, Oyo's army extended its frontiers to the Guinea coast.

What then were these kingdoms like when the Portuguese first established contact with them? Pacheco Pereira reported in 1505: "Here at the Senegal you find the first black people. This is the kingdom of Wolof, a hundred

leagues long and eight broad. The kingdom of Wolof can put into the field an army of about 10,000 cavalry and 100,000 infantry." It would appear from the early sixteenth-century accounts of Alvise da Cadamosto, a Venetian explorer in the service of Prince Henry of Portugal, that the kingdom consisted of five polities, all under a single ruler. Valentine Fernandes, a Lisbon printer of Moravian origin, writing in the same period, furnishes us with further details. He says the king had many subjects under him and administered his state with the aid of Muslim "dignitaries after the fashion of dukes and counts" and "white bischerigs who are priests and preachers of Mahomet, and can read and write." He adds that some of the ordinary people had embraced Islam, though the majority of them were sticking to their animistic beliefs. It is not surprising that some of the people should be Muslims, since the kingdom was situated to the south of Takrur, into which Islam had penetrated as early as A.D. 1000.

The Portuguese found the fifteen-hundred-mile-long stretch from Gambia to the borders of modern Ghana only sparsely settled; it appears that no state of any size emerged along that coast before the end of the fifteenth century. But in the area of modern Ghana, between the Pra and Volta rivers, the explorers-traders came upon the cluster of Akan states described earlier.

The three contiguous Akan states of Aguafo, Fetu, and Asebu were similar in organization: at the head of each state was a king (he lived in a capital a few miles from the coast), who was assisted by a council of elders. Eustace de la Fosse, writing in 1479, reports taking security from the "Mansa and Caramansa," who, he adds, "are the king and viceroy of Aguafo," and it was with the viceroy that Don Diego de Azambuja negotiated for the plot at Elmina, on which the castle São Jorge was built in 1482. Each of these states had trading villages or outlets, some of which became European settlements.

In contrast, the Fante state seems to have been composed of a series of inland townships, or quarters, within about three to five miles of one another. Collectively, they made up the capital district of Mankessim (alternatively Fantyn), and each quarter was under a chief, or *braffo*, who was advised by the family or clan heads. One *braffo* was recognized as overall leader, though his authority was limited, and he had to consult the others before he could declare war or make peace. It is also evident from the oral traditions and from a shrine that has survived near Mankessim that all the Fante recognized one national god, whom they called Nanaam. Orders emanating from the chief priest of Nanaam were binding on all the Fante. Thus, the government of the Fante was a sort of theocracy with political power being controlled by the chief ruler and the chief priests. Like the other states, the Fante also had some coastal outlets; these were Anomabu, Little Fantyn, and Kormantin. The Fante remained in Mankessim until the last three decades of the seventeenth century when, probably as a result of population pressure, they began to move out of the townships to establish kingdoms within a twenty- or thirty-mile radius of the capital.

No sizable states had emerged in the area between the mouth of the Volta River and Yorubaland by the middle of the fifteenth century, but in the western and midwestern regions of Nigeria, the Portuguese found the Yoruba and Edo peoples living in what were probably the most advanced and certainly the most interesting states of the Guinea coast: Ife, Benin, and Oyo. The oldest of these was Ife. Indeed, the Yoruba-speaking peoples regard Ife as the center of the world and the cradle of their civilization. According to one of their traditional accounts, it was there that God's children landed and set about to create the world. The most senior of these children was Oduduwa, whom they regarded as the first ruler, or *oni*, of Ife. He is said to have had sixteen children, whom he sent out to found the Yoruba states.

From a careful analysis of these oral traditions and the terra-cotta art of Ife, Willett has concluded that these oral traditions represent the arrival of "a small, but influential group of people," probably from the east or northeast. He postulates further that these people found the indigenous Yoruba and Igbo peoples already working in terra cotta, and that they introduced the art of bronze casting and the ideas of divine kingship, and that these new arrivals founded Ife, from which place the other Yoruba kingdoms would be created. Whether founded by the Yoruba or by invaders from the east, Ife never developed into a kingdom, for reasons that are still not apparent. It remained throughout essentially a city-state ruled by a "divine" king, who, as a Portuguese observer put it, was held "in great reveration as is the Supreme Pontiff with us." Nevertheless, Ife is of vital interest because it has remained from its foundation the religious center of all the Yoruba peoples and because it was there that the Yoruba's world-acclaimed sculpture in bronze, wood, and terra cotta was first developed.

From there this unique art spread to the whole of West Africa. The bronze sculptures, their supreme achievement, were made by the lost-wax process. The best of these were created in the classical period of Ife art, which conventionally has been said to have lasted from the beginning of the thirteenth to the middle of the fourteenth century. However, in view of the bronze sculptures recently discovered at Igbo-Ukwu, which have been dated by the radiocarbon process to the ninth century A.D., many scholars are beginning to accept an earlier date for Ife's classical period, probably before our millennium, bringing it closer to the Nok culture.

To the southeast of Ife, in the forest area, Benin emerged. Whereas Ife remained a city-state, Benin had developed into a sizable kingdom by the middle of the fifteenth century. Pereira, who visited Benin four times, wrote in 1505:

> A league up this river on the left two tributaries enter the main stream: if you ascend the second of these for twelve leagues you find a town called Huguatoo [Gwato], of some 2,000 souls: this is the harbor of a great city of Beny [Benin], which lies nine leagues in the interior with a good road between them. Small ships of fifty tons can go as far as Huguatoo. This city is about a league long from gate to gate; it has no wall but is surrounded by a large moat, very wide and deep, which suffices for its defense . . . . Its houses are made of mud walls covered with palm leaves. The Kingdom of Beny is about eighty leagues long and forty wide; it is usually at war with its neighbors. . . .

It seems clear from the traditional accounts of Benin that there are at least two periods of Benin history. All that can be pieced together is that during the first period Benin was a city-state under the rule of the Ogiso dynasty and that this family was replaced by the Oba dynasty sometime before 1300. Establishing themselves among the Edo-speaking peoples, who were organized only into clans, lineages, and village groups, the new Oba kings claimed supernatural powers. They soon succeeded in converting the city-state into the sizable and thriving kingdom that the Portuguese found on their arrival in the 1470's.

The oral traditions of Benin, Ife, and Oyo shed some light on how the Oba dynasty came to power. The histories of all three kingdoms agree that after a period of anarchy, the people of Benin beseeched the *oni* of Ife, Oduduwa himself, for a ruler, and he sent his son Oranmiyan. But believing that it would be better for a native of Benin to rule there, Oranmiyan married a daughter of one of the local chiefs and shortly thereafter had a son, Eweka, to whom he gave the throne. Oranmiyan then returned to Ife and from there went on to establish the kingdom of Oyo. Eweka thus became the first *oba* of Benin, but he had to obtain his insignia of office from the *oni* of Ife. It seems obvious from this account that the founders of the Oba dynasty of Benin, like the founders of Oyo, came from Ife.

To govern this kingdom, it would appear that the Oba kings developed certain political institutions that were an amalgam of Ife traditions and local political and social ideas. At the head of the kingdom was the *oba*, who, like the rulers of the early Sudanese states and those of Ife, was a "divine" king. As the English explorer Thomas Wyndham observed in 1553: "And here to speak of the great reverence they give to their king, it is such, that if we would give as much to our Saviour Christ, we should remove from our heads many plagues which we daily deserve. . . ."

The king was assisted by three ranking classes. The first class was the *uzama*, or king makers, whose position dates from Benin's early dynastic era. They had to perform certain important state rituals, including the installation of the *oba*. The second group was the *eghaevbo n'ogbe*, or palace chiefs, who were responsible not only for the *oba*'s regalia, his wives and children, his personal relations, and his doctors and divine men but also for the administration of the provinces, or fiefs. The third estate was the *eghaevbo n'ore*, or town chiefs, whose leader was the *iyase*, the prime minister and commander in chief of the army, and from whom other war leaders as well as other governors of provinces were chosen. Since most of these officials were appointed by the *oba* himself, he enjoyed considerable powers, though he still had to ensure his position by playing one group against another.

Provincial Benin, that is the conquered territories, was divided into three administrative units. At the base was the village under a village head; at the intermediate level was the chiefdom made up of a number of villages, each administered by a chief appointed by the king; at a higher level were the fiefs, or provinces, each consisting of a number of chiefdoms and directed by either a town or palace chief. This system of administration remained without any fundamental changes until the late nineteenth century.

Regarding Benin's achievements in art, the local oral tradition admits to learning the art of bronze casting from Ife. It is related that Oguola, the fifth *oba* of the second dynasty, who reigned during the end of the fourteenth century, sent to the *oni* of Ife for a bronzesmith to teach his people. The *oni* is said to have agreed and sent Iguegha, who is worshiped to this day in Benin as the patron of bronzesmiths. In fact, the style of the early Benin bronzes is quite similar to that of Ife, but by the sixteenth century, using the same lost-wax process known in Ife, Benin artists had

evolved a distinctive style of their own, which was less naturalistic and more formal. As in Ife, the people of Benin also worked in wood, ivory, and raffia.

Despite the widespread tradition that attributes the founding of both Benin and Oyo to Oranmiyan, it is now generally agreed that Oyo's founding occurred nearly a century later, between the last two decades of the fourteenth and the first three decades of the fifteenth centuries. That it had grown into a fairly large kingdom by the end of the fifteenth century through expansion northward must have been due partly to the ability of Oyo's founding kings and partly, as we have seen, to its position in an area best suited for the domination of the trade routes from the north. Their art was derived from Ife, but as Frank Willett has pointed out, it shows "gradually declining naturalism, as if the social pressures which produced the naturalism of Classical Ife have gradually weakened."

Oyo's political institutions were based, as in the other kingdoms of West Africa, upon a "divine" king. The *alafin* ruled the kingdom with the advice of a council composed of seven notables known as the *oyo mesi* under the leadership of the *bashorun*, or prime minister. The *oyo mesi* was not only responsible for the election of the *alafin*, but according to a historian of Yoruba tradition, Samuel Johnson, its members "represent the voice of the nation, on them developed the chief duty of protecting the interests of the kingdom." The *alafin* could not declare war or peace without their consent. Moreover, should the *bashorun* ever declare three times, "the gods reject you, the people reject you, the earth rejects you," the *alafin* was obliged to commit suicide. However, some safeguards were instituted against the abuse of this power. Firstly, one of the members of the *oyo mesi*, known as "the *alafin*'s friend," had to die with the *alafin*. Secondly, both the *alafin* and the council were controlled by the *ogboni*, a secret earth cult consisting of all members of the *oyo mesi*, heads of the other cults, rich traders, and prominent diviners. This society had to ratify certain decisions of the *oyo mesi*, among them the rejection of the *alafin* by the *bashorun*. It seems clear that the people of Oyo devised a system that had checks and balances built into it to eliminate arbitrary or dictatorial exercise of power.

In summation, the people of West Africa, stimulated by trade and ruled and inspired by talented leaders, did form states and develop political institutions that were truly unique and truly African between 500 and 1450. Some of them also developed artistic skills, which in their aesthetic sensitivities were comparable, if not superior, to those of contemporary Europe.

THE ART OF IFE

Long before the Renaissance burst upon Europe, one of the world's great art traditions arose among the Yoruba and Edo peoples of what is now western Nigeria. Beginning perhaps as early as the ninth century (and deriving influences possibly from the earlier Nok culture), artists in the city-state of Ife, the Yoruba's religious center, produced masterpieces in bronze, wood, ivory, and terra cotta, like the life-sized bronze head at right. With artists at Benin and Oyo, to whom they taught their skills, they achieved for several centuries a naturalism and monumentality comparable to the qualities found in classical sculpture.

Details of two sensitively designed bronzes, made by the lost-wax process, reflect the sophisticated cultures of the ancient Yoruban societies. Opposite is a Benin bronze of a mounted warrior in a plumed headdress, possibly a visitor from the north. An oni, or king, of Ife is seen at right.

In earlier times members of the Ife royal family painted their faces for certain festivals with an extract of blister beetles, which raised welts like those on the almost life-sized head above; the terra cotta may originally have been part of a figure.

The subject of the handsome terra-cotta head opposite is shrouded in Ife legend. One version says it represents Lajuwa, a usurper who gained power by deceit after the death of an oni. Eventually the rightful successor had him executed.

The majestic figure of a king at right, regarded by many experts as the finest Ife bronze yet discovered, sat for centuries on a bank of the Niger River at Tada. The 21-inch-high work, cast perhaps before A.D. 1000, was held sacred by the villagers, who believed that the founder of the Nupe kingdom had brought it as a symbol of his rule. Ritual washings wore away its limbs.

197

THE GOLDEN IMPERATIVE

Asante gold weights

THE SERPENT OF WAGADU

Ghana, the first empire to rise in West Africa, flourished from the sixth to the thirteenth century, reaping most of its profits from gold-rich lands to the south. This legend recounts Ghana's downfall. Wagadu, which still survives, is a city in Upper Volta.

The prosperity of Ghana was not a human work. The empire owed its wealth to an enormous serpent, which everyone worshiped. The reptile was named Bida and lived in a pit. Tradition dictated that each year he must be given as a propitiatory offering the most beautiful girl of the empire, adorned with all her finery. Each clan, each tribe, fulfilled by turns this sorrowful sacrifice. . . .

Wagadu was a region of miraculous prosperity. Rains of water brought nourishment to the earth and carried it to the cotton, the sorghum, and the fruit trees, which, thanks to this sustenance, produced magnificent harvests; rains of gold bestowed the metal from which were chiseled the heads of walking sticks for men as well as their spurs, and the jewels and rings of women. The dense population was a mosaic in which moved the Bambara, overly eloquent warriors; the Sarakholle, raconteurs and philosophers; the Kasonke, a race of artists; and the Poulho, great lords fiercely attached to the pastoral life. The Poulho women wore heavy amber beads, in necklaces on their bronzed chests and set at the crests of their enormous hairdos, like stars in the firmament. The Mousso had a light and supple stride, accentuated by the slow dance of their arms, which moved in the muslin sleeves of

their *boubous.* They wore gold as bracelets, as necklaces, as rings on their feet, and as earrings. . . . All the cities of the empire were protected by a magic invisible barrier that held invaders in check.

Thus one year it happened that the martyr of the serpent of Wagadu was to be a young girl of unparalleled beauty named Sia. She was the fiancée of Amadou Sefedokote, Amadou the Taciturn. Sia, at sixteen, was already a fine young woman. . . . The most beautiful jewels were put to shame by her fine appearance, the sweetness of her voice, the curve of her breasts, and the graceful proportions of her hips. And Amadou the Taciturn loved his fiancée more than his taboo. It was with suffering that he watched approaching the dawn of the day on which Sia was to be swallowed by the sacred serpent of Wagadu.

On the eve Amadou spent a night of torments. An immense sadness seized him and he threw himself on his tara [a bed made of tree stalks joined together with strips of bark], his head boiling with bitter thoughts. . . .

The sun rose slowly in the east; its clear, straight rays encircled it with a halo shaded with purple. With great fright Amadou saw the day filter through a slit made by the door of his room. He left his hut like an automaton. He took his saber from its sheath of mottled leather, which preserved it from rust. And all day, in order to escape his grief, he sharpened his sword on a gritty stone. Toward evening the saber was so sharp that it cut the wind.

When the sun had set, without the knowledge of anyone, Amadou went near the large pit, surrounded with offerings,

where Bida lived. In haste he built a straw hut sheltered behind a screen of trees. There, he hid himself.

The ancient ones had formed a procession that was to carry Sia to the ritual sacrifice. Darkness had drowned the huts, deepening around them, and night had swallowed everything in its depths, even the thoughts of men. And suddenly, the deep tones of a tam-tam shattered the night with its arrows, which struck through the shadows, pouring out their significant meaning. It was the signal of the hour of the sacrifice. The tam-tams had tried to say it in the lively rhythms, which on other nights bathed with the moon had carried the long line of girls toward the marriage hut—in the same way their sweet song was beat out. But the tam-tams in their gay motif sent forth this time the lamentations of sorrow. . . . Sia was wrapped with the loincloth, which during her free time she had made under the shade of the yellow fig tree with the blue leaves in the hope of making it her marriage costume. During the night while one could distinguish only the lugubrious echoes of a weeping tam-tam, Sia went forward slowly, pushed toward death by the inexorable escort of the ancient ones. When they were a few steps from the refuge of Bida, they abandoned the young girl after the most ancient of the ancients had pronounced the solemn sentence, full of resignation: "Remain here and forgive us."

Sia no longer had the use of her legs. She knelt down, her hands over her eyes in the naive gesture of the hare, which, head thrust in a thicket, believes it possible to escape danger because he no longer sees it.

Soon the pointed head of Bida emerged from the pit. The serpent then rose through the darkness; with a rapid thrust, it moved toward the inert ball that the young girl had become, shielded in her loincloth.

Bida scented its prey with caution and brusquely dashed back into its home. An instant afterward, the long, flexible body of the serpent spurted out like an arrow, belly glistening; there was a moment of pause, then the hideous animal drenched the young girl with its venom, and with an imperceptible movement, plunged down into its pit again.

The sticky liquid that the serpent had spit, shook Sia Tounkara with repugnance. Screaming, she tried vainly to disentangle herself from her loincloth and her *boubou*, which were enveloped in the same horrible paste that stuck to her and froze her with terror.

But Amadou the Taciturn awaited in the darkness. . . . Although he was very much afraid, his jaws frozen, he maintained his senses. He knew that Bida only struck its victim on the third appearance. He now held himself tensed, and opened his eyes wide, because the moment of combat approached.

From the pit arose a gray arrow, vertical and oblique all at the same time, which threw itself on Sia, circling her with an astonishing precision. But Bida was not as fast as Amadou, and with one stroke of his flawless saber the head of the serpent of Wagadu was cut off! Bida regenerated with the rapidity of drops of rain following one upon another, a second, a third, a fifth, seventh head, all animated by the same intention of swallowing the young girl, but none of them was able to withstand the saber of Amadou, who loved his fiancée more than his fetish.

The last head cut off flew away saying: "For seven years, seven months, and seven days, Ghana will receive neither rains of water nor rains of gold," and Bida fell into the Boure [a river where the Mandingos find gold].

The body of Bida was convulsed in enormous coils of which the successive waves died on the edge of the pit. In a final movement, it left its refuge, with the effect that the tail broke off and flew away. It fell in the valley of the Faleme [where the golden riches of the Senegal are found]. . . .

For seven years, seven months, and seven days, no rain watered Ghana. The rivers dried up, the valleys became barren, famine and thirst decimated men, who fled toward lands where life was possible.

Thus did Ghana end—the most famous empire and the cradle of African civilization. Its splendors became only evocations, the sad dreams of the African guitar under the shrouds of sand.

FATHER OF BRIGHT COUNTRY

The great medieval empire of Mali began as a small Mandingo chieftaincy in the late ninth century. In 1203 it was conquered and annexed by Sumanguru Kante, ruler of the Susu kingdom. As related in the following story, taken from an epic of old Mali, Sundiata returned thirty-two years later to crush Sumanguru (given here in its variant form, Soumaoro) and the Susu (Sosso) at the battle of Kirina (Krina). In the tradition of heroic legends, Sumanguru's legendary ancestors are repeatedly invoked, and he is called the son of the buffalo and the lion, references to the totems of his mother and father. The epic is part of West Africa's oral history and has been preserved since ancient times by the griots, now mostly a class of professional musicians, but formerly the counselors of kings. The griots memorized constitutions, customs, and governmental history, and tutored the children of Mali's princely class.

Sundiata went and pitched camp at Dayala in the valley of the Niger. Now it was he who was blocking Soumaoro's road to the south. . . .

Soumaoro advanced as far as Krina, near the village of Dayala on the Niger and decided to assert his rights before joining battle. Soumaoro knew that Sundiata also was a sorcerer, so, instead of sending an embassy, he committed his words to one of his owls. The night bird came and perched on the roof of Djata's [Sundiata's] tent and spoke. The son of Sogolon [another epithet for Sundiata] in his turn sent his own to Soumaoro. Here is the dialogue of the sorcerer kings:

"Stop, young man. Henceforth I am the king of Mali. If you want peace, return to where you came from," said Soumaoro.

"I am coming back, Soumaoro, to recapture my kingdom. If you want peace you will make amends to my allies and return to Sosso where you are the king."

"I am king of Mali by force of arms. My rights have been established by conquest."

"Then I will take Mali from you by force of arms and chase you from my kingdom."

"Know, then, that I am the wild yam of the rocks; nothing will make me leave Mali."

"Know, also that I have in my camp seven master smiths who will shatter the rocks. Then, yam, I will eat you."

"I am the poisonous mushroom that makes the fearless vomit."

"As for me, I am the ravenous cock, the poison does not matter to me."

"Behave yourself, little boy, or you will burn your foot, for I am the red-hot cinder."

"But me, I am the rain that extinguishes the cinder; I am the boisterous torrent that will carry you off."

"I am the mighty silk-cotton tree that looks from on high on the tops of other trees."

"And I, I am the strangling creeper that climbs to the top of the forest giant."

"Enough of this argument. You shall not have Mali."

"Know that there is not room for two kings on the same skin, Soumaoro; you will let me have your place."

"Very well, since you want war I will wage war against you, but I would have you know that I have killed nine kings whose heads adorn my room. What a pity that your head should take its place beside those of your fellow madcaps."

Equestrian sculpture by the Dogon of Mali
MUSEUM OF PRIMITIVE ART

"Prepare yourself, Soumaoro, for it will be long before the calamity that is going to crash down upon you and yours comes to an end."

Thus Sundiata and Soumaoro spoke together. After the war of mouths, swords had to decide the issue. . . .

Sundiata wanted to have done with Soumaoro before the rainy season, so he struck camp and marched on Krina where Soumaoro was encamped. . . . The great battle was for the next day.

In the evening, to raise the men's spirits, Djata gave a great feast, for he was anxious that his men should wake up happy in the morning. Several oxen were slaughtered and that evening Balla Fasseke [Sundiata's *griot*], in front of the whole army, called to mind the history of old Mali. He praised Sundiata, seated amidst his lieutenants, in this manner:

"Now I address myself to you, Maghan Sundiata, I speak to you king of Mali, to whom dethroned monarchs flock. The time foretold to you by the jinn is now coming. Sundiata, kingdoms and empires are in the likeness of man; like him they are born, they grow and disappear. Each sovereign embodies one moment of that life. Formerly, the kings of Ghana extended their kingdom over all the lands inhabited by the black man, but the circle has closed and the Cisses of Wagadou are nothing more than petty princes in a desolate land. Today, another kingdom looms up, powerful, the kingdom of Sosso. Humbled kings have borne their tribute to Sosso, Soumaoro's arrogance knows no more bounds and his cruelty is equal to his ambition. . . . The kingship of Sosso is but the growth of yesterday, whereas that of Mali dates from the time of Bilali [Bilal]. Each kingdom has its childhood, but Soumaoro wants to force the pace, and so Sosso will collapse under him like a horse worn out beneath its rider. . . .

"You are the outgrowth of Mali just as the silk-cotton [kapok] tree is the growth of the earth, born of deep and mighty roots. To face the tempest the tree must have long roots and gnarled branches. Maghan Sundiata, has not the tree grown? . . .

"You are the son of Nare Maghan, but you are also the son of your mother Sogolon, the buffalo-woman, before whom powerless sorcerers shrank in fear. You have the strength and majesty of the lion, you have the might of the buffalo. . . .

"Tomorrow allow me to sing the 'Song of the Vultures' over the bodies of the thousands of Sossos whom your sword will have laid low before evening." . . .

At break of day, Fakoli came and woke up Sundiata to tell him that Soumaoro had begun to move his *sofas* [infantry] out of Krina. The son of Sogolon appeared dressed like a hunter king. He wore tight-fitting, ochre-colored trousers. He gave the order to draw up the *sofas* across the plain, and while his chiefs bustled about, [two officers] came into Djata's tent.

"Brother," said Manding Bory, "have you got the bow ready?"

"Yes," replied Sundiata. "Look."

He unhooked his bow from the wall, along with the deadly arrow. It was not an iron arrow at all, but was made of wood and pointed with the spur of a white cock. The cock's spur was the Tana of Soumaoro, the secret which Nana Triban had managed to draw out of the king of Sosso. . . .

The sun had risen on the other side of the river and already lit the whole plain. Sundiata's troops deployed from the edge of the river across the plain, but Soumaoro's army was so big that other *sofas* remaining in Krina had ascended the ramparts to see the battle. Soumaoro was already distinguishable in the distance by his tall headdress, and the wings of his enormous army brushed the river on one side and the hills on the other. . . . Sundiata did not deploy all his forces. The bowmen of Wagadou and the Djallonkes stood at the rear ready to spill out on the left towards the hills as the battle spread. Fakoli Koroma [king of the Koroma tribe and a defector from the army of Soumaoro, his uncle] and Kamandjan were in the front line with Sundiata and his cavalry.

With his powerful voice Sundiata cried, "*An gnewa!* [Forward!]" The order was repeated from tribe to tribe and the army started off. Soumaoro stood on the right with his cavalry.

Djata and his cavalry charged with great dash but they were stopped by the horsemen of Diaghan and a struggle to the death began. Tabon Wana and the archers of Wagadou stretched out their lines towards the hills and the battle spread over the entire plain, while an unrelenting sun climbed in the sky. The horses of Mema were extremely agile, and they reared forward with their fore hooves raised and swooped down on the horsemen of Diaghan, who rolled on the ground trampled under the horses' hooves. Presently the men of Diaghan gave ground and fell back towards the rear. The enemy center was broken.

It was then that Manding Bory galloped up to announce to Sundiata that Soumaoro, having thrown in all his reserve, had swept down on Fakoli and his smiths. . . .

His eyes red with anger, Sundiata pulled his cavalry over to the left in the direction of the hills where Fakoli was valiantly enduring his uncle's blows. But wherever the son of the buffalo passed, death rejoiced. . . . [Sundiata] looked for Soumaoro and caught sight of him in the middle of the fray. Sundiata struck out right and left and the Sossos scrambled out of his way. The king of Sosso, who did not want Sundiata to get near him, retreated far behind his men, but Sundiata followed him with his eyes. He stopped and bent his bow. The arrow flew and grazed Soumaoro on the shoulder. The cock's spur no more than scratched him, but the effect was immediate and Soumaoro felt his powers leave him. His eyes met Sundiata's. Now trembling like a man in the grip of a fever, the vanquished Soumaoro looked up towards the sun. A great black bird flew over above the fray and he understood. It was a bird of misfortune.

"The bird of Krina," he muttered.

The king of Sosso let out a great cry and, turning his horse's head, he took to flight. The Sossos saw the king and fled in their turn. It was a rout. Death hovered over the great plain and blood poured out of a thousand wounds. Who can tell how many Sossos perished at Krina? The rout was complete and Sundiata then dashed off in pursuit of Soumaoro. . . .

When Djata had been joined by all the army he marched on Sosso. Soumaoro's city, Sosso, the impregnable city, the city of smiths skilled in wielding the spear. . . .

Sosso was a magnificent city. In the open plain her triple rampart with awe-inspiring towers reached into the sky. The city comprised a hundred and eighty-eight fortresses and the palace of Soumaoro loomed above the whole city like a gigantic tower. . . .

From the top of a hill, Djata and his general staff gazed upon the fearsome city of the sorcerer-king. The army encamped in the plain opposite the great gate of the city and fires were lit in the camp. Djata resolved to take Sosso in the course of a morning. He fed his men a double ration and the tam-tams beat all night to stir up the victors of Krina.

At daybreak the towers of the ramparts were black with *sofas*. Others were positioned on the ramparts themselves. They were the archers. The Mandingoes were masters in the art of storming a town. In the front line Sundiata placed the *sofas* of Mali, while those who held the ladders were in the second line protected by the shields of the spearmen. The main body of the army was to attack the city gate. When all was ready, Djata gave the order to attack. The drums resounded, the horns blared and like a tide the Mandingo front line moved off, giving mighty shouts. With their shields raised above their heads the Mandingoes advanced up to the foot of the wall, then the Sossos began to rain large stones down on the assailants. From the rear, the bowmen of Wagadou shot arrows at the ramparts. The attack spread and the town was assaulted at all points. Sundiata had a murderous reserve; they were the bowmen whom the king of the Bobos had sent shortly before Krina. The archers of Bobo are the best in the world. On one knee the archers fired flaming arrows over the ramparts. Within the walls the thatched huts took fire and the smoke swirled up. The ladders stood against the curtain wall and the first Mandingo *sofas* were already at the top. Seized by panic through seeing the town on fire, the Sossos hesitated a moment. The huge tower surmounting the gate surrendered, for Fakoli's smiths had made themselves masters of it. . . . They opened the gates to the main body of the army. . . .

Soumaoro's palace was now at Sundiata's mercy. While everywhere the Sossos were begging for quarter, Sundiata, preceded by Balla Fasseke, entered Soumaoro's tower. The *griot* knew every nook and cranny of the palace from his captivity and he led Sundiata to Soumaoro's magic chamber. . . .

The inmates of the chamber had lost their power. The snake in the pitcher was in the throes of death, the owls from the perch were flapping pitifully about on the ground. Everything was dying in the sorcerer's abode. It was all up with the power of Soumaoro. Sundiata had all Soumaoro's fetishes taken down and before the palace were gathered together all Soumaoro's wives, all princesses taken from their families by force. The prisoners, their hands tied behind their backs, were already herded together. Just as he had wished, Sundiata had taken Sosso in the course of a morning. When everything was outside of the town and all that there was to take had been taken out, Sundiata gave the order to complete its destruction. The last houses were set fire to and prisoners were employed in the razing of the walls. . . .

Yes, Sosso was razed to the ground. It has disappeared, the proud city of Soumaoro. A ghastly wilderness extends over the places where kings came and humbled themselves before the sorcerer king. . . .

Sosso vanished from the earth and it was Sundiata, the son of the buffalo, who gave these places over to solitude. After the destruction of Soumaoro's capital the world knew no other master but Sundiata.

THE LAND OF ODUDUWA

The first sizable kingdoms to develop in the area southeast of Ghana and Mali were the Yoruba states of Ife, Oyo, and Benin. Today the Yoruba peoples form the dominant stock in Nigeria's western region; they are also found in its northern region, as well as in Dahomey and northern Togo. They share a common culture, language, and belief in their descent from a common ancestor, Oduduwa, the first ruler of Ife. Although the Yoruba have many different creation myths, all describe Ife as the cradle of their culture and the center of the world. The version excerpted below is told by E. Bolaji Idowu, who teaches at University College in Ibadan, Nigeria.

The King of Ile-Ife is regarded by most of the Yoruba as the Father of the race as well as their spiritual leader. It is generally believed that he derives his status from *Oduduwa* whom the Yoruba believe to be their original ancestor and a priest-king of Ile-Ife. There is traditional evidence that in the ancient days, the priest-king of Ile-Ife was the one in whom resided all authority, religious and secular, and that he held a pontifical sway over all. Even after the scepter had branched off and part-authority went to Oyo and elsewhere, the Yoruba continue to look upon Ile-Ife as "the Home," the unique, sacred spot which was the source and fountain of all . . . .

We shall now proceed to tell the story of the creation of the earth and its fullness. What is now our earth was once a watery, marshy waste. Up above was the skyey heaven which was the abode of Olodumare [the Supreme Being] and the divinities, with some other beings. The watery waste constituted, in a way, the sporting place for those dwellers above. Upon it they used to descend by strands of spider's web which also formed bridges by which they walked over it. Some of them came down from time to time for the purpose of hunting.

What moved Olodumare to think of creating the solid earth, no one knows. However, He conceived the idea and at once carried it into effect. He summoned Orisa-nla, the arch-divinity, to His presence and charged him with the duty: for material, He gave him a leaf packet of loose earth (some say that the loose earth was in a snail's shell), and for tools a five-toed hen and a pigeon.

When Orisa-nla arrived, he threw the loose earth on a suitable spot on the watery waste. Then he let loose the hen and the pigeon; and these immediately began the work of scattering and spreading the loose earth. This they did until a great portion of the waste was covered. When enough of it had been covered, Orisa-nla went back and reported to Olodumare that the work had been accomplished. Whereupon, Olodumare dispatched the chameleon to go down and inspect what had been done. The

chameleon, it must be noted, was chosen on the merit of the extraordinary carefulness and delicacy with which it moves about, and the still more extraordinary way in which it can take in any situation immediately. From the first visit, the chameleon took back the report that although the earth was indeed wide enough, it was not yet sufficiently dry for any further operation; from the second visit, however, it returned with the cheering report that it was both "wide enough" and sufficiently dry.

The sacred spot where the work began was named Ife—"That which is wide," from the Yoruba word *fe*, meaning "to be wide." And that, according to the tradition, was how Ife, the Holy City of the Yoruba, got its name. The prefix *Ile-* [meaning "house"] was added much later on to signify that it was the original home of all and to distinguish it from the other towns called Ife which have come into existence as a result of migrations.

The creation of the earth was completed in four days; the fifth day was therefore set apart for the worship of the Deity and for rest. When Olodumare was satisfied that the work had indeed been accomplished, He sent Orisa-nla back to equip and embellish the earth. This time, He sent Orunmila to accompany him and be his counselor. To Orisa-nla, Olodumare handed the primeval *Igi Ope* (Palm Tree). This he was to plant—its juice would give drink, its seed would give oil as well as kernels for food. He gave him also three other trees which were full of sap. These were *Ire* (Silk Rubber Tree), *Awun* (Whitewood), and *Dodo*. These also were to be planted and propagated: their juices would give drink. For as yet, there was no rain upon the earth. The original hen and pigeon which had been used in spreading the loose earth should now increase and multiply and provide meat for the dwellers on earth.

Orisa-nla came down and did as he was told. When all was ready, Oreluere, one of the beings who had been prepared beforehand, was commissioned to lead a

party of those beings down to the earth. He brought them down as he was instructed and those became the nucleus of the human occupation of the earth.

When the affairs of the earth had been running for some time and its inhabitants were multiplying, it was discovered that there was not enough water for use. Therefore, Orisa-nla appealed to Olodumare and, as a result, rain began to fall upon the earth.

Orisa-nla was assigned another special job. He was made the "creator" of human physical features for the future. It is not clear from the oral traditions when he first began to do the work. However, he got the job; and his allotted duty was thenceforth to mould man's physical form from the dust of the earth. He thus became the sculptor-divinity. But the right to give life Olodumare reserved to Himself alone for ever. . . .

The word [*olodumare*] is said to be a contraction of the phrase-name Olodu-omo-ere—"Olodu, the offspring of the boa." This suggestion is based upon a myth which derives from the natural phenomenon of the rainbow. The Yoruba believe, generally, that the rainbow is produced by a very large boa: the reptile discharges from its inside the sulfurous matter which sets all its surroundings aglow and causes a reflection, which is the rainbow (*Osumare*), in the sky. The matter which is so discharged is known as *Imi Osumare* ("rainbow-excrement") and is considered very valuable for making people wealthy and prosperous. It is the Yoruba equivalent of the "philosopher's stone"! . . . It is, however, very rarely obtained, in spite of the fact that it is so much earnestly sought after, one reason being that anyone who approached the spot at the moment when it is on the ground would be consumed forthwith; and another that the reptile itself has the miserly habit of swallowing it all up again when the ritual is over! . . .

The myth has it that the name of this personage who is above was originally Olodu. He was the offspring of the large primordial boa, and was a prodigy from birth. Very early he acquired a reputation for prowess and goodness. For some reason, the earth could no longer contain him, and so he went to dwell in heaven. There he exceedingly increased in all good and divine qualities. But before he went up, both he and his parent had entered into a covenant that they would always remember, and from time to time communicate with, each other. The rainbow which occurs in the sky is the sign of that age-long covenant and communion between Olodu and the boa, a sign that the covenant remains for ever. . . . ,

[There are] two other very important names by which Olodumare is known. These are Olofin-Orun and Olorun. . . . The name Olorun is the one commonly used in popular language.

HOW BRONZES ARE MADE

It was at Ife that the renowned Yoruba sculpture in bronze, wood, and terra cotta first developed. The Ife bronzes, which most probably were made before the beginning of our millennium, were cast by the lost-wax process, which has since been widely used in West Africa. According to oral tradition, the artisans of Benin—a sizable Yoruba-ruled kingdom by the mid-1400's—learned lost-wax bronze casting from their Ife neighbors. However, whereas it is certain that there was artistic contact between the two states, there is now considerable evidence to indicate that the influence was in both directions. Ife bronzes are characterized by a sophisticated naturalism; Benin's, by stylization. The neighboring Hausa people of northern Nigeria give this oral account of the technique.

In the name of Allah the Compassionate, the Merciful. This account will show how the [Benin] figures are made. This work is one to cause wonder. Now this kind of work is done with clay, and wax, and red metal [copper], and solder [zinc], and lead, and fire. The first thing to be done if one of the figures is to be made, is to get clay and work it most thoroughly, and get the little stones which are in it worked out. It is well worked in

the hands. Next the shape of the top of a head is constructed [from the clay], and then the jaws on the same piece as the top of the head. Then the nose is shaped, and the eyes and the lips made. Then a certain stick which has been shaped like a knife is put [against the model] and it is smoothed [with this]. A very little water is put on when it is being thus smoothed until it is perfect; then it is set in the sun to dry. Next wax is melted and poured over it [the clay model],

Messenger of Death, a Benin bronze plaque
WERNER FORMAN

[and] then it is gone over [again] with the knife. As it [the wax] hardens it is smoothed over. When it has been well done, then a fire is kindled, [and] a knife put in the fire. When it is slightly warm it is taken up and pressed over the wax in order that it may adhere well [to the clay foundation]. The eyes get the finishing touches, [and] the eyebrows, and mouth and chin and beard. Then this stick like a knife is got out [and] dipped

in water [and] pressed against the wax, [and] passed over it—it is well smoothed [and] shines [all over]. If the model is of a woman's head then the hair adornment is put on. How the adornment of the hair is made, is as follows. Wax is rolled out till it is like a string—water is used; it forms a long piece. Then he [the smith] cuts it into pieces [and] fastens them on top of the head. Then he takes a razor [and] cuts [them the required length]. Next he cuts off other short pieces of wax [and] sticks them along the head. Then he rolls out another bit of wax with water, making it long like a rope. He divides it in two [down the middle, not across], lays them side by side, and puts them on the top of the first upright pieces and sticks [the whole] on. The part left over he cuts off [and] casts aside. Then he prepares a certain broad piece of wax and makes ears out of it [and] fixes them on. But whenever he is about to stick any piece on, first he puts the knife in the fire and presses it against the wax. Then he sits down—this [part of the work] is completed. There remains the pouring in of the metal. When he has finished [the part just described] he takes up mud [and] covers the whole head with it; leaving only a small hole. He puts it in the sun to dry—this part is finished. There remains the pouring in of the metal.

This description is of the pouring in of the metal. The way the metal is poured in is [as follows]. When the fire has been brought it is poured into the melting-furnace, [and] the bellows are set to work [and] the fire blown [and] charcoal poured in. Then the model is lifted [and] placed on the fire. Water is poured into a pot or cup. When the model has become heated then the wax inside melts. Then it is taken up, the tongs, or some [take] a stick, are placed across the pot [of water], and the figure put on top, and the wax keeps dropping out. And it is held so till all the wax has melted and dropped into the water. Then a great quantity of charcoal is poured [into the furnace]. The figure [in clay] is set on the fire.

Bars of metal are continually being cut with a hammer; many pieces are broken up in this way, [and] put in the smelting-pot. Then they scrape out a hole in the charcoal and put the smelting-pot in, replace the charcoal again, [and] cover up. The [mud] figure is brought and set. [It is set] on the fire. They keep blowing the bellows, and this clay lump is turned till red hot. Then the metal has melted, then the figure is taken up, a hole is dug, [and] it is placed in it so that it is firmly set. The hole left in the clay is cleared out and the melted metal poured in. If it is filled, that is well; if not, more is added to fill it. If full then [the work] is finished. Next it is set aside to cool, then [the outside covering of clay] is broken off. Then you see a beautiful figure. That is it. The work of Ali is completed.

A CHILD IS . . .

Central to Yoruba philosophy is belief in a cycle of reincarnation. Deceased ancestors are said to be reborn into the same family. Thus, having children carries additional genealogical significance. Three months after the birth of a child, the parents consult an oracle to find out which ancestor the child has brought back to life. This poem was translated by Ulli Beier, a distinguished African-ist who specializes in Yoruba literature.

A child is like a rare bird.
A child is precious like coral.
A child is precious like brass.
You cannot buy a child on the market.
Not for all the money in the world.
The child you can buy for money is
    a slave.
We may have twenty slaves,
We may have thirty laborers,
Only a child brings us joy.
One's child is one's child.
The buttocks of our child are not so flat
That we should tie the beads on another
    child's hips.
One's child is one's child.
It may have a watery head or a square
    head,
One's child is one's child.

It is better to leave behind a child,
Than let the slaves inherit one's house.
A child is the beginning and end of
    happiness.
One must not rejoice too soon over
    a child.
Only the one who is buried by his child,
Is the one who has truly born a child.
On the day of our death, our hand
    cannot hold a single cowrie.
We need a child to inherit our
    belongings.

THE ILLUSTRIOUS METAL

The wealth of Ghana and of the subsequent empires that flourished in the western and central Sudan during the Middle Ages was largely dependent on these states' roles as middlemen in the lucrative gold trade. Gold was a basic commodity in trans-Saharan commerce from the eighth to the fifteenth century, during which period the Sudan furnished a major share of the world's gold. One of the best reports on gold production is by William Bosman, a seventeenth-century Dutchman who spent fourteen years on the Guinea coast, where he was an official for the Dutch West India Company. There he observed methods that had been in use for hundreds of years. The following extract on the subject is from his New and Accurate Description of the Coast of Guinea *first published in English in London in 1705.*

This Illustrious Metal is generally found in three sorts of places: First, the best is found in or betwixt particular Hills; and the *Negroes* apprehending where the Gold is, dig Pits; and separate it from the Earth which comes out with it.

The second place is in, at, and about some Rivers and Water-falls; whose violence washeth down great Quantities of Earth, which carry the Gold with it.

The third is on the Sea shore; where (as at *Elmina* and *Axim*) there are little Branches or Rivulets into which the Gold is driven from Mountainous Places, as well as to the Rivers; and after violent Showers of Rain in the Night, next Morning these places are sure to be vis-

ited by hundreds of *Negro*-Women naked, except a Cloth wrapped about them to hide what Modesty obligeth. Each of these Women is furnished with large and small Troughs or Tray, which they first fill full of Earth and Sand, which they wash with repeated fresh Water, till they have cleansed it from all its Earth; and if there be any Gold, its Ponderosity forces it to the bottom of the Trough; which if they find, it is thrown into the small Tray, and so they go to washing it again: which Operation generally holds them till Noon: Some of them not getting above the value of Sixpence; some of them find pieces of six or seven Shillings, though not frequently; and often they entirely loose their labor. Thus the digging of Pits, the gathering it, at or about the Rivers, and this last mentioned manner, are all the ways they know to come at Gold.

The Gold thus digged or found, is of two sorts; one is called Dust-Gold, or Gold-Dust, which is almost as fine as Flower, and is the best, bearing also the greatest Price in *Europe:* The other sort is in pieces of different sizes; some being hardly the weight of a Farthing, others weighing as heavy as twenty or thirty Guineas; though of the last sort not many occur. The *Negroes* indeed tell us, that in the Country Pieces as heavy as one or two hundred Guineas, are found. These Lumps or Pieces are called Mountain-Gold; which being melted, touch better than Dust-Gold; but the multitude of small Stones which always adhere

to 'em, occasion a great loss in the melt-
ing; for which reason Gold-Dust is most
esteemed. Thus much of the good and
pure Gold; and now to touch upon the
false. The first sort is that mixed with
Silver or Copper, and cast into *Fetiches*
[ingots]. . . . These *Fetiches* are cut into
small bits by the *Negroes*. . . . The *Negroe*
Women know the exact value of these
bits so well at sight, that they never are
mistaken; and accordingly they tell them
to each other without weighing, as we do
coined Money.

YORUBA PROVERBS

*Proverbs have been called the national poetry
of the Yoruba. They are highly refined con-
trivances; however, they also embody an
ethical code, and most are sententious observations on men, manners, and morals. The
sound of the language may be heard in the
following example: "Owe li esin oro bi oro
ba no owe li afi iwa a, owe on oro ni
irin." It means "a proverb is the horse of
conversation; when the conversation [flags],
a proverb revives it: proverbs and conversation follow each other." This group was compiled by Richard Burton in the last century.*

Mouth not keeping to mouth, and lip
not keeping to lip, bring trouble to the
jaws.
(Talk is silver, silence is gold.)

When the day dawns the trader betakes
himself to his trade;
The spinner takes her distaff [or spindle],
the warrior takes his shield;
The weaver bends over his Asa, or sley
[stoops to his batten];
The farmer awakes, he and his hoe-
handle;
The hunter awakes with his quiver and
bow.
(A correct and picturesque description
of the daybreak scene in every Yoruba
town. It also instructs that no one should
remain idle.)

When the spear sees the battle, it dances;
when the lance sees the battle, it joys.

The thread follows the needle.

The calabash having saved them [in time
of famine], they said, "Let us cut it for a
drinking cup."

He fled from the sword and hid in the
scabbard.
("Out of the frying pan into the fire.")

There is no market in which the dove
with the prominent breast has not traded.
(The cowry, on account of its circula-
tion as currency, is compared with the
dove.)

Peace is the father of friendship.

Wrangling is the father of fighting.

One here, two there, [so gathers] a vast
multitude.

The jaw is the house of laughter.
(The jaw is here compared with a happy
family.)

The young cannot teach tradition to the
old.

I have tied the leopard skin round my
waist; you cannot sell me.
(Meaning, I have the protection of powerful friends; you cannot ruin me with
law expenses.)

One who does not understand the yellow
palm-bird says the yellow palm-bird is
noisy.
(Men are prone to despise what they do
not understand.)

As a calabash receives the sediment of
water, so an elder must exercise fore-
bearance.

"SCUFFLES OFTEN OCCUR"

*Ijala is one of the many types of oral poetry
recited by Yoruba-speaking people. Myth-
ically and ritually these chants are associated
with the worship of Ogun, the Yoruba god of
iron, who is believed to have been a hunter*

An itinerant weaver at a portable loom

during his earthly life, and who, as a god, oversees all iron implements. Ijala chants are primarily performed at hunters' celebrations, but they also figure at happy occasions not specifically connected with Ogun or the hunt, such as weddings, naming of children, and housewarmings. The subject matter of the chants depends on the type of festivity: there are salutes to animals and birds, praise songs honoring royal lineages, and benedictions for social occasions. There is also a type of ijala having no central theme and devoted to random observations on Yoruba life. The next example, compiled by S. A. Babalola, himself a Yoruba, belongs to the last category. The Ata Ari, Apateere, and Ologbongan referred to are villages near Ibadan. At Ikeeku, also near Ibadan, water is deep underground. The "prospective chief is not a fool" because he watches the drummer's beating hand and thereby cannot be tricked into taking a false step. The sekere musician rattles a bottle gourd covered with strings of tiny cowry shells.

Scuffles often occur when people sing at Ata Ari.

Unless you have a bucket with a long strong rope tied to its handle, you cannot have water at Apateere.

Unless you dig a water-hole of your own, you cannot have water to drink at Ikeeku.

Isn't the pond near Ologbongan? Verify this from anyone you see.

Verify this, I say, from anyone you see.

For a dance, the appropriate dress is an *agbada.*

For a social visit, the appropriate dress is a caftan.

The fitting place for a hat is the head, the fitting place for a string of beads is the waist.

The hips of a hiking trader on the move are never at ease.

A hawker's head is usually bald in the middle.

A minstrel's eyes show no signs of any shyness.

The hips of a corn-grinder in action Never stay erect.

A pepper-grinder's head does not stay motionless.

A drummer drumming trickishly, to catch out his dancer,

Is matched by the dancing prospective chief who is not a fool.

A drummer was one day drumming before another man's wife.

As he drummed, he peered from the edge of the woman's wrapper, to catch a glimpse of her waist beads.

As he drummed, he lifted up the edge of the woman's cloth to look upon the woman's seat.

However, by the time he got back to his house,

A *sekere* music man had abducted his wife, so he clasped his hands together and heaved a long protracted sigh.

A YORUBA PRAISE SONG

The most common type of Yoruba poetry is the oriki, a poetic word used to describe and extol a person or god. In the course of his life every Yoruban, commoner or prince, acquires a set of oriki, or praise names. These are chanted by professional musicians. The most poetic oriki are those dedicated to the orisha, the Yoruba deities who mediate between Olodumare, the supreme god, and man. The orisha are usually hero-kings, or ancestors, or founders of cities. The following oriki, translated by Ulli Beier, is that of Oshun, one of the three river wives of Shango, the deity of thunder. Oshun is a beautiful coquette, a healer, and a mother goddess. Here she is also identified with Iyalode, the title of a female chief in Yoruba towns. She is associated with brass, and her color is yellow.

We call her and she replies with wisdom.
She can cure those whom the doctor has failed.
She cures the sick with cold water.
When she cures the child, she does not charge the father.
We can remain in the world without fear.
Iyalode who cures children—help me to have my own child.
Her medicines are free—she feeds honey to the children.
She is rich and her words are sweet.
Large forest with plenty of food.
Let a child embrace my body.
The touch of a child's hand is sweet.

Owner of brass.
Owner of parrots' feathers.
Owner of money.

My mother, you are beautiful, very beautiful.
Your eyes sparkle like brass.
Your skin is soft and smooth,
You are black like velvet.

Everybody greets you when you descend on the world.
Everybody sings your praises.

YORUBA RIDDLES

Riddles are often used at the beginning of a storytelling session, where they test the acuity of the audience and arouse interest. The following Yoruba riddles and their surprise answers were translated by Ulli Beier.

We call the dead—they answer.
We call the living—they do not answer.
(Dry leaves sound when trodden on. Fresh ones don't.)

We are going to Ife—we face Ife.
We are returning from Ife—we still face Ife.
(Climbing and descending a palm tree one faces the same direction.)

We are pounding yam—
The dog is dancing.
(A woman's breasts dance when she is pounding yams.)

The black one is squatting,
The red one is licking his bottom.
(Cooking pot on the fire is licked by the flame.)

Two tiny birds
Jump over two hundred trees.
(A man's eyes can carry him far.)

The bereaved one has stopped weeping.
The compassionate friend is still crying.
(After the rain stops, the leaves continue to drip.)

The essence of authority: Golden regalia worn by an Asante ruler in modern Ghana

THE
LONG
HERITAGE

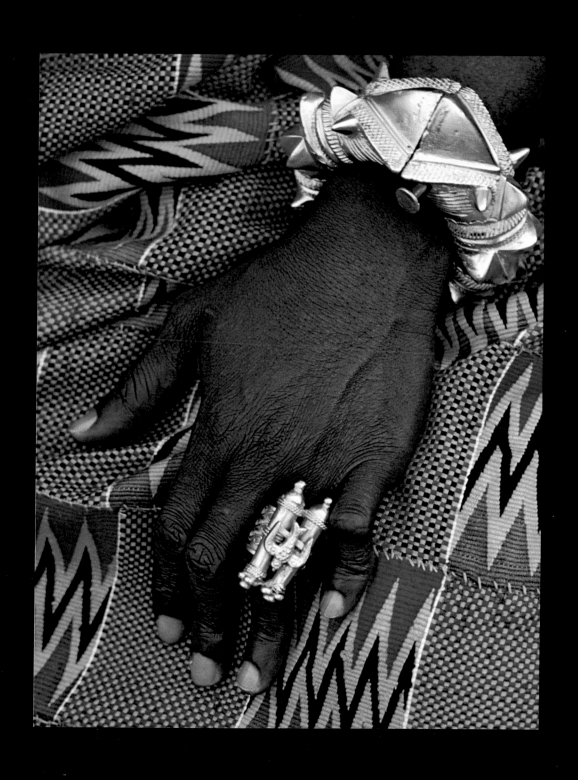

ERA OF EMPIRES

During the one thousand years that Europe was experiencing the Middle Ages and the Renaissance, kingdoms and empires, conquering armies and powerful rulers, rose and fell in the fertile lands of West Africa south of the Sahara. Travelers from North Africa made legendary such names as Ghana, Mali, and Songhai, and told of the glories of busy cities like Kumbi Saleh, Gao, Jenne, and Timbuktu. Among the rulers were some of Africa's greatest: Sundiata, Mansa Musa, Sunni Ali, Askia Muhammad. In 1591 a Moroccan armed force overran the area, and West Africa's great age ended. Even though some of its cities had disappeared by the nineteenth century, memories lived on in oral accounts and Arab travelers' writings.

Wealth from trade financed large armies, and warfare was common. The cavalryman at left, with a shield and wearing chain mail, is from a northern Nigerian area that was once part of the Hausa states.
KEN HEYMAN

Timbuktu, rich trade and cultural center of Mansa Musa's Mali empire, was sacked and razed by many conquerors. The sketch above, drawn by René Caillié in 1828, gives only a hint of its great past.

The university in the Sankore quarter of Timbuktu was famed throughout the Muslim world. But other cities were also centers of Islamic learning, where youths like the ones seen at left studied the Koran.

The Great Mosque at right, dating from the fourteenth century, is at Jenne on the Niger River. Despite Islam's sway, local religious practices persisted outside the cities and even in court ceremonies.

A modern-day caravan approaches Timbuktu. Camels, introduced to the Sahara from the Near East in Roman times, permitted the opening of new routes across waterless stretches.
PHOTO TRENDS

THE GOLD TRADE

As far back as history records, there were trade contacts between North Africa and the savanna region south of the Sahara. By 1000 B.C. caravans of bullocks or horses, guided by desert dwellers, were carrying goods from oasis to oasis between the areas. In the south agriculture and iron had created a base for a populous and expanding civilization. The earliest traders to the south might have brought salt, an eagerly sought commodity, and just as early they might have been paid for it with gold. In time the Sudanese trading towns became important suppliers of gold to the Mediterranean area, and Ghana, the first of the West African kingdoms, was known as the Land of Gold. The gold-producing regions, including Wangara near the upper Niger and Senegal rivers, actually lay south of Ghana, and sites were often kept secret from the northern traders. Wangara was later enfolded in the Mali and Songhai empires, and until the discovery of the New World, caravans to North Africa from those Sudanese states brought European kingdoms the major part of their gold.

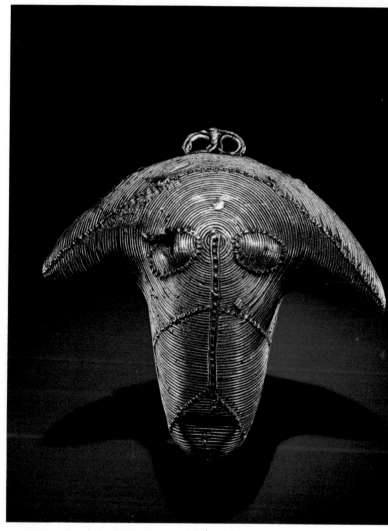

In addition to trading gold, West Africans themselves also worked the metal into many dazzling objects of splendid artistry. The ornamental pendant mask above was made by the Baule of the Ivory Coast, a people that formerly lived in the Asante kingdom of present-day Ghana.
MUSEUM OF PRIMITIVE ART—LEE BOLTIN

raditional gold emblems of high office adorn the asantehene, *or paramount chief of Asante.*
TO RESEARCHERS—THOMAS D. W. FRIEDMANN

Canoes up to forty feet long plied Nigeria's waters. This nineteenth-century view shows an Ibo craft, its flags decorated with the enemy's emblem, dismembered limbs, and other oddments.

THE
GUINEA COAST

When Portuguese navigators first reached the West African coast in the fifteenth century, they called it by the Moroccan Berber phrase *Akal n-Iguinawen,* "Land of the Blacks." For generations thereafter the Guinea coast, a center of gold and slave trade, was the only part of sub-Saharan Africa even vaguely known to most Westerners. Inland, through the great belt of forest and northward to the old empires of the Sudan, was a vast network of trade routes, linking a multitude of kingdoms, city-states, and communities of many different peoples. Only in the last century has the white man, or for that matter other Africans, recognized the variety of sophisticated cultures that flourished in West Africa.

The Benin River (left) winds through the Nigerian forest and the heart of the once-powerful kingdom of Benin. Benin's artists excelled in naturalistic sculpture, as shown in this sixteenth-century bronze portrait of a queen mother at right.

Chapter Six

THE NIGER TO THE NILE

(c. A.D. 500–1600)

by

Basil Davidson

EASTWARD FROM THE WESTERN SUDAN, from the states of the upper and middle Niger, from the lands of ancient Ghana and Mali and Songhai, the same broad plains of grass and sifting soil flow for two thousand miles until they reach and overleap the waters of the Nile. These plains of the central Sudan traverse Hausaland and Bornu, their populous heart and center, encircle the marsh-trimmed mirrors of Lake Chad, and lead on thirstily through the solitudes of Kanem and Zaghawa and Wadai, lands where the world is altogether flat but for the slow deception of long-dry riverbeds.

Then, as though reflecting the drama of this great region's history, the plains confront the sudden glacis of Darfur, where green peaks rise into the mists of Jebel Marra's 10,100-foot summit. But at once the land falls away to plains again. They flow on now into the hard cattle country of little water and infrequent pasture that is Kordofan. Beyond Kordofan they come to the oases lands of Nubia and the White Nile. They cross these and continue to the Blue Nile and the highlands of Ethiopia. And that, at last, is their frontier.

The peoples of the central Sudan, like their neighbors in the western Sudan, have an interrelated history much the same in kind and content. Its dominant themes are those of political adventure and ambition; of swift conquest and defeat among peoples to whom good horsemanship and fine horses have always mattered much; of ceaseless movement and migration brought to rest and stability only where long-distance trade routes crossed and became knit together within the defensive walls of market towns or royal capitals. Its poets and scholars, Muslim but rooted in African tradition, have told similar stories of empires and warriors, of battles and booty, of the joys of home.

the Sudan corridor, diverse peoples like these Hausa villagers and Tuareg nomads are neighbors.

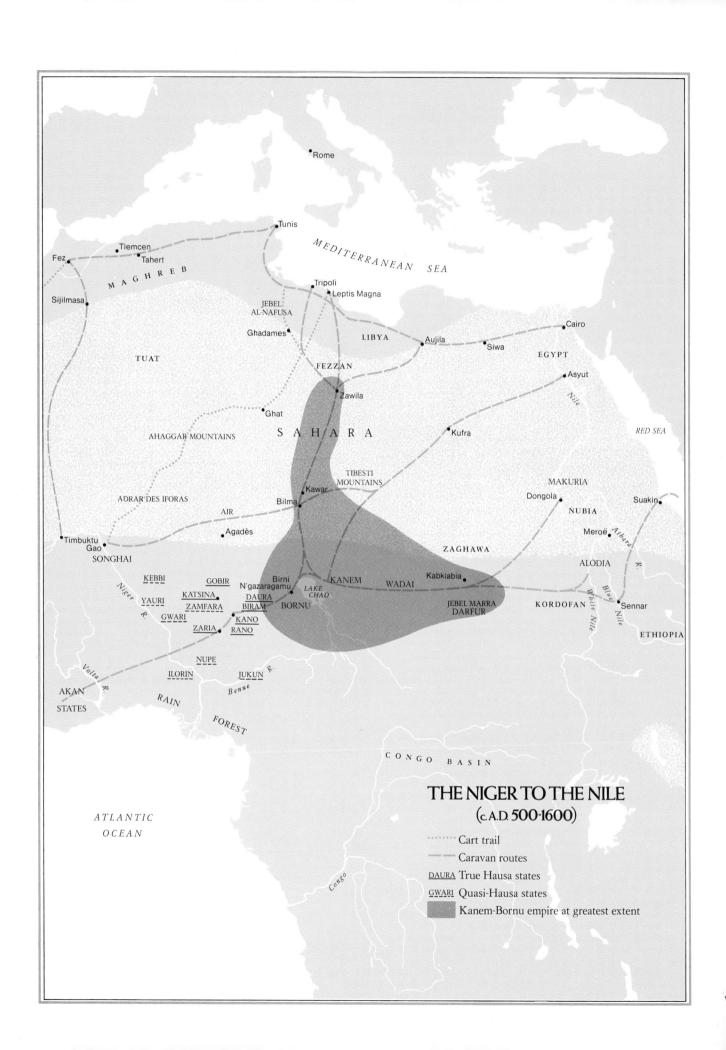

Rome

MEDITERRANEAN SEA

Tunis

Fez
Tlemcen
Tahert
MAGHREB
Sijilmasa

Tripoli
Leptis Magna
JEBEL
AL-NAFUSA
Ghadames
LIBYA
Aujila
Cairo
Siwa
EGYPT
Asyut

TUAT
FEZZAN
Zawila

SAHARA
Kufra
Nile

AHAGGAR MOUNTAINS
RED SEA

TIBESTI
MOUNTAINS
MAKURIA
Dongola
Suakin

ADRAR DES IFORAS
Kawar
Bilma
NUBIA
Meroë

AIR
Agadès
ZAGHAWA
ALODIA

Timbuktu
Gao
SONGHAI

Kabkiabia
KANEM
WADAI
KORDOFAN
Sennar

KEBBI
GOBIR
Birni
N'gazaragamu
LAKE
CHAD
BORNU
JEBEL MARRA
DARFUR
ETHIOPIA

YAURI
KATSINA
DAURA
ZAMFARA
BIRAM
GWARI
ZARIA
KANO
RANO

NUPE
ILORIN
JUKUN
Benue R.

AKAN
STATES
Volta R.
RAIN

FOREST

ATLANTIC
OCEAN

CONGO BASIN

Congo

THE NIGER TO THE NILE
(c. A.D. 500-1600)

.... Cart trail

— — — Caravan routes

<u>DAURA</u> True Hausa states

<u>GWARI</u> Quasi-Hausa states

▓ Kanem-Bornu empire at greatest extent

"The clash of spears had long been doubtful, yet it ended in glory. . . . These were our deeds: they lived in the memory of all. Oh, triumphant expedition! But the greatest joy is still to tell, joy most precious, the recovery of my lost love, a part of myself! Silks from India are less soft than is her skin, her noble form is timid as a fawn. . . ." It was thus that a Bornu ruler returning from a fight set down his praise poem in due and proper verse. The poem is from the nineteenth century, but could have been written any time back to about A.D. 1000.

In contrast with the oral traditions and written records of many parts of Africa, the histories of the central Sudan are for the most part dynastic. They are principally concerned with powerful monarchs and their rise to power, with the enclosure of broad areas of trade and tribute within systems of centralized rule, with the impact of Islam upon methods of government or upon social and moral attitudes and customs. The characteristic note of these chronicles is epic. "On the next day, all the soldiers mounted their horses after equipping themselves and their horses with armor, with breastplates, shields and their best clothing," wrote a courtier of the great Idris Alooma (1570–1602), who was *mai*, or ruler, of Kanem-Bornu at the same time that Queen Elizabeth I was reigning over England. "When we had all ridden a short distance we met the messengers of the lord of Stambul, the Sultan of Turkey. . . . Our troops charged toward them, and they galloped their horses toward us. This continued for a long time until the infantry were tired of standing still. . . ."

Nearly two centuries later, passing far eastward through the Sudanic sultanate of Sennar on the Blue Nile, the Scottish traveler James Bruce described the cavalry of the Funj people as though he were speaking of the same scene. Each lancer possessed a shirt of mail and a helmet of beaten copper, and their horses were "all above sixteen hands high, of the breed of the old Saracen horses, all finely made and as strong as our coach horses, but exceedingly nimble in their motion."

This sort of history may read agreeably, but it has the disadvantage of telling little about everyday life. In countries pestered by royal ambition, whether in Africa or not, peaceful or productive citizens figure little in the records. Yet the deeper truths, revealed by archeological discoveries over the past twenty years or so and by the very recent probing of modern historians, are reasonably clear in their general shape and outline.

From very early times the Niger-Nile region formed a zone of migration and slow settlement, where indigenous Stone Age peoples were joined by groups from the southern Sahara and other neighboring regions. This mingling gave rise in remote antiquity to new peoples, ancestors of the peoples who inhabit the region today. By A.D. 500 they had begun to acquire their characteristic cultures, modes of speech, religious beliefs, political systems, and notions about themselves. By A.D. 1000 they had assumed patterns of community life that would give rise to all subsequent development down to the twentieth century, even now marking these peoples with a distinctive quality.

Central to the history of much of the region is the record of the Kanuri and their thousand-year predominance in the Lake Chad region. The Kanuri played the same role here, in the sense of being the "core" people of a masterful centralizing polity, that the Soninke played in Ghana, the Mandinka (or Mandingo, as they are frequently known) in Mali, and the Songhai in the middle Niger area.

Peripherally, there were many other peoples. There were nomads of the southern Sahara, seminomads of the grasslands, and sedentary farmers in the forest zone to the west and south, some of the last group being culturally linked to the peoples of the northern Congo Basin. Several of these smaller societies early acquired small centralizing polities of their own, opposed the Kanuri in their bid for mastery, and fought them in many wars and raids. Others, somewhat farther away, stayed altogether free of Kanuri overlordship. Even then the Kanuri influence continued.

Prominent among these more distant neighbors were the Hausa-speaking groups to the west; the Nupe and Jukun astride the Benue valley to the south; the Berber raiders and traders of Aïr and Bilma, the little kingships of the central-southern Sahara. And woven into their midst, at least from the middle of the fifteenth century, there were groups of Fulbe, or Fulani, as their Hausa neighbors and subsequent historians have called them; their origins were far in the west. These Fulani were sometimes to play a vigorous role in religion and politics.

All these peoples belong to the "Country of the Blacks," as the region is commonly known; however, there is considerable variation in skin pigmentation of its inhabitants, ranging from the relative pallor of the Fulani to the luminous "black" of the Hausa. Despite these apparent differences, they shared a common pastoralist culture, which continues much the same even today. The people of the central Sudan early took advantage of grasslands, which were largely free of the menace of tsetse flies, to raise sizable herds of cattle, and many were farmers whose skills in growing millet and other crops were developed two thou-

The young nomad at left wears the elaborate facial ornament of the Fulani, a widely dispersed people dwelling in minority enclaves from Senegal to Lake Chad. His copper-colored skin, straight hair, and slender frame are common among his own Bororo group; however, other Fulani often show strongly Negroid characteristics. The diversity reflects a continued racial intermixing that has marked Fulani history. Their social organization, too, follows differing forms: many Fulani live in sedentary villages, and some have become aggressive state builders; the Bororo are pastoralists, basing their wealth and communal life around large herds of cattle, like that pictured opposite.

BOTH: VICTOR ENGLEBERT

sand years ago and more. Some of them acquired the techniques of ironworking not much later than that.

Two factors influenced the development of those among them who formed kingdoms and organized under some type of governmental rule: long-distance trade and Islam. As A. Adu Boahen has argued in his preceding chapter on the western Sudan, these elements are fundamental to West African history as a whole; but the roots of the Niger-Nile region have supported a distinctively different cultural flowering from that in the western Sudan. So far as the first of these shaping factors is concerned, this difference is explained by the fact that the north-south routes of the trans-Saharan commerce were supplemented in the central Sudan by an important system of lateral communications from the region of Wadai through Darfur to such crossroads towns as Sennar, which linked the region with routes running to Egypt, the Red Sea, and the Horn of Africa.

At any rate, since the rise of the post-Meroitic Christian kingdoms of Nubia after A.D. 540, and probably much earlier during Meroitic times, there was trade and travel along well-known routes reaching between Lake Chad and the Nile. Little or nothing is known of those who may have passed that way, if only because detailed histories of Meroë

and the Nubian kingdoms are almost entirely lost; today there remains just a scattering of potsherds to indicate the connection. Sherds of probable Meroitic origin have been picked up in long-dry wadis east of Lake Chad, but at present the sole sure fragmentary evidence of a Christian presence (or of links with Christian Nubia) is a single piece of pottery, found in the ruins of one of the old Kanuri capitals east of the lake. According to A.D.H. Bivar, a noted British Africanist, it bears the characteristic cream slip of the pottery from the Nubian state of Makuria, which flourished between about A.D. 600 and 1300. That so little material evidence has survived is disappointing, especially in view of the known trading enterprise of the Nubian kingdoms. Yet the hint of influence from the Nile remains curiously insistent in central Sudanese civilization, not least of all in the old Kanuri skills of building in brick, such as the Meroites and Nubians possessed.

Of early north-south connections there are far more sure indicators, though these, too, are tantalizingly rare and often imprecise. During Carthaginian and Roman times in North Africa, the Garamantes of the central Fezzan seem mainly to have used a trail going southwestward from their country through the Ahaggar massif to the Adrar des

Iforas mountains and probably onward to the middle Niger. But to the east, the central-southern Sahara also offered valuable commodities and oases to lure and sustain the trader (for example, the salt deposits of the Bilma oasis in the modern Niger Republic). The existence of many later links between the Fezzan and the Chad area makes it very probable that the Garamantes had also come this way.

Writing soon after 450 B.C., the Greek historian Herodotus says that the Garamantes "hunt the Ethiopian [among classical writers the generic term for "African"] hole-men, or troglodytes, in four-horse chariots, for these troglodytes are exceedingly swift of foot—more so than any people of whom we have any information. They eat snakes and lizards and other reptiles." These cave dwellers were possibly the Tebu people, between whose homeland in the Tibesti Mountains and the Fezzan there are at least two sites where ancient wall paintings of horse chariots are found. If the Garamantes themselves had left any written records, they would no doubt have revealed much more information on the subject. Roman records are almost as silent. An expedition led by one Julius Maternus of Leptis Magna reached the "land of Agisymba." Judging by the report that they found rhinoceroses in abundance there, the adventurers must have been somewhere in the Sudan; whatever else they may have learned about this land, aside from its being a country where black people lived, remains unknown.

Yet early north-south links seem probable. Though lacking gold, the Lake Chad region could provide elephant ivory, and it probably did. There had once been great numbers of elephants in North Africa as well as in the Sudan, but Mediterranean demand for ivory may well have depleted the local supply. (So honored was the creature in Leptis Magna that the authorities erected a statue of an elephant in one of their streets.) Accordingly, behind the history of the Niger-to-the-Nile region there hangs a shadowy backdrop painted with the symbols of ancient trade and contact with North Africa and the Nile, and possibly, though on this the records are entirely silent, with the Congo Basin and southern Nigeria.

If the central Sudan was a trading crossroads from ancient times, it was little used for a long time, and its indigenous peoples were left to evolve their own early structures of self-rule and development. How and when they did this remains a matter for conjecture. All that can be affirmed is that toward the ninth century, four or five protostates can be

People living along the shores of Lake Chad are farmers, but they supplement their diet with fish and, occasionally, the meat of the hippopotamus, an amphibious beast that once inhabited the shallow waters in great numbers. The engraving at right shows hunters closing in for a kill. The hippo's habitat, which seasonally varies in size from 4,000 to 10,000 square miles, was once an inland ocean.

BARTH, *Travels in Central Africa*, 1857

discerned in the region around Lake Chad. These began to be dominated by the Kanuri people, operating under powerful chiefs of the Saifuwa lineage. The Saifuwa were able to rise to power over their neighbors for reasons far from certain, though a good central position commanding trade routes west and east and a relatively fertile land were no doubt high on the list.

Their manner of organization also played a determining role. Like the early kings of Ghana, and afterward of Mali and Songhai, the Saifuwa must have drawn their initial strength among the Kanuri from a ritual authority. Saifuwa seniority came, in other words, from their standing in the line of divinely sanctioned ancestors, who were in turn the "owners" of the land.

The Saifuwa were thus the intermediaries between the spiritual power and the people, or so they succeeded in presenting themselves; and from that position of strength, evidently reached late in the ninth century, they were able to accumulate the consequential powers of secular rule, both political and military. The traditions are vague or silent on the ways in which they did this. But it may be inferred from later African examples, which are far better known, that they became kings because the Kanuri (or at least their clan leaders) were agreed on the need for stronger, and hence

more unified, means of getting tribute and controlling trade: in short, for assuring themselves of all those desiderata that gave rise to regular governments in Africa and elsewhere. The Kanuri chose to achieve these ends by putting government into the hands of kings.

Stronger than their neighbors, the Kanuri under their early Saifuwa kings embarked on conquest and began the building of an empire, at this time mainly in the region of Kanem to the east of Lake Chad. By the eleventh century, however, Islam was beginning to be a major factor in West African history. The expansion of that faith, which had followed the Muslim conquests in North Africa, profoundly influenced all it touched, including the trans-Saharan commerce and, eventually, the rise of the larger Kanem-Bornu empire.

Kharijite Berbers, dissenters from Abbasid religio-political rule, led the way in opening up the Sahara and, ultimately, the Sudan beyond. They gathered in states greatly given to trading enterprise. Sijilmasa and Tahert became crossroad city-states in the western and central Maghreb, while in the Fezzan two small Kharijite states in the neighborhood of Jebel al-Nafusa and Zawila, only a short distance from the ancient but long-since-abandoned homeland of the Garamantes, took shape toward the end of the eighth century.

Closely linked to one another by religious ties and trading interests, these little states rapidly assumed command of the middle Saharan trade routes. In the steps of the Garamantes they revived the old route southwestward to the Niger, and they pioneered a new route, though perhaps following the trace of one far older, south through the oases of Kawar and Bilma to the borders of Chad and the central Sudan.

This Kharijite primacy in trans-Saharan trade—a trade now to become far greater than before—was due in part to Egypt's abandonment of the Nile-to-the-Niger transversal Saharan route. During the late ninth century caravans appear to have ceased making regular use of this road, which had led from the northern Nile through the Kufra oasis and then on to Gao on the middle Niger, mainly because its perils were considerably greater than those of the alternate routes being opened up throughout the Fezzan and the Maghreb. Partly, too, the Kharijite states owed their success to stubborn enterprise, itself the product of their zealot culture.

One scrap of evidence that seems to affirm their central position in the whole great trading system, now in the course of growth, is the fact that a ninth-century governor of Nafusa could speak "the language of Kanem," presumably Kanuri, in addition to Arabic and his native Berber. Another indication of Saharan contacts with the Mediterranean coast is the fact that Cairo's east gate during the high days of that city's prosperity under the Fatimids was called the Bab al-Zawila, the "Gate of Zawila."

Thus Nafusa and Zawila, like Tahert and Sijilmasa, put the peoples of the western and central Sudan in touch with a worldwide system of trade. For Sudanese kings and traders, business partnership with Muslims meant a growing acquaintance with the manners and attitudes of Islam, and they became attuned to techniques of commercial credit and contract, such as were now becoming indispensable to a trade conducted over distances as great as these were and in volume ever larger than before. As with later incursions of Christianity in Africa, early Islam traveled in the trader's knapsack.

There was, of course, much more significance to these outside contacts than that. At least by the tenth century Islam could teach Sudanese potentates a good deal about new techniques of centralizing government, whether in respect to law or administration. Beyond that it could offer them membership into a wider world of power and prestige than any they had known before, thus broadening the horizons of their provincial obscurity. It could bring them the services of scribes and scholars, and it could lend a some-

Shrouded in the indigo robes that have given his people the name "blue men," a Tuareg strums a three-stringed lutelike instrument.
PHOTO RESEARCHERS—HECTOR ACEBES

times dazzling glint to their majesty and pomp. In other words, Islam could provide a new and necessary cultural framework in which to construct a stronger, more centralized system of government and a more autonomous basis for royal rule. This is not to derogate from the spiritual attractions of Islam. Yet, however real these attractions were, they could not have prevailed without their more secular attendants.

The first Kanuri king to accept Islam for himself and his court was Umme Jilma; Saifuwa traditions award him a reign in the late eleventh century. Thenceforward the Saifuwa kings were all Muslims. They made the pilgrimage to Mecca, some of them more than once. They introduced Muslim laws and customs, being careful (like their contemporaries in the western Sudan) not grossly to offend the sensibilities of their non-Muslim subjects, who would remain a large majority until very recent times. They welcomed scholars from the great schools of Cairo and the Maghreb, and probably from Spain. They encouraged the founding of their own Koranic schools. Gradually, through this cautious spread of Islam in court and market place, they undercut the power of rival nobles who relied upon the religious loyalties of Kanuri tradition. More and more, they gathered to themselves the attributes of supreme monarchs rather than the more limited privileges and powers of leaders of councils of lineage peers. And they tied themselves ever more successfully into the trans-Saharan trade.

At least from the eleventh century these kings had regular contact with the Fatimid rulers of Ifriqiya. Fatimid records tell of presents received from the "Malik al-Sudan," which in this context undoubtedly refers to the *mai*, or king, of the Kanuri. Such presents were mostly *'abid*, a word that may be loosely translated as "slaves," so long as modern implications are not read into the word. These *'abid* were mainly men who had forfeited their civic rights and status for one reason or other, commonly by capture in raiding warfare, and who were used as royal bodyguards. Relatively few in number, they were selected for good health and strength, and were expensive to buy and maintain. Yet Ifriqiya's Fatimid governors, always anxious to re-ensure themselves against uncertain local loyalties, were able to assemble enough *'abid* from the Sudan to maintain a regular company of troops.

These small but successful attempts at diplomacy encouraged the Kanuri kings to extend their hegemony across the northern desert. Late in the twelfth century the Fatimid rulers of Cairo were overthrown by the forces of the Syrian Saladin (Salah al-Din). Not long afterward these voracious, predominately Asian, mercenaries began looting the Kharijite states of the Fezzan. Evidently they continued in this way for a long time. They "set the country ablaze," in the words of a thirteenth-century writer, and greatly disturbed the desert trade. Reacting at last in 1258, the king of Kanem "sent emissaries to kill [one of these mercenaries], and [so] delivered the land from strife. His head was sent to Kanem and exhibited to the people," a detail that suggests that "the people," or least the traders, had by this time lost a lot of sleep over the plundering of their trans-Saharan commerce. After that, Zawila is said to have come under Kanuri control, while the Kanuri kings of this blossoming empire of Kanem-Bornu saw to it that they continued to enjoy fruitful relations with the Hafsid rulers of Tunisia.

Such was the formative framework, so far as external factors were concerned, affecting the Hausa to the west of the Kanuri, as well as many peoples to the east of them. Potent even in early times, the influence of long-distance communications grew in later centuries. Even if the written records are mainly lost, the remaining ones still give strong evidence of these connections. Thus, the earliest attested example of diplomatic correspondence in the central and western Sudan is a letter from a Kanuri king to the Sultan Barquq, of the Mameluk dynasty of Egypt, written sometime around A.D. 1391; it would not have been unique. And when, much later, Mai Idris Alooma's court scribe celebrates a meeting with messengers from the Ottoman sultan in Istambul, he is speaking for a tradition of far-ranging correspondence, which is already very old.

Yet the cultures that took shape in Kanem, as elsewhere in the central Sudan, were far more than copies of their prestigious examples beyond the desert. Although increasingly marked by Islam after the twelfth century, these cultures were no more Arab or Berber than were those of Mali and Songhai. On the contrary, they were the expression of local and indigenous factors of development that have never ceased to mark them with a depth and resonance that is all their own. This was the originality, the power of local beliefs and skills, which explains their long endurance through the years. Islam might show the way to a wider world, whether spiritual or social: all these peoples continued nonetheless to stand, and stand firmly, on their own sense of identity and purpose. Their history shows this very clearly.

Like its neighbors to the east and west, the Kanuri state used Islam to modify and strengthen structures already firmly in place. It was a transformation that took place slowly. King Umme might accept Islam. His successor, Dunama I, might twice make the pilgrimage, and according to tradition, suffer drowning in the Red Sea while on a third trip to Mecca. Those who followed might reinforce their links with the Fezzan and Tunisia or with Libya and Egypt. Yet they continued to owe their power to local concepts of authority and its use. For then and long afterward the king was little more than primus inter pares, or prime minister, of a ruling council of lineage peers. This council numbered twelve, and something is known of its organization. Under the *mai* they formed a government that Ives Urvoy, the first twentieth-century historian to concern himself with these matters, aptly called "the administrative council of the Saifuwa family firm."

As the early empire crystallized, these councilors acquired regular titles and "departments," governorships of provinces, and commands of armed forces. Among such titled offices were the *kaigama*, "lord of the south," who was commander of the kingdom's army; the *galadima*, "governor of the west," who administered the country west of the lake that was later called Bornu; and the *chiroma*, who, in some sense, was the king's deputy and also nominated heir to the throne. Some of these titles have survived to this day. A modern visitor to the palace of the emir of Kano in northern Nigeria will be asked to obtain a pass from the office of the *madaki*, a Hausa corruption of the Bornu title *mai dawaki*, "the lord of the cavalry"; once inside, he may find not only the emir, but also the emir's *chiroma*. In Bornu the survivals are still more numerous.

In early times the Saifuwa made their *main* capital—for they had several, like all such states resting upon a network of tributary power over long distances—at N'jimi, whose exact location is unknown, but was undoubtedly near the eastern borders of Lake Chad. Here they developed a court at which the *magira*, or queen mother, had much authority, as did also the *gumsa*, the king's senior wife, and where the Saifuwa "family council" met. Here, too, as Islam grew in influence, *'ulama*, or learned men, wrestled with the growing problems of juridical and economic development. From time to time the court shifted its residence, following the king to one or other of the regional capitals, whose imposing brick ruins may still be seen by anyone who can take the time to go there—though it seems that the builders of a new Africa are fast making away with the bricks.

This pattern of government expanded greatly in the thirteenth century, when Kanuri power ranged far to the east of Lake Chad, as well as some way to the west, and had its northern outposts as distant as the Fezzan. Kings numbered eighteen to twenty-one in lists established by Ronald Cohen, an American cultural anthropologist, were all entitled *Dunama*, "the Great," and were the leaders of a large imperial enterprise. Their reign dates were probably between about A.D. 1150 and the beginning of the next century. They were succeeded by others—down to about number thirty in Cohen's lists—who enjoyed a similarly wide-ranging power.

But what proved good for the Kanuri proved also good for some of their neighbors. Even before A.D. 1400 there were several vassal peoples, among them the Bulala, who were east of Chad and who had grown strong enough to contest Kanuri overlordship; coupled with dynastic strife, this challenge led to a major shift in the fortunes of the Saifuwa and their dependents. Driven out of that portion of Kanem east of Chad, they took refuge in the territory governed by the *galadima* west of the lake. Here in Bornu they developed a new capital at Birni N'gazaragamu, which is today situated near the border between Nigeria and the Republic of Niger. From this place, surrounded by a tough brick wall, the Kanuri successors were to rule until well into the nineteenth century. Having recuperated their dynastic

Bornu's ablest warriors guarded the royal personage, who by custom never defended himself, it being deemed beneath his dignity.
DENHAM, *Travels and Discoveries in Africa*, 1827

and military strength, their kings were able to embark on fresh imperial adventures not long before A.D. 1500. Again they thrust their armies east of Chad, subduing the Bulala and possibly pushing on as far as Darfur. And once more they mastered the southerly terminals of the Saharan trails to the Fezzan and Libya.

This new Kanuri empire reached its zenith under the sixtieth king in Cohen's lists. This was the memorable Mai Idris Alooma, who reigned in the last quarter of the sixteenth century, and whose power possibly reached as far east as Kordofan. The empire largely remained at this pinnacle of power until about A.D. 1750, when Al-Hajj Ali Dunama saw the outset of a new time of troubles. The last ruler of the Saifuwa dynasty, the seventy-fifth king, died shortly after 1846, ending more than one thousand years of royal succession.

More telling than the events of this dynastic history are the changes in structure that enabled these Bornu kings to reassert the primacy of their forebears in Kanem. From

Bornu foot soldiers, even in the 1800's when this engraving was made, continued to rely on the lance and the bow in waging war.

DENHAM, *Travels and Discoveries in Africa,* 1827

about 1450 there came the same political evolution that, a little later, was to characterize Songhai under Askia Muhammad I. This is the gradual and cautious development of administrative power by appointment rather than by right of birth. In ways that remain to be understood in detail, the grand council of Saifuwa peers begins to lose its authority to a king, who is still a constitutional monarch in that he is bound by law and custom, as well as by the balance of internal power within the structure, but is no longer merely primus inter pares. While continuing to uphold Kanuri religion, if only because it is Kanuri religion that lies at the root of his power, he relies increasingly on Islam for the shaping of new forms of delegated power, which stand outside the customary lineage network.

Adapting Muslim examples in Egypt and elsewhere,

commoners and "slaves," who are sometimes eunuchs, begin to form an administrative corps of "king's men," whose loyalty is not to any lineage but to the person of the king himself. The *kaigama*, for example, was almost certainly considered to be of noble lineage in early times. A Kanuri praise song composed shortly before 1700 celebrates him as "the chief slave" of the king: "star of the morning, holder of the principal of the king's offices, less than the king certainly, yet greater than all the prosperous men. . . ."

Having such men at his command, the king can begin to offset the authority of his princely rivals and nobles, and even displace them in their governorships and commands. Building on the same method, he selects captives for a troop of "king's soldiers," and so provides himself with an armed force whose loyalties are likewise outside the lineage structure. Mai Idris Alooma even imported Turkish musketry instructors and formed a little corps of musketeers.

With all this increase in prestige and power, royal expenses multiply. Long-service soldiers prove expensive, and so do their armaments and horses. A growing administration drains the royal purse, while heightened prestige calls for still larger palaces and still higher walls of clay and timber. Royal hospitality has to be lavish if it is not to seem ridiculous. Somehow there has to be ever more revenue from taxation and tributes, and so the imperial process acquires a momentum of its own. Only the corresponding growth and rivalry of neighboring peoples will bring it to a halt. This did not happen to the Kanuri empire until the eighteenth century.

Important among neighboring state systems, which developed by much the same constellation of local and intrusive factors of growth, were those of the Hausa, lying west and southwest of Bornu. Although the early formative factors in Hausaland were similar to those of the Kanuri, the results were markedly different.

Like the Kanuri, the Hausa emerged around or soon after the middle of the first millennium A.D. from a mingling of ancestral stocks; some of their ancestors may have come from Bornu or Kanem or possibly farther east. Like them, the early Hausa were pastoralists and farmers, workers in iron, and traders, who took a lead among other ethnic groups in the localities where they had settled and proved able to dominate large areas. Unlike the Kanuri, however, the Hausa evolved no single unifying system. Their independent cities, each governing lands extending a long way from its walled center, were rivals rather than allies, and this rivalry, thanks to the competition fostered by long-distance trade, grew stronger with time. Enterprising in commerce, skilled in handicrafts, shrewd in their handling of community affairs, these city-states were to become a most notable element in the whole West African scene.

At the very beginning, according to Hausa traditions, there were seven true states: Biram, Gobir, Daura, Kano, Katsina, Rano, and Zaria. Their rulers were all grandsons of a "founding-hero" called Bayagidda, also said to have been the son of a princess of Bornu, an early pointer to the influence of Bornu that recurs throughout their history. Then, at some later time, there likewise appeared seven "illegitimate" Hausa states: Kebbi, Kamfara, Gwari, Jukun, Nupe, Yauri and Ilorin (referring here to Yoruba, north of the forest). Their founders had not been among the progeny of Bayagidda, but had adopted Hausa ideas and institutions. These traditions manifestly point to an early period of population movements and cultural interchange.

From the first, it seems, these emergent Hausa communities acquired their separate identities in stockaded villages, or *birni*, where initially villagers and nearby farmers took shelter in times of trouble. About a thousand years ago these *birni* appear to have grown into towns governed by kings. Here they developed their language and their customs, their beliefs and political structures. This is indicated by detailed Kano traditions, which now begin to be supported by new archeological research. By 1300, in any case, these towns had become the centers of states with frontiers between them. If such frontiers for a long time marked out little more than claims to spheres of interest, they were already well enough defined to set the pattern of possession and rivalry between power systems whose institutions remained closely similar.

Although the legitimate states of Kano, Katsina, and Zaria took the lead sometime before the fifteenth century, all the Hausa city-states manifested a dominant interest in local and long-distance trade, at which their men excelled, and they served both as emporiums and as centers of handicraft manufacture in textiles, leather, metals, and other goods. After 1400, with Islam becoming increasingly more influential, they were also centers of learning, and the level of intellectual discourse there was high enough to attract noted scholars from distant places. Except for a time in the sixteenth century when western Hausaland and even Kano came under the influence and partial control of the Songhai emperor Askia Muhammad I, the Hausa states looked generally to Bornu and its rulers for new ideas about government and for solutions to new problems. Some of the states even came under official Bornu overlordship.

Here, as elsewhere, society was becoming more deeply stratified; kings were acquiring more power; new forms of servitude were beginning to appear. Of King Abdullahi Burja, who ruled in Kano between about 1438 and 1452 and who was probably under strong Bornu influence, the traditions say that he set up "slave settlements" by regularly raiding their non-Muslim enemies for captives who could be put to productive work. This was clearly an innovation that reflected the growth of deeper social divisions, just as it did in Bornu. But it would be wrong to see in this the transformation of Kano's economy to one based on slavery. The actual status of slaves probably differed little in practice from that of neighboring free villagers, and nothing like a plantation economy ever developed.

A few decades later King Muhammad Rumfa of Kano established a nine-man council of state that was possibly modeled on Saifuwa practice. No doubt to emphasize his power, he built himself a new palace, which appeared grand and glorious to his courtiers and was to be the model of other and later palaces in Hausaland. More important in the long run, Rumfa also gave a strong thrust to that process of appointing "king's men"—whether commoners, eunuchs, or other "slaves"—who stood outside the aristocratic establishment and enabled Kano and other Hausa states to evolve the intricate checks and balances of their monarchial systems.

Such innovations, and the socioeconomic reasons that provoked them, called for the introduction of new laws and customs. Learned men were expected to show how this could best be done. Intellectuals at court might have been ornamental, but they were looked to for practical advice as well. According to the Kano Chronicle, soon after 1450 a number of Fulani priests "came to Hausaland from Mali, bringing with them books of divinity and etymology"; they initiated a period of Fulani intellectual leadership that persists to this day.

But the scholar best remembered as an influence on the remodeling of Hausa institutions was, as it happened, neither from the western Sudan nor from Bornu. He was Muhammad al-Majhili, a renowned jurist of Tlemcen in western Algeria, who sojourned in Kano at the end of the fifteenth century; he wrote for Muhammad Rumfa a book whose title is reasonably translated as *The Obligations of Princes*. A little later, as the previous chapter has shown, Al-Majhili went to Gao and gave advice to Askia Muhammad I.

Evolving in this way, the stronger of these states flourished by trade and tribute. They became vital components in the whole long-distance commerce of West Africa. Al-

The establishment of one state's hegemony over another was often accompanied by the taking of slaves to fill the ranks of armies and to perform civilian tasks in the societies of the conquerors. As the centuries passed, slaves also became a major source of revenue for the ruling classes. In this 1891 engraving, rifle-bearing African traders lead off their captives, having decimated the ill-defended village.
Illustrated American, MAY 2, 1891

though they often quarreled with each other, their wars stopped short of large-scale destruction. Menaced from time to time by Songhai or Bornu, they managed for the most part to retain their independence. Much can be guessed from their traditions.

Happily for history, however, there appeared in 1550 the celebrated eyewitness description of Leo Africanus. It is unlikely to have been a very reliable description, as it was written many years after Leo's visit to Hausaland and for a European audience with no means of critical judgment, as Leo must well have known; but it was and is the only one of its kind and therefore the best. Published in Venice nearly a quarter of a century after the writing was finished, this work startled mercantile Europe with a vision of distant

power and wealth in much the same way as Columbus' reports on the Americas had done fifty years earlier.

Leo Africanus, whose given name was Al-Hasan ibn Muhammad al-Wazzan az-Zayyati, had visited Timbuktu at the age of seventeen with an uncle who was a Moroccan ambassador. Soon after 1500 (the date remains uncertain) he made another journey to the Sudan, at which time he passed through Hausaland. By now he was about thirty and in the diplomatic service of the king of Fez in Morocco.

While sailing westward from Tripoli in 1518, he was captured by a Christian pirate named Pietro Bovadiglia. Realizing that he had an important prisoner on his hands, Bovadiglia turned the future Leo over to Pope Leo X, who imprisoned him for a year in Rome's Castel Sant' Angelo on the banks of the Tiber. There, the young captive was instructed in Christianity by three bishops; in 1518 he was baptized as Giovanni Leo de' Medici, after the pope. Soon afterward he began making notes for a book about his African travels. This he completed in 1526; the notes are lost, but what appears to be the finished manuscript came to light in 1931. The manuscript had been edited sometime before 1550 by a leading Venetian administrator, Giovanni Ramusio, who brushed up the author's faulty Italian (Ramusio also gave Leo the name by which he is remembered) and published the result.

Ramusio's volume had an instant and widespread success, and was subsequently translated into numerous European languages, including an English version by John Pory, whose 1600 edition is quoted throughout this text. Considering the history of its production, the story is a lively one and may still be read with pleasure. In it the Hausa states of the early sixteenth century are vividly depicted. Gobir, Leo Africanus found, was rich in cattle and people, many of them living in thriving towns. "Heere are also great store of artificers and linnen weavers: and heere are such shooes made . . . the greatest part whereof be carried to Tombuto [Timbuktu] and Gago [Gao]."

Leo described another state later absorbed by Katsina as "very populous, and having a king raigning over it, which maintaineth a garison of seven thousand archers, and five hundred horsemen. . . .", or cavalry, that is, hired as mercenaries from some other state. "The inhabitants are very rich, and have continuall traffique with the nations adjoining. Southward thereof lieth a region greatly abounding with gold," is a reference to Hausa trade with the gold-producing country of the Akan in present-day Ghana.

Kano appeared to Leo as a great capital whose "walles and houses whereof are built for the most part of a kind of chalke [baked clay]." (These structures can be seen today.) "The inhabitants are rich merchants and most civill people," just as the German explorer Heinrich Barth would find them more than three centuries later, and just as they are now. Of Zaria he writes: "The inhabitants are rich and have great traffique unto other nations." Bornu has "a most puissant prince. . . . Horsemen he hath in continuall readines to the number of three thousand, & an huge number of footmen; for all his subjects are so serviceable and obedient unto him, that whensoever he commandeth them, they will . . . follow him. . . ." The Bornu king, Leo, says, engaged in raiding for captives who could be sold as slaves. He invited merchants of Barbary, and willed them to bring him great store of horses: for in this countrey they use to exchange horses for slaves, and to give fifteen and sometime twentie. And by this means there were abundance of horses brought: howbeit the merchants were constrained to stay for their slaves till the king returned home conquerour with a great number of captives, and satisfied his creditors for their horses. And often times it falleth out that the merchants must stay three months togither, before the king returneth from the warres, but they are all that while maintained at the kings charges. Sometimes he bringeth not home slaves enough to satisfie the merchants: and otherwhiles they are constrained to awaite there a whole yeere togither; for the king maketh invasions but every yeere once, & that at one set and appointed time of the yeere. Yea I myselfe met with sundree merchants heere, who despairing of the kings paiment, bicause they had trusted him a whole yeere; determined never to come thither with horses againe. And yet the king seemeth marvellous rich; for his spurres, his bridles, platters, dishes, pots, and other vessels wherein his meate and drinke are brought to the table, are all of pure golde; yea, and the chaines of his dogs and hounds are of golde also.

The little that is known of Hausa rule before A.D. 1600 suggests that its cost continued to grow, as pomp and majesty kept pace with military reinforcement. Later evidence supports that analysis. For example, under Muhammad Sharifa, king of Kano from 1703 to 1731, tradition says that taxes and tribute had increased to such a point that "the Arabs left the town and went to Katsina, and most of the poorer people fled the country." No doubt this exaggerates the situation. But the fact that many Hausa freemen did indeed become acutely discontented with their lot is strongly suggested by the relative ease with which the Fulani jihad, launched in 1804, would succeed.

Yet if taxes and tribute continued to grow heavier, such evidence as there is indicates that the constraining power of Hausa checks and balances within the governing system itself did also. These checks and balances turned upon a shrewdly managed structure of offices, whether filled by appointment or inheritance, whereby the king could maneuver in favor of his own decisions, but could seldom or never act as an autocrat. On one side were the leaders of traditional Hausa lineages—the kingmakers of the past—whereas on the other were slave officials, eunuchs, and similar courtiers, whose privileges depended only upon royal power. Thus Dr. Michael G. Smith, a British anthropolo-

The brick ruin below is thought to have been an ancient Christian monastery. It is north of the Jebel Marra massif in Darfur, an area now within the sphere of Islam and under the local rule of the melik *at left.*

BOTH: BASIL DAVIDSON

gist, has concluded from his study of the evidence that, "in the seventeenth and eighteenth century, a Hausa ruler concentrated his attention on rival chiefdoms [within his state], and on his senior kinsmen or free officials. The ruler took such steps as he could to deprive lineage rivals of power and to reduce powerful officials," playing the one off against the other as opportunity might allow.

Much the same was undoubtedly true of Bornu, just as it was of Songhai after the reforms of Askia Muhammad I. Here, as in contemporary Europe, kings might wish to be dictators, but found in practice that they had to maneuver and mollify the ruling oligarchies, whether free or slave, upon whom they always depended. In so far as the term is valid for monarchies of that period, these were of a constitutional type: they depended upon an institutional structure within which the kings, though always having the last word, could act only by a systematized consent.

In other, lesser polities, east of Lake Chad and the old lands of Kanem, it was probably much the same, though very little is as yet known about them. The state of Darfur appears to have emerged in distant times as a relay intermediary in the Nile-Niger trade. Darfur traditions speak of a dynasty called the Daju, identified only in vague and contradictory legend, which was followed by the slightly better-documented Tunjur dynasty, based in the hills to the north of Darfur's Jebel Marra. Some of these early kings were probably in contact, and perhaps in partnership, with

the later rulers of Meroë. In addition, a fine brick complex erected on one of the hills in the Jebel Dar Furnung north of Jebel Marra seems to have been built as a Christian monastery, an indication that the Christian kingdom of Makuria had established a far-western mission settlement there.

Islam evidently came to power in Darfur during the sixteenth century, perhaps under one of Mai Idris Alooma's ancestors or under Idris himself; and there emerged at Jebel Marra a new dynasty known as the Keira, which was undoubtedly ruled with a Muslim constitution similar to that of Bornu. The earliest of these Keira kings, to whom tradition gives the name of Sulaiman Solong, appears to have ruled in the middle of the seventeenth century. He or his successors took over an earlier tradition of building in brick that may have started in Meroë, but in any case had long since passed westward to Kanem and Bornu. By the reign of the seventh Keira monarch, Muhammad Teirab, the kingdom had acquired enough centralized power and wealth to erect imposing, fortified stone structures. Some of these, notably to the southwest of Kabkabia on the western flank of Jebel Marra, were still in a fair state of preservation when the present writer saw them in 1957.

The evidence is inconclusive as to whether or not the kings of Bornu were able during the sixteenth century to bring Darfur, even briefly, within their sphere of influence and tribute, but there is no doubt about one major point. From sometime before A.D. 1500 the history of the peoples of the grasslands east of Darfur, and of Darfur itself, belongs to the tragic afterglow of Christian Nubian civilization.

Already seven centuries old when the kingdom of Makuria collapsed at the end of the fourteenth century Nubia's kingdoms stood for a remarkable African achievement. Internal written records have never been recovered, but surviving Arabic memoirs tell a little of what they were like. Writing in A.D. 1208, Abu Salih the Armenian claimed that Alodia, the southernmost of the three kingdoms, had four hundred churches as well as many monasteries, and praised the wealth and comfort of its capital. Archeological finds during the 1960's have added greatly to the list of its noble church buildings and saved at Faras in the north a large number of superb religious frescoes.

Of the final decades of Christian Nubia almost nothing is known. The Ethiopians, barricaded behind high mountain passes, were able to survive the Muslim onslaught and upheaval and, eventually, to turn the tables on their rivals, notably the sultanate of Adel, located in what is northern Somalia today. But the Nubians had no such natural defenses. Invaded by Mameluk armies from the north, infil-

A hunting party of Sudanese men and boys runs through grass bordering the Blue Nile. Their uncompromising environment offers little more than a seminomadic subsistence economy, largely based on the management of cattle and the gathering of durra, millet, and other grains.
BLACK STAR—HOYNINGEN-HUENE

trated by Muslim migrants moving down the Blue Nile in the south, Christian Nubian civilization disappeared during the fifteenth century into a historical mist that no research has yet managed to penetrate. When at last the mist begins to clear late in the fifteenth century, the scene has altogether changed, and the Islamization of Nubia is far advanced. Nomad peoples dominate Makuria. Control southward from the riverain frontier of Alodia is held by the Funj, a people of uncertain but possibly southern Nilotic origins who had also accepted Islam. In 1503–1504 their first listed ruler, Amara Dunqas, founded his capital at Sennar. Here the Funj kings would rule until the nineteenth century.

These disturbances meant little to the western peoples. Although the ancient trading route from the Nile through Darfur to Chad ceased to feed their commerce, they continued to thrive upon the north-south Saharan routes. By 1600 they were just reaching the apogee of cultures formed a thousand years earlier. Beginning in the seventeenth century, they would come slowly to grips with the challenge of a wider western world from which they were still separated by the vast distances of inner Africa. With modern reassessment of written and oral records, and the aids of archeology, historians can now set forth these cultures not only in outline but also in considerable detail. Here, as Ahmad ibn Fartua, Idris Alooma's chronicler, remarked nearly four centuries ago about his own written history of Bornu, "we have mentioned very little, passing over much

from fear of being lengthy and verbose. But the thoughtful reader will understand that beyond the river lies the sea."

If one were to embark on that sea, however, there would be interesting things to speculate about as well as to say. King Idris Alooma and England's Queen Elizabeth I certainly talked different languages, but were their basic administrative and political problems so very dissimilar? Both, after all, were much concerned with the overweening power of nobles and the need for loyal servants; both had a great deal of trouble with each.

In a very different direction, southward into the far interior of Africa, other comparisons with Kanem-Bornu's social order might be found. For there, too, south of the Congo forests in geophysical circumstances not markedly different from those of the Sudan, the sixteenth and seventeenth centuries saw the emergence of another cluster of kingdoms much concerned with trade. Undoubtedly, at least two great differences divided them: in the Sudan there was the formative influence of Islam, reaching into every field of organized life, whereas in the south there was the ever-destructive tsetse fly. Yet the basic nature of the problems of centralizing rule might have been much the same, and the solutions—superficialities aside—of the same order.

The story of the kingdoms and lesser polities of the far interior belong rightly to another chapter. Yet that of the Nile-Niger region, as of the remainder of West Africa, can undoubtedly help to illuminate it.

MERCHANTS AND POTENTATES

DESERT CARAVANS

The central Sudan was the hub of an elaborate system of trails that linked the emporiums of North Africa and the Sahara with the whole of the Sudan from the Niger to the Nile. The steady stream of caravans that made the perilous desert crossing is the subject of this selection. It comes from an unpublished study by Dr. Samir Zoghby, assistant director of the African Section, the Library of Congress.

The history of commerce is strewn with trails with exotic connotations. The Silk Road, the Spice Road, the Gold Road, and the Salt Road have always intrigued our imagination, goaded by such romantic figures as Marco Polo and Vasco da Gama, and, in Islam, the Maqarri brothers and Ibn Battuta.

There were basically four types of caravans in the trans-Saharan trade: military, religious, small commercial, and large commercial. The military was essentially of the *ghazw* [raiding] type, which was also considered as a commercial enterprise and was as thoroughly prepared. The religious caravan was mainly composed of pilgrims on their way to Mecca or sometimes to the tomb of a venerated *marabout* [or holy man]. The small commercial caravans consisted usually of five to one hundred camels, while the large annual ones had from five hundred to two thousand camels. The smaller the caravan, the greater the speed. [A Adu] Boahen states that: ". . . the average rate was fifteen to sixteen miles [per eight hour day] for a heavily laden caravan, seventeen to eighteen for a moderately laden, and twenty to twenty-two a day of ten hours for a lightly laden caravan. As a rule the caravans left the Barbary states between September and October, and departed from the Sudan at the commencement of the rainy season in April or May. Barring accidents and undue delays, the journey lasted from seventy to ninety days depending on the size of the caravan and the weight of each camel load."

The commercial caravans and especially the large commercial ones were very elaborate endeavors. Careful arrangements were made, associations were formed for the trip, and some traders delegated their representatives who traditionally kept one third of the benefit. Sometimes the large caravans were made up of smaller caravans traveling together for safety.

Though the trans-Saharan trade did not have to wait for the camel, it was the latter that made the intensive contacts between the two shores of the Sahara possible. There were usually two types of camel in the caravan. One was the white or greyish *mehari*, which is built for speed, with its elegant frame; and the burden camel for carrying goods, which was brown and stocky. Great care was taken to select camel drivers who loaded and unloaded the beasts, as a wounded or ill-loaded camel could delay and even endanger the caravan.

Four factors have been the cause of most deaths during those tremendous trips. The variations in temperature—as high as 110° F. by day to as low as 20° F. at night—claimed many victims. Sandstorms were reported to have buried entire caravans in oblivion, such as the army sent by Al-Mansur to invade the Songhai before the commando raid of Juder (1591). Thirst, however, has been pictured as the most horrible danger in the desert. Since the ratio of a gallon of water a day per man is the minimum safe allowance, water was a vital necessity. The problem was tackled from two angles. Springs were kept in good order and protected by the "Pinkertons" of the desert and ample water supplies were carried along. Goatskins were filled with water, but as Al-Yaqut reported, sandstorms usually dried up the goatskins, so the merchants resorted to killing camels, specially the ones who had just quenched their thirst, and drinking the somewhat greenish water found in their stomachs.

A different type of Saharan danger was the threat of nomadic robbers. To counter this threat, the merchants selected their guides and camel drivers from the areas crossed. They also concluded agreements with the leaders of the predominant tribes for safe-conduct. The nomads, who realized the importance of the trails, requested seasonable "ransoms," fearing to scare away the customers. At Ghadames, each commercial concern had its special protector and catered to his needs.

The livelihood of these tribes hinged on the power of the two foci of power both north and south of the Sahara. When the Maghreb states were strong, they were able to control the nomads by closing the passes leading to the Tell. Similarly, when the Sudanic empires were powerful, they contained and controlled the nomads and even occupied their strongholds when they upset the trade routes, such as when Ghana occupied Awdaghast in 990.

The desert routes were controlled by

the Tuareg. The western Sahara, from Sijilmasa to Ghana, was the preserve of the Bani Masufa, while the central Sahara between Tuat and the Ahaggar Mountains was controlled by the Ahaggar Tuareg, and the Ajjer Tuareg controlled the trails north of Ghat. . . .

Another trail which became important later on, specially after the collapse of Awdaghast [1055], was the route Sijilmasa-Taghaza-Ghana. The stop at Taghaza allowed the traders to load salt slabs to be sold in the Sudan. Farther east, the Fezzan-Kawar trail was less heavily used, but still reflected a pale shadow of its old frame as the Garamantian Road, the more so since it was the easiest and shortest route from the Mediterranean into Central Africa. The trail *Darb al-Arbi'* in linking Kanem with Asyut in Egypt was discontinued, according to Ibn Hawqal, during the tenth century due to sandstorms and raiders, and the route Cairo-Tunis-Fez-Sijilmasa was adopted.

Once the caravans reached the southern termini, the camels were unloaded, and the goods to the south followed two paths: they were either shipped by canoes down the Niger, whenever possible, or loaded on asses and bullocks, as the camels could not resist the tsetse fly. Once the forest was reached, the goods were once more unloaded and carried by headload to their destination in the forest area.

SEARCHING FOR THE SOURCE

In 1447, while staying at the oases of Tuat (which he had reached from Hono, or Honein, on the coast), an Italian named Antonio Malfante wrote this informative letter to a friend in Genoa. Malfante, who was evidently employed as an agent for one of the Italian banking corporations of the day, had ventured into the Sahara primarily to find the source of the gold that was pouring into Europe from the western Sudan. However, neither he nor any other outsider—until the nineteenth century—would discover

the precise location of the mines from which the Sudan kingdoms obtained their gold. The letter, originally written in Latin, provides an engaging account of life in the oases and in the "Land of the Blacks" farther south.

After we had come from the sea, that is from Hono, we journeyed on horseback, always southwards, for about twelve days. For seven days we encountered no dwelling—nothing but sandy plains; we proceeded as though at sea, guided by the sun during the day, at night by the stars. At the end of the seventh day, we arrived at a *ksour* [a village], where dwelt very poor people who supported themselves on water and a little sandy ground. They sow little, living upon the numerous date palms. At this *ksour* we had come into Tueto [the Tuat oases]. In this place there are eighteen quarters, enclosed within one wall, and ruled by an oligarchy. Each ruler of a quarter protects his followers, whether they be in the right or no. The quarters closely adjoin each other and are jealous of their privileges. Everyone arriving here places himself under the protection of one of these rulers, who will protect him to the death: thus merchants enjoy very great security, much greater, in my opinion, than in kingdoms such as Themmicenno [Tlemcen] and Thunisie [Tunis].

Though I am a Christian, no one ever addressed an insulting word to me. They said they had never seen a Christian before. It is true that on my first arrival they were scornful of me, because they all wished to see me, saying with wonder "This Christian has a countenance like ours"—for they believed that Christians had disguised faces. Their curiosity was soon satisfied, and now I can go alone anywhere, with no one to say an evil word to me.

There are many Jews, who lead a good life here, for they are under the protection of the several rulers, each of whom defends his own clients. Thus they enjoy very secure social standing. Trade is in their hands, and many of them are to be trusted with the greatest confidence.

This locality is a mart of the country of the Moors, to which merchants come to sell their goods: gold is carried hither, and bought by those who come up from the coast. This place is De Amamento [Tamentit], and there are many rich men here. The generality, however, are very poor, for they do not sow, nor do they harvest anything, save the dates upon which they subsist. They eat no meat but that of castrated camels, which are scarce and very dear.

It is true that the Arabs with whom I came from the coast brought with them corn and barley which they sell throughout the year . . . .

It never rains here: if it did, the houses, being built of salt in the place of reeds, would be destroyed. It is scarcely ever cold here: in summer the heat is extreme, wherefore they are almost all blacks. The children of both sexes go naked up to the age of fifteen. These people observe the religion and law of Muhammad. In the vicinity there are 150 to 200 *ksour*.

In the lands of the blacks, as well as here, dwell the Philistines [the Tuareg], who live, like the Arabs, in tents. They are without number, and hold sway over the land of Gazola [the Sahara] from the borders of Egypt to the shores of the Ocean . . . and over all the neighboring towns of the blacks. They are fair, strong in body and very handsome in appearance. They ride without stirrups, with simple spurs. They are governed by kings, whose heirs are the sons of their sisters—for such is their law. They keep their mouths and noses covered. I have seen many of them here, and have asked them through an interpreter why they cover their mouths and noses thus. They replied: "We have inherited this custom from our ancestors." They are sworn enemies of the Jews, who do not dare to pass hither. Their faith is that of the Blacks. Their sustenance is milk and flesh, no corn or barley, but much rice. Their sheep, cattle, and camels are without number. One breed of camel, white as snow, can cover in one day a distance which would take a horseman four days to travel. Great warriors, these people are continually at war amongst themselves.

The states which are under their rule border upon the land of the Blacks. I shall speak of those known to men here, and which have inhabitants of the faith of Muhammad. In all, the great majority are Blacks, but there are a small number of whites [Berbers].

First, Thegida [Takedda], which comprises one province and three *ksour;* Checoli, which is as large.

Chuchiam [probably Gao], Thambet [Timbuktu], Geni [Jenne], and Meli [Mali], said to have nine towns;

Thora, Oden, Dendi, Sagoto, Bofon, Igdem, Bembo, all these are great cities, capitals of extensive lands and towns under their rule.

These adhere to the law of Muhammad.

To the south of these are innumerable great cities and territories, the inhabitants of which are all blacks and idolaters, continually at war with each other in defense of their law and slaves which the blacks take in their internecine wars are sold at a very low price, the maximum being two *doubles* a head. . . .

"It is not long since I was in Cuchia [Gao], distant fifty days' journey from here, where there are Moors," my patron said to me. "A heathen king, with five hundred thousand men, came from the south to lay siege to the city of Vallo. Upon the hill within the city were fifty Moors, almost all blacks. They saw that they were by day surrounded by a human river, by night by a girdle of flames and looked upon themselves as already defeated and enslaved. But their king, who was in the city, was a great magician and necromancer; he concluded with the besieger a pact by which each was to produce by incantation a black goat. The two goats would engage in battle, and the master of that which was beaten, was likewise to consider himself defeated. The besieger emerged victorious from the contest, and, taking the town, did not allow one soul to escape, but put the

Tuareg pounding millet, a staple of their diet
VICTOR ENGLEBERT

entire population to the sword. He found much treasure there. The town to-day is almost completely deserted save for a poverty-stricken few who have come to dwell there."

Of such were the stories which I heard daily in plenty. The wares for which there is a demand here are many: but the principal articles are copper, and salt in slabs, bars, and cakes. The copper of Romania [the Byzantine empire], which is obtained through Alexandria, is always in great demand throughout the land of the Blacks. I frequently inquired what they did with it, but no one could give me a definite answer. I believe it is that there are so many peoples that there is almost nothing but is of use to them.

The Egyptian merchants come to trade in the land of the Blacks with half a million head of cattle and camels—a figure which is not fantastic in this region.

The place where I am is good for trade, as the Egyptians and other merchants come hither from the land of the Blacks bringing gold, which they exchange for copper and other goods. Thus everything sells well; until there is nothing left for sale. The people here will neither sell nor buy unless at a profit of one hundred per cent. For this reason, I have lost, Laus Deo!, on the goods I brought here, two thousand *doubles.*

From what I can understand, these

people neighbor on India [probably Ethiopia]. Indian merchants come hither, and converse through interpreters. These Indians are Christians, adorers of the cross. It is said that in the land of the Blacks there are forty dialects, so that they are unable to understand each other.

I often inquired where the gold was found and collected; my patron always replied "I was fourteen years in the land of the Blacks, and I have never heard nor seen anyone who could reply from definite knowledge. That is my experience, as to how it is found and collected. What appears plain is that it comes from a distant land, and, as I believe, from a definite zone." He also said that he had been in places where silver was as valuable as gold.

This land is twenty-eight days' journey from Cambacies [probably Ghadames], and is the city with the best market. It is twenty-five days from Tunis, from Tripoli in Barbary twenty days, from Trimicen [Tlemcen] thirty days, from Fecia [Fez] twenty days, from Zaffi, Zamor and Messa twenty days on horseback. I finish for the present; elsewhere and at another time, God willing, I will recount much more to you orally. I am always at your orders in Christ.

UMME JILMA, "ANGEL OF GOD"

The Kanuri states of Kanem and Bornu and the Hausa states were the dominant powers in the central Sudan. Kanem, which lies to the north of Lake Chad, was at the southern end of a main trans-Saharan trail. Its ruling dynasty, the Saifuwa, converted to Islam during the reign of Umme Jilma (1085–1097), the mai, or king, who is said to have died in Egypt while on the hadj to Mecca. This Kanuri praise song, honoring Kanem's first Muslim mai, is the oldest of its genre.

O! Sultan, the good, whose sleep is light as that of a hare:
Sultan, truly a Sultan, who stays not in the house of his father's sister:
Of noble birth from both his father and mother:

Of noble birth indeed, of noble birth
    from both his parents:
Where you sit costly carpets are spread
    for you; above your head is a canopy
    of gold:
O! Sultan, who can discomfit one like
    pebbles on one's eyelashes:
O! Sultan, Angel of God.
As there is a protector of the camel's
    tongue, do you protect us:
The friend of youth:
Whose writing slate is made of "kabwi"
    wood;
At night a warrior on a coal-black horse;
    but when day dawns he is to be seen
    with his Koran in his hand.
We wait upon your blessing:
Babuma Amadu said to Mai Aji Fannami
    at the Sugu war,
"Sultan, even if you are mounted on your
    bay horse called 'Kite Kiteram,'
Birni Njimi [the capital] is a long way off
    if you want to run away."

KANEM AT ITS HEIGHT

By the mid-thirteenth century the mai *of
Kanem controlled the entire Fezzan as well as
the trade route to Tripoli. His kingdom
stretched eastward as far as Wadai in present-day Chad, westward as far as Kano, and
included Bornu, southwest of Lake Chad.
This territorial expansion furthered the dis-
semination of the Islamic culture throughout
the Sudan. As related in the following passage by Al-Maqrizi (1364–1442), a Cairo-
born historian, the Muslim population of
Kanem even built a college and hostel in
Cairo. It housed Kanuri students of Islamic
law and pilgrims on their way to Mecca. The*
mai *still retained much pre-Islamic ritual,
such as addressing his subjects from behind a
screen. Al-Maqrizi's account also contains
the first reference to money in Kanem-Bornu.*

All the Sudanese derive their origin from
Fut the son of Ham. Their tribes number nineteen. . . . The inhabitants of
Kanem are a great people, and for the
most part Muslims. Their city is called
Njimi. . . . [Their king] is a nomad in
mode of life. When he sits on his throne

his courtiers prostrate themselves before
him, and fall on their faces. His army,
horse and foot and transport, numbers
100,000. . . . The King of Kanem has five
feudatory kings subject to him. . . .

Their king in the year 700 A.H. [A.D.
1300] was al-Hajj Ibrahim of the sons of
Saif ibn Dhi Yazan, who occupied the
throne of Kanem, which is the seat of
power of Bornu. There reigned after him
his son al-Hajj Idris. Then Idris' brother,
Daud ibn Ibrahim; then Umar ibn Idris;
then the brother of the latter [and so on].

The first seat of this empire on the
side which is near to Egypt is called
Zuwila [the Zawila oasis in the Libyan
Fezzan]. Between this town and the
town of Kaukau [probably Gao], which
is on the opposite [western] frontier, the
distance is three months' march. The inhabitants of Kanem cover the head with
a veil. The king does not show himself
except at the time of the two religious
festivals, in the morning and afternoon;
the rest of the year he is not seen and
those who talk to him are placed behind
a screen. The principal food of this people is rice which grows wild in the country. They have also cheese, guinea corn,
figs, limes, melons, pumpkins and fresh
dates. As regards money, they use a kind
of cloth which they make and which is
called "Wendy." Each piece is ten cubits
long, but for facility of exchange it is cut
up into pieces of a quarter of a cubit or
smaller. Other substances such as shells
of different kinds and pieces of copper
or gold are equally used in commerce
and their value is estimated in an equivalent amount of cloth. In this country the
pumpkins are so big that they are used as
boats to cross the Nile. . . .

They are of the sect of the Imam
Malik. They are particular in enforcing
justice and extremely severe as regards
religion. In the year 640 A.H. [A.D. 1242],
they built in the town of Fustat [Cairo], a
college for people belonging to the sect
if the Imam Malik known as the college
of Ibn Rashid. It is in this college that
members of this nation reside if they
come to Cairo.

SONG OF THE BORNU SLAVES

*A new era of Kanuri history was inaugurated
in the late 1300's, when the Saifuwa were
forced to retreat into Bornu. Kanem was taken
over by the Bulala people and was not re-
conquered by the Kanuri until the early
1500's. During these centuries Bornu became
a chief factor in the trans-Saharan trade. Its
principal export was slaves; its main import,
horses. As the female slaves crossed the desert
from their beloved Bornu, they sang of* rubee,
or "gold," and of the longed-for atka, *or
freedom document. This song, recorded in the
1840's, was put into verse by John Green-
leaf Whittier. It reflects the desperation of
generations of Bornuan slaves as they trekked
their way to servitude in unknown lands.*

Where are we going? Where are we
    going?
    Where are we going, Rubee?
Hear us, save us, make us free;
Send our Atka down from thee!
Here the Ghiblee wind is blowing,
Strange and large the world is growing!
    Tell us, Rubee, where are we going?
    Where are we going, Rubee?

Bornou! Bornou! Where is Bornou?
    Where are we going, Rubee?
Bornou-land was rich and good,
Wells of water, fields of food;
Bornou-land we see no longer,
Here we thirst, and here we hunger,
Here the Moor man smites in anger;
    Where are we going, Rubee?

Where are we going? Where are we going?
    Hear us, save us, Rubee!
Moons of marches from our eyes,
Bornou-land behind us lies;
Hot the desert wind is blowing,
Wild the waves of sand are flowing!
Hear us! tell us, Where are we going?
    Where are we going, Rubee?

A MOST EXCELLENT PRINCE

*The Bornu empire reached its apogee in the
late sixteenth century during the reign of*

*Idris ibn Ali (1570–1602), better known as
Idris Alooma. The deeds and talents of this
black monarch are particularly well known
through the chronicles kept by his chief imam,
Ahmad ibn Fartua. Many are recorded in
the following extract from Fartua's* History
of the First Twelve Years of Mai Idris
Alooma. *The* mai *was a zealous Muslim,
and in the words of his imam, he was "an
accomplished diplomat and was conversant
with correct procedure and methods of nego-
tiation." Idris Alooma also excelled as a military tactician. He introduced firearms into the
Lake Chad area and was the first to employ
camels on the plains of Bornu. These innovations helped him subdue such troublesome elements as the So, the indigenous people of
Bornu. At Idris Alooma's death, his empire
had no equal between the Niger and the Nile.*

*At one of the provincial residences of the sultan of Bornu, all regular business stops when the
royal procession arrives. The sultan's attendants carry ceremonial umbrellas and feather fans.*
BARTH, *Travels in Central Africa,* 1857

Our Sultan Haj Idris ibn 'Ali ibn Idris
sought to follow the example of our Lord
and Master Muhammad, the chosen
(may the blessing of God and peace rest
on him and on all the prophets) in regard
to the holy wars which the Prophet
(upon whom be the blessing of God and
peace) undertook; for God has guided
and directed him towards making all his
acts, and bearing, and endeavor follow
the set road and redound to His glory.

Look how God . . . made easy his path,
as we heard from our Sheikhs who have
passed away, for the accomplishment of
wonders and varied exploits such as no
former king had wrought onwards from
the days of Sultan al Haj Daud ibn
Nigale, who fled to the realm of Bornu.
So we will recall what we have learnt so
far as we can. . . . .

How then about the exemplary punishment he meted out to the tribe of So,
in accord with God's command to fight
unbelievers, who are close to Muslims
and vexatious to them. . . .

Or again his war with the people of
Kano, what time they built many "stockades" in their land, seeking to harm the
land of Bornu. They kept raiding and
carrying off plunder, flying to their
stockades and walled towns; and there
hiding their gains among their own possessions.

So they did, till our Sultan attacked
them with lofty purpose and aim, and
destroyed all their defenses except the
great "stockade" called "Dala."

So also his exploits when he fought
the Barbara, till the earth in its fulness
became too narrow for them and the
desert too small for them, so that they
found no sufficient place in which to
pasture their flocks or dwell. . . .

The people of the land of Jawan
brought him a horse as a present, in fear
and submission. So they were brought
before him and departed assured of his
protection.

Look too at his journey to the house
of God, that he might win a sure glory.
Thus leaving the kingdom he loved and
an envied pomp, he went East turning
his back on delights and paying his debts
to God (be He exalted).

So he made the pilgrimage and visited
Tayiba [Medina], the Tayiba of the
Prophet, the chosen one (upon whom be
peace and the blessing of God), the
unique, the victorious over the vicis-
situdes of day and night.

He was enriched by visiting the tomb
of the pious Sahabe the chosen [the companions of the prophet Muhammad], the

perfect ones (may the Lord be favorable
and beneficent to them), and he bought
in the noble city a house and date grove,
and settled there some slaves, yearning
after a plenteous reward from the Great
Master. . . .

Among the benefits which God (Most
High) of His bounty and beneficence,
generosity, and constancy conferred
upon the Sultan was the acquisition
of Turkish musketeers and numerous
household slaves who became skilled in
firing muskets.

Hence the Sultan was able to kill the
people of Amsaka [south of Lake Chad]
with muskets, and there was no need for
other weapons, so that God gave him a
great victory by reason of his superiority
in arms.

Among the most surprising of his acts
was the stand he took against obscenity
and adultery, so that no such thing took
place openly in his time. Formerly the
people had been indifferent to such of-
fenses, committed openly or secretly by
day or night. In fact he was a power
among his people and from him came
their strength.

So he wiped away the disgrace, and the
face of the age was blank with astonish-

ment. He cleared away and reformed as far as he could the known wrong doing. . . .

Owing to the Mai's noble precepts all the people had recourse to the sacred Sheria [canon law of Islam], putting aside worldly intrigue in their disputes and affairs, big or little.

From all we have heard, formerly most of the disputes were settled by the chiefs, not by the "Ulema" [learned men].

For example, he stopped wrong doing, hatred and treachery, and fighting between Muslims, in the case of the Kuburi and Kayi. They had been fighting bitterly over their respective prestige, but on the Sultan's accession, he sternly forbade them to fight till they became as brothers in God. . . .

He also came to the people of the hills of Zajadu and the hills of N'garasa, called N'guma, who had allied themselves with the sons of Sultan Daud and his grandsons and relatives and made raids on the land of Bornu, killing men and enslaving women and children right down to the time of our Sultan. . . . He scattered their host, and divided them, but of the N'guma he spared all and established them in settlements under his direction as his subjects nor did they resist or became recalcitrant.

The tribe of N'gizim, the people of Mugulum, and the people of Gamazan and others of the N'gizim stock who were neighbors were insolent and rebellious, till our Sultan went out to them with a large host, destroyed their crops, and burnt their houses in the wet season. Thus they felt the pinch of a ruined country, yielded to him obedience, and submitted to his rule.

He introduced units of measure for corn among these people by the power and might of God. The N'gizim who dwelt in the West, known as Binawa, would not desist from enslaving Muslims in their country and doing other evil and base actions. They kept seizing the walled towns of the Yedi as fortresses and places of refuge and hiding, using them as bases treacherously to attack the

Muslims by day and night, without ceasing or respite. But when our Sultan ascended the throne, he and his Wazir in chief Kursu took counsel to stem the torrent of their guile and deceit, so that they left off their wickedness, and some followed the Sultan, others the Wazir Kursu, others various leaders who had waged "Holy War" with the Sultan.

To some the Sultan gave orders to settle, and devote their time to agriculture. . . .

Know, my brethren, that in what we have told you, we have failed to tell all. We have but told you a part of the story of the deeds of the early years of our Sultan's reign, with hand and pen. . . .

Thus we have cut short the recital of all his wars, in this brief compilation. . . .

We have ceased to doubt that our Sultan al Haj Idris ibn 'Ali accomplished much more than his grandfather. . . .

We have seen that the deeds of the Sultan (may God on high enrich His bounty with plenteous beneficence and favor) were such that if an account of this era were narrated and set forth, we should never hear the like recorded of the reign of any of our former kings. . . .

Anyone whose claims to greatness in comparison with his sires, were as the claim of our Sultan would have just cause for pride. It is no mere theory that he surpasses them all and has no peer, exalted above them in his wise counsel, and prompt action. . . .

So it is. Our Sultan the Amir ul Muminin and Khalifa of the Lord of the worlds, who visited the two noble sacred cities Sultan Idris ibn 'Ali, ibn Idris (may God enoble him in both worlds), sought to attack his enemies the So N'gafata, and destroy and scatter them. He therefore built the big town near Damasak and put Shetima Biri Getirama in command, together with his son Ajima Gasma ibn Biri. He made four gates in the town and placed a keeper in charge of each gate—and quartered there a detachment of his army. He ordered all his chiefs who were powerful and possessed of a defense force, to build houses,

and leave part of their equipment there as for instance, the horses, and quilted-armor for them and coats of mail.

After he had done this he gave the town the name of Sansana ul Kabir. The people who lived in it were strenuous fighters in "Holy War." They went out morning and evening, seeking the enemy, fending them off, until God designed the ruin of their towns.

The Sultan again built another town to the North of Birni near Sansana and South of it. It was a large town. He placed there Chikama Buma, and made two gates only, the Eastern gate and the Western gate and no more.

He handed over to Chikama Buma many slaves of the Kardi so that by reason of their numbers there was little room. . . .

When our Sultan had finished building the two above mentioned towns, he turned his thoughts toward a policy of cutting off root and branch these evil doers. . . .

In regard to the character of our Sultan, the Amir ul Muminin Haj Idris ibn 'Ali (may the Lord enoble him and endow him with excellence), God laid upon him the obligation to wage Holy War and raid, as a special favor from Him (be He exalted), and gave him good hope of heavenly reward. He did not choose this world in preference to the next, when he had any affair in hand and took counsel and thought. If he found a precedent in the Kura'an or Hadiths upon which the four rightly directed Imams who have gone before agreed, he did it following the example of those who had gone before; if he did not find any precedent in the Kura'an or traditions, he would leave off, and turn aside from his course altogether.

Such were his two lines of action. He kept no secrets from those in whom he reposed confidence. As regards this, if he was upon a journey and heard any news of the enemy by night or day, he did not rest but went forth among his people to the source of the news with the army following him; leading himself for fear any misfortune should befall which he was able to avoid, or in his power to save. He relied on his Lord in everything and he was his support, sure that nothing would happen except by the foreknowledge of God (be He exalted). Hence he was a brave warrior who advanced everywhere, appearing promptly without pausing or beating round, until what he proposed was accomplished. Such was his character and his disposition.

Among the gifts with which God had endowed him, was an impressive appearance. All his followers, small or great, never felt contented except in his presence. Even though he sent large armies in one direction and went in some other direction with a small force himself, his captains were not content to go without him, however large the number of the army.

Thus whatever journey he undertook himself with a small force, leaving the large numbers to go by some other route, they would not agree to remain with the people apart from him. Their hearts did not rest being in a dilemma between the two courses, until God joined them again to their king. (May God give him great victory.) We know this by testing it in many different fields....

Sultan Abdul Jelil, the son of Abdul Jelil of the tribe of Bulala, came to Sima to war with a small army. A fierce fight ensued. People's hearts were in their throats. Then the Amir al Muminin Haj Idris ibn 'Ali, came to them at nine o'-clock on a Thursday in their distress. The enemy were broken and fled like donkeys running away from a hyena. Thus were the Bulala terrified at seeing the dust of the king to the East of them going up to the sky. The Sultan (may God exalt his powers and make his victory great) followed them far, till the horses and mounts grew weary....

He returned in the evening. Had God not favored the host of Bornu, He had not helped them by sending to them the king, even as He helped the host of our lord and master and Prophet, Muhammad the chosen, (may God's blessing rest on him and peace), on the day of

Sisaban by the hand of his nephew and son-in-law Haidara, our lord and master 'Ali ibn Abi Talib (may God most high be pleased with him). Had it not been for the Sultan misfortune had happened. So he brought joy to the hearts of the men of Bornu and he made their eyes cool. So they congratulated each other and fell on each other's necks on the Thursday, and Friday and Saturday.

The king gave them robes of gladness in accordance with the universal joy. He then returned to Bornu.

Such is the story we have heard about this Thursday and the fight that took place on the third of the month Shawwal. This was one of the remarkable achievements of our Sultan and with this was the fact that the horses which he left behind him when he went to war were much more numerous than those which he took with him. The same was the case with pack animals. The shields were all left at home and were not sent after him.

Such was his policy and his method, with which God had endowed him from birth....

May God increase the Sultan's majesty and the beauty of his renown and greatness; his goodness and his victoriousness; by the grace of our lord and master Muhammad upon whom be the blessing of God and peace, and by the grace of his companions, the chosen ones, who followed, and of those who followed them; and by the grace of Jibrail and Michail and Israfil and all the prophets and messengers of God. May the blessing of God and peace rest on them all Amen! Amen!! Amen!!!

Such is the account we have given of the character of our Sultan and his wars in the time when he was king. We have written it after there has passed of his reign twelve years.

THE YERIMA'S PRAISE SONG

Among the dignitaries attached to the Bornu court were the galadima, *the* mastrema, *the* kaigama, *and the* yerima, *who were, respectively, the wardens of the western, eastern, southern, and northern sectors of the realm. They, as well as other royal officials, were honored with praise songs sung by the mai's balladeers, the most important of whom were the* ngijima. *At the height of Bornu prosperity these singers occupied exalted positions. They walked at the sultan's side during processions and enjoyed the special honor of being allowed to point at him with their official sticks. The yerima addressed in this song served under Mai Idris Alooma.*

Yerima Malumi, he is the strength of the Capital:

Yerima who owns the town of Kurkuri of many jujube trees:

You are the Yerima who owns Dal Karia:

Yerima, you are the owner of Sugugu:

Star of the morning, whose light illumines the East and the West:

These are all attributes of Yerima Malumi:

Yerima, if your father is alive, Dal Karia is yours:

And even if he dies, Dal Karia is yours:

Yerima, for whom a he-goat gives milk and a bull gives milk:

That is what it is to be Yerima.

Is the Kaigama the big man? No, no, the Yerima is the big man:

It is said that people argued on this point:

Where is Adam, Fanta's son? Seek him:

And Yusuf, Palmata's son? Seek him:

And Dunama, Fana's son? Seek him:

They got these three witnesses and they gave their evidence.

[They said], Yerima is like the moon at its full.

That is what it is to be the Yerima:

His father and mother are both of noble birth:

The Yerima is a chief who has his stables in the North, that is the Yerima.

Who is the Kaigama? The Kaigama is a slave.

You Yerima the owner of Firi Kimo and of Firi Mayamiram.

And of Yeri Arbasan, and of Mafi Gudu.

And of Barkawal and Belle:

And the owner of Ngilwasu, and Damaya of the Fan Palms.

Zari the Yerima's town is the gateway [to Bornu] defended with many spears:

Zari the Yerima's town where guns are as numerous as the fruit of the fan palms:

Zari the Yerima's town where those who sit in council with him are as numerous as the "Kindil" [Acacia] trees:

Zari the Yerima's town where vendettas are as numerous as the Acacia Verek trees:

Zari the Yerima's town where silks and silver head-ornaments abound:

Zari the Yerima's town full of milch cows and arrow shafts.

STAR OF THE MORNING

In addition to being the warden of the south section of the Bornu empire, the kaigama *was the commander in chief of the army. He was the sultan's chief slave, but as was the case with many other slaves of royal masters, he held a position of high esteem and responsi-*

bility. *Kaigama Anterashi, celebrated in the following praise song, was in office during the second half of the seventeenth century.*

Kaigama Anterashi,
He is the Star of the morning:

Chief slave, the rallying point of the spearmen:

The hub of war:

His town Chirami, his personality that of a Sultan:

Morning and evening he is in the midst of the noise [of war]:

A chieftain, the glowing embers of the Sultan's Council:

[His friendship] a death-trap: his friend short-lived:

If a hawk snatches up a chicken,

Following its tracks devolves on the Kaigama:

Holder of the principal of the [Sultan's] offices:

Less than the Sultan, certainly, but greater than all the prosperous men:

If the chief slave wages war, he does not do so in vain.

If he does not engage in war, his idleness is not useless:

Chief slave, if I say to you "Slave,"

I mean the slave of the Sultan:

Chief slave, if I say to you "Bush-cow,"

You are a [man with the heart of] a bush-cow among men:

Chief slave, [if I say] your town is Ngumfane, I mean that you are the forehead of

A Bornu ruler in the robes of his high office
DENHAM, *Narrative of an Expedition,* 1826

all the slaves:

Chief slave, patience is your attribute:

Your patience like that of a dromedary:

Chief slave, in your hand is a large-headed spear:

Chief slave, you practice witch-craft but its source is in the palm of your hand:

Chief slave, my master, war is your hobby:

Your play, play with a shining spear:

You owner of the town of Zarara, your attributes those of a Sultan:

You and a Sultan do not eat from one calabash,

Neither do you eat what a Sultan leaves:

Sun [of greatness], seat [of power]:

Embers of the Sultan's assembly:

If the Sultan counts as ten large whole Kola-nuts,

The Kaigama counts as twenty halves:

If he and the Sultan are sitting together
and their horses are fighting:

He will not catch the Sultan's horse:

Nor will the Sultan catch his:

Some other man will catch them:

These are [the privileges of] a chief slave.

You are the father of all the minor chiefs:

And the older brother of all the great
chiefs:

Chief slave, owner of the town of Ala
and of Alari:

Who lives between the Rivers Shari and
Sharwa:

Chief slave, Commander of Bornu's
army:

Should the Sultan come out of an old
woman's dilapidated hut even,

After him will come the holder of the
office of Kaigama:

Should [the link in] the office of Kaigama break, the Fuguma will join it up
anew:

Fuguma of the games that never cease:

His play not that of the women.

Nor of boys:

They are games played with a polished
spear:

You [Fuguma] have lit the fires of war,
and are feeling their heat:

Other men look on at you from behind a
screen:

You [Kaigama] Chief slave, owner of the
town of Fefelo and of Kafe Fello,

Provide a thousand calabashes of food
for your followers:

The Ngijima, Babuma and Zakkama,

All three have sung their song:

For the success of the holder of the office
of Kaigama:

For the success of Anterashi, son of Lima:

And he has given them seventy slaves.

REMAINS OF THE PAST

*Archeological findings, such as those de-
scribed in the following article on the old
Kanuri capitals, are invaluable supplements
to oral tradition and chronicles. The authors
of this study are A.D.H. Bivar, a noted Africanist, and Peter L. Shinnie, professor of
archeology at the University of Khartoum,
Sudan. In 1959 they visited all the sites
mentioned except N'guru in northern Nigeria.*

Though the picture of the Kanuri nation
forming in Kanem, to the east of Chad,
in the early middle ages and its subsequent move west to Bornu is reasonably
clear, the origins of the Kanuri remain
obscure and much of the early history is
a highly dubious myth. . . .

Much remains to be done to elucidate
these problems, and archaeology should
be able to make its contribution. . . .

The most conspicuous of the remains
left by the Kanuri from earlier times
are the ruins of red brick buildings. This
type of building, rare until modern times
in Africa and presumably of alien origin,
is known from a number of sites stretching westwards from the Nile. . . .

These sites are, in Nigeria, Birni
N'gazargamo, Gambaru, and N'guru, in
the Republic of Niger, Garoumele, and
in the Republic of Chad, Tie.

Birni N'gazargamo is the best known
as it is the largest of the sites and its history—or at least the dates at which it was
first occupied and finally abandoned—
are certain. . . .

The outline of the history of the site
is reasonably clear. It is known to have
been founded in about A.D. 1470 by Ali,
son of Dunama, and remained the capital
of the kings of Bornu until its capture
and destruction by the Fulani in 1812.

In its present state it is an impressive
sight. It consists of an enormous earth
rampart enclosing a rough circle. This
rampart still stands about 7 meters high
and the distance across the enclosure is
about 2 kilometers. There are five en-
trances. Traces of ditch can be seen in a
few places along the outside of the rampart and it is likely that originally it ran
the whole way along but is now silted
up. Inside this vast enclosure are a number of red brick ruins consisting of a
large complex in the center and a number
of other smaller buildings scattered
throughout the enclosed area. . . .

It can be safely assumed that the main
complex was the palace of the Mais
[kings] of Bornu, that the other red brick
buildings were the residences of other
leading persons, and that the majority of
the inhabitants of the town lived in the
flimsy grass huts typical of the neighborhood, or in houses of sun-dried brick.
These have left no surface indications.
The plan gives as much information of
the nature of the main central building
as can be ascertained. Failing excavation,
nothing useful can be said about the
usage of the various rooms, nor as to details of internal layout or of any features
not visible on the surface. The only additional information is that the small building to the south-east of the main complex is known to the local inhabitants as
a mosque and, though there is nothing
in the layout, as it can now be seen, to
support such a view, they may be right.
This mosque seems to be an afterthought
and the bricks, though of the same size,
look to be of different manufacture and
perhaps made of clay from another source.
Excavation may answer this question. . . .

Gambaru, which is only 3 miles from
Birni N'gazargamo and to its east, is
clearly a site of a later period. Tradition,
for what it is worth, collected by [H.R.]

Palmer describes it as having been built by Queen Amsa, mother of Idris Aloma, in an attempt to separate him from the court and thus to protect his moral character. If this is so it must be a building of the sixteenth century and this date, rather later than that given for the founding of Birni N'gazargamo, corresponds well with what one can deduce from an inspection of the two structures. Gambaru is in a much better state of repair than the older site and there is some suspicion in our minds that the walls have been restored and repaired at some comparatively recent date. . . .

The site of Garoumele is in the Republic of Niger, immediately to the west of the road that runs from Niamey to N'guigmi at the north end of Chad. . . .

[Ives] Urvoy says that this site was the residence of the kings of Kanem before the foundation of Birni N'gazargamo. He recounts that after the flight from Kanem, Omar Said and Kade Alounou (1388-9) wandered on the south and west confines of Bornu; then their successors established themselves at . . . [Garoumele]. If this is so, it makes the site considerably older than those of Bornu and geographical considerations make this highly likely. The story presumably comes from oral tradition and may well be right, but the archaeological evidence is at present too scanty to make a reasoned judgment. There are few Kanuri in the area today, though there are a number of Kanembu villages along the shore of the lake. . . .

During the course of our journey, we had much in mind the question of the location of Njimi, known to have been the capital of the Kanuri before the settlement at Birni N'gazargamo. . . .

Knowledge of the town of Njimi is derived from the Bornu Arabic text known as the *Kanem Wars of Idris Aloma*, where it is implied that it is in Kanem, i.e. east of Lake Chad: from several other Bornu chronicles and king-lists: and from the Arab geographers. The name is also well remembered in Kanuri oral tradition. . . .

Since the countryside [of Kanem] is in many ways different from that of Bornu and is little visited, it is perhaps worth giving some description of it. This may help to explain some aspects of the development and early history of the Kanuri state.

The country falls into two areas; that of the dunes, often as much as 30 meters high and composed of fine sand, covered for the most part with long grass, tamarisk, or patches of acacia scrub; and the flats, which are depressions of black cotton-soil, surrounded by girdles of palm trees, and with water freely available from shallow wells. Settlements are generally situated on the higher dunes to obtain the benefit of the evening breeze. Water for the towns is carried up on camels from below. The flats are humid and oppressive, but they have shade and with good cultivation can produce a remarkable variety of vegetables. They have the appearance of former lakes, and may still hold water in a generous rainy season. The human inhabitants of the dunes are the Goraan, living in conical grass huts and matting shelters, and possessing cattle, goats, and camels. By contrast, along the flats the people are mainly cattle-raising Kanembu.

The archaeological site at Tie . . . is chiefly characterized by its quantity of scattered brick. It is situated at the crest of a large dune formation, and is nearly 2 miles from possible sources of water. The total area is nearly square being some 243 meters by 218 meters. There are no certain traces of a surrounding wall, but to the north and north-east the boundary is more sharply defined. Elsewhere it is vague and irregular. Apart from the two main buildings at the northeast of the site, and four small mounds along its northern edge, there are few signs of substantial buildings. The area to the west seems likely, however, to have been covered by a number of smallish huts. . . .

Local opinion at Mao attributes this site, and indeed all the others which characteristically make use of baked brick, as of the Bulala period (c. A.D. 1300-1600). If this attribution were correct, it would be natural to connect the demolition of Tie with some episode in the Kanem wars of Mai Idris [Aloma], and therefore probably attributable to the 1570's.

SARKI THE SNAKE

The Hausa emerged around A.D. 500, at about the same time as the Kanuri, their neighbors to the east. They evolved from an intermingling of diverse peoples who possibly came from the Sahara and the Nilotic Sudan and who merged with the autochthons, including people of the So culture. This admixture accounts for the wide variety of physical types found among the Hausa. Their oft-told "Legend of Daura," which follows, recounts the origin of the seven "true" Hausa states and seems to reflect the infiltration and merging of different peoples that occurred early in Hausa history. It comes from the as yet undated Girgam, a written record kept by the kings of Daura, traditionally the first Hausa state and now a tiny emirate east of Katsina. The killing of the snake Sarki probably suggests a change in religious beliefs, and the marriage of the queen of Daura to the hero Abuyazidu could represent a shift from matrilineal to patrilineal succession.

There was once a prince of Bagdad called Abuyazidu [Bayagidda] who quarreled with his father and left his home in the east. After some time his wanderings brought him to Bornu. There he was given a daughter of the Sultan in marriage, Magira by name. He stayed in Bornu and his affairs prospered so much that in the course of time he became rich and powerful. His wealth and authority only excited hatred and envy, however, and the Sultan began to plot against his life. But Magira, being a daughter of the palace, heard was was afoot and warned her husband. Although she was with child, they decided that the only safety lay in flight. So with nothing but a mule to carry their possessions and a slave-girl to wait on them, they took the road to

Bornu descendants of the Hilalian invaders
DENHAM, *Narrative of an Expedition*, 1827

the west. When they reached a place called Garun Gabas Magira's days were fulfilled and she gave birth to a son. Abuyazidu left her there and, taking the concubine with him, continued his journey.

After a time Abuyazidu came to the town of Daura which was then ruled by a woman, and last of a line of nine Queens. He lodged in the house of an old woman called Waira and in the evening he asked her for water. "Young man" said the old woman "in this town there is no water to be had except on Fridays. Only when all the people are assembled can we draw water."

"Nevertheless" he said "I am going to get some now. Give me a bucket."

He took the bucket which she gave him and went to the well. Now a gigantic snake called "Sarki" [the Hausa word for "king"] lived in the well and when it heard the bucket being lowered it lifted its head out of the well and tried to strike Abuyazidu. But he drew his sword and struck off its head which he then hid. After that he drew water for himself and his horse, gave what was left to the old woman, and went to bed.

Next day as soon as it was light the townspeople saw that the snake was dead. They marveled at its size and the news was quickly taken to the Queen. Escorted by all her warriors, she rode down to the place and she too marveled at the size of the snake which was still lying half in and half out of the well. "I swear" she said "that if I find the man who killed this snake I will divide the town into two and give half of it to him."

"It was I" said one of the bystanders at once.

"Where is its head then?" said the Queen. "If you cannot produce the head you are lying." The man remained silent. Others also came forward and said that they had killed the snake but none of them could produce the head and their claims were all rejected.

At length the old woman Waira spoke up. "Yesterday evening" she said "a stranger came and lodged at my house with a strange animal as big as an ox. He took my bucket, went to the well, drew water, drank some himself, watered his animal, and gave the rest to me. Perhaps it was he who killed the snake."

"Let him be found" said the Queen. When Abuyazidu appeared she asked him if he had killed the snake. He said that he had and when she demanded its head he produced it from where it was hidden. "I made a promise" she said "that I would divide my town in two and give half to him who did this deed."

"Do not divide the town" he said "because I for my part will be amply rewarded if you will deign to take me as your consort." And so it came about that Abuyazidu, Prince of Bagdad, married the Queen of Daura.

After the marriage Abuyazidu took up his residence in the palace. He was given the title of Makas-Sarki, the slayer of the snake, but after a time he came to be known simply as Sarki.

The concubine who had come from Bornu with Abuyazidu now gave birth to a boy. As the Queen seemed to be barren, the girl was confident that one day her son would become Chief so she called him Karabgari or Take-the-Town. But a year or two later the Queen also conceived and in due course she too brought forth a boy. Her son she named Bawogarior or Give-back-the-Town.

In the fulness of time Makas-Sarki and the Queen died and they were succeeded by their son. Bawogari thus became the first Chief of Daura and he in turn had six sons. The eldest Gazaura succeeded him in Daura. The second, by the same mother, was Bagaudu and he became the founder of Kano. The third was Gunguma and he became the founder of Zazzau [Zaria]. The fourth was Duma and he became the founder of Gobir. The fifth was Kumayau and he became the founder of Katsina. The youngest was Zuma Kogi and he became the founder of Rano.

Daura, Kano, Zazzau, Gobir, Katsina, and Rano are six of the seven original Hausa States. The seventh is Garun Gabas and that was founded by the son of Abuyazidu's first wife Magira, the daughter of the Sultan of Bornu, whom he had to leave behind when he was on his way from Bornu to Daura.

These are the origins of the *Hausa Bakwai* or seven original states of Hausaland.

BARBUSHE THE HUNTER

Of all the Hausa states, Kano is the one whose history is best known. This is because of the renowned Kano Chronicle, source of the following story. The selection describes the original inhabitants of Kano and the infiltration, around A.D. 1000, of immigrants from Daura, led by Bagaudu, grandson of Prince Abuyazidu. Like all African folk myths, it mixes fact with fantasy. Barbushe, the hunter-priest of the local god, is portrayed as a giant able to carry several elephants on his head; this suggests his importance in the community. Most likely the legend symbolizes a conflict that arose when aliens tried to become the overlords of the inhabitants.

This is the history of the lords of this country called Kano. Barbushe, once its chief, was of the stock of Dala, [who was] a black man of great stature and might, a hunter, who slew elephants with his stick and carried them on his head about nine miles. Dala was of unknown race, but came to this land, and built a house on Dala hill [thenceforth a sacred rock also called Dala]. There he lived—he and his wives. He had seven children—four boys and three girls—of whom the eldest was Garageje. This Garageje was the grandfather of Buzame, who was the father of Barbushe. Barbushe succeeded his forefathers in the knowledge of the lore of Dala, for he was skilled in the various pagan rites. By his wonders and sorceries and the power he gained over his brethren he became chief and lord over them. Among the lesser chiefs with him were Gurzago. . . . After him came Gagina who was so strong that he caught elephants with rope. . . . From Toda to Dan Bakoshi and from Doji to Dankwoi all the people flocked to Barbushe on the two nights of Idi—for he was all-powerful at the sacrificial rites.

Now the name of the place sacred to their god was Kakua. The god's name was Tchunburburai. It was a tree called Shamuz. The man who remained near this tree day and night was called Mai-Tchunburburai. The tree was surrounded by a wall, and no man could come within it save Barbushe. Whoever else entered, he entered but to die. Barbushe never descended from Dala except on the two days of Idi. When the days drew near, the people came in from east and west and south and north, men and women alike. Some brought a black dog, some a black fowl, others a black he-goat, when they met together on the day of Jajibere at the foot of Dala hill at eve. When darkness came, Barbushe went forth from his house with his drummers. He cried aloud and said: "Great Father of us all, we have come nigh to thy dwelling in supplication, Tchunburburai," and the people said: "Look on Tchunburburai, ye men of Kano. Look toward Dala." Then Barbushe descended, and the people went with him

to the god. And when they drew near, they sacrificed that which they had brought with them. Barbushe entered the sacred place—he alone—and said "I am the heir of Dala, like it or no, follow me ye must, perforce." And all the people said: "Dweller on the rock, our lord Amane, we follow thee perforce." Thus they spoke and marched round the sacred place till the dawn, when they arose, naked as they were, and ate. Then would Barbushe come forth and tell them of all that would befall through the coming year, even concerning the stranger who should come to this land, whether good or ill. And he foretold how their dominion should be wrested from them, and their tree cast down and burnt, and how this mosque should be built. "A man shall come," said he, "to this land with an army, and gain the mastery over us." They answered, "Why do you say this? it is an evil saying." Barbushe held his peace. "In sooth," said he, "you will see him in the sacred place of Tchunburburai; if he comes not in your time, assuredly he will come in the time of your children, and will conquer all in this country, and forget you and yours and exalt himself and his people for years to come." Then were they exceeding cast down. They knew well that he did not lie. So they believed him and said: "What can we do to avert this great calamity?" He replied, "There is no cure but resignation." They resigned themselves. But the people were still grieving over this loss of dominion at some distant time, when Bagoda, a generation later, came with his host to Kano. There is a dispute, however. Some deny this, and say that it was Bagoda's grandson who first reached Kano, and that he and his son died at Sheme. He, at all events, entered Kano territory first. When he came, he found none of Barbushe's men, save Janbere, Hambarau, Gertsangi, Jandamissa, and Kanfatau. These said, "Is this man he of whom Barbushe told us?" Jambere said, "I swear by Tchunburburai if you allow this people within our land, verily they will rule you, till

you are of no account." The people refused to hearken to the words of Jambere and allowed the strangers to enter the country, saying: "Where will Bagoda find strength to conquer us?"

So Bagoda and his host settled in Garazawa and built houses there. . . . Now the chiefs whom Bagoda found holding sway over this land acknowledged no supreme lord save Tchunburburai and the grove of Jakara. Jakara was called "Kurmin Bakkin Rua," because its water was black, and it was surrounded by the grove.

The pagans stood in awe of the terrors of their god and this grove, which stretched from Gorondumasa to Dausara. The branches and limbs of its trees were still—save, if trouble were coming on this land, it would shriek thrice, and smoke would issue forth in Tchunburburai, which was in the midst of the water. Then they would bring a black dog and sacrifice it at the foot of Tchunburburai. They sacrificed a black he-goat in the grove. If the shrieks and smoke continued, the trouble would indeed reach them, but if they ceased, then the trouble was stayed. The name of the grove was Matsama and the name of Tchunburburai was Randaya.

The greatest of the chiefs of the country was Mazauda, the grandfather of Sarkin Makafi. Gijigiji was the blacksmith; Bugazau was the brewer; Hanburki doctored every sickness; Danbuntunia, the watchman of the town at night, was the progenitor of the Kurmawa. Tsoron Maje was "Sarkin Samri," and Jandodo was "Sarkin Makada Gundua da Kuru." Beside these there was Maguji, who begot the Maguzawa, and was the miner and smelter among them. Again there was Asanni the forefather of minstrels and chief of the dancers. Bakonyaki was the archer. Awar, grandfather of the Awrawa, worked salt of Awar. He was Sarkin Rua of this whole country. In all there were eleven of these pagan chiefs, and each was head of a large clan. They were the original stock of Kano.

YAJI'S REVENGE

Most of the Hausa people are settled in northern Nigeria and in the adjacent regions of the Republic of Niger, which is Hausaland proper. Today they are among the world's most fervid Muslims, and Islam figures prominently in their culture. This excerpt, also from the Kano Chronicle, describes the first and ephemeral introduction of Muhammad's teachings in Hausaland. It states that Islam came to Kano during the reign of Sarki Yaji (1349–1385). However, it is also possible that Muslim influences had penetrated from Bornu, which had been Islamized since the reign of Umme Jilma in the eleventh century. This passage ends with the legend of Kano's sizable community of blind.

The eleventh Sarki was Yaji, called Ali. His mother was Maganarku. He was called Yaji because he had a bad temper when he was a boy, and the name stuck to him. He drove the Serikin Rano from Zamma Gaba, went to Rano, and reigned at Bunu two years. Then he removed to Kur together with the Ajawa and Worjawa and Aurawa. He stayed there. In Yaji's time the Wangarawa [Mandingo] came from Melle [Mali], bringing the Muhammadan religion. The name of their leader was Abdurahaman Zaite. Others were Yakubu, Mandawali, Famori, Bilkasim, Kanaji, Dukere, Sheshe, Kebe, Murtuku, Liman Jibjin Yallabu, the father of Serikin Pawa, Gurdumus, Auta, Laual, Liman Madatai and others —about forty in all. When they came they commanded the Sarki to observe the times of prayer. He complied, and made Gurdamus his Liman [leader of prayer], and Laual his Muezzin. Auta cut the throats of whatever flesh was eaten. Mandawali was Liman of all the Wangarawa and of the chief men of Kano. Zaite was their Alkali [judge]. The Sarki commanded every town in Kano country to observe the times of prayer. So they all did so. A mosque was built [at Kur, the capital] beneath the sacred tree facing east, and prayers were made at the five appointed times in it. The Sarkin Garazawa was opposed to prayer, and when the Moslems after praying had gone home, he would come with his men and defile the whole mosque and cover it with filth. Danbugi was told off to patrol round the mosque with well-armed men from evening until morning. He kept up a constant halloo. For all that the pagans tried to win him and his men over. Some of his men followed the pagans and went away, but he and the rest refused. The defilement continued till Sheshe said to Famori, "There is no cure for this but prayer." The people assented. They gathered together on a Tuesday in the mosque at the evening hour of prayer and prayed against the pagans until sunrise. They only came away when the sun was well up. Allah received graciously the prayers addressed to him. The chief of the pagans was struck blind that day, and afterwards all the pagans who were present at the defilement—they and all their women. After this they were all afraid. Yaji turned the chief of the pagans out of his office and said to him, "Be thou Sarki among the blind."

THE ISLAMIZATION OF KANO

Yaji's progress in encouraging Islam was destroyed by his son, who was a pagan. However, during the reign of the illustrious Sarki Muhammad Rumfa (1465–1499) a new wave of missionaries entered Kano, and Islam became firmly entrenched as the state religion. As related in the subsequent chapter from the Chronicle, Kano's sacred tree—probably that worshiped by Barbushe and his tribe—was finally cut down and replaced by a mosque.

The twentieth Sarki was Mohamma, son of Yakubu, commonly called Rimfa. His mother's name was Fasima Berana. He was a good man, just and learned. He can have no equal in might, from the time of the founding of Kano, until it shall end. In his time the Sherifs came to Kano. They were Abdu Rahaman and his people. There is a story that the Prophet appeared to Abdu Rahaman in a dream and said to him, "Get up and go west and establish Islam." Abdu Rahaman got up

A branched sword, its blade ornamented with markings that seem to have been inspired by Arabic characters, was fashioned in Chad.
GALERIE KAMER, COLLECTION OF MR. AND MRS. JOHN DE MENIL

and took a handful of the soil of Medina, and put it in a cloth, and brought it to Hausaland.

Whenever he came to a town, he took a handful of the soil of the country and put it beside that of Medina. If they did not correspond he passed that town. So he journeyed until he came to Kano. And when he compared the soil of Kano with Medina soil they resembled one another and became as one soil. So he said, "This is the country that I saw in my dream." And he took up his abode at Panisau. Then he sent in to the Sarkin Kano. The Sarkin Kano Rimfa went out together with his men, and escorted Abdu Rahaman back to the city together with his men, of whom the chief were Hanatari, Gemindodo, Gadangami, Fokai and others, ten in all. Abdu Rahaman lived in Kano and established Islam. He brought with him many books. He ordered Rimfa to build a mosque for Friday, and to cut down the sacred tree and build a minaret [or mosque-tower] on the site. And when he had established the

Faith of Islam, and learned men had grown numerous in Kano, and all the country round had accepted the Faith, Abdu Karimi returned to Massar, leaving Sidi Fari as his deputy to carry on his work.

Rimfa was the author of twelve innovations in Kano. He built the Dakin Rimfa. The next year he extended the walls towards the Kofan [gate of] Mata from the Kofan Dagachi and continued the work to Kofan Gertawasa and Kofan Kawayi, and from the Kofan Naissa to the Kofan Kansakali. The next year he entered his house [i.e. he built a new palace, still called the *Gidan Rimfa*]. He established the Kurmi Market. He was the first Sarki who used "Dawakin Zaggi" in the war with Katsina. He was the first Sarki who practiced "Kame." He appointed Durman to go round the dwellings of the Indabawa and take every first-born virgin for him. He was the first Sarki to have a thousand wives. He began the custom of "Kulle" [wife-seclusion]. He began the "Tara-ta-Kano." He was the first to have "Ka-kaki" [long trumpets] and "Figinni," [ostrich-feather fans] and ostrich-feather sandals. It was in his reign that the Sallam Idi was first celebrated in Kano at Shadakoko. He began the custom of giving to eunuchs the offices of state, among them, Dan Kusuba, Dan Jigawa, Dan Tarbana, Sarkin Gabbas, Sarkin Tudu, Sarkin Rua, Maaji, Sarkin Bai, Sarkin Kofa. There were four eunuchs without a title. He said to them, "I make you chiefs of the Treasury." The name of one was Turaki, another was Aljira; the names of the other two were Al-Soro and Kashe Kusa.

The Gladima Dabuli built a house at Goda, and the Madawaki Badosa built a house at Hori. Chiroma Bugaya built a house at Dabazaro. Surely there was no Sarki more powerful than Rimfa! He was sung as "The Arab Sarki, of wide sway." In his time occurred the first war with Katsina. It lasted eleven years, without either side winning. He ruled thirty-seven years.

AN EPISTLE ON KINGSHIP

In addition to constructing mosques and encouraging the ritual and belief of Islam, Muhammad Rumfa sought the advice of Muslim scholars concerning the ruling of his kingdom. When Sheikh Muhammad al-Majhili, the famed theologian, preacher, and jurist from Algeria, came to Kano toward the end of Rumfa's reign, the sarki *commissioned him to write a treatise on Islamic government. A passage from the resultant work, whose English title is* The Obligations of Princes, *is quoted below. This North African "Machiavelli" helped Rumfa evolve a monarchical system, with built-in checks and balances, which was to characterize the governmental organization of all Hausa states.*

The sojourn of a prince in the city breeds all manner of trouble and harm. The bird of prey abides in open and wild places. Vigorous is the cock as he struts round his domains. The eagle can only win his realm by firm resolve, and the cock's voice is strong as he masters the hens. Ride, then, the horses of resolution upon the saddles of prudence. Cherish the land from the spoiling drought, from the raging wind, the dust-laden storm, the raucous thunder, the gleaming lightning, the shattering fireball and the beating rain. Kingdoms are held by the sword, not by delays. Can fear be thrust back except by causing fear?

Allow only the nearest of your friends to bring you food and drink and bed and clothes. Do not part with your coat of mail and weapons and let no one approach you save men of trust and virtue. Never sleep in a place of peril. Have near to guard you at all times a band of faithful and gallant men, sentries, bowmen, horse and foot. Times of alarm are not like times of safety. Conceal your secrets from other people until you are master of your undertaking.

THE TWO ROGUES

Islam drew Hausaland into the commercial center of the network linking the Sahara and the western Sudan. Kano, and especially Katsina, prospered through their contacts with the north and the west. The Hausa traders were noted for their shrewdness, a quality shared by Dan-Kano and Dan-Katsina, the protagonists in the following folk tale. Both are bent on acquiring valuable trade goods without paying market value. The chief currency of Hausaland was cowry shells. Since these were not found locally, they had to be imported. For centuries the main source of foreign exchange used to buy cowries was the revenue—often in the form of gold—obtained from the sale of slaves, which were exported to Saharan oases, North Africa, and the Middle East.

There were once two rogues, one of whom came from Kano and the other from Katsina.

One day the rogue from Kano peeled the bark off a boabab tree and took it to the dye-pits and dyed it and beat it to give it a glaze and then wrapped it up in paper to make it look like the best broadcloth.

While the rogue from Kano was doing this, the rogue from Katsina was filling a goatskin with pebbles. Having done that, he covered the pebbles over with a couple of hundred cowries and tied up the mouth of the bag and set off for the market.

On the way to the market the two rogues happened to meet.

"Where are you going to, my friend?" asked the Kano man.

"I'm going to market" said the Katsina man. "Why—what have you got to sell?"

"Best blue broadcloth" said the Kano man.

"Well now, I was going to market to buy broadcloth" said the Katsina man. "I've got my money here" he went on, pointing to his bag "twenty thousand of it."

In this way the two rogues struck a bargain on the road and exchanged their wares before they reached the market. On parting company each thought that that he had got the better of the other and so when they had gone a short distance they turned aside to see what they

The great trading center of Kano, famed for its brilliantly colored textiles and leather goods
BARTH, *Travels in Central Africa*, 1857

had obtained. The Kano man found that he had got a bag of stones and the Katsina man found that he had got a parcel of bark. . . .

At this they both retraced their steps and when they met again they said: "We are each as crafty as the other and so from now on we had better join forces and seek our fortune together."

So the two rogues joined forces and took the road together. When they came to a town they got themselves water-bottles and staffs and begging-bowls and then, pretending to be blind beggars, they set off again.

They were going along, deep in the bush, when they came to a place where some traders had pitched their camp. They did not show themselves to the traders, however, but hid in the bush near the camp.

When night fell, the two rogues came out of hiding and entered the traders' camp with their eyes closed, pretending that they were blind beggars. The traders let them stay in the camp and in due course went off to sleep. As soon as they were asleep, the two rogues opened their eyes and removed all the traders' goods and carried them over to a dry well into which they threw them.

At daybreak next day the traders got up and found that they had been robbed of all their goods. The blind men also got up and began saying "Where are our water-bottles? Let's hope they haven't been stolen."

This made the traders very angry. "Here we are" they cried "robbed of all we possess and all you miserable beggars can think about is whether your water-bottles have been taken too. It's too much: get out of here before we kick you

out." So the two rogues groped their way out of the traders' camp.

Soon afterwards the traders departed, loudly bemoaning the fact they had been robbed. As soon as they had gone, the two rogues opened their eyes again and hurried over to the well into which they had thrown the traders' goods.

"Dan-Katsina" said the Kano man "down you go."

"No Dan-Kano" said Dan-Katsina "you go."

"No you" said Dan-Kano.

So Dan-Katsina went down the well and tied the goods which were at the bottom to a rope which Dan-Kano lowered to him. Dan-Kano thereupon hauled the goods to the top and carried them a little way away from the well and stacked them. After that, each time he went back to the well, he took a large stone with him and these stones he collected in a heap near the head of the well.

When they had been working for some time, Dan-Kano called down the well to his companion. "Dan-Katsina" he said "when the stuff is finished, and you are ready to come up yourself, let me know and I'll haul you up very carefully so that you don't bump yourself against the side."

"Very well" said Dan-Katsina.

They worked away like this until the last bale had been hauled up. But Dan-Katsina did not tell Dan-Kano this. Instead he said: "The next load is going to be a pretty heavy one, Dan-Kano, but after that there are no more." He then crawled into the last of the bales and hid himself inside.

Dan-Kano now hauled up the last bale and carried it over to where he had stacked the others. He did not realize

that Dan-Katsina was hiding inside it. Then he went back to where he had collected the pile of stones and started hurling them down into the well where he thought Dan-Katsina still was.

While Dan-Kano was busy throwing all the stones which he had collected down the well, Dan-Katsina crept out of the bale in which he had hidden and quickly started removing the rest of the goods and hiding them in another place. When Dan-Kano came back, therefore, he found that the goods had all vanished.

"Well I'll be blowed!" he said to himself. "While I was dealing with Dan-Katsina, someone else must have come along and taken my things from here."

The thought then occurred to Dan-Kano that as the thief couldn't be far away and would need an animal to move all the stuff he would probably come hurrying back if he heard a donkey braying. So Dan-Kano went into some nearby scrub and started braying like a donkey. Sure enough, Dan-Katsina soon came hurrying up saying: "Steady Neddy! Hold hard there! Come on boy!" When they saw one another, Dan-Kano said: "Dan-Katsina, you're a scoundrel" and Dan-Katsina said: "Dan-Kano, you're another."

The two rogues now collected their goods and took them to Dan-Kano's house. When they got there Dan-Katsina said: "I want to go on and visit my home, Dan-Kano, so we'll leave the stuff here and I'll come back in three months' time and then we'll split it."

"Very well" said Dan-Kano.

When Dan-Katsina had been gone for two months, Dan-Kano had a grave dug in his compound which he covered over with potsherds and old calabashes. When the three months were nearly up he retired into this grave and his family heaped earth over the potsherds and calabashes.

A few days later Dan-Katsina appeared and asked Dan-Kano's family where he was.

"Haven't you heard?" they said. "Dan-Kano is dead. He died four days ago."

"Indeed?" said Dan-Katsina. "Well then take me to his grave so that I can see it for myself."

When he was taken to the grave Dan-Katsina burst into loud lamentations. "So Dan-Kano has gone the way of all flesh!" he cried. "God's will be done. But you know" he went on, addressing Dan-Kano's relations "you ought to cut thorn and cover up the grave because otherwise hyenas will come and dig him up, poor soul."

"We'll do it tomorrow" said the relations.

"Now take me to my lodging" said Dan-Katsina "for tomorrow I must go home."

The relations prepared a lodging for Dan-Katsina in Dan-Kano's house and brought him stew and dumpling and milk gruel. He did not touch the food, however, because he said that, with his friend in his grave, he couldn't bring himself to eat anything.

In the middle of the night, when all the household were asleep, Dan-Katsina got up and crept out of the house and went to Dan-Kano's grave. There he started growling—Grrr, Grrr, Grrr—and went down on all fours and scrabbled at the earth which covered the grave as if he was a hyena trying to get in.

Inside the grave, Dan-Kano heard the noise outside and was filled with terror. "Help!" he cried. "Mercy! I'm going to be eaten by a hyena. Let me out of here."

"All right" said Dan-Katsina. "Out you come."

And so in the end the two rogues, Dan-Kano and Dan-Katsina, had to divide the goods which they had stolen from the traders equally between them.

"WILDE WOODIE HAUSALAND"

Leo Africanus was an energetic Moorish diplomat when he made two journeys through the Sudan in the early sixteenth century. He later produced an informative travelogue entitled The History and Description of Africa, *from which the following accounts of four of the seven "true" Hausa states— namely Guber, or Gobir; Cano, or Kano; Casena, or Katsina; and Zegzeg, or Zaria— are taken. Leo's given name was actually Al-Hasan ibn Muhammad al-Wazzan az-Zayyati, but in 1518 he was captured by a Christian pirate, taken to Rome, and there he was converted to Christianity and baptized Giovanni Leo de' Medici. In 1526 he completed in Italian his account of Africa; it was edited and published in 1550 by Giovanni Ramusio, a prominent Venetian administrator, who was the first to call him Leo Africanus. This translation was made in 1600 by John Pory.*

Of the kingdome of Guber: It standeth eastward of the kingdome of Gago almost three hundred miles; betweene which two kingdomes lieth a vast desert being much destitute of water, for it is about fortie miles distant from Niger. The kingdome of Guber is environed with high mountaines, and containeth many villages inhabited by shepherds, and other herdsmen. Abundance of cattell here are both great and small: but of a lower stature then the cattell in other places. Heere are also great store of artificers and linnen weavers: and heere are such shooes [probably leather sandals] made as the ancient Romans were woont to weare, the greatest part whereof be carried to Tombuto and Gago. Likewise heere is abundance of rice, and of certaine other graine and pulse, the like whereof I never saw in Italie. But I thinke it groweth in some places in Spaine. At the inundation of Niger all the fields of this region are overflowed, and then the inhabitants cast their seede into the water onely....

Of the province of Cano: The great province of Cano standeth eastward of the river Niger almost five hundred miles. The greatest part of the inhabitants dwelling in villages are some of them herdsmen and others husbandmen. Heere groweth abundance of corne, of rice, and of cotton. Also heere are many deserts and wilde woodie mountaines containing many springs of water. In these woods growe plentie of wilde citrons and limons, which differ not much in taste from the best of all. In the midst of this province standeth a towne called by the same name, the walles and houses whereof are built for the most part of a kinde of chalke [baked clay]. The inhabitants are rich merchants and most civill people. Their king was in times past of great puissance, and had mighty troupes of horsemen at his command; but he hath since beene constrained to pay tribute unto the kings of Zegzeg and Casena....

Of the kingdome of Casena: Casena bordering eastward upon the kingdome last described, is full of mountaines, and drie fields, which yeeld notwithstanding great store of barlie and millseed. The inhabitants are extremely black [having great noses and blabber lips.] They dwell in most forlorne and base cottages: neither shall you finde any of their villages containing above three hundred families. And besides their base estate they are mightily oppressed with famine....

Of the kingdome of Zegzeg: The southeast part thereof bordereth upon Cano, and it is distant from Casena almost an hundred and fiftie miles. The inhabitants are rich and have great traffique unto other nations. Some part of this kingdome is plaine, and the residue mountainous, but the mountaines are extremely cold, and the plains intolerably hot. And because they can hardly indure the sharpnes of winter, they kindle great fires in the midst of their houses, laying the coles thereof under their high bedsteads, and so betaking themselves to sleepe. Their fields abounding with water, are exceeding fruitful, & their houses are built like the houses of the kingdome of Casena. They had a king of their own....

BORTORIMI AND THE SPIDER

The wily, wiry spider is one of the most popular animals in African folklore. In Hausa legend he is generally depicted as an unscrupulous, vindictive creature, like the insect of this tale. The spider is, however, a Hausa hero, for he embodies such admired gifts of endurance as cunning, a huge capacity for eating, and a genius for satisfying his needs.

There was once a certain Man whose name was Bortorimi, a Giant was he, there was no one like him in all the world, for, when he used to go to the forest, he would kill some twenty Elephants, and bring them home for his meal. One day the Spider sent his Wife—the female Spider—to Bortorimi's house to get fire. So she went, and while she was there, they gave her a great piece of meat, so she took it home with her. Then the Spider said "Who has given you that meat?" And she replied "I got it at Bortorimi's house." Immediately the Spider said "Put out your fire." And when she had done so, she returned to Bortorimi's house, and said that the fire had gone out. So more meat was given to her.

Then the Spider himself went to Bortorimi's house, but when Bortorimi gave him some meat he ate it all up at once, and did not bring any home. When he had eaten it, he said to Bortorimi "Where do you get this meat?" And the other replied "Over there in the forest, a great way off." "I see," said the Spider, "may I accompany you next time?" And Bortorimi said "Very well," but that he would not be going until the next morning, [so the Spider went home].

But the Spider could not wait until the dawn had come, so he pulled the roof off his hut, and set it on fire, and this made the whole place as light as if day had broken, although it was really not even dawn, but midnight. Then the Spider ran to Bortorimi's house, and stood outside, and called out "Hey, Bortorimi, Bortorimi, awake, awake, it is dawn." But Bortorimi replied "Oh! come, Spider, now I was watching you when you took the roof off your house and burned it." So the Spider went home again.

Soon afterwards he mounted a rock and made the first "Call to Prayer," and said that dawn had come. Then he went and roused Bortorimi, saying "everyone is astir, they are calling to prayer, wake

up." But Bortorimi said "Oh! dear Spider, can you not have patience?" and he refused to go.

Now Bortorimi's nose was as big as a house, there was a market inside it. At daybreak they started off, and when they had come to a certain great river, Bortorimi said to the Spider "Drink your fill." And when the Spider had drunk all he wanted, Bortorimi pouted his lips and drank up all the water, leaving only the mud. Then they went on, and at last they reached the depths of the forest where the Elephants used to feed.

When they had arrived at the spot, Bortorimi said to the Spider, "Go and spy on the Animals there, and abuse them, and when you have done so, and they chase you, run and get inside my nose." "Very well," said the Spider, and off he went and abused the Elephants, calling out "Hey, you Animals, you are not properly born." Immediately they charged down upon the Spider, but he went off at a run, and jumped into Bortorimi's nose, and Bortorimi captured the whole herd and killed them.

Now as soon as the Spider got inside the nose (where there was a market) he began his tricks, saying that he was a King's Son, and so he ought to have a present of ground-nuts to eat, and the Old Woman selling them gave him some.

Just then Bortorimi finished killing the Elephants, and he began calling out "Spider, Spider, come out." So the Spider emerged, and Bortorimi said to him "Now choose the Elephant that you are going to take." But the Spider said that he could not carry one, so Bortorimi heaped them all together and carried the lot. When they had got home, Bortorimi said "Now Spider, here is yours," and the Spider skinned the Elephant, and roasted it, and ate every bit, he would not give any to his Wife.

As soon as the Spider had eaten it, he returned to Bortorimi's house, and said "O, Bortorimi, are you not going back to the hunting-ground?" But Bortorimi said "Umm, I shall not return, this is enough for me."

HAUSA PROVERBS

Today Hausa is the lingua franca of the central Sudan and as such is one of Black Africa's most important tongues. Proverbs such as abokin sarki sarki ne," *a friend of a chief is a chief," and those that follow, would be readily understood by millions of Africans.*

Each end of the fire has its smoke.
(Everything has its own consequences.)

Even the Niger has an island.
(The mightiest things do not have it all their own way.)

Everything done to a free man he will pay back except digging a grave.
(A free man kicks till death stops him.)

God made beautiful the silk cotton tree, the rubber tree must cease being angry.
(Quarrel not with what God ordains.)

Although a man doesn't own a camel, he knows [the word for] "kneel."
(It is evident to the meanest intelligence.)

Before one comes out of water one does not squeeze [one's] loincloth.
(Wait to finish the work before cleaning up.)

Where the boy picked up a cowry there he goes on digging.
(Exploiting a "pocket.")

It's the squeezing that makes the drum sound sweet.
("I won't," implies ability to choose.)

The road to the Gold Coast, far away and profitable.
(Long journeys make heavy purses.)

The man who looks like going is sent.
(Give your orders to those who are likely to obey them.)

If music changes so does the dance.
(One must move with the times.)

South of the Sahara and Lake Chad, a Musgu horn player summons an audience.

CROSSROADS
OF
EMPIRE

EAST MEETS WEST

Complementing the Black empires of the western Sudan, there arose in the corridor of rolling grasslands that stretch from the Niger to the Nilotic Sudan a string of equally dynamic kingdoms, notably Kanem-Bornu, the Hausa galaxy, Darfur, and Sennar. Like their western neighbors, these central Sudanese states were strongly tied to the trans-Saharan trade. They were also the chief entrepôts in a brisk intercourse between the Niger and the Nile, their societies a synthesis of African cultures east and west. They generated social and political systems as sophisticated as those of medieval Europe. Their walled towns were centers of Islamic learning; their treasuries supported retinues of armored knights and caparisoned steeds; their courts were theatrical in their ceremony and splendor.

As shown in the 1815 engraving above, the sultan of Bornu gave audience from a cagelike pavilion. His aides wore padding and huge headgear, since ample bellies and large heads were the fashion at court.

After 1500 Christian Alodia fell to the Funj, who founded the Muslim kingdom of Sennar, named after its capital on the Blue Nile. The Funj dynasty, one of whose members is pictured at right, ruled until 1821.

RAPHO-GUILLUMETTE-GEORG GERSTER

The wall painting above was executed over a thousand years ago in a church at Faras, once the capital of the Christian kingdom of Nobatia. The mural, which is dominated by the crowned figure of Archangel Michael, is shown with its chief excavator, Polish archeologist Kasimierz Michalowski. The ruined palace below, at Jebel Marra, belonged to Muhammad Teirab, an eighteenth-century Darfur king.

BASIL DAVIDSON

WIND, SAND, AND SALT

Before salt became readily available in the twentieth century, it was the "prince of commodities" in the saltless Sudan. Mined by Tuareg oases dwellers of the Sahara and sold in the south, it was as important a trade item as gold. Indeed, salt generated wealth in transit, as states that lay along the caravan routes imposed high tariffs on the merchandise passing through their lands. Ibn Battuta, a visitor to northern Mali in 1352, has left us this impression of the thriving salt city of Taghaza: "Its houses and mosques," he noted, "are built of blocks of salt, roofed with camel skins. There are no trees there, nothing but sand. In the sand is a salt mine; they dig for the salt, and find it in thick slabs . . . as though they had been tool-squared. . . . The negroes come up from their country and take away the salt from there. . . . [They] use salt as a medium of exchange . . . they cut it up into pieces and buy and sell with it. The business done at Taghaza . . . amounts to an enormous figure in terms of hundredweights of gold-dust."

The Tuareg are the undisputed masters of the salt trade. Navigating by the sun, stars, dunes, and rocks, they cross the Sahara to the markets of the Sudan. There they barter their blocks of salt (left) for millet, sugar, tea, and cotton. Caravans like that below once comprised as many as 25,000 camels, or "ships of the desert."

Contrary to the usual Muslim practice, Tuareg men, rather than women, swathe their faces in cloth. Warriors, each in a tagilmust, or "mouth muffler," are shown in the engravings opposite and at right. Left, traders at the salt-rich oasis of Bilma mend their clothes behind a wind screen of pack saddles, while a servant pounds millet.

LYONS, *L'Afrique*, 1821

FACES OF THE SUDAN

The "Country of the Blacks" is the home of peoples of different physical types whose economies have long nurtured pastoralists, farmers, traders, and ironworkers. These peoples organized prototypical Sudanese states as early as the ninth century A.D. and recognized "divine" kings as rulers. But it was the spread of Islam in the eleventh century that signaled the Sudan's entry into the mainstream of world commerce. By the thirteenth century most of the region's merchants were Muslims, who also diffused the faith. Many kings espoused Islam, thereby commanding the allegiance of a larger number of subjects than those restricted to local kinship ties. The new religion encouraged the growth of an educated class, which formed the bureaucratic cadres of the Sudan's emerging nations and empires. However, until the nineteenth century, Islam's hold on most Sudanese peoples was superficial; their culture and beliefs remained basically those of their ancestors.

Ethiopia, still a "Christian island in a Muslim sea," has about 14,000 churches, served by some 250,000 clerics. The priest above holds a characteristic processional cross, allegedly that of King Lalibela. He wears the turbanlike temtem, *standard garb for married priests and* debteras, *laymen who are experts in the liturgy and traditional wisdom of the Church. At right, Hausa traders confer at the market of Kano in northern Nigeria.*

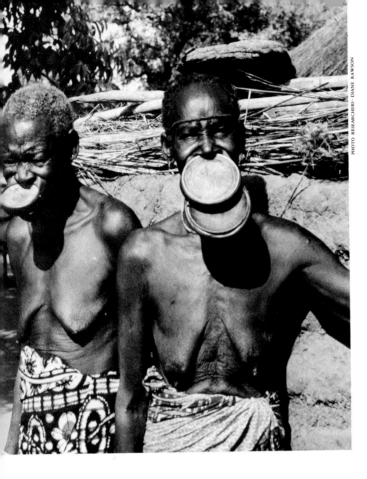

PHOTO RESEARCHERS—DIANE RAWSON

PHOTO RESEARCHERS—VICTOR ENGLEBERT

The epitome of feminine pulchritude among the Sara of Chad was the wearing of lip plates, inserted during childhood. The custom may have originated as part of initiation or as a device to discourage enslavement by the Arabs. Their use is waning; they are worn mainly by the aged, as above. At right is a young Tuareg.

Below left is a Fulani from Niger; at right is a Dangaleat girl from Chad. Both belong to predominantly cattle-owning societies.

BOTH: RAPHO-GUILLUMETTE—MARC AND EVELYNE BERNHEIM